THE MANAGEMENT OF INVESTMENT DECISIONS

Donald B. Trone

William R. Allbright

Philip R. Taylor

IRWIN
Professional Publishing

Chicago • Bogotá • Boston • Buenos Aires • Caracas
London • Madrid • Mexico City • Sydney • Toronto

Irwin Book Team

Marketing manager: *Angela Wells*
Project editor: *Beth Yates*
Production supervisor: *Dina L. Treadaway*
Assistant manager, desktop services:
  Jon Christopher

Designer: *Laurie J. Entringer*
Compositor: *Douglas & Gayle Limited*
Typeface: *11/13 Times Roman*
Printer: *R. R. Donnelley & Sons Company*

Library of Congress Cataloging In-Publication Data

Trone, Donald B.
  The management of investment decisions / Donald B. Trone, William R. Allbright, Philip R. Taylor.
    p. cm.
  Includes index.
  ISBN 0-7863-0392-1
  1. Investments. 2. Investment analysis. I. Allbright, William
R., 1957. II. Taylor, Philip R. III. Title
HG4521.T693 1996
332.6'78—dc20   95–10474

Printed in the United States of America

1 2 3 4 5 6 7 8 9 0 DO 2 1 0 9 8 7 6 5

From Don Trone:

To my family, particularly Tara and Tim, who have taught me the true meaning of *compound interest.*

To my staff at the Investment Management Council. It can never be called "work" when you have the privilege of serving with such outstanding individuals.

And, to the people of Callan Associates Inc. In particular, I wish to thank Ronald D. Peyton, Edwin C. Callan, and James J. O'Leary (deceased February, 1994). These three men provided me the prerequisites for the undertaking of this book: inspiration, leadership, and friendship.

From Bill Allbright:

To my wife, Shannon. I will be forever indebted for her encouragement, patience, and understanding. Her listening ear proved to be the most valuable resource in the preparation of this book. Also, to my wonderful and loving children, Elizabeth and Tyler—you both are the reason I kept going when I had no more to give. I am truly blessed with a full quiver!

I also deeply appreciate my faithful clients who have allowed me the freedom to take the time to write this book, the trust to apply the principles and concepts outlined in this book, and the words of encouragement and acts of appreciation that motivated me to undertake this project. To have a job that brings such great reward and satisfaction from so many wonderful and supportive people is a blessing never to be taken for granted.

From Phil Taylor:

To the Clients of PR Taylor, who have uniformly embraced *the prudent process* and their *role* in it.

To the Staff of PR Taylor, whose work with clients is distinguished by a commitment to excellence and *shared responsibility for the process.*

Especially to Lisa and Kelly, whose long-standing support of our firm and this project made it all possible.

ABOUT THE AUTHORS

Donald B. Trone is the founder and executive director of the Investment Management Council, a division of Callan Associates Inc. Don is responsible for developing investment consulting services for the middle and upper retail markets and for establishing working relationships with outside independent consulting firms. Don and Bill Allbright are co-authors of the industry bestseller, *Procedural Prudence*. Don graduated as president of his class from The United States Coast Guard Academy and with honors from the U.S. Naval Flight Training program in Pensacola, Florida. He had a distinguished 10-year career as a Coast Guard officer and helicopter pilot, and is credited with flying over 100 search and rescue missions. Don received his master's degree from the American College.

William R. Allbright is president of Allbright & Hart Financial Advisors, Inc., based in Dallas, Texas. His firm specializes in financial and investment consulting for individuals, qualified retirement plans, and charitable organizations. This consulting service entails utilization of the principles described throughout this book. Bill received his BBA in accounting (with Honors) from Texas Tech University and a Juris Doctor degree from Southern Methodist University. Bill is a CPA and an attorney licensed in the State of Texas. He is also certified as an investment management consultant by the Institute of Investment Management Consultants and is a member of the Investment Management Council. He is a frequent lecturer on the topics of asset management and ERISA procedures, and he periodically acts as an expert witness regarding these issues.

Philip R. Taylor is founder and President of P. R. Taylor, Inc., an investment banking and investment consulting firm headquartered in Palo Alto, California, with offices in New York, Dallas, Walnut Creek, and Tampa. The firm's principals have billions of dollars of money management experience for major banks, institutions, and endowments. As a member of the Investment Management Council, P. R. Taylor brings its institutional experience and Callan's institutional resources to bear on the middle market. Mr. Taylor is a founding member of the Hoover Institution's Council for Global Economic and Political Transition. Previously, he was corporate counsel, director of taxes, and a director of business development for Tandem Computers, Incorporated, where he was responsible for negotiating major international corporate transactions. He was also a member of Tandem's Finance and Legal Policy Committee. Earlier, he was senior tax counsel and manager of tax planning for Hewlett-Packard Company, international tax counsel at Ashland Oil, Inc., and financial consultant at Inland Steel Company. Mr. Taylor holds a J.D. degree from the University of Virginia and a mechanical engineering degree from Northwestern University. He is a member of the California Bar.

ACKNOWLEDGMENTS

We have had the great fortune of working with countless professionals in the investment services industry who have heavily influenced our thinking. Whenever possible, we have tried to attribute ideas to the originator. But we know, regrettably, that we will fail to properly recognize numerous friends and colleagues. For that we are sorry, and offer our sincere apologies in advance.

We do wish to thank and gratefully acknowledge the following individuals for their assistance in preparing this book.

Bo Abesamis
Carol Allen
Albert Bellas
Cheryl Bott
Deanne Christopulos
Brian Cunningham
Eric Davison
Ann Deluce
Mike Devine
Art Fenton

Ron Gold
John Gonzales
Charles Hart
William Hoisington, Esq.
Lynn Hopewell
Marti Jensen
Kenny Kahn
Michelle Lee
Jim McKee
Peggy Newton

Greg Patterson	Rich Todd
Amy Paul	Paul Troup
Ronald D. Peyton	Jim Van Heuit
Roger Raulin	Dick Vosbrug
Gary Robertson	Steve Weinstein
Joel Schwarz	Thurmon White
Dick Smith	Elaine Yeary
Sue Stevens	

We would particularly like to thank Roger Hewins and Amy Clifford for their extensive editing, rewriting, and substantive contributions.

Graphics and illustrations by Maria Fortuno.

And Melina DiChiara who fed us during the final days of editing.

Donald B. Trone
William R. Allbright
Philip R. Taylor

INTRODUCTION

This book seeks to fulfill the requests of numerous professional advisers for a practical manual that lays out the step-by-step process for the proper management of investment decisions.[1] The premise is that you can assist your clients in achieving their objectives by engaging them in the straightforward process which contributes most to investment success: *asset allocation, the development of thoughtful investment policy statements, the selection of appropriate money managers, and the monitoring of service providers.*

Our message is appropriate whether investment guidance is incidental to your normal practice or the mainstay. For the experienced adviser, the methodology we employ, as well as the checklists and the illustrations, should be of tremendous assistance in sharpening your existing skills. For the inexperienced adviser, the process about which we write is

---

[1]For the purposes of this text, we include within the definition of a professional adviser: attorneys, accountants, actuaries, pension administrators and record keepers, investment consultants, financial planners, and broker-consultants.

simple and straightforward, and can be easily mastered and applied in the real world.

Indeed, the first important lesson is recognizing that your client's investment decisions need thoughtful management, no less than other critical areas within the client's business, family, or charitable interests. Certainly the portfolios would seem to compel an enlightened management focus. Successful and sophisticated investors have learned over the last 20 years to concentrate their energy and resources on *managing* their investment decisions, rather than on trying to choose winning stocks or top-performing money managers.

Furthermore, the law has now caught up with prudent investment practices. Fiduciaries and trustees (of which you as an adviser may be included) are required to manage investment assets along the lines of the proven investment process outlined in this book. To do otherwise is to risk personal liability and, in extreme cases, criminal sanctions. The good news is that the legally prudent management of investment decisions should lead to long term investment success as well.

We do not include topics on making money or on portfolio management. These are subjects that are more appropriately left to money managers (mutual funds), business schools, and the financial press. There are plenty of people in this world who are willing to offer their expertise in that area, but there is a critical shortage of knowledgeable advisers to whom clients can turn for practical, objective, jargon-free guidance. We seek to fill that void.

Many investors have neither an understanding of the implications of their investment strategies nor access to appropriate resources for guidance. We will have been successful if we accomplish no more than to encourage you to engage in a prudent investment process and to teach your clients to do the same. Fortunately, the process is within the easy grasp of any of your clients, regardless of their account size or level of sophistication.

Managing investment decisions has always been a difficult endeavor. When someone else's money is involved, it can be an even more arduous task, given the additional challenge of meeting serious legal standards for investment management. Few would argue that the task appears to be increasingly complex, forcing you and your clients to contend with a host of new investment markets and opportunities. In this environment of seemingly endless choices, it is easy to lose the forest for the trees. Fiduciaries struggle to comply with the rules that govern their activities while trying to fulfill the desires and wishes of donors, grantors, and corporate and public sponsors of retirement plans. What are those rules? Where should your clients look for practical guidance in meeting the letter and intent of the law? What should your role be in fulfilling their responsibilities?

In a highly dynamic environment, we believe the development of a successful investment strategy demands a simple process for managing investment decisions. Yet, many of your clients, like the investors of every past age, still search for the money manager with the magic elixir to assure investment success. This search leads to a frenzy of meaningless activity, rarely resulting in sustainable performance and usually frustrating the potentially valuable efforts of even the best money managers.

We want to share with all individuals and institutions the successful investment management techniques that multibillion dollar institutions now routinely employ to achieve consistent, steady asset growth over time. Although the theories underlying this procedural process were developed by Nobel Prize winners in finance and economics, this is not an academic treatise. Rather, it is meant to be a practical reference tool.

All of the concepts discussed herein are within the easy grasp of any college graduate—simple, yet powerful. We make every attempt to avoid arcane language and higher mathematics. You won't find any quadratic equations, and you won't need to pull out a college text on set theory. As the adviser, you'll find that you should spend the bulk of your time assisting your clients in defining their objectives and the risks they are prepared to take to meet them. Furthermore, with a realistic policy in place to manage your client's investment decisions, you'll spend far less time implementing and monitoring those decisions. The long-term investment success of your clients and your peace of mind should speak for themselves.

In Chapter 1, we outline the steps of the prudent investment process, with an emphasis on *process,* both to achieve investment objectives and to avoid fiduciary liability. In Chapter 2, we describe the investor or fiduciary's primary responsibility as one of *management*. The investor's time should be spent managing the overall investment process; it is not necessary to acquire the skills of a money manager.

In Chapters 3 through 8, we examine each step of the process in more detail. We discuss techniques on how to inquire into the investor's current circumstances, constraints, and goals. We define asset allocation and describe its overwhelming importance. We detail the straightforward method for choosing the allocation that is appropriate for each particular investor. We consider the factors to be incorporated in a well-developed investment policy statement that will serve as the business plan for implementing, monitoring, and adapting the investment strategy to changing circumstances. Chapters 6 and 7 lay out a due diligence process for evaluating and selecting money managers to implement the chosen investment strategy. In Chapter 8, we describe the investor's need, and the fiduciary's legal obligation, to monitor all aspects of the investment plan, including the performance of the portfolio and that of the individual money managers.

In Chapters 9 through 12, we cover topics that are tangential to the decision-making process. We explain the myriad of expenses that any investment portfolio will incur, with a view towards uncovering the numerous undisclosed costs of typical investment management. In Chapter 10, we discuss the role of investment management consultants. In Chapter 11, we describe common breaches of fiduciary duties, and outline the legal principles governing the activities of fiduciaries and explain how these principles parallel the prudent process outlined in this book. Chapter 12 addresses the implementation of socially responsible investment strategies.

Chapters 13 through 17 outline the unique investment management requirements of the different market segments. Chapter 13 discusses the concerns of wealthy families and the differences between the individual and institutional investor. Chapter 14 illustrates the various approaches taken by professionally advised foundations and endowments. Chapter 15 covers the ever-increasing market for defined benefit and defined contribution pension plans. Chapters 16 and 17 describe the practices of public retirement funds (state and municipal retirement funds) and Taft-Hartley funds (union pensions).

Our concluding chapter provides a glimpse into the future. It is not our intention to predict the future, but rather to give you an indication of developing trends that are expected to continue.

Managing the investment process should be like managing any other business activity: Investors have to determine *their* objectives, the resources for achieving them, and the process to go through to get there. Most importantly, we believe it is essential for your clients to be able to evaluate any new investment procedure or opportunity in the context of their individualized investment policy. Otherwise, the avalanche of financial products is sure to overwhelm even the most diligent investor. Deviations from the process in order to consider the latest Wall Street innovations will be nonproductive at best and will likely disrupt the strategy that was adopted for achieving long-term investment success.

CONTENTS

CHAPTER 7
Step 4 cont.—Implementation: Structure and Alternative Investments 173

CHAPTER 8
Step 5—Monitoring the Portfolio   201

CHAPTER 9
Controlling Investment Expenses   223

CHAPTER 12
Managing a Socially Responsible Investment Agenda   285

CHAPTER 13
High Net Worth Families   295

CHAPTER 14
Endowments and Foundations   311

CHAPTER 15
Defined Benefit and Defined Contribution Plans   321

1

THE PROCEDURALLY PRUDENT PROCESS

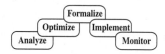

*"It's not whether you win or lose that counts,
but who gets the blame."*
Will Rogers

*"An investment philosophy is a system of general beliefs about how
investment funds should be managed. Unfortunately, most people have no
clear thought-out investment philosophy and do not follow a plan."*
T. Rowe Price

There is certainly no shortage of books, brokers, barkers, or barbers who are willing to share with you the secrets of making money. Individuals who would ordinarily hesitate to stop and give directions to a lost tourist have no reservations about striking up a conversation with a stranger on where the market closed, complete with their own commentary and opinions. The subject of investing has universal appeal and is politically correct in almost any setting. Yet despite all that has been written and professed about making money, there is very little information available on the management of investment decisions.

This book is about the process that a fiduciary, trustee, or curious investor should follow to successfully manage investment decisions—not about making money. The distinction is subtle, yet critically important, particularly for the individual or committee charged with managing someone else's money. When a person has a legal and/or moral responsibility for an investment portfolio, that person's primary role is one of management. Simply stated, the role is to set policy, to select appropriate professional money managers (including mutual funds), and to monitor the results. In contrast, hired professional money managers are those persons charged with making investment decisions.

This important concept of management is further reinforced by existing and proposed fiduciary statutes. For most fiduciaries and trustees, the legal requirements for prudent investment management parallel the course of action that would be followed by an informed professional investor. The courts will judge a fiduciary on the process that was followed in managing investment decisions—not on the ultimate investment results.

While managing sound investment decisions is not an easy task, in this chapter we will describe a process that provides clear guidance to practical, readily identifiable, and easily adaptable steps. The process is virtually the same for all types of portfolios, regardless of asset size or intended use. (The differences that do exist between the management of different portfolios are detailed in later chapters.) While the procedures discussed will not guarantee investment success, they will significantly increase the odds of building and structuring an investment portfolio that will withstand the test of private and public scrutiny.

The Process

Superior investment returns are a result of developing a prudent process or strategy, and then sticking with it. In order for fiduciaries and investors to manage better (informed) investment decisions, procedurally prudent judgments must replace intuition and/or emotional decisions influenced by market noise, press-appointed investment gurus, or product peddlers.

The process incorporates both modern investment management theory and the legal elements of fiduciary conduct. It reflects management techniques followed for over 20 years by the multibillion dollar pension funds, major foundations, and endowments able to afford the benefits of professional investment counsel.

Hierarchy of Decisions

Figure 1–1 outlines the hierarchy of decisions that reflects a synthesis of modern investment management theory. The model is truly hierarchical—there is a priority to the decisions that have to be managed.

- The initial, and most critical, decision for the investor is to establish an investment time horizon. That is, the investor must decide how long a particular investment strategy can be followed. The shorter the time horizon, the less appropriate are equities, or any other asset class with high return variations. Conversely, the longer the time horizon, the more an investor can afford an allocation to equities.

- Once the time horizon has been established, the next decision is in which asset classes the portfolio should be invested. The time horizon and the selection of asset classes are closely linked. For time periods of less than five years, prudent choices of asset classes will often be limited to securities with less return volatility, such as short-term fixed income and cash.

- The third decision is the allocation of the portfolio between each asset class. If the investor has chosen equities, fixed income, and cash as the appropriate asset classes, then what

---

FIGURE 1–1
Hierarchy of Decisions

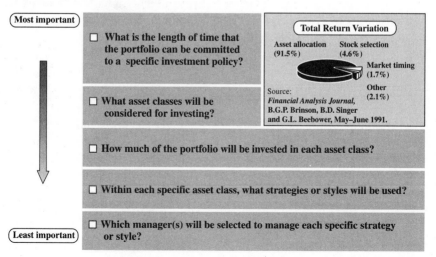

Source: Copyright © 1993, Investment Management Council.

percentage of the portfolio will be allocated to each? For example, the decision may be to place 60 percent in equities, 30 percent in fixed income, and the balance in cash.

- Of lesser consequence is the decision to diversify a particular asset class among sub-asset classes. However, this decision will still have a positive impact on the long-term performance of a portfolio and will minimize interim total return fluctuations. In the above example, if 60 percent of the portfolio is going to be allocated to equities, there are several equity sub-asset class styles that should be considered for diversification: value, core, growth, and small cap.

- The last decision, and the decision that will have the least impact on the long-term performance of the portfolio, is which money manager or mutual fund to select. What?!!! Is this a misprint? No. One of the most common mistakes made by investors is reversing this hierarchy of decisions by placing far too much emphasis on the selection of money managers—or, worse yet, selecting money managers and then, by default, having the asset class and sub-asset class decided by the money manager.

For example, if an investment committee hires a growth equity manager and charges the manager with structuring a balanced account, guess what type of portfolio the investment committee is going to end up with? A portfolio heavily allocated to equities with a growth tilt. The proper procedure would have been for the committee to set the allocation and then to search for money managers that are specialists in each of the respective asset classes and sub-asset classes.

Another reason why the money manager decision has such a low priority is there is no reliable way to predict the future performance of a money manager or mutual fund. There is a reason why the disclosure "Past performance is no indication of future performance" is printed on every mutual fund prospectus and money manager proposal—because it's true. By the time a hot mutual fund, money manager, or even asset class graces the top ten list of the financial press, the overwhelming odds are that within a short period of time the performance will decline.

Fiduciary Code of Conduct

As previously mentioned, our investment management process incorporates the legal elements of fiduciary conduct—those standards codified under the Employee Retirement Income Security Act of 1974 (ERISA) and the more recently adopted Restatement Third, Trusts (Prudent Man Rule) [hereafter referred to as Third Restatement].[1] There are a number of common threads that are woven into the fabric of these two statutes, and from them one can derive a uniform code (see Figure 1–2).

By combining the hierarchy of decisions with the Uniform Code of Fiduciary Conduct, a five-step process emerges that encapsulates the components of both. The five steps are integrated—no one step can be effectively implemented without drawing upon information developed in the previous step. The following is a summary of each of these steps (see Figure 1–3), with details provided in later chapters.

FIGURE 1-2
Uniform Code of Fiduciary Conduct

Uniform Code of Fiduciary Conduct

1. **Prepare written investment policies and document the process used to derive investment decisions.**

2. **Diversify portfolio assets with regards to the specific risk/return objectives of participants/beneficiaries.**

3. **Use professional money managers ("prudent experts") to make investment decisions.**

4. **Control and account for all investment expenses.**

5. **Monitor the activities of all money managers and service providers.**

6. **Avoid conflicts of interest.**

---

[1] As of the printing of this book, The Restatement Third, Trusts (Prudent Man Rule) has been adopted by Alabama, California, Delaware, Florida, Georgia, Illinois, Iowa, Kansas, Minnesota, Montana, Nevada, New York, South Carolina, Tennessee, Virginia, and Washington.

FIGURE 1–3
Steps in the Investment Management Process

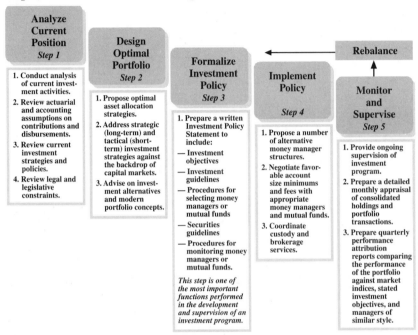

Source: Copyright ©1993, Investment Management Council.

Steps in the Investment Management Process

Step 1—Analyze the Current Situation

Investment decisions should never be managed in isolation or in a vacuum. All factors that may have a bearing on the decisions should be identified, analyzed, and integrated into the process, including the determination of the portfolio's objectives.

The portfolio's investment objectives specify the results that the investor or fiduciary would equate with a successful investment program. These differ from the broad statements of purpose or aspirations constituting the portfolio's mission in that the objectives must be a list of quantifiable investment results expected to be achieved over a specified time horizon. For example, a common objective for investment committees of retirement plans and foundations is to produce a total rate of return that exceeds the rate of inflation by a certain amount.

Objectives are typically set for the total portfolio as well as for the various asset classes and each individual money manager or mutual fund. Objectives serve three purposes: (*a*) they are necessary inputs to the asset allocation decision (step 2 of the process); (*b*) they are important components to the investment policy statement (step 3); and (*c*) they facilitate the performance evaluation process (step 5).

In addition to determining the portfolio's missions and objectives, the investor should analyze information and details relating to:

1. The length of time a particular investment strategy can be followed (time horizon) until there is a significant disbursement.
2. The portfolio's cash flow (contributions/withdrawals).
3. Regulations, trust documents, or legal instruments that may constrain investments to remain within certain asset classes, mandate certain asset mixes, or establish specific security guidelines.
4. The types of risk to which the portfolio is exposed and the types of risk the investor is willing to accept.

Of the foregoing, the analysis of risk is often the first topic of concern among investors and fiduciaries. Risk can never be completely avoided, but it can be managed through the proper implementation of this process. "Therefore, the duty of caution does not call for avoidance of risk by trustees but for their prudent management of risk." [2]

In gathering the necessary data to analyze investment objectives, it is advisable to consult with all professional advisors that may be involved in working with the investor or fiduciary. The *attorney* should review legal documents that pertain to the assets to be invested and comment on any restrictions that limit the type or allocation of assets. The *accountant* should update cash flow statements and balance sheets—highlighting any information that may materially impact investment decisions. The *actuary* (for defined benefit plans or self-insurance trusts) should submit the latest report on accrued and estimated liabilities. And a competent *investment consultant* should conduct a fiduciary audit to uncover any procedural omissions or prohibited transactions.

---

[2] Restatement Third, Sec. 227, comment e, p. 18.

Step 2—Design Optimal Portfolio

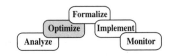

Step 2 involves determining the optimal portfolio mix (asset allocation) that satisfies the investment objectives. A portfolio's asset mix or asset allocation refers to the percentages that are invested in various asset classes, such as domestic stocks, domestic bonds, cash, real estate, international stocks, international bonds, and so on. As will be emphasized throughout this text, *the investor's or fiduciary's choice of an asset mix outweighs all other decisions in terms of the ultimate impact on a portfolio's investment performance.*

The investor's role is to choose the appropriate combination of assets that optimizes risk and return objectives. The chosen asset allocation will be that unique portfolio that maximizes the investor's return subject to a particular level of risk tolerance. We use the acronym RATE to define the key investor-specific inputs:[3]

R   Risk tolerance of investor

A   Asset class preferences

T   Time horizon of investment objectives

E   Expected or desired rate of return

R   Risk
We first consider what many consider the element of primary importance in setting a long-range asset allocation strategy: the *investor's risk tolerance.* There are many different ways to define risk, but we have found the most effective way is to ask, "How much money are you willing to lose in a given year?" The primary function and role of the investor is to manage risk, not to maximize investment returns (which is the proper role of the money manager). An investor's attitude toward risk is central to maintaining a strategic, long-term asset allocation.

A   Asset Classes
Investors must specify the asset categories they want represented in their investment portfolio. Portfolio theory and the successful experience of large institutional investors suggest that investors should consider the

---

[3] The investment consultant who deserves credit for developing this acronym is Bryan Brand, who maintains a thriving practice in Chesterfield, Missouri.

broad asset classes (equities, fixed income, and cash) as a starting point, and then add to the list those asset classes in which they can *afford* to invest. For instance, would the size of the portfolio justify an allocation to foreign bonds, which have relatively high transaction costs and currency risk? Does the size of the portfolio allow for the cost-effective investment in certain illiquid alternative investments?

Similarly, it is the investor or fiduciary who knows what restrictions should be placed on the composition of the chosen asset classes. For example, trust, statutory, or regulatory requirements may prohibit ownership of certain types of securities. Just as important, the personal biases of key decision makers must be considered. In all cases, investors should *not* invest in an asset class they do not understand. Either the investor should know how an asset type is expected to perform under varying market conditions or the investor must engage an experienced consultant to explain the pitfalls as well as the opportunities. The investment de jour should not be selected simply because of its present appeal.

T   Time Horizon

The investor's choice of time horizon is often the key variable in determining the ratio of equity to fixed income investments. Even if the investor has a very high risk tolerance, the investor shouldn't invest in stocks if the money is needed next year. One must consider the timing of the possible unexpected as well as expected requirements for use of the portfolio's assets. The investor's management role centers on determining the likely and possible drawdowns of the portfolio's resources—an inquiry that must be pursued with an insider's view.

The time horizons of many investment portfolios are arguably 20 years or longer. In practice, however, five-year horizons are typically chosen for the planning of the portfolio's assets. This is because an investor or fiduciary is not likely to continue to follow a policy that may not be working for 20 years. In addition, there is difficulty in forecasting with any assurance for a longer period.

E   Expected Return

When investment objectives are identified, either a specified rate of return is determined or a relative rate of return is established. For example, the investment committee for a hospital may determine that it has to earn 9 percent on its assets to have the necessary resources to build a new hospital wing in five years. Or the same committee may establish a relative rate of return exceeding the rate of inflation by 5 percent so that the hospital building fund is able to maintain purchasing power. An investment strategy that is out of sync with the risk tolerance of its sponsors or investment committee is doomed to fail. On the other hand, once a specific or relative rate of return has been established, it is the committee's responsibility to choose an allocation whose expected returns accomplish the objectives.

Optimization Models
Computer optimization models exist that mathematically determine alternative optimal asset mixes from which to choose. These models are based on capital markets forecasts and investor specific inputs (RATE).[4] Due to the great disparity between different models, the investor is cautioned to carefully research the investment expertise of the source. The adage "garbage in—garbage out" has never been more applicable.

   When the optimization is run, rarely is there one solution that meets all of the investor's different objectives. Typically, an investor's risk and return objectives are mutually exclusive of one another. The investor wants to assume a minimal level of risk—"I never want to lose money in any given year." But the investor also wants a relatively high rate of return—"I want to earn at least 9 percent on my money." In this example, a risk level of "no losses in a given year" has a return expectation of 7 percent. The return expectation of 9 percent carries with it a potential loss (worst case scenario) in a given year of −6.7 percent.[5] Trying to balance this risk tolerance with the desired rate of return is an excellent example of just one of the many critical roles that an investor and/or investment committee has to manage.

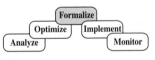

Step 3—Formalize Investment Policy Statement

This is the most important step in the process and is also the most glaring omission fiduciaries and investors make. There are a number of excellent reasons why a well written investment policy statement (IPS) is so important.

---

[4] Key capital markets variables are expected returns, standard deviations of returns, and cross-correlations of returns between the considered asset classes.

[5] Based on capital markets expectations developed by Callan Associates Inc., with a statistical level of confidence of 90 percent. How these models are developed is discussed in more detail in Chapter 4.

ERISA case law and the Third Restatement clearly reference the development and maintenance of an IPS as a critical fiduciary function.[6] One of the first documents that an auditor from the Department of Labor (DOL) or Internal Revenue Service (IRS) will likely check is the IPS. The lack of an IPS, or a poorly written IPS, is prima facie evidence that other aspects of the investment program may also not be in compliance.

For the individual investor, the IPS provides logical guidance during implementation of an investment strategy. Often intelligent investors make the mistake of entering into periods of emotionally driven binges of buying and selling because they have no formal guideposts to mark their investment boundaries.

For the investment committee, particularly one with a high turnover of members, the IPS ensures continuity of the investment strategy and may keep future members from second guessing the actions of original members. For foundation and/or endowment committees, the IPS also provides donors the best proof of the organization's stewardship.

"Investment policies must be simple, forthright, and understandable to a competent stranger."[7] It should detail the desired investment mix and management structure, provide a strategy for automatically rebalancing the assets, provide for clear and enforceable performance standards for money managers, and define the duties and responsibilities for all parties involved in the management of the portfolio's assets.

The IPS should be viewed as the business plan and the essential management tool for directing and communicating the activities of the portfolio. First and foremost, its purpose is to explicitly state the investor's *realistic* long-term investment goals. Properly designed, an investment policy is far more than a mere perfunctory description of the investor's investment program. Rather, it is the formal, long-range strategic plan that allows the investor to coordinate the management of the portfolio's investment programs in a logical and consistent framework. Its prescriptive mandates for money managers provide the essential link between the investor's objectives and the realities of capital markets.

Investment committees must develop their investment policies with the understanding that they will be implemented in a complex and dynamic financial environment. The investment policy will produce its greatest benefits during periods of adverse market performance.

---

[6] ERISA Sec. 402(b)(1) and Restatement Third, Sec. 227, comment d, p. 14.

[7] John W. Guy, *How to Invest Someone Else's Money* (Burr Ridge, IL: Irwin Professional Publishing, 1994) p. 75.

Committee members will be less tempted to alter an otherwise sound program by irrational fears; the investment policy will act as a stabilizer. Its mere existence should force fiduciaries to pause and consider the external and internal circumstances that prompted the development of the existing policy in the first place and whether the current poor market conditions were actually predictable—not in their timing, but in their intensity and unexpectedness. This is what the substance of good policy review should be all about: the framework that will allow cooler heads and a longer-term outlook to prevail.

In periods of financial market prosperity, such as the 80s, almost any investment program, no matter how inconsistently it was designed, likely generated impressive results. In those circumstances, the advantages of a comprehensive investment policy and the time devoted to its development may have appeared marginal. However, even under favorable market conditions, the investment policy may temper the temptation to increase the aggressiveness of an investment program, as fiduciaries extrapolate the current market trends into the future.

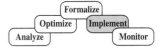

Step 4—Implementation

Once the IPS has been approved, searches are commenced to select appropriate money managers (including mutual funds), a custodian, and transaction brokers. Most investors consider this step the sexiest part of the process. However, decisions made at this level will not have as much impact on the long-term performance of the portfolio as the asset allocation decisions made in step 2 and then formalized in step 3.

Effective management skills are most critical in the implementation stage, *not* because one needs to become the money manager for the portfolio—just the opposite. The successful investor will intuitively follow the time-proven maxim of doing what one knows best and delegating the rest to others.[8] However, for some reason (perhaps the perceived glamour of making investment decisions), the investor or investment committee often takes on direct responsibility for investing some or all of the funds rather than delegating those tasks to outside professional money managers.

---

[8] Peter F. Drucker has labeled this important approach "making strength productive" and stresses that it "is the unique purpose of any organization." *The Effective Executive* (New York: Harper & Row, 1967), pp. 71-99.

Yet, as we have pointed out, the investor's primary function is to set policy, and the primary function of the money manager(s) is to maximize returns within mandated investment parameters. Mastering the skills of effective money management requires years of studying and an understanding of the capital markets. To achieve even marginal success as a money manager requires a serious allocation of time and money, well beyond the resources of most investors.

Key Tenets to Implementing a Successful Investment Strategy

• When selecting money managers or mutual funds, the investor should consider using specialists, not generalists. Over the last 20 years, large institutional portfolios have transitioned almost completely from single balanced managers to multiple manager investment programs. In the past, many balanced managers made both asset mix and security structure decisions for their clients. Today, the asset allocation decision and sub-asset class implementation (with each manager pursuing a distinct investment style) are primarily in the domain of the investment committee. Incidentally, a comparison of fees also reveals that the fees paid to the combination of specialists is often less than the median balanced manager's fee.

• When asset size permits, take advantage of diversifying between different investment styles within an asset class—for example, diversifying the equity component of a portfolio between growth and value styles.

• Notwithstanding the above, keep the implementation strategy simple. Overdiversifying a portfolio will increase costs and make implementation and monitoring of the portfolio more difficult.

• Have investment decisions made by professionals, particularly if the investor is a fiduciary or trustee. ERISA and the Third Restatement do not require the use of professional money managers (mutual funds), but fiduciaries can be held to the same level of expertise. The law provides fiduciaries with "safe harbor rules" that, when followed, offer fiduciaries protection from certain forms of liability.

• Follow a due diligence process when interviewing and selecting managers. Money management firms hire the best and brightest minds in the country, and every firm will appear to have an incredible story to sell. If there is no structure to the selection process, the investor will have a very difficult time determining the most appropriate manager.

(In the consulting industry, the final selection process performed by unsophisticated investment committees is often referred to as the beauty pageant.)

• When possible, avoid load funds or any investment service where the advisor or consultant is compensated by commissions. The growing availability of no-load funds and fee-based advisors should enable the investor to find competent objective services, regardless of portfolio size.

• Be assured of best execution for all transactions. The largest expense, next to money manager fees, is transaction costs. Fiduciaries are specifically charged with controlling investment expenses. The investor should know who is receiving compensation from transactions, what percentage of the transactions is being used by money managers to pay for research and other services, and, for investors working with brokers in wrap fee programs or receiving other consultant-related services, what percentage of the portfolio is required to be traded through the sponsoring broker.

• Ensure that the portfolio's assets are properly safeguarded. There is a difference between holding assets at a brokerage firm and using a trust company. A trust company is required to segregate each client's assets and hold them in a separate account. Brokerage firms, on the other hand, can commingle a client's assets with the general assets of the brokerage firm.

Step 5—Monitoring and Supervision

Monitoring the resulting performance of selected money managers and/or mutual funds and evaluating the continuing viability of meeting the investor's objectives constitute the final step of the investment management process. For the fiduciary, monitoring the activities of hired money managers and service vendors is an ongoing requirement. An effective monitoring program should provide the investor with sufficient information to evaluate the program's strengths and weaknesses, and to keep the program on track in achieving the portfolio's objectives.

The truly effective investor or fiduciary realizes that a crucial element of the decision-making process is establishing appropriate performance measurement standards:

1. To facilitate good investor-money manager communications and to confirm the mutually agreed-upon goals of the investment policy.
2. To show whether the assets are being managed as directed by that policy with respect to the portfolio's risk tolerance and expected return.
3. To support the qualitative judgments about the continued confidence, or lack of it, in the money manager's abilities.
4. To support the periodic consideration of the continuing appropriateness of the investment policy.

A common mistake made by investors is the failure to compare money managers to appropriate peer groups, or comparing managers to benchmarks that may be totally irrelevant. For example, equity managers should not always be hired or fired by the mere comparison of their performance to the S&P 500. Equity managers that follow a growth strategy should be compared against other growth managers. There will be times when the median returns of all growth managers over- and underperform the S&P 500.

Monitoring the specific performance of money managers and service vendors includes an analysis of not only "what happened?" but also "why?". The analysis combines the disciplines of performance measurement—the science—with performance evaluation—the art. Performance measurement is primarily a technical accounting function that computes the return of the total portfolio and component parts. Performance evaluation uses the information generated by performance measurement to determine what contributed to or detracted from the portfolio's return.

Review Procedures

A long-term investment strategy requires alteration only when the underlying factors of the investment objectives change. These changes tend to be infrequent, if not rare, and reviews directed toward constantly reassessing existing policy tend to be counterproductive. The investment committee should be particularly cautious of making changes during periods of market extremes. The tendency to tinker can lead to ill-advised short-run decisions.

Despite the infrequent need for policy modifications, periodic reviews can serve a very productive purpose. When aimed at educating fiduciaries and other decision makers, reviews can reinforce the logic of current policy and therefore reduce the chances of unnecessary alterations. In addition, whenever significant events occur that warrant a review, one should see that they are examined in an orderly fashion.

At least monthly, investors should analyze their custodian's appraisal report containing the current market value of holdings and the previous month's transactions and expenses. Particular attention should be paid to transactions (buys and sells) initiated by hired money managers and compared against the manager's stated investment strategy.

On a quarterly basis, one should compare the asset allocation of the portfolio and the performance of hired money manager(s) to benchmarks established in the IPS. If the situation warrants, the portfolio should be rebalanced back to the strategic asset allocation of the IPS. (If the IPS calls for a 60/40 allocation to equities and fixed income, and the quarterly report shows an existing asset mix of 70/30, then equities should be sold off and fixed income purchased.)

At least annually, there should be a formal review to determine whether investment objectives are being attained or have changed. One should be particularly sensitive of the need to determine whether the investment strategy still holds the highest probability of meeting short-term liquidity needs and long-term objectives.

Summary

Regardless of portfolio size, the investor benefits from a clear understanding of the role one should play in the management of investment decisions. Only by following a structured process can one be certain that all critical components of an investment strategy are being properly implemented. The sole purpose of this book is to provide the investor with the knowledge and confidence to apply this process on a routine basis.

The role of the investor and the fiduciary is to maximize the benefits to be gained from the process—that is, to maximize the likelihood of achieving one's goals and investment objectives. The degree of commitment to the necessary tasks outlined in the process will ultimately determine investment success. It will be the actions of the investor, not those of the money managers, that will have the greatest impact on the ultimate value of the portfolio.

Of course, investment success alone should be reason enough for one to apply the concepts discussed above. For fiduciaries who need additional incentive, in Chapter 11 we discuss the formidable scheme of legal sanctions, including personal liability, that awaits those who breach their fiduciary duties.

2

ROLE AND RESPONSIBILITY OF FIDUCIARIES, TRUSTEES, AND INVESTMENT COMMITTEE MEMBERS

"We ought not to rest satisfied with mediocrity, when excellence is within our reach."[1]

Joseph Story (1821)

*"[T]he real need in most investment relationships is not for more **investment** management, but for more **management** management, and this set of skills is far more likely to be found among corporate executives, foundation trustees, and makers of trusts with general management experience and orientation than among investment management specialists."*[2]

Charles D. Ellis, Managing Partner
of Greenwich Associates

Trustees, investment committee members, and fiduciaries (together, hereafter referred to as fiduciaries) have the most important, yet most misunderstood role in the investment process. The importance of their role stems from providing the essential management of the investment process, without which the other components of the investment plan can be neither defined, implemented, nor evaluated.

---

[1] Joseph Story, *The Miscellaneous Writings of Joseph Story* (Boston: James Monroe and Company, 1835) p. 433.

[2] Charles D. Ellis, *Investment Policy: "How to Win the Loser's Game,"* 2nd ed. (Homewood, IL: Business One Irwin, 1993), p. 3.

19

This chapter defines the proper role of the fiduciary. Straightforward terms are used to describe what fiduciaries should be doing to best assure investment success, and why. The emphasis is on the fiduciary (or investor) as the *manager* of the investment process—a role that does not require expertise as an investment specialist. As legal standards become more compatible with the tasks required for investment success, good management of the investment process, by itself, will reduce most concerns about fiduciary liability for investment decisions.

Fiduciaries have struggled to fathom their proper role in the investment management process. They have a tendency to micromanage their money managers or try to get up to date on the latest Wall Street investment theory or product. Yesterday, it was portfolio insurance, hedging techniques, and money market preferred stock; today, it's CMOs, negative convexity, derivatives, and alternative investment classes; tomorrow, it might be neural network investment strategies, chaos and fractal theories, and nonlinear forecasting.

How should well-informed fiduciaries spend their time? Setting and meeting investment objectives is much like meeting the goals of any business—a strong management team is needed that clearly understands the investment environment, the purpose and direction of the organization, and the unique resources upon which the fiduciary has to draw to meet the organization's goals. Fiduciaries are responsible for the general management of the assets. Their most important tasks—that is, the responsibilities that cannot be delegated—are

1. Determining the portfolio's mission and objectives.
2. Choosing an appropriate asset allocation strategy.
3. Establishing explicit written investment policies consistent with the objectives.
4. Selecting investment managers to implement the investment policy.
5. Monitoring investment results.

Who Is a Fiduciary?

General Definition

A fiduciary is defined as someone acting in a position of trust on behalf of, or for the benefit of, a third party. *The American Heritage*

Dictionary definition of a fiduciary is: "of, pertaining to, or involving one who holds something in trust for another . . . a person who stands in a special relation of trust, confidence, or responsibility in his obligations to others, as a company director or an agent of a principal," and "[a] member of a board elected or appointed to direct the funds and policy of an institution."

ERISA Definition

With respect to qualified retirement plans, ERISA defines the term *fiduciary* as any person who, with respect to a plan,

1. Exercises any discretionary authority or discretionary control regarding management of the plan, or exercises any authority or control (discretionary or otherwise) regarding management or disposition of its assets; or

2. Renders investment advice regarding plan assets for a fee or other compensation, direct or indirect, or has any authority or responsibility to do so; or

3. Has any discretionary authority or discretionary responsibility in the administration of such plan. [3]

The term *fiduciary* also includes any person designated as a named fiduciary. Under ERISA, one or more persons must be specified as the "named fiduciary" who has authority to control and manage the operation and administration of the plan. Contrary to the concept that a person may be a fiduciary for some purposes but not others (limited by function), named fiduciaries are deemed to hold fiduciary status for all purposes.

ERISA provisions allow named fiduciaries to allocate or delegate certain functions pursuant to procedures established in plan documents.[4] In certain instances, a named fiduciary can be protected from liability by designating another person to undertake fiduciary responsibility. (As an example, fiduciaries are encouraged to delegate investment decisions to qualified professional money managers, see the "Safe Harbor Rules" discussed in Chapter 6.)

---

[3] ERISA Sec. 3(21)(A), 29 U.S.C. Sec. 1002(21)(A) (1985).
[4] 29 C.F.R. Sec. 2509.75-8 at FR-13, FR-14.

A review of basic principles reveals that "Congress's intention in adopting ERISA was to spread a broad protective net of fiduciary responsibility."[5] ERISA language is designed to be broad in scope so that numerous categories of occupations and services rise to the level of fiduciary status—insurance companies, contract service providers, brokerage firms, investment counselors, employers, union officials, attorneys, and banks.[6] A comprehensive analysis of fiduciary status is provided as an appendix to this chapter.

General Fiduciary Status

There is no question that trustees under ERISA or the Third Restatement are fiduciaries and subject to the traditional duties of reasonable care and undivided loyalty under the statutory and common laws of trust and agency.[7] The issue and "trap for the unwary" is the extent to which persons other than trustees are deemed fiduciaries and possibly subject to the same duties.

How does one decide whether activities arise to create fiduciary status? Fiduciary status is determined by a "facts and circumstances" test specific to each situation. Someone could be found to be a fiduciary to one particular client without necessarily being a fiduciary for other clients, even though he/she may be performing similar services for each client. Thus a definitive, all-inclusive description of a fiduciary is impossible.

In general, the issue is whether one has control or influence over a client's investment decisions, or if the client is dependent on the adviser's services as the primary basis for its decisions. The resolution of that question turns on the factors discussed in Table 2–1.[8]

Determining fiduciary status is a complicated area that requires expert legal advice. This outline of pertinent issues is merely intended to heighten the awareness of circumstances necessitating the expert assistance of competent counsel. Legal advice regarding one's status

---

[5] District 65, UAW v. Harper & Row, Publishers, 670 F.Supp. 550, 555 (S.D.N.Y. 1987).

[6] Jane Kheel Stanley, "The Definition of a Fiduciary Under ERISA: Basic Principles," *Real Property, Probate and Trust Journal* 27 (1992).

[7] The duty of loyalty is discussed in Chapter 11. Generally, it requires that trustees act in a manner that puts their clients' interests above their own and that they act solely for the benefit of the client. The duty of reasonable care requires adherence to the prudent investor standard.

[8] Research paper prepared by Tim Patterson, Esq., of the law firm Cooley Godward Castro Huddleson & Tatum, San Francisco.

TABLE 2–1   Factors That May Determine Fiduciary Status

Factors	Facts Favoring Fiduciary Status	Facts Contrary to Fiduciary Status
1. Range of recommendations	Specific recommendations as to securities and money managers.	General advice or choice of reasonable investment and/or manager options.
2. Scope of services	Retainer arrangement for regular advice on variety of substantive issues over extended period of time; individualized advice based on client's circumstances; agreements that services serve as primary basis for decisions.	Project-related work; general work that client must adapt to its specific situation; agreements that services do not serve as primary basis for investment decisions.
3. Experience and investment sophistication of board	Unsophisticated; little investment experience; always follows recommendations of advisors.	Experienced and sophisticated; expresses own opinions; modifies options; seeks other opinions; engages other regular advisors.

as a fiduciary should be sought not only because the consequences of fiduciary status can be onerous (i.e., you can be held liable for the breaches of your co-fiduciaries), but good legal counsel may also be able to provide advice on how to alter the scope of one's activities and delivery of services to lessen the likelihood of fiduciary status.

Primary Duties of Fiduciaries

The role of the fiduciary is to manage the process—to look at the entire portfolio, to ensure that priority items are accomplished in a timely fashion by the most capable parties, and to measure results against agreed-upon goals.

Trustees can get immersed (some would say, submerged) in issues of portfolio operations, and, as a result, end up delegating or even abdicating their primary responsibilities for investment management. By default or otherwise, they defer critical asset allocation and other policy decisions to outside vendors who can hardly do more than reflect their own individual biases or time horizons (sometimes very different than those of the client). The fiduciary then spends countless hours at committee meetings listening to unfocused stories of last year's fortunes or travesties presented by eager or forlorn salespeople who, in turn, may not be attuned to their client's particular circumstances.

The management of investment decisions should not be delegated to product salespeople for several reasons. First, most of the decisions in the investment process have a qualitative as well as a quantitative aspect to them. Deferring to an outsider to make the fundamental decisions only assures cookie-cutter services, not the individual attention the situation demands. As an example, there are many ways to measure risk. Regardless of the quantitative measures favored, committee members know far better than anyone else the likelihood of their staying with an investment program whose results are less than stellar. The committee's feel will be an important factor determining risk tolerance for optimizing the asset allocation of the investment portfolio.

Similarly, only the committee members know the complete history of the investment program, the personalities and management structure of their organization, and the internal biases that have developed because of their successes and failures. Each committee member is likely to have a business to run or other tasks to perform. The only successful investment program will be one to which the committee members are committed for the long haul.

Second, committee members are in the best position to know what is unusual and important about their investment objectives. Do they view the contribution and investment strategy as an integral part of their balance sheet? For what contingencies have they planned? This type of information is part of the knowledge that must be brought into the process of formulating long-range investment policy.

Third, product salespeople have their own businesses to run, businesses that require them to be immersed in the details of meeting their business or investment objectives. The likelihood of them having the interest or the time to carefully consider the committee's specific circumstances is not great. While their input may be valuable in setting some objectives, they should not be expected to do the committee's job.

Fiduciaries do not have to possess superhuman qualities to successfully perform this management role, nor do they need "extensive experience in securities analysis or portfolio management."[9] What is required is

1. A sincere commitment and the courage to develop a consensus formulation of their organization's true concerns, interests, and objectives.

2. A personal interest in understanding the basics of capital market expectations.

3. The discipline to develop the long-term investment policies that can be expected to achieve their investment objectives.

4. The patience to evaluate events calmly in the context of long-term trends and institutional goals.[10] Policy revisions are rarely time sensitive. In fact, the greater the seeming urgency of policy changes, the more likely those changes are really active portfolio management decisions (proper role of the money manager) posing as policy issues.

5. The knowledge of and the discipline to implement the prudent investment process described in this text.

6. An understanding of their strengths (i.e., investment resources, staff, technological insight, effective consultant relationships, and so on) and those of their advisors to determine the realistic expectations/demands for performance.

7. The ability to "get the right things done," otherwise known as effective management. The prudent process itself facilitates effective management by distinguishing important from unimportant tasks as well as the priorities for accomplishing them.

Since the difference between a good manager and a great manager may merely be that "a great manager gets things done,"[11] every investment policy must be implemented. As the manager of the investment program, the fiduciary's role is to develop the investment philosophy and long-term strategic plan for the fund and to implement a stable, productive investment program designed to achieve those objectives.

---

[9] Ellis, *Investment Policy,* p. 3.

[10] John W. Guy, *How to Invest Someone Else's Money* (Burr Ridge IL: Irwin Professional Publishing, 1994), p. 159.

[11] Quote often attributed to David Packard, cofounder of Hewlett-Packard Company.

Delegation of Fiduciary Duties

The advantages and necessity of engaging experts to assist the fiduciary in managing the portfolio are widely understood by successful investors. In the past, the fiduciary's right to delegate was often prohibited under the common law of trusts; however, today's legal standards generally reflect modern thinking about delegation. Fiduciaries are encouraged to delegate if the item to be delegated is outside their sphere of knowledge, and they may rely on experts to aid in the achievement of the portfolio's objectives. The fiduciary's inquiry with respect to delegation should be

1. Is delegation allowed or required under the law governing one's activities?
2. What is the proper procedure for delegating tasks?

With respect to the first question, the historical anti-delegation rule of the law of trusts reveals a legal standard grossly out of step with reality for trustees still subject to its prohibitions. Seeking to modernize trust investment law and to restore flexibility to accommodate changing financial circumstances, modern statutes and the courts now take quite a different view of the propriety and role of delegation.[12] They recognize that fiduciaries cannot be experts in all aspects of investments and administration, nor can they possess knowledge in the entire range of activities integral to the operation of a trust, endowment, or employee benefit plan.[13]

> A trustee has a duty personally to perform the responsibilities of the trusteeship *except as a prudent person* might delegate those responsibilities to others. In deciding whether, to whom and in what manner to delegate fiduciary authority in the administration of a trust, and thereafter in supervising agents, the trustee is under a duty to the beneficiaries to exercise fiduciary discretion *and to act as a prudent person would act in similar circumstances.*[14]

The Treasury Department's regulations governing fiduciaries of *private foundations* implicitly grant permission to delegate by according the fiduciary protection from liability if he or she relies on the advice

---

[12] For a detailed discussion of delegation and the liability incurred for delegating, see "When the Fiduciary's Agent Errs — Who Pays the Bill — Fiduciary, Agent, or Beneficiary?", *Real Property, Probate and Trust Journal* 28, no. 3 (Fall 1993).

[13] ERISA Sec. 402(c)(2) and (3).

[14] Restatement Third, Sec. 171, *Duty with Respect to Delegation.*

of "qualified investment counsel."[15] In the case of nonprofit institutions, delegation is also permitted in those states which have adopted the Uniform Management of Institutional Funds Act (UMIFA). For pension plans, ERISA provides explicit authority to delegate:

> Any employee benefit plan may provide: . . .that a person who is a named fiduciary with respect to control or management of the assets of the plan may appoint an investment manager or managers to manage (including the power to acquire and dispose of) any assets of a plan.[16]

Trustees will generally not be held liable for the acts or omissions of the investment manager, nor will they be responsible for the investment of trust or plan assets under the management of the investment manager, unless the appointment is imprudent or the fiduciary fails to monitor the conduct of the manager.[17] Once a fiduciary has delegated a "proper task,"[18] the law of personal trusts and the modern statutes are in complete agreement that

1. The delegation must be to a qualified person.
2. The delegation must be accomplished prudently.
3. The fiduciary must continue to monitor the conduct of the appointee.

These rules require the fiduciary to focus on the fact that delegation is like any other business decision. The mere fact that one is allowed, or even required, to delegate in certain circumstances doesn't mean any delegation will suffice.

Documentation

Fiduciary standards of care create the necessity for written documentation evidencing the fiduciary's diligence and informed consideration of the pertinent factors in the decision-making process. The

---

[15] Treas. Reg. § 53.4944-1(b)(2)(v).

[16] ERISA Sec. 402(c)(3), 29 U.S.C. Sec. 1102(c)(3).

[17] Restatement Third, Sec. 171, comment a; ERISA Sec. 405(d)(1) (under ERISA, a fiduciary can also be liable under the co-fiduciary rules of Section 405(a)).

[18] Under the modern statutes this could be "any task," taking into account the circumstances surrounding the decision.

documents that must be maintained depend on the overall circum-stances of the investment plan and on the nature of the individual investment decisions.

Elaborate procedures and a paper trail to show how these proce-dures were followed will not always be sufficient to demonstrate prudence in the event of a legal challenge or audit. To avoid liability, a fiduciary will also need to demonstrate a rational basis for the decisions taken based on the particular circumstances. For example, investment deci-sions based purely on convenience or cost will not satisfy the standard. Nor can one hope to justify the use of an investment manager, product, or asset allocation by documenting its use by other fiduciaries. The fact that others have used the product is not a legitimate basis for its use by another fiduciary with different risk tolerance levels, resources, goals, and objectives.

It becomes rather straightforward to see what substantive detail is required to support an honest, informed decision-making process for later reflection and evaluation. Of course, the crucial investment policy statement and ongoing written performance evaluations should be saved. In addition, the fiduciary should document all material factors considered in the deliberation of investment alternatives, including

1. The current and projected resources and obligations of the investment plan and the reasonableness of the underlying related assumptions.
2. The rationale for the choice of performance goals, time horizons, and permissible asset classes and the sensitivity to variations in each.
3. The basis for the validity of the capital markets expectations data utilized in determining an optional asset allocation.
4. The purpose the money manager(s) or service(s) is/are intended to play in the total portfolio, and the performance objectives or conditions that must be met to achieve that purpose.
5. The factors considered in the choice of money managers or investment vehicles.

Whether one is choosing a performance objective, policy asset allo-cation, permissible asset classes, or individual money managers, the prudence (and likely success) of the investment management decisions will be determined by the *quality* of the surrounding decision-making process. The purpose of documentation is to highlight the substantive elements of the decision-making process, providing solid evidence of the thoughtful process employed by careful fiduciaries in their management of investment funds. The factors discussed above are really no more or less than what informed decision makers would consider in managing their own funds. In fact, these are the same factors considered by successful investors, regardless of whether they are subject to fiduciary standards of conduct.

Common Mistakes Made by Fiduciaries

Separate from possible breaches (see Chapter 11), there are a number of common mistakes that fiduciaries may make in the investment process. An awareness of these mistakes will help the fiduciary avoid such mistakes in the future.

Micro-Management.   A common fiduciary mistake is to micromanage the portfolio rather than take a holistic view of the process. Often, fiduciaries get involved in the minutiae of monitoring which stocks and bonds have been chosen for their portfolios but have no particular benchmark for distinguishing good results from bad. For example, when an investment manager alters the allocated pool of stocks, the fiduciary's interest may be piqued by the likely discovery that some of the stocks sold have increased in value since they were sold, and that stocks that were purchased (or held) have decreased in value—all within the last two months! Is this really as important as a view toward the overall results the manager is achieving? Probably not.

An Investment Policy Statement is Not Developed.   Without a business plan, not only does the fiduciary not know where he or she is going, neither does anyone else. The money managers do the best they can without competent managerial guidance, but the simple fact is they cannot do the fiduciary's job. The resulting pragmatism (i.e., treating every investment decision on its merits and in isolation) not only wastes enormous time but leads to frustration and futility.[19] Clean and explicit long-term investment policies can only be developed by the fiduciary's adequate communication of the organization's objectives.

---

[19] Peter F. Drucker, "The Elements of Decision Making" in *The Effective Executive* (New York: Harper & Row, 1967), p. 125.

Wasted Time for Routine Meetings. Time is a fiduciary's most valuable resource. It should be used to discuss policies, abnormalities, missed objectives, or education. Agendas, accompanied by necessary reports and proposals circulated in advance, are essential to the effective management of the process. Fiduciaries must let the prudent process guide their selection of relevant information from the barrage of data and opinions in the marketplace. Anything less will surely result in poor decisions unsupported by any process, with the only way of improving the results being to start over.

Characteristics of a Successful Investment Committee

The role of the investor or investment committee is one of management. Consequently, the attributes current or prospective committee members should possess are those contributing directly to this need for professional management. Rather than requiring specialized money management skills, prudent investment management merely couples basic management disciplines with a desire to learn the goals and limitations of the overall investment management process. Investment expertise is not essential.

The successful investment committee, like any good management team, will focus first on determining the right things to do, rather than on how to do things right, and then on prioritizing the means for accomplishing them. Even more importantly, the successful investment committee will have little difficulty deciding what not to do. Because they either participated in the actual development of a thoughtful investment plan or at least understood its overall financial framework and goals, they will waste far less time pursuing the latest hot money manager or financial instrument. The committee understands the need to provide clear direction to the money managers and will resist the temptation to micromanage. They will involve experts with different mind-sets (images of the world) to assist them in setting goals and in evaluating their performance towards achieving them.[20]

---

[20] Peter Schwartz, *The Art of the Long View: Planning for the Future in an Uncertain World* (New York: Doubleday, 1991) p. 53.

To develop a well-functioning investment committee, what are the specific characteristics to look for in individual committee members? As the decision makers for investment management, the individual members share every executive's challenge to be effective. And, as pointed out by Peter Drucker, they must possess neither brilliance nor creativity, nor are those talents enough to carry the day:

> **Yet men of high effectiveness** are conspicuous by their absence [on investment committees]. High intelligence is common enough among executives. Imagination is far from rare. The level of knowledge tends to be high. But there seems to be little correlation between a man's effectiveness and his intelligence, his imagination or his knowledge. Brilliant men are often strikingly ineffectual; they fail to realize that the brilliant insight is not by itself achievement.
>
> *Intelligence, imagination, and knowledge are essential resources, but only effectiveness converts them into results.* By themselves, they only set limits to what can be attained. [21]

Although it may make good reading, there is no single set of personality traits that can be ascribed to the effective committee member. They ". . . differ as widely as do ineffectual ones, are indeed indistinguishable from ineffectual executives in type, personality and talents."[22]

The most important characteristic of effective investment committee members, and the only characteristic they are likely to share in common, is the ability (demonstrated in another context) to get the right things done. That ability must be joined with a genuine interest, perhaps enthusiasm, for establishing and achieving investment objectives. Together, effective management ability *and* an interest in achieving investment results will assure that committee members obtain the investment knowledge necessary to achieve the committee's goals. This is a leadership role requiring dedication and serious purpose. The problem is not the setting of priorities, but keeping the pressures of a seemingly urgent crisis from crowding out time for important and thoughtful reflection on the future. The key question then is, how do you recognize the committee member likely to be most effective?

The most valuable committee members will have demonstrated (in some field) a keen eye for identifying and prioritizing strategic issues, a systematic approach for crafting and choosing between alternative

---

[21] Drucker, *The Effective Executive*, pp.1–2. Bracketed phrase inserted. Emphasis added.
[22] Ibid., p. 22.

solutions, and the discipline to follow through for purposeful performance. These committee members might have earned their wings in almost any discipline. The general requirements for effective management practices are the same for the university dean as for the trustee of the university's endowment fund, for the corporate CEO or hospital administrator as for their respective pension plan's investment committee.

In every case, their previous success will illustrate acquired habits of effectiveness that transcend day-to-day activities. They will attribute their success in part to a focus on valuable outside results that can be accomplished in a reasonable time frame, to a concentration on the priorities that build on their strengths and make a real difference, and to a thoughtful systematic process for making fundamental decisions based on dissenting opinions rather than on a consensus of the facts. In effect, they will have practiced the habits that should be emphasized in ongoing fiduciary training programs.

Importance of Education and Training for Investment Committee Members

Successful investment performance merely requires effective management of the process by knowledgeable investment committees. It does not require mastery of any particular investment skill, but competence in the understanding and execution of the investment process. The process itself draws upon the systematic decision making and management approach of other successful enterprises.

As for knowledge, we are not talking about the generalized knowledge of an educated person one might want as a guest at the dinner table. Quite the contrary. By knowledge, we mean information effective in action and focused on results.[23] The information and tools necessary to achieve investment success are available and tested. Almost anyone with management experience committed to making this knowledge productive can do so and apply it in their own circumstances.

Yet effective investment committees are rare. The management skills that many investors and volunteers could bring to the table are often inexplicably left at the door. The reason seems to be a general

---

[23] Peter F. Drucker, *Post-Capitalist Society* (New York: Harper Business, 1993), pp. 45, 46, 190, and 211.

fascination with the perceived excitement and glamour of buying stocks and bonds, or otherwise *making* investment decisions. As a result, the decision-management process of few investment committees bears any resemblance to that familiar to the same committee members in the business endeavors that prompted their appointments in the first place. Why? Lack of intelligence and talent is not the problem. Rather, it is one of differentiating comparatively minor elements of the investment process from major overall strategies, and product-based financial knowledge from investment fundamentals.

The solution lies in education and training in the effective practices of investment management and in the basic fundamentals of investments, and should emphasize that courage, as much as analysis, dictates the important rules for identifying priorities. The good news is that *effective* investment management can be learned. First, effectiveness (in investment management as in other management disciplines) is neither a part of one's knowledge itself nor a skill, but rather "a practice which one learns through doing the same elementary things over and over again."[24] Consequently, anyone with ordinary intelligence can learn to manage investment decisions effectively.

Fiduciary training should concentrate on methods to streamline the investment decision-making process, highlighting priorities and the relative contributions of each task. Real world examples should make clear the desirability (sometimes the necessity) of delegating to investment consultants much of the spade work and analysis that committee members need for effective decision making.

Investment basics should be presented in digestible modules so they are easily understood by the nonprofessional and supported by interactive computer models that give members an intuitive feel for iterative changes. Prototype policies and implementation structures should be presented so committee members do not have to initiate each step in the process with a blank sheet of paper.

Training modules should prepare committee members to develop a mission statement and objectives reflecting the real needs of their investment fund and organization. These will outline the steps for a detailed inquiry into the strengths and weaknesses of the sponsoring organization to the extent they have a bearing on the likely demands of the investment

---

[24] Drucker, *The Effective Executive*, p. 21.

fund. Training modules should also illustrate the interaction between the risk profile and expected returns for the investment fund and the likely impact on the plan sponsor's contributions or financial statements.

Effective committee members must acquire knowledge and skills that are applied in a systematic process to achieve the desired results. Effective decisions are, above all, a matter of systems—the right steps in the right sequence. Training in the disciplined prudent process as discussed in this text will enable the ordinarily competent person with some managerial skills to be effective. The truly gifted person may well acquire a mastery of the practices leading to attendant improvements in the process itself.

Summary

What is required of thee? *To walk humbly and with knowledge that the process will determine favorable results.* The strategy and initial approach that is taken will have the greatest impact on the results obtained. The role and responsibility of the fiduciary cannot be taken lightly, nor can it be abdicated by default to an inappropriate decision maker, service provider, or money manager. The management of the investment process requires a macro view that avoids the allure of hot investment trends that do not have as much impact on performance as one would hope or think.

APPENDIX

ADDITIONAL LEGAL NOTES ON ERISA FIDUCIARY STATUS

Because ERISA is considered an important touchstone for the general protection of beneficiary rights, an understanding of ERISA's expansive reach is necessary to understand state and other regulation of fiduciary responsibility.

In general, fiduciary status can be discerned from an analysis of the titles held and/or the functions performed (and the context in which they are performed) by persons responsible for the investment process.

Title Held

Recognizing that certain positions are inherently fiduciary in nature, a person may be deemed a fiduciary solely by reason of the position or title held. Plan trustees and administrators are considered fiduciaries, and courts generally presume the positions of named fiduciary and investment manager are fiduciary in nature. Only where the facts conclusively establish a lack of authority, control, and responsibility would holders of these titles escape the fiduciary designation.

The "cases make clear that, particularly in the case of plan trustees, it is easier under ERISA to assume fiduciary status than to shed it."[25] In the first place, fiduciary status cannot be informally terminated. In fact, fiduciary liability does not necessarily end even upon resignation. Resignations will only be effective if done in compliance with strict legal standards. For instance, tendering a resignation letter would not be sufficient, by itself. Compliance with specific plan provisions is essential. In any case, a fiduciary's attempted resignation may be rendered ineffective by his continued relationship with the plan.

Function Performed

ERISA provides a functional definition of a fiduciary based on (1) the person's authority, control, or responsibility over a plan, or (2) the services (investment advice) rendered to a plan. Regardless of a person's title or the absence of special formalities (e.g., formal appointment as a trustee),[26] a person can be a fiduciary if so "determined by focusing on the function performed, rather than on the title held."[27]

---

[25] Stanley, "The Definition of a Fiduciary," p. 257.

[26] Donovan v. Mercer, 747 F.2d 304 (5th Cir. 1984).

[27] Blatt v. Marshall & Lassman, 812 F.2d 810, 812 (2d Cir. 1987).

The "control or authority" definition encompasses plan trustees, plan administrators, the members of plan investment or administration committees, investment managers, and each person who selects, appoints, supervises, or monitors such individuals.[28] It is clear that fiduciary status is not limited to those who have direct access to plan assets or hold a particular title. The definition can even include persons involved in the management or administration of investment funds, such as plan consultants, who ordinarily would not be viewed as fiduciaries.

Fiduciary status is determined by objective standards. "It matters not that the person may subjectively believe that he or she is not a fiduciary as long as the requirements under the regulations are met."[29] Nor does it matter whether the person has acknowledged fiduciary status in writing or otherwise. For example, company officials sponsoring an ERISA plan may be fiduciaries to the extent they retain authority for the selection and retention of named fiduciaries. They have retained, in essence, "discretionary authority or control" over the management of the plan.[30]

Similarly, under the "rendering investment advice for a fee" definition, there is no clear line to categorize those activities that give rise to fiduciary status and those that do not. The DOL regulations[31] defining *investment advice* assuredly pick up the normal activities that a layperson would categorize as investment advice, such as valuing or making recommendations for the purchase or sale of securities. However, the regulations and the case law go far beyond those circumstances, sweeping in other activities that might not ordinarily be described as investment advice, including normal sales presentations.

---

[28] Donovan v. Mercer, *supra* note 25.

[29] Farm King Supply, Inc. Integrated Profit Sharing Plan and Trust v. Edward D. Jones & Co., 884 F.2d 288 (7th Cir. 1989).

[30] 29 C.F.R. Sec. 2509.75-8 at D-4. See Newton v. Van Otterloo, 756 F.Supp. 1121, 1132 (N.D. Ind., 1991) (power to appoint and remove fiduciaries makes company's board of directors fiduciaries).

[31] 29 C.F.R. Sec. 2510.3-21(c)(1) provides that a person shall be deemed to be rendering "investment advice" to an employee benefit plan, only if:

(i) Such person renders advice to the plan as to the value of securities or other property, or makes recommendations as to the advisability of investing in, purchasing, or selling securities or other property; and

(ii) Such person either directly or indirectly (e.g., through or together with any affiliate)—

(A) Has discretionary authority or control, whether or not pursuant to agreement, arrangement or understanding, with respect to purchasing or selling securities or other property for the plan; or

(B) Renders any advice described in paragraph (c)(1)(i) of this section on a regular basis to the plan pursuant to a mutual agreement, arrangement, or understanding, written or otherwise, between such person and the plan or a fiduciary with respect to the plan, that such services will serve as a primary basis for investment decisions with respect to plan assets, and that such person will render individualized investment advice to the plan based on the particular needs of the plan regarding such matters as, among other things, investment policies or strategy, overall portfolio composition, or diversification of plan investments.

Delegation

Under ERISA, fiduciaries are allowed to delegate authority to another fiduciary and may avoid responsibility and liability for the actions of that other fiduciary. However, attempted delegations of authority may be ineffective to transfer liability to another person if a court or regulatory body subsequently determines that the other person is not really a fiduciary. Furthermore, anyone found to be a fiduciary (whether a trustee or not, and regardless of whether they *think* they are a fiduciary) is, of course, held to a higher standard of care than would otherwise be the case. For example, they cannot avoid ERISA's prudent man rule by contract, nor can they be protected by contractual provisions excusing their negligence, regardless of the extent to which such protection might otherwise be valid.

On the other hand, absent the conduct that falls within the ERISA definition of a fiduciary, the liability of a fiduciary who is *not* a named fiduciary is generally limited to the functions performed with respect to the plan, and the fiduciary will not be personally liable for all phases of the management and administration of the plan.[32]

---

[32] 29 C.F.R. Sec. 2509.75-8 at FR-16. Cf. Birmingham v. Soggy-Swiss Intern. Corp. Retirement Plan, 718 F.2d 515, 521–522 (2d Cir. 1983) (the very purpose of designating a named fiduciary is to focus liability for mismanagement with a measure of certainty by limiting the exposure of liability to that named individual).

CHAPTER

3

STEP 1—ANALYZING THE CURRENT POSITION

"The journey of 1000 nights begins with the first step."
Chinese Proverb

"Nothing is particularly hard if you divide it into small jobs."
Ray Kroc

The investment management process begins with a thorough understanding of the investor's current situation and future needs. To implement the process (or verify that a process has been followed) it is necessary to obtain a complete understanding of the investor's current financial position, legal and regulatory constraints, and investment profile. This understanding is obtained from an in-depth analysis of the current facts and circumstances pertaining to the funds to be invested.

To be successful, investors must avoid ad hoc approaches to their investment decisions. Otherwise the result may be "a short-term focus on issues of only minor consequence to the ultimate success of the plan, while consideration of more important matters goes relatively unattended."[1] As with any business plan, definitive objectives must be

---

[1] Jeffrey V. Bailey, "Investment Policy: The Missing Link," in *Pension Fund Investment Management: A Handbook for Sponsors and Their Advisors*, ed. Frank J. Fabozzi (Chicago: Probus Publishing Company, 1990), p. 12.

established. Here, the investor plays a key management role in defining objectives that are realistic and consistent with the portfolio's current and future resources, and with the investor's values and priorities.

Types of Investment Portfolios

The starting point is to determine the legal character or ownership of the investable assets, which reveals quite a bit about what is and isn't permissible or appropriate among potential asset classes or strategies. Generally, portfolios fall into one of the following four categories:

1. *Retirement plans.* There are five subcategories:

    • Qualified retirement plans (approved by the IRS) established by private corporations, partnerships, associations, or individuals and include defined benefit plans and defined contribution plans (401(k) plans).

    • Public retirement plans established by state, county, or municipal entities and include defined benefit plans and defined contribution plans (457 plans).

    • Retirement plans established by nonprofit organizations, such as churches, hospitals, and schools and include defined contribution plans (403(b) plans).

    • Individual retirement accounts (IRAs) and IRA rollovers, which are typically included in the overall analysis of an individual's portfolio.

    • Nonqualified retirement plans or supplemental funds, which are not tax deferred and include those plans that have been established as supplemental retirement or bonus portfolios by corporations (e.g., SERPs and Rabbi Trusts).

2. *Individual or family wealth.* There is no specific dollar amount that necessitates the application of the principles described in this book. However, a significant financial event may occur that precipitates the desire to have a thorough understanding of the investment management process (e.g., receiving the right to a lump-sum retirement distribution, an inheritance, a divorce, or the proceeds from the sale of a

business or winning the lottery).[2] Also included would be family trusts. Different and competing needs may exist between the current beneficiary (life estate) and any future beneficiaries (remaindermen).

3. *Foundations/endowments/charitable trusts.* These are trusts funded for the sole purpose of accomplishing certain charitable endeavors and are established according to the requirements of specific IRS and state codes.

4. *Miscellaneous asset pools.* These may be corporate or municipal accounts established to fund short to intermediate financial objectives, or restricted assets earmarked for specific uses or objectives (e.g., depreciation reserves, working capital reserves, or escrow arrangements). Also included would be the general accounts of insurance companies or reserves of self-insurance trusts established by professional entities.

Each of the different pools may have one or more persons designated as fiduciaries or trustees. Depending on the purpose and nature of the trust, the fiduciary may have specific investment duties that should be performed. An audit checklist of the more common fiduciary requirements is provided in Appendix 3–1.

Financial Statements

No matter how the portfolio may be owned or characterized by legal structure, it is helpful to build a balance sheet of the portfolio to determine assets and liabilities (see Table 3–1). This can then be expanded to include an income statement showing the yearly or periodic cash flows—contributions or disbursements.

Two basic questions arise from the analysis of financial statements: "Where is the money now?" and "How is it being managed?" The answers should help determine how the assets are currently allocated, the costs for managing the investments, and the performance of previous investment decisions.

---

[2] This book is not designed to be a financial planning treatise. It is primarily designed as an aid in reducing risk and increasing return of a relatively large pool of money.

TABLE 3–1   Balance Sheet and Cash Flow Projections

Individual's Balance Sheet

Assets:

Cash	$ 78,000
Fixed income	500,000
Domestic equities	1,125,000
International equities	267,000
Investment real estate	250,000
Residence	750,000
Total assets	$2,970,000

Liabilities:

Unfunded income taxes	($ 12,500)
Residential mortgage	(128,000)
Total liabilities	($ 140,500)

Net worth   **$2,829,500**

Defined Benefit Plan's Cash Flow Projections:

Sources:

Contributions		
Current year	$ 462,000	
Prior year	818,000	$1,280,000
Investment income		
Interest	$ 745,000	
Dividends	925,000	1,670,000
Total sources		$2,950,000

Uses:

Benefit payments		($1,500,000)
Expenses:		
Money managers	$ 235,000	
Custodian	92,000	
Actuary	65,000	
Consultant	24,000	
PBGC premiums	75,000	
Legal	15,000	
Accounting	5,000	($ 511,000)
Total uses		($2,011,000)

Surplus   **$ 939,000**

Current Asset and Style Allocation

The initial challenge is the labeling of the investor's current portfolio—determining which investments, money managers, or mutual funds fall within each broad and subasset class. As mentioned in Chapter 1, the investor's asset mix will have far more impact on the long-term performance of the portfolio than any other factor, including the selection of money managers.

Most investors are familiar with the distinction between the broad asset classes—equities, fixed income, and cash. But they may not be aware of the different styles of money management that have emerged and correspond to the subasset classes.[3]

Thirty years ago, money was managed, for the most part, by large institutions, specifically banks and insurance companies. With the passage of ERISA in 1974, sponsors of retirement plans were charged to follow a more procedurally prudent process for the management of the plan assets. Investment committees began to devote more attention to the performance of their money managers and sought ways to diversify their needs.

The outgrowth was the formation of new, smaller money management firms that drew upon the talent pool of the larger institutions. The new firms became specialists in one or more specific subasset classes instead of trying to invest across a broad asset class. Within a relatively short period of time, the practice by investment committees of unbundling investment services and hiring specialists became the norm. (This same pattern is being repeated today in the defined contribution marketplace.)

The investment consulting industry began its growth primarily as a result of the proliferation of these money management specialists. Committees wanted to know (1) how each of the firms compared to one another, (2) how they could find information on these new firms, and (3) most importantly, how to structure an efficient portfolio using specialists. An outgrowth of the consulting research was the development of styles, or peer groups.

---

[3] There are no industry standards on how to segregate money managers into styles, and there are only a handful of investment consulting firms that have the research capabilities and depth of staff to do the required analysis. The style definitions used in this book were developed by Callan Associates Inc.

For a money manager to be included within a style group (the same analysis is applied to mutual funds), different aspects of the analysis must produce consistent results. The typical examination includes (1) risk and return statistics, (2) portfolio (securities) characteristics, (3) descriptive information provided by the managers in question-naires and marketing material, and (4) on-site interviews by the consulting firm conducting the analysis.

Each style has a specific risk/reward profile that enables further refinement of an asset allocation strategy. Note in Figure 3–1 that the return premiums of each of the equity styles do not change in synchronization with the others. In particular, growth and value managers move in opposite directions—in statistical terms, there is a negative correlation between the two, a desirable trait for diversification purposes.

For example, in 1983, the median return of growth managers under-performed the S&P 500 (indicated by the zero baseline) by approximately 2.2 percent. In addition, value managers outperformed both growth and core managers. Two years later, growth managers rebounded and outperformed the entire lot.

Another reason for the rise in popularity of style analysis was to enable investors to make better comparisons between money managers. Without an understanding of the impact that styles have on investment performance, an unsuspecting investor could reap rewards on a poor manager that happened to be following a hot investment style, or disparage a good manager whose style was out of favor.

Domestic Equity.   Managers are generally stylized by the characteristics of the securities the money manager is purchasing for the portfolio. The more common analysis includes a comparison of the average capitalization weightings and market ratios (e.g., price/book and price/earnings). (See Figure 3–2.)

- *Value*: Managers buy securities that are considered out of favor, or not efficiently priced, relative to the stock market. Common portfolio characteristics include a low price/book ratio and low price/earnings ratio.
- *Yield*: Managers focus on selecting securities with high sustainable dividend yields. The portfolio characteristics of value and yield are very similar, except for a higher average dividend yield. (Utility stocks typically make up a portion of the portfolio.)

FIGURE 3–1 **Benefits of Investment Style Diversification**

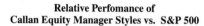

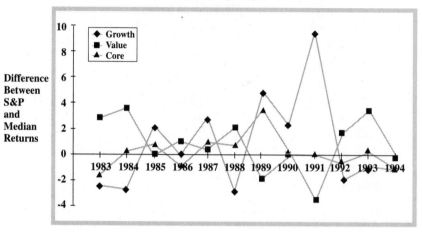

Source: Copyright©1995, Investment Management Council.

FIGURE 3–2 **Equity Style Matrix**

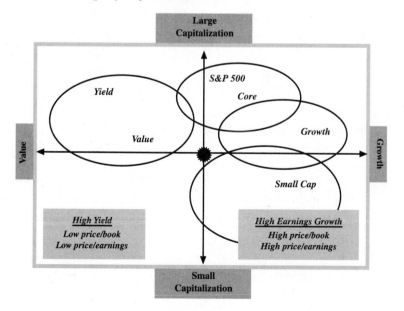

- *Core*: Managers tend to mimic the portfolio characteristics of the S&P 500, except that the portfolio does not hold as many securities. Industry classifications tend to be similar to the index.
- *Growth*: Managers concentrate on the selection of securities whose growth rates are anticipated to be greater than those of the overall stock market. Common portfolio characteristics include higher price/book ratios and higher price/earnings ratios.
- *Small cap*: Managers concentrate on buying companies whose capitalization is less than $1 billion. Small cap managers show unique return characteristics largely because of the uncertainty surrounding the expectations of small company stocks: there is less research on the firms, product lines are usually less diversified, and there is less known about the management of the firm.

Within each of these equity styles, managers can be further subdivided into the type of process they follow in selecting securities.

- *Top-down*: Managers begin their fundamental analysis with a macro examination of the global markets. From this analysis the manager identifies the sectors (e.g., consumer cyclicals) that are likely to benefit from anticipated changes, and within the selected sectors the individual companies that are likely to outperform their peers.
- *Bottom-up*: Managers search for securities that meet specified fundamental characteristics. So a portfolio does not concentrate on securities from the same sectors, security selection is made against the backdrop of a macro examination.
- *Concentrator*: Managers hold fewer securities and consolidate their bets on only a few sectors of the market or in a few securities. As a result, performance often varies considerably from the broad market indexes.

Domestic Fixed Income.   Managers can actively manage or add value to a bond portfolio by (1) changing the average credit quality of the portfolio; (2) swapping bonds between different sectors—government, municipal, agency, and corporate; (3) changing the average maturity/duration of the portfolio; and (4) negotiating favorable trading spreads.

Duration is defined as the present value of the bond's coupon payments and principal repayment. The higher the coupon payment and the closer the principal repayment, the shorter the bond's duration. Duration is an excellent measure of how the bond's price will change in response to a change in interest rates. A bond with a duration of six years will exhibit twice the percentage change in the bond's price as a bond with a duration of three years. Fixed income portfolios with longer maturities tend to have longer durations, and consequently exhibit more price volatility than portfolios with shorter durations. (See Figure 3–3.)

- *Defensive*: Managers concentrate their portfolios on short duration bonds, typically less than five years. The maturity of the bonds ranges from two to five years. Preferred sectors are government and high quality corporate bonds.
- *Intermediate*: Managers concentrate their portfolios on bonds with a duration ranging from 3 to 10 years. The maturity of the bonds ranges from 4 to 10 years. Preferred sectors are government and medium to high-quality corporate bonds.

FIGURE 3-3   Fixed Income Styles

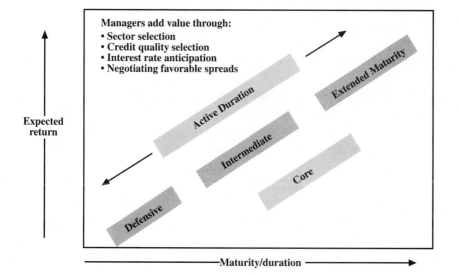

Historically, intermediate managers have been able to capture 80 percent of the return of long-term portfolios with considerably less risk.

- *Extended maturity*: Managers concentrate their portfolios on bonds with a duration ranging from 10 to 25 years. The maturity of the bonds is greater than 10 years. Preferred sectors are government and medium to high quality corporate bonds.

- *Core*: Managers maintain the portfolio's duration close to that of a broad market index, such as the Lehman Government/ Corporate Index, yet may hold different sectors from those represented by the index. Value is added by over- or under-weighting the sectors relative to the index and identifying undervalued issues that may be going through credit improvements.

- *Active Duration*: Managers add value by adapting the duration of the portfolio to anticipated changes in interest rates. If interest rates are anticipated to rise, the duration will be shortened. These managers aggressively work the yield curve, paying particular attention to the forecasted direction of interest rates.

- *High yield*: Managers invest in fixed-income securities with below-investment-grade ratings: for example, Standard & Poor's ratings of AA or less, and Moody's of less than BBB. Many managers will add value by identifying undervalued securities, or securities that are about to be upgraded due to corporate earnings improvement or other features of the particular issue (bond price should be increasing for reasons other than decreasing interest rates). Performance variations in this style are larger, but there are also potentially higher returns.

- *Mortgage-backed*: Managers focus their research on mortgage-backed securities, including the more complicated issues such as mortgage pass-throughs and collateralized mortgage obligations (CMOs). This is a highly specialized style in which convexity and prepayment risks increase the complexity of the markets.

Figure 3–4 shows a risk/reward profile depicting both the equity and fixed income styles.

FIGURE 3–4   Risk Return Profiles

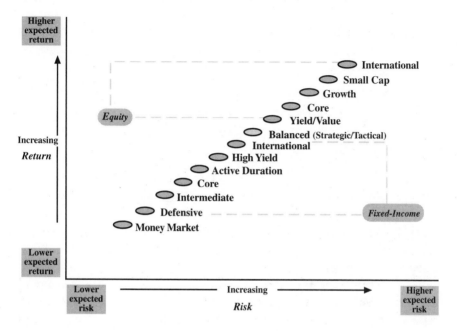

Source: Copyright©1994, Investment Management Council.

Analysis Specific to Retirement Plans

It is important to review and understand the salient features of retirement plan documents (e.g., lump-sum features, vesting, loan provisions, payment provisions in the event of the death of a participant, and contribution and distribution timing). Chapter 15 provides additional details on defined benefit and defined contribution plans.

For a defined benefit plan, it is important to determine the nature of the employment base and the possible cyclical nature of the sponsoring business. Those businesses within industries that go through periods of boom and bust would probably adopt a more conservative investment strategy than those businesses that enjoy steady expansion. Or a plan that has a history of contributions exceeding withdrawals/distributions can adopt a more risky allocation than the plan whose work force is nearing retirement age.

Plans that offer lump-sum payments to terminating participants require an additional examination of participant demographics. These plans include (1) most all defined contribution plans, (2) defined benefit plans that provide lump-sum alternatives in lieu of monthly benefit options, and (3) plans that have special provisions for early retirements. Particular attention must be focused on

- Age of the participants.
- Length of service by participants.
- Vested benefits of participants broken down by length of service.
- Vested benefits of top account balances broken down by age.

It is convenient to build histograms (Figure 3–5) of the results to graphically show the probable point in time when distributions will exceed contributions, or the time when there will most likely be a significant outflow of portfolio assets. This information is critical since it will determine the overall time horizon for the plan assets, which, in turn, will impact the risk tolerance level. For example, if the average age of all participants in a profit sharing plan is 45, but 40 percent of the plan assets benefit only the top six participants, who are all over age 63, then the time horizon would be considered short. It would be imprudent to invest the plan assets as if they were entirely for the 45-year-olds.

Costs and Historical Performance

Another aspect in analyzing how the portfolio is currently structured is determining the costs for managing the assets. Understanding the composition of the different layers of expenses is important since they have a direct impact on performance. Each of the following investment expenses is detailed in Chapter 9, "Controlling Investment Expenses":

- Custody, including custodial and transaction fees, and the annual expenses of the money market account used for cash sweeps.
- Brokerage, including execution and commission costs, and the use (or the lack of use) of directed brokerage (soft dollars and commission recapture programs).

FIGURE 3–5   Histograms of Age Distribution and Employee Service

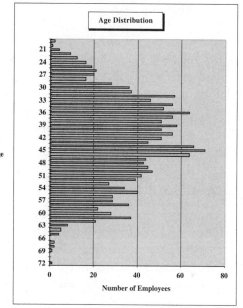

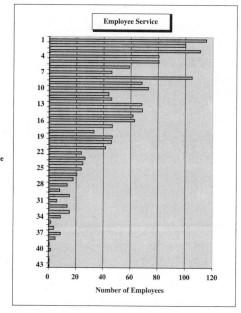

- Money manager's fees and/or the annual expenses of mutual funds (including front- and back-end loads).
- Investment consulting fees.

Performance.   As the assets are examined and the costs are evaluated, it is also helpful to analyze the portfolio's historical performance. Specifically, the goal is to review the decision-making process that has been followed and determine whether it has been successful in accomplishing the portfolio's specific investment objectives. (Chapter 8 details procedures for calculating portfolio performance.)

Documents and Data Gathering

The ownership classification of the assets will dictate the different documents that should be reviewed in step 1. Each of the various ownership alternatives (mentioned at the beginning of this chapter) requires the collection of specific items needed in the evaluation process. Appendix 3–2 contains sample checklists that can be utilized depending upon the particular pool of money involved.

One of the most convenient ways to determine asset allocation, costs, and performance is to request at least 13 months of custodial statements. (Thirteen months are necessary to ensure that beginning and ending market values are shown for a full 12-month period.) The custodial statement should provide asset mix, beginning and ending market values, book value (initial purchase price), expenses (deductions from the account), transactions (if trades are stated), and deposits and withdrawals. One deficiency to look for is the lack of accrued but unpaid income (e.g., accrued interest on bonds) that may require adjustments to the performance calculations.

Investment Risk Profile

Advisors working with investors should have an understanding of the various elements of risk with which the investor is contending, or which are of concern. The term *risk* has many different connotations, depending on the investor's frame of reference, circumstances, and objectives. Typically, the investment industry defines *risk* in terms of performance volatility, or the probability of not meeting the investor's specific investment objectives. However, asset allocation decisions based solely on the statistical definition of risk—standard deviation—can lead to a one-dimensional view that does not always ensure adequate equity exposure for portfolios that require higher returns.

> [T]he current misunderstanding of what truly constitutes risk in a given situation often leads to portfolios with less than optimal equity contents and, therefore, lower long-term returns than might otherwise be achieved...Volatility per se...tells us nothing about risk until coupled with consequence. The determining question in structuring a portfolio is the consequence of loss; this is far more important than the chance of loss.[4]

Risk, therefore, warrants an expanded definition to adequately convey the potential meanings it may have to different investors, and to catalog the different elements of risk with which the investor may have to contend. (See Figure 3–6.)

Liquidity Risk. The inability to raise cash to meet essential outlays is the primary risk that is common to all investors. Every portfolio is going to have its own unique cash flow requirements, which is why investment portfolios cannot be managed in a cookie-cutter fashion. Since the timing and amount of inflows and outflows of cash distinguish one portfolio from another, realistic cash flow projections are critical in planning for the appropriate asset allocation.

Asset Allocation Risk. A close corollary to liquidity risk, it asks the question: Have the assets been optimally diversified to meet return expectations? A common mistake is to adopt an asset allocation strategy that has a low probability of meeting future cash flow needs. Or a suitable asset mix was established, but the portfolio was not periodically rebalanced to maintain the desired risk/return profile. For example, during a bull market, the equity portion of the overall portfolio will rise, therefore exposing the portfolio to more risk than originally intended.

Board Room Risk. No one wants to be remembered as the member of an investment committee that lost money, or as the family member who mismanaged the family fortune. Consequently, "the risk tolerance of a fund...is the risk tolerance of the majority of the board of directors at

---

[4] Robert H. Jeffrey, "A New Paradigm for Portfolio Risk," The Journal of Portfolio Management, Fall 1994.

FIGURE 3–6   Elements of Investment Risk

Liquidity Risk	Will there be sufficient cash to meet disbursement/ expense requirements?
Boardroom Risk	Are decision makers willing to ride out short-term volatility in favor of appropriate long-term strategies?
Purchasing Power Risk	Has an investment strategy been employed that will, at the very least, keep pace with inflation?
Funding Risk	What is the probability that anticipated contributions will not be made?
Risk versus Return	Are investment returns consistent with level of risk taken?
Asset Allocation Risk	Are assets optimally allocated to meet required return and risk parameters?
Lost Opportunity Risk	Have market timing strategies been inappropriately employed, exposing the investor to missed opportunities in the market?

Source: Copyright©1993, Investment Management Council.

the moment of most severe market adversity."[5] Decision makers are faced with the difficult task of making long-term investment decisions that carry the risk of highly visible negative short-term market fluctuations. This is often the unspoken fear that keeps fiduciaries from making the difficult decisions that have to be made. A corollary term is *symmetry risk*—the risk that outsiders will criticize the board's decisions as being different from everyone else's. Fiduciaries must always remember that they are charged with making decisions for the primary benefit of the participant or beneficiary, even at the risk of making a politically unpopular decision.

Lost Opportunity Risk.   Every time an investor deviates or procrastinates in implementing an appropriate investment strategy, the investor is exposed to lost opportunity risks. Inevitably, allocations made to an asset class will generate losses, but remember: The goal is to efficiently

---

[5] Charles D. Ellis, *Investment Policy: "How to Win the Loser's Game,"* Business One Irwin (Burr Ridge, IL) 1985 and 1993, p. 27.

position the *entire* portfolio to minimize risk and maximize return. Also included in this category is the risk associated with market timing—the attempt made by some investors to time the beginning and ending of each subsequent bear and bull market. The consensus among professional investment consultants is that attempts to time the market are statistically stacked against the investor.

Purchasing Power Risk.   The costs of goods and services will inevitably increase due to inflation, and if these increases are not planned for, larger amounts of the portfolio will have to be liquidated in order to meet cash flow needs. "Safety of capital includes not only the objective of protecting the trust property from the risk of loss of nominal value but, ordinarily, also a goal of preserving its real value—that is, seeking to avoid or reduce loss of the trust estate's purchasing power as a result of inflation."[6]

Funding Risk.   Retirement plans have to be sensitive to the risk that the sponsoring organization will not be able to make required contributions. Public retirement plans are at the mercy of elected officials, who often view retirement assets as belonging to the government entity, not the participants (Chapter 16). Taft-Hartley plans rely on multiple employers to make contributions—employers that are often significantly impacted by boom-and-bust cycles (Chapter 17). And corporate retirement funds run the risk that the sponsor will go out of business, with defined benefit payments falling on the shoulders of the Pension Benefit Guarantee Corporation (PBGC). Individuals face funding risk due to the possible death of the primary wage earner. This disruption in cash flow or contributions can alter the investment plan.

Risk versus Return.   Investors should not continue with an investment program that does not reward the investor for the amount of risk that is taken. Performance evaluation should not be limited to analyzing just the absolute returns, but should incorporate the risks the money manager (mutual fund) took with the money. Or, worded differently, investors should be as sensitive to the potential risks of an investment strategy as they are to the potential gains. The offense committed by some brokerage firms is not that they sell bad products, but that they sell the products by overemphasizing the potential gains and not adequately explaining the risks.

---

[6] Restatement Third, Sec. 227, comment e, p. 18.

Summary

A good test to determine whether sufficient information has been collected to move on to step 2 is to answer satisfactorily the following questions.

1. What is the timing of contributions and disbursements? Is there a specific point in time when disbursements will be greater than contributions and liquidity becomes critical? What is the certainty of future contributions?
2. Do legal documents impose any asset or allocation restrictions?
3. Do the actuarial reports, spending policies, trust documents, and/or budgets establish a minimal investment return expectation?
4. What are the current costs for investment-related services? What are the costs for money management, custody, brokerage, and consulting? Are there any soft dollar agreements, and what has been the average costs for transactions?
5. What different risks must the investor manage?

To set the investment management process in motion, it is necessary that all facts and circumstances surrounding the current situation be discovered. In many respects this is achieved only by acting as a junior detective and overturning the stones and kicking the tires. It is necessary to attain a full and complete understanding of the asset make up, legal structure, and overall objectives before moving on to determine an optimal asset allocation or money manager lineup. This is limited to an examination not only of quantitative financial data, but also of the qualitative elements of the investor's risk tolerance.

APPENDIX 3–1
FIDUCIARY INVESTMENT COMPLIANCE CHECKLIST

The following checklist is to assist investment fiduciaries who are subject to ERISA or Third Restatement duties. The checklist is also useful for public fund fiduciaries, but they should check state statutes for additional requirements.

An overview of the broad fiduciary requirements includes

Uniform Code of Fiduciary Conduct
1. **Prepare written investment policies, and document the investment decision-making process.**
2. **Diversify assets with regard to specific risk/return objectives of participants and beneficiaries.**
3. **Use prudent experts to make investment decisions.**
4. **Control investment expenses, and ensure the "best execution" of investment transactions.**
5. **Monitor the activities of all money managers and service providers.**
6. **Avoid all conflicts of interest.**

I. Review of Plan or Trust Documents
❑ A. Fiduciaries and trustees are named and responsibilities are assigned among named fiduciaries and trustees.
❑ B. Plan/trust documents allow for the fiduciaries to designate persons other than named fiduciaries to be responsible for certain functions; for example, appointment of professional money managers.
  ❑ 1. Vendor agreements are in writing and do not exceed terms of greater than three years.
  ❑ 2. Vendor agreements are being followed (e.g., fee charges, reports, etc.).
❑ C. Written evidence is maintained of consistent supervision and evaluation of investment program.
  ❑ 1. Minutes of meetings of trustees or investment committee are maintained and are current.
  ❑ 2. Appropriate documentation is in place regarding monitoring of plan assets.
❑ D. Investigation is made into any possible prohibited transactions, specifically whether a fiduciary or party in interest is receiving any direct or indirect benefit from use or sale of plan assets.

II. Review of Investment Policy Statement (IPS)

An investment policy must be established and should be in writing [ERISA Sections 402(a)(1), 402(b)(1)–(2), 404(A)(1)(D); Restatement, Third, Sec. 227(a)].

- ❑ A. Investment objectives are identified.
- ❑ B. Asset allocation guidelines are identified.
    - ❑ 1. Risk tolerance or variability of returns.
    - ❑ 2. Asset classes appropriate for consideration.
    - ❑ 3. Time horizon to achieve objectives or to meet distribution requirements.
    - ❑ 4. Expected return on investments compared to designated benchmarks.

Plan assets must be diversified [ERISA Sec. 404(a)(1)(C); Restatement, Third, Sec. 227(b)].

- ❑ C. Strategic asset allocation is set and rebalancing variance limit is identified.
- ❑ D. Securities guidelines are identified for each asset class.
- ❑ E. Restricted securities are identified.

Investment decisions must be made with the skill of a prudent expert [ERISA Sec. 404(a)(1)(B); Restatement Third, Sec. 171].

- ❑ F. Procedures are established (due diligence) for selecting prudent experts to make investment decisions.
    - ❑ 1. Performance numbers are reviewed and are time-weighted composite of actual results. Long-term performance outperforms appropriate market indices.
    - ❑ 2. Performance is compared relative to risk assumed. Managers have positive alpha or high Sharpe ratio. Standard deviation of manager is reported and understood.
    - ❑ 3. Performance is compared against managers of like style or strategy. Long-term performance is in upper median of Callan, or similar major manager consultant universe.
    - ❑ 4. Manager follows specific investment style that corresponds to evaluated performance record.
    - ❑ 5. Manager and/or custodian is able to properly service account.
    - ❑ 6. The track record evaluated is attributable to specific investment manager assigned to portfolio.

Note: In order to meet safe harbor provisions [ERISA Sec. 405(d)(1)], money managers must

- ❑ a. Be a registered investment advisor under the Investment Adviser's Act of 1940, insurance company, a bank, or an investment company (mutual fund).
- ❑ b. Be prudently selected (due diligence procedures outlined above).

        ❑ c. Be given power to manage, acquire, and dispose of the plan assets.

        ❑ d. Acknowledge responsibility in writing.

        ❑ e. Be properly monitored and supervised.

❑ G. Control procedures are established.

    ❑ 1. Responsibilities of money manager.

        ❑ a. Vote proxies, if instructed.

        ❑ b. Annually submit an ADV Part II.

        ❑ c. Notify fiduciaries when involved in any litigation or violation of securities regulations.

        ❑ d. Appropriately register (if required) in state.

    ❑ 2. Monitoring of money managers.

        ❑ a. Manager's adherence to IPS.

        ❑ b. Material changes to manager's organization.

        ❑ c. Comparisons of manager's performance to indices, managers of similar style, and IPS objectives.

    ❑ 3. Review of costs and fees for reasonableness of services provided. Investment expenses must be controlled [ERISA Sec. 404(a); Restatement Third, Sec. 227(c)(3)].

        ❑ a. Administrative costs.

        ❑ b. Money management fees.

        ❑ c. Custody fees.

        ❑ d. Brokerage costs (best execution).

        ❑ e. Soft dollar arrangements that are acknowledged and understood.

III. Specific to ERISA Fiduciaries

❑ A. Funding status of plan is noted—over- or underfunded.

    ❑ 1. Actuarial assumptions are verified (if defined benefit plan).

    ❑ 2. Contributions and allocations are appropriate (if defined contribution plan).

    ❑ 3. If participant directed, investment choices are appropriate under ERISA Sec. 404(c).

❑ B. Short term liquidity needs are identified.

    ❑ 1. Matching assets with age of participants.

    ❑ 2. Employment contracts and vesting schedules.

❑ C. Flow of funds (contributions and distributions) are noted for one, three, and five years.

❑ D. Summary plan description.

    ❑ 1. Verify that it is consistent with plan documents.

    ❑ 2. Should be written in easy-to-understand language.

❑ 3. Should have been provided to each participant.
❑ E. Annual return has been timely filed with IRS.
    ❑ 1. Forms 5500, 5500-C, and 5500-R.
    ❑ 2. Review any IRS correspondence regarding plan.
❑ F. Summary annual report.
    ❑ 1. Has been provided to participants within 270 days after the end of each plan year.
    ❑ 2. Review previous annual reports for consistency.
❑ G. Required ERISA bonding is in force [ERISA Sec. 412(a)].
❑ H. Loan provisions do not violate prohibited transaction rules and meet minimum requirements [ERISA Sec. 406(a)–(b); DOL Reg. §2550.408(b)-(1)].
    ❑ 1. Plan documents permit the use of loans.
    ❑ 2. Loans are available to all participants.
    ❑ 3. Loans are not available to highly compensated employees in greater amounts than to other employees.
    ❑ 4. Loans bear a reasonable rate of interest.
    ❑ 5. Loans are adequately secured.
❑ I. Plan investment assets are subject to jurisdiction of U.S. district courts— no foreign assets unless held by a U.S. intermediary [ERISA Sec. 404(a)(2)].
❑ J. Prohibited transactions under I.R.C. Sec. 4975 (and regulations) are avoided.
❑ K. Claim review procedures are specified for benefit payment controversies [ERISA Sec. 503].
    ❑ 1. Specific steps are clear and provided to participants. (Note: This has become a fertile area of inquiry by lawyers representing disgruntled participants.)

APPENDIX 3–2
FACT FINDING AND DATA GATHERING

I. *Retirement Plans.*
  A. Qualified Plans. Review the following documents:
    1. Trust agreement and amendments;
    2. IRS Form 5500, including schedules.
    3. Independent accountant's audit report, if required by IRS.
    4. Plan documents.
    5. Summary Plan Description.
    6. Actuarial report (defined benefit plans only), which identifies interest rate and investment earning assumptions and the funding status of the plan.
  B. Public Plans. Similar to qualified plans plus:
    1. Audited reports showing the timing of contributions and disbursements.
    2. Funding status.
    3. Participant demographics.
  C. Funded Nonqualified Retirement Accounts (SERPs, Rabbi Trusts, Top Hat plans, etc.). Similar to qualified plans plus:
    1. Financial health and viability of company sponsor to be able to continue to fund obligation.
    2. Disparity between participant formulas and calculations.
  D. Individual Retirement Accounts (IRAs). (See Individual Accounts, below.)
II. *Individual (or Couple) Accounts.*
  The individual or couple should provide:
  A. Income history—both earned and unearned.
  B. Date of birth(s). This is critical in developing the time horizon for the portfolio. Many times, time horizon for an individual investor may be thought of in terms of number of years between now and retirement. This

---

Notes:
  1. The plan documents will indicate the timing of contributions and disbursements, which is critical in developing the investment strategy appropriate for the plan assets. In order to appropriately determine the time horizon for a plan that pays lump-sum benefits upon retirement, it may be helpful to construct two tables—one depicting the participant balances based on the top 10 to 15 percent in account size and the second depicting the participant balances of the top 10 to 15 percent participant age groups.
  2. In order to understand participant demographics, it is also useful to prepare two histograms—one that depicts years of service and one that provides an age distribution. This helps determine time horizon and constitutes the necessary due diligence to analyze plan participant characteristics. (See Table 3–5).

is not the case. The true time horizon should be based on the individual's life expectancy (giving consideration to parents' and grandparents' longevity) and/or intended bequests.

C. Copy of prior years' tax returns (Form 1040), brokerage statements, and/or other relevant reports. Tax returns can many times be a discovery tool since they will list dividends and capital gain transactions. Although the number of shares owned may not be known, it is possible to arrive at the shares owned based on the total dividends reported.

III. *Family Trust.*

As in the individual situation, the family trust needs to be analyzed in terms of its income history and beneficiary profile.

A. The governing trust document, including amendments, to determine:
    1. Beneficiaries—current and future.
    2. Mandatory and discretionary distribution dates and contingencies.
    3. Payment requirements of interest and principal.
    4. Investment restrictions and prohibitions.
B. Audit report prepared by an independent or family accountant (if available).
C. IRS Form 1041, including supporting schedules.
D. A list of all beneficiaries and their birth dates. A family tree may be necessary to reflect relationships and beneficiaries. As with the individual, the birth dates of the beneficiaries may determine the time horizon. These are needed for all current and future beneficiaries, including a class of beneficiaries (e.g., after-born grandchildren).

IV. *Foundations/Endowments/Charitable Trusts.*

In a charitable setting, the pool of money needs to be examined by gathering the following documents:

A. Trust agreement, including amendments.
B. IRS forms, filings, and audit reports.
C. Term of years, if remainder or lead trust.
D. Independent annual audited financial statement.

Note: Charitable entities may have political reasons (or justifications) for using certain custodians, money managers, or investments. Although a charitable gift may be complete from a tax standpoint, from a practical standpoint, there are usually ties or unwritten requirements that the donor made when the gift was funded.

APPENDIX 3–3
PORTFOLIO PLANNING SURVEY FOR INDIVIDUALS

CONFIDENTIAL

Date Prepared: _____

CLIENT NAME

Client Address:

_____

_____

_____

_____

_____

_____

Phone: _____ Fax: _____

PERSON(S) COMPLETING PPS

Phone: _____ Fax: _____

Introduction

The critical first phase of our investment management service involves a portfolio planning process that leads to the development of a written policy. This Investment Policy Statement (IPS) details your investment goals and objectives and your long-range plan for achieving them. In essence, it becomes the link between your needs and the realities of the investment markets. In addition, it serves as a directive for implementing your portfolio strategy and establishes a rationale for making subsequent investment decisions, judgments, and evaluations.

We believe that the creation and execution of a reasonable and logical investment policy is absolutely critical to the long-term success of your investment program. Therefore, it must be crafted with skill, a common perspective of the realities of the financial world, and a clear understanding of the financial and psychological factors that influence the needs of the portfolio.

This questionnaire is designed to assist us in assessing your goals, analyzing your present investment allocation, and designing an appropriate investment policy for your portfolio. With your help, we trust that you will find its completion to be an enlightening first step in the development of your long-term investment policy.

Personal Data

Individual	*Spouse*
Name: _____	Name: _____
Date of Birth: _____	Date of Birth: _____
SSN: _____	SSN: _____
Home Address: _____	Home Address: _____
Home Phone: _____	Home Phone: _____
Occupation: _____	Occupation: _____
Employer: _____	Employer: _____
Business Address: _____	Business Address: _____
Business Phone: _____	Business Phone: _____
Business Fax: _____	Business Fax: _____

Children / Dependents

Name	*Date of Birth*	*SSN*
_____	_____	_____
_____	_____	_____
_____	_____	_____
_____	_____	_____
_____	_____	_____

Advisors

Attorney:_____

      Phone:_____

      Address: _____

Accountant: _____

      Phone: _____

      Address: _____

Trust Officer: _____

      Phone:_____

      Address:_____

Documents

Please identify location of following documents:

1. Existing wills of individual and spouse: _____

2. Trust instruments: _____

3. Life insurance policies: _____

4. Information on retirement plans: _____

5. Income tax returns for past five years:

6. Business agreements and documents regarding interests in corporations, partnerships, and sole proprietorships: _____

   _____

   _____

7. Prenuptial and/or postnuptial agreements, separation agreements, divorce papers: _____

   _____

Financial Data

Attach schedule to show detail

	Individual	*Spouse*
Salary and Bonus:	$	$
Assets **Investable Assets:** Cash Equivalents, Taxable Bonds, Tax-Free Bonds, Stocks, Limited Partnerships, IRAs/Keoghs and Insurance (Cash Value)	$	$
Non-Investable Assets: Real estate (residence), personal property, company benefits (stock options, 401(k), pension and profit sharing), and business interests	$	$
Total Assets:		
Liabilities: Notes payable and mortgages	$	$
Total Liabilities:		

Net Worth:

$	−	$	=	$
Total Assets		Total Liabilities		Net Worth

1. What is the total amount of investment funds that will be included in this portfolio?

   $ _____

   What percentage of the total net worth is represented by this portfolio?

   _____ %

2. Is there an immediate or near term need for income from this portfolio?

   ☐ Yes ☐ No

3. Will significant cash disbursements and/or contributions be made over the next five years? If yes, please attach a schedule.

   ☐ Yes ☐ No

4. Is this a taxable portfolio?

   ☐ Yes ☐ No

   If yes, what tax rate should be used for planning purposes?

   _____ %

5. What is the portfolio's investment time horizon? Investment time horizon refers to the minimum length of time the portfolio is reasonably expected to be invested before being liquidated, or alternatively, the period of time during which the investment objective for this portfolio will continue without substantial modification.

   ☐ Less Than Five Years

   ☐ Greater Than Five Years

6. Asset class preferences for asset simulation model.

   Provide any asset class limitations

   Asset Classes:

	Minimum	Maximum
Cash	____ %	____ %
Defensive fixed income	____ %	____ %
Global fixed income	____ %	____ %
High yield fixed income	____ %	____ %
Large cap equities	____ %	____ %
Small cap equities	____ %	____ %
International	____ %	____ %
Real estate	____ %	____ %
Closely held assets	____ %	____ %

7. To what extent can this portfolio be invested in long-term, illiquid investments? Up to what percent?

   _____ %

8. What percent of your investments are you likely to need within five years?

   _____ %

9. This portfolio should be structured with a goal of producing an annual rate of return of _____ %.

   Rate of return:
   _____ %

   The portfolio should be structured with a goal of producing an annual rate of return that is _____ % above the rate of inflation.

   Rate above inflation:
   _____ %

   Anticipated rate of inflation over the next five years?

   Anticipated inflation:
   _____ %

10. For each of the following attributes, circle the number that most correctly reflects your level of concern. The more important the concern, the higher the number. You may use each number more than once.

	Most					*Least*
Capital preservation	6	5	4	3	2	1
Growth	6	5	4	3	2	1
Tax minimization	6	5	4	3	2	1
Inflation protection	6	5	4	3	2	1
Current income	6	5	4	3	2	1
Aggressive growth	6	5	4	3	2	1

11. Investment risk can be viewed in many different ways. Please check any of the following that most closely define your view of risk.

_____ The possibility of not achieving a targeted rate of return.

_____ The loss of buying power over a long period of time.

_____ Wide swings in the market value of your portfolio over short (1 month) periods of time.

_____ Loss of principal.

12. Several investment portfolio performance records are presented below. Please check the one that most nearly approximates the goals of this portfolio.

	Expected Average Rate of Return	*Expected Annual Rate of Return**	*Annual Worst Case Scenario***
_____Very low	4.8	4.4– 5.2%	3.5%
_____	6.9	5.0– 8.8%	0.2%
_____Low	6.8	4.5– 9.1%	−1.3%
_____	8.0	5.2–10.8%	−1.9%
_____Average	7.6	4.9–10.3%	−1.9%
_____	8.4	5.1–11.7%	−3.0%
_____High	8.3	4.7–11.9%	−4.3%
_____	8.9	4.9–12.9%	−4.7%
_____Very high	9.1	4.5–13.7%	−6.7%
_____	9.8	4.2–15.4%	−9.1%

* Return ranges are based on +/- one standard deviation. This translates to a probability of the return falling within these limits, 2 out of every 3 years.

** There is a 95% probability that the annualized return will be better than the "worst case scenario."

13. What is the minimum annual rate of return that can be tolerated?

    `_____%`

14. Once the portfolio's strategic asset allocation is determined and implemented, which is the most appropriate for portfolio rebalancing?

    _____ Rebalancing (subject to established tolerance bands) back to the original strategic asset allocation model.

    _____ Tactical rebalancing to adjust for perceived under- or overvaluations in the stock and bond markets.

15. Are there currently any investment concerns or conflicts you would like to have addressed? If yes, please describe below.

    _____

    _____

    _____

    _____

    _____

16. How involved do you want to be in the investment management process?

    _____ Actively involved.

    _____ Participate only in decision-making process.

    _____ Assign total responsibility to investment consultant.

17. What is the greatest advantage to your current investment program?

    _____

    _____

    _____

    _____

    _____

18. What is the greatest disadvantage to your current investment program?

    _____

    _____

    _____

    _____

    _____

4

STEP 2—DESIGNING THE OPTIMAL PORTFOLIO

"[I]t is generally agreed by theoreticians and practitioners
alike that the asset allocation decision is by far
the most important made by the investor".[1]

William F. Sharpe, *Nobel Prize winner*

"The single most important dimension of
investment policy is asset mix, particularly the ratio
of fixed-income investments to equity investments."[2]

Charles D. Ellis

In the last chapter, we discussed the crucial step of analyzing the investor's current situation, including the intended purpose of the portfolio, investment constraints, and return objectives. Combining these preparatory steps with a good grasp of the behavior of capital markets, we are now ready to move to the next step in the investment process: designing the

---

[1] William F. Sharpe, "Asset Allocation," in *Managing Investment Portfolios: A Dynamic Process,* 2nd ed., ed. John L. Maginn and Donald L. Tuttle (Boston: Warren, Gorham & Lamont, 1990), p. 7-3.

[2] Charles D. Ellis, *Investment Policy: "How to Win the Loser's Game,"* 2nd ed. (Homewood, IL: Business One Irwin, 1993), at 35.

71

investor's optimal asset allocation. Asset allocation is the systematic process of designing an optimal portfolio mix that satisfies the investor's specific risk and return parameters.

The asset allocation process and the computerized analytical tools that support it will improve an investor's understanding of the trade-offs inherent in various combinations of investable assets. For instance, should one invest in stocks, bonds, or cash, and how much should be invested in each category? What about real estate or international assets? The asset allocation process prepares an investor to make an educated choice of asset categories in which to invest and the amount of money to be invested in each.

General

Asset allocation itself is just another name for investment diversification; however, optimal asset allocation strategies can achieve far superior results than just random diversification. If investment funds are allocated to each asset class according to sound policies of modern investment practice, the resultant asset allocation will not only reduce risk ("avoid putting all your eggs in one basket"), it can actually improve investment returns through the choice of asset classes ("which baskets") and reinforce the necessity for monitoring the results ("watch the baskets").

The theoretical underpinnings of asset allocation are quite straightforward. They originated in 1952 when Dr. Harry Markowitz, Nobel Prize-winning economist and the revered father of modern portfolio theory, discovered that an investment portfolio could be constructed with less risk than the weighted average of its component parts.[3] This is possible because all assets do not move up and down together in perfect synchronization. For instance, equity and fixed-income markets often move in different directions. The imperfect correlations of their returns will dampen the volatility of the overall portfolio.

> [E]ffective diversification depends not only on the number of assets in a trust portfolio but also on the ways and degrees in which their responses to economic events tend to reinforce, cancel or neutralize one another.[4]

---

[3] Harry M. Markowitz, *Portfolio Selection: Efficient Diversification of Investments* (New Haven, CT: Cowles Foundation for Research in Economics at Yale University, 1959); and Harry M. Markowitz, "Portfolio Selection," *Journal of Finance*, March 1952.

[4] Markowitz, *Portfolio Selection*.

At that time, all publications discussing preferred investment practices looked pretty much the same as the newspaper and magazine articles appealing to the retail investor today. That is, they harped on investment return and ignored risk. However, Dr. Markowitz recognized that the singular focus on return did not square with reality: "it occurred to me that I should consider risk as well as reward."

His resulting thesis (and the innovative basis for his Nobel Prize 40 years later) expressed the concept quite simply: "Investors like potential return and dislike risk," and with that, he became the first scholar, money manager, or business manager of investment portfolios to consider risk and reward as part of a cohesive whole. If that revelation seems too trivial, remember that today, over 40 years later, most everything one reads in the financial press and in the glossy publications of money managers and mutual funds still touts investment returns, with rarely a comment about the risk taken.

Asset allocation is now widely understood by successful investors to be the single most important determinant of the long-term performance of any investment portfolio. As described by Nobel laureate William Sharpe:

> Different investors approach asset allocation in different ways. Thus generalizations about its importance are difficult to make. Moreover there are alternative ways of measuring the importance of most investment decisions, including the asset allocation decision. *Despite these complications, it is generally agreed by theoreticians and practitioners alike that the asset allocation decision is by far the most important made by the investor.* [5]

The overwhelming importance of asset allocation has been demonstrated by comprehensive studies conducted on the investment returns actually achieved by large pension plans. The seminal work on performance attribution is the 1986 Brinson, Hood, and Beebower study that found asset allocation accounted for 93.6 percent of the total variation in returns for a typical large pension plan. [6] The fact that only three asset classes were considered in detail serves to strengthen the conservative nature of the already startling conclusion. As indicated by William

---

[5] Sharpe, "Asset Allocation," p. 7-3.

[6] Gary P. Brinson, L. Randolph Hood, and Gilbert L. Beebower, "Determinants of Portfolio Performance," *Financial Analysts Journal,* July/August 1986, and Gary P. Brinson, L. Randolph Hood, and Gilbert L. Beebower, "Determinants of Portfolio Performance II: An Update," *Financial Analysts Journal,* May/June 1991. (This article is an update of the former article).

Sharpe: "Had allocation across more classes been considered, the percentage would in all likelihood have been even larger."[7] Thus less than 7 percent of the fund's performance was due to the choice of individual stocks and bonds, market timing, security selection, transaction costs, and other miscellaneous items combined.

Whether asset allocation is of overwhelming importance or only the most important decision made by an investor is a distinction without a difference. Regardless of the relative sophistication of the investor, modern asset allocation techniques allow investors to control risk and improve performance substantially, with even small shifts in portfolio mix.

Thoughtful asset allocation strategies have enabled many investors to weather the storms of the 1987 stock market crash, the 1990 stock market decline and the 1994 bond market debacle with equanimity, while other investors have panicked and abandoned their positions. During these periods of extreme volatility, the investor's asset allocations were the most important determinant of both the risk and the return of their portfolios.

Fiduciaries and other investors are bombarded with a proliferation of investment products and services that appeal to our baser instincts desiring more reward for no risk. The higher returns of these products are usually packaged with the promise (often oral) of no greater risk than simpler, more familiar investment vehicles. Frequently, the investors' naïveté is later revealed in *The Wall Street Journal* when hundreds get caught in the inevitable buzz saw that ties risk to reward. Many more suffer their losses in private, all unnecessarily. (The current uproar over losses with financial derivatives as experienced by Orange County is only the latest debacle in a seemingly unending stream.)

Investors should understand there is only one way to increase the returns of their otherwise randomly diversified portfolios without a corresponding increase in portfolio risk: *asset allocation, the only free lunch!* The importance of asset allocation provides further support for our suggestion in Chapter 1 that fiduciaries and investors should first follow the straightforward steps of the basic prudent process before worrying about the details of more sophisticated implementations of their investment strategy. The process sets the priorities for consideration of investment issues, and the asset allocation that results from that process alone will allow investors to achieve the majority of their investment objectives.

---

[7] Sharpe, "Asset Allocation," p. 7-5.

Process for Choosing the Optimal Asset Allocation

The allocation process begins with a thoughtful decision focusing on the relative attractiveness of broad asset categories for a particular investor. It continues with further diversification to optimize the holdings within each of the various broad asset classes chosen for investment. The deliberate construction of a portfolio by this method will enable an investor to identify and anticipate possible return and risk outcomes.

TABLE 4–1 Broad Asset Classes

Large Cap Equity Those equity securities similar in capitalization to those in the Standard & Poor's 500 Index.

Small Capitalization Managers who invest in companies with relatively small capitalization (the average market capitalization is approximately $400 million).

International Equity This asset class is composed of securities held by Morgan Stanley Capital International's EAFE Index. The investments include approximately 1,000 securities representing the stock exchanges of Europe, Australia, New Zealand, and the Far East.

Broad Domestic Fixed-Income Securities in this asset class are a composite of all publicly issued, fixed-rate, nonconvertible, domestic bonds. The issues are rated at least BBB, have a minimum outstanding principal of $100 million for U.S. government issues or $50 million for other bonds, and have a maturity of at least one year.

Defensive Domestic Fixed-Income Fixed income securities whose average maturity is two to five years are included in this asset class.

International Fixed-Income The proxy used for this asset class is the Salomon Brothers Non–U.S. Dollar World Government Bond Index. This index excludes U.S. bonds and includes all fixed-rate government bonds in 10 countries having remaining maturities of one year or longer with amounts outstanding of at least the equivalent of $100 million U.S. dollars. The index is capitalization-weighted and is expressed in terms of U.S. dollars.

Cash Equivalents These are instruments or investments of such high liquidity and safety that they are virtually as good as cash. Examples are a money market fund and a treasury bill. The Financial Accounting Standards Board (FASB) defined cash equivalents for financial reporting purposes as any highly liquid security with a known market value and a maturity, when acquired, of less than three months.

Real Estate Consists of open- and closed-end commingled funds managed by real estate firms.

Asset allocation is the investor's choice of investment categories (asset classes) in which to invest and the percentage to allocate to each category. For instance, Table 4–1 represents the broad classes that are typically considered by most investors. With this variety and more from which to choose, the $64 thousand question is how should an investor make choices among the alternatives?

In general, an investor should make these choices with an understanding of the range of potential investment outcomes, both for the individual asset categories (i.e., stocks, bonds, and so on) and for the portfolio as a whole. One must consider the likely effect of economic and capital market conditions on each of the individual asset categories and how the investment returns will impact each other. The reasonably likely portfolio outcomes must be consistent with the investor's objectives, risk tolerance, and legal responsibilities.

Consequently, one person's asset allocation is not necessarily even an interesting starting point for developing one's own. In the first place, each investor is going to have a cash flow schedule (contributions and disbursements) that is unique. Second, other investors may not have had sufficient resources to correctly produce and evaluate their alternatives. Third, and most importantly, those decisions assuredly did not take another investor's individual needs and goals into account.

As we shall see, any number of so-called optimal portfolios (which minimize risk for a given level of return) can be constructed by taking into account general economic conditions and the expected risk/return profiles of specific asset classes. (See Figure 4–2.) However, to achieve the investor's investment objectives, one must also carefully consider the investor's own circumstances and needs in the asset allocation process.

The risk of a portfolio can be less than the average or weighted average risk of the individual asset classes comprising the portfolios. In fact, in some cases the portfolio risk can be even less than the risk of the least risky asset class (e.g., U.S. bonds) in the portfolio. Note that, in Figure 4–1, the standard deviation for the 100 percent U.S. bond investment is greater than the 40/60 equity/fixed-income mix, and, in addition, the 40/60 diversified portfolio has a greater rate of return than the all-fixed-income portfolio.

This remarkable result is made possible by a simple fact understood by observers of market movements: the prices of assets comprising different asset classes seldom move in synchronized fashion and often move independently or even in opposite directions. We say the returns of these assets are not perfectly correlated. For example, by adding equities (high variability of returns) to a portfolio of fixed income (lower variability of returns), the resultant portfolio may exhibit less variability of returns and higher expected compound returns than the original portfolio of fixed income alone.

FIGURE 4–1   Efficient Frontier

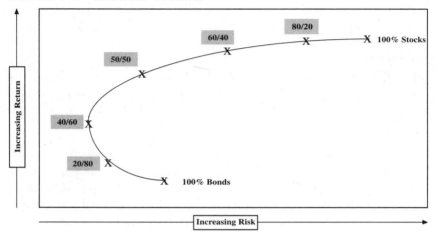

Source: Copyright © 1993, Investment Management Council

FIGURE 4–2   Asset Allocation Variables

Capital Markets Expectations	Principal Investor Inputs	
1. Projected returns of asset classes	R	Risk tolerance
2. Projected levels of variability of returns (standard deviation)	A	Asset class preferences
3. Projected correlations (related movement) of asset classes	T	Time horizon of major disbursements
Callan: Risk premium model overlayed with econometric forecasts.	E	Expected returns

Source: Copyright © 1994, Investment Management Council.

Inputs to the Allocation Decision

Asset allocation decisions can be modeled using optimization software that is readily available in the retail marketplace. (See Appendix 4–1 for a listing of software sources.) The software enables the investor to adopt an appropriate asset mix representing an ideal blend of the investor's risk and return parameters. There is no uniformity in the programming or capabilities of the software; however, most models require consideration of two fundamental sets of inputs: (1) projected capital market conditions (usually set by an investment consultant) and (2) the investor's specific expectations and constraints (see Figure 4–2). The careful analytic consideration (whether formal or informal) of these two sets of data is referred to as the *integrated asset allocation process.*[8] The idea is to consider all major aspects of the decision in a consistent manner.

Capital Markets Expectations

The choice of an optimal asset allocation strategy must be built on carefully developed expectations for the capital markets and the way in which the individual asset classes are expected to perform in relation to and in combination with each other. The development of optimized asset allocations requires estimates of the risk (standard deviation of returns) of each asset class, the expected return of each asset class, and the correlations of each asset class's return with that of each of the other asset classes.

Experience suggests that for predicting future values, historical data on different asset classes appears to be quite useful with respect to standard deviations, "reasonably useful for correlations, and virtually useless for expected returns."[9] Simple extrapolations of historical data are not only likely to be poor estimates of future performance, they may also lead to the development of expectations that cannot be met. To provide an investor with any assurance that one is constructing an asset allocation on reasonable estimates, more professional approaches are clearly called for and, indeed, are provided by the major consulting organizations. In general, these approaches combine an analysis of historical returns with possible economic scenarios and expected long-term market equilibrium results, taking into account reasonable relationships among expected returns, risks, and correlations.

---

[8] Sharpe, "Asset Allocation," p. 7-21.
[9] Sharpe, "Asset Allocation," p. 7-37.

Table 4–2 shows historical returns for each of the broad asset classes in column one. The next two columns show returns for the last 10 and 5 years, respectively. The far right-hand column shows the projected returns of the same asset classes over the next five years. [10] Notice that the consulting firm that developed these projections is taking the position that the 1990s will not see the same returns as the 1980s, and that future returns will likely regress to their historical averages.

TABLE 4–2 **Comparative Study of Capital Markets**

Asset Class	Historical Returns* (Time Period)	10-Year Returns** (1985–1994)	5-Year Returns** (1990–1994)	Projected Returns (5-Yr. Forecast)
Large cap equities	10.2[h] (1926–1994)	14.4[a]	8.7[a]	9.8
Small cap equities	13.6[a] (1981–1994)	13.6[a]	10.5[a]	10.8
International equities	12.8[b] (1972–1994)	17.6[b]	1.5[b]	10.7**
Defensive fixed income	9.2[e] (1978–1994)	8.0[e]	6.7[e]	7.2
Broad fixed income	5.4[h] (1926–1994)	9.8[d]	7.7[d]	7.5
High yield fixed income	12.2[e] (1985–1994)	12.2[e]	12.0[e]	8.0
Global fixed income	12.3[c] (1985–1994)	12.3[c]	9.7[c]	7.5
Real estate (composite)	7.4[a] (1972–1994)	3.6[a]	−0.6[a]	8.6
Cash (90-Day T-Bill)*	3.7[h] (1926–1994)	6.1[f]	5.0[f]	4.8
Inflation	3.1[h] (1926–1994)	3.5[g]	3.4[g]	4.0

*Data from 1926–1994 reflects 30-day T-Bill; 10-year and 5-year historical returns reflect 90 day T-Bill.
**Reflects 85% MSCI EAFE and 15% Morgan Stanley Emerging Markets Free.
Data Source Key: [a]Callan Associates Inc.; [b]Morgan Stanley; [c]Salomon Brothers; [d]Lehman; [e]Merrill Lynch; [f]Federal Reserve; [g]DOL; [h]Ibbotson Associates, Inc. Copyright. © 1995, Investment Management Council.

---

[10] Expected returns were developed by Callan Associates Inc. for the period 1994–1998.

FIGURE 4–3   Scenario Assumptions

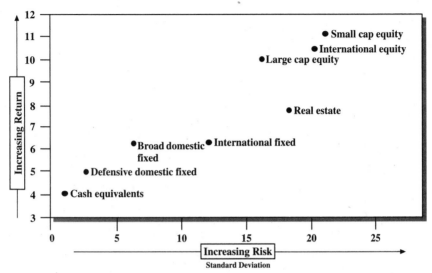

Source: Copyright © 1994, Investment Management Council.

When the projected returns are plotted against the projected volatility of the returns (standard deviation), you can see the relative risk/return profile of each of the broad asset classes (see Figure 4–3). Those assets which offer the least return and least risk fall in the bottom left hand portion of the graph, and those with the most risk and most volatility are in the upper right hand side of the graph.

The expected correlation of returns between asset classes is the third critical capital markets parameter (expected return and standard deviation being the first two). When adding asset classes to a portfolio, those assets that possess a low correlation to the assets that already comprise the portfolio should receive preference. A correlation of 1.0 would indicate that the two asset classes are highly correlated to one another and, therefore, from a diversification standpoint, it would be preferable not to include both in a portfolio. A correlation of .10 or any negative correlation would provide the total portfolio greater diversification benefits.

TABLE 4–3 Correlation Table

Asset Class	(1)	(2)	(3)	(4)	(5)	(6)	(7)
(1) Large cap equity	1.00	0.89	0.60	0.37	0.21	0.04	0.11
(2) Small cap equity	0.89	1.00	0.52	0.26	0.06	0.05	−0.14
(3) International equity	0.60	0.52	1.00	0.41	0.27	0.51	−0.10
(4) Broad domestic fixed	0.37	0.26	0.41	1.00	0.92	0.44	−0.04
(5) Defensive domestic fixed	0.21	0.06	0.27	0.92	1.00	0.42	0.10
(6) International fixed	0.04	0.05	0.51	0.44	0.42	1.00	−0.31
(7) Cash equivalents	0.11	−0.14	−0.10	−0.04	0.10	−0.31	1.00

Source: Callan Associates Inc. projected correlations for the period 1994–1998.

One look at Table 4–3 reveals that it is nearly impossible for the nonprofessional to make even an educated guess of reasonable correlation estimates. Professional estimates will likely consider the "well-known tendency for near-term future risks and correlations to be more like those of the recent past than those of the distant past."[11]

Principal Investor Inputs

In Chapter 2, we described the role of the fiduciary or investor as the manager of the investment process:

> The *role* of the fiduciary is to maximize the benefits to be gained from the process—that is, to maximize the likelihood of achieving the objectives of the investment funds for which one is responsible.

Asset allocation is still as much an art as it is a science in spite of the rigor and specificity of the decision-making process for choosing optimal asset allocations. Recent advances in portfolio theory, technological tools, and more comprehensive databases have not reduced the asset allocation decision to one of merely finding the computerized, mathematical solution to the problem. Quite the contrary. First of all, the outputs of the computerized optimization models can only be as good as the inputs. Most of the capital markets data are just that: statistical data, not facts. They provide extremely valuable insights but not unassailable truths on which to bet the ranch.

---

[11] Sharpe, "Asset Allocation," p. 7-39.

Second, the investor's inputs are anything but absolutes. To be valuable, they require thoughtful inquiry, and most likely experience and re-evaluation, to ascertain whether one has covered the important bases to build a sound investment strategy. And last, but not least, the computer models themselves tend to be extremely sensitive to small changes in input variables and thus exacerbate the problems mentioned above. The key is that these technological advances should be used for what they are—tools and analytical frames of reference that enable investors and fiduciaries to effectively manage the most important decision in the investment process: asset allocation. The variability of the investors' individual circumstances means there is no one right asset allocation answer, nor is there a legitimate shortcut to the process itself.

To assist investors in remembering their specific inputs to the asset allocation model, we use the acronym RATE:

R Risk tolerance

A Asset classes to be considered

T Time horizon

E Expected or needed investment return

R Risk Tolerance

Risk tolerance can be measured in a variety of ways, but regardless of how it is measured, the higher it is, the greater an investor's perceived ability or willingness to take on risk in order to obtain a higher expected portfolio return.

We have found the best way to measure risk is to ask the investor, "What percentage of the portfolio are you willing to lose in a given year?" The initial response is invariably zero. We then show the investor the corresponding return (approximately 7.0 percent) that is associated with constructing a portfolio with a zero loss limit. The reaction is often that the return would not be satisfactory. So we then ask, "What rate of return would meet your needs?" The response often ranges between 9 and 10 percent. The loss limits (worst case scenario in a given year) associated with these returns fall between -9 and -11 percent of the portfolio's value. With these two extremes identified (the loss limit and the return expectation), we then begin to bracket the specific risk/return level with which the investor is most comfortable.

Even with the insight that results from education in investment fundamentals, it is not enough to say, "I need to take *this level of risk* to achieve my desired returns." If the investor later abandons the program because of unwelcomed volatility, the investor will likely forfeit his or her chances of achieving desired investment objectives. And investors are far more likely to abandon an investment program for its volatility of returns than for any other reason. Consequently, this manifestation of risk (i.e., aversion to losses) is the crucial parameter for the investor's determination of an optimal asset allocation. The investor's ability to stay-the-course is strongly influenced by

1. The investor's expectations regarding the variation in value (up and down) most likely to be experienced over time.
2. The degree to which an investor perceives that actual results are in line with those expectations.
3. The investor's emotional ability to accept the inevitable decline in value (albeit temporary) and possible loss actually experienced in asset returns.

Although it is difficult for the investor to know his or her bottom-line loss until it has been experienced, education in portfolio management fundamentals will undoubtedly change perceptions of and tolerance for risk. In other words, knowing what is likely to happen seems to prepare investors to accept it.

A Asset classes

The investor must specify the choice of asset classes that will comprise the set of feasible investment opportunities. Portfolio theory suggests the most appropriate asset classes to be used as a starting point are broad market indices representing the full capitalization-weighted range of investment opportunities available to the portfolio. From that starting point, it is the investor who knows in the first instance what restrictions should be put on the composition of the chosen asset classes. For example, settlor, statutory, or regulatory requirements may prohibit ownership in certain types of securities.

Table 4–1 on page 75 shows the broad asset classes. In some cases these broad asset classes can be broken down into several subasset classes. For instance, the large cap equity class can be implemented with a combination of core equity, growth equity, or value equity managers (described in greater detail in Chapter 6). However, these issues should not detract the investor from the main asset allocation decision; rather, they should be thought of as decisions to be considered later, in implementing the chosen strategic asset allocation.

Choosing asset classes is usually an iterative decision. In the first step, after eliminating inappropriate or restricted asset classes, the remaining asset classes will likely constitute a broad global mix from which to choose. An investor should then evaluate several optimized portfolios (see Figure 4–5) to determine the relative contribution to increased returns/decreased risk provided by other asset classes. The referenced costs (such as the fiduciary's additional time commitment required to manage the successful implementation of some of these investment classes) may well be worth the increased return and risk diversification benefits, but require careful analysis in light of the investor's particular circumstances. Careful documentation of this analysis will also ensure that these decisions will be revisited properly when circumstances change.

T Time Horizon

The investor's time horizon is the primary variable in determining the allocation between stock and fixed income investments. For shorter investment horizons, investors are likely to get the mix right without any fancy optimization models. One should intuitively and correctly understand that stocks are more risky (returns are more volatile) than short-term T-bills and cash. Consequently, if an investor's investment horizon is less than five years, in most cases one should not invest in stocks, or even fixed-income investments with maturities in excess of the investment horizon.

However, both individual and institutional investors tend to underestimate their time horizons. Individuals (with finite lives) tend to confuse their retirement horizons with their investment horizons, the latter usually being much longer. The start of retirement plan distributions does not determine an investor's time horizon; rather, it is the time over which one will consume the investment returns. For a retiring couple, this may be another 20 to 40 years; for an institution, arguably an infinite time horizon:

> It would appear to make more sense for a pension plan to focus not on an investment horizon, which may in fact be infinite, but rather on its usual decision period. How long will it be before the next major decision is made?[12]

---

[12] William F. Sharpe, "The Risk Factor: Identifying and Adapting to the Risk Capacity of the Client," *Asset Allocation for Institutional Portfolios* (Charlottesville, VA, The Institute of Chartered Financial Analysts, 1987).

And, indeed, the time horizon must be a period over which the investor agrees to stay with a particular asset allocation if the portfolio is performing within the probable expectations established beforehand. It is simply unrealistic to expect any investor to hold an assessment for 20 years! All the more so for an investment committee whose members change over time and whose judgments may be subject to scrutiny by influential observers (i.e., their bosses or the public) less enamored with the teachings of modern portfolio theory.

Investors are likely to design their asset allocations around appropriate longer time horizons if they understand the power of time to decrease the risk of, and to increase the compound returns to their portfolios. As Figure 4–4 illustrates, as an investor's time horizon lengthens, the expected return from stocks will stay the same, but the risk of varying returns (standard deviation) will decline dramatically. All things being equal, one should tend to invest more in equity classes as time horizons lengthen.

FIGURE 4–4 **Equity Returns and Volatility Over Various Time Periods**

Domestic Equity Performance Data
1926–1994

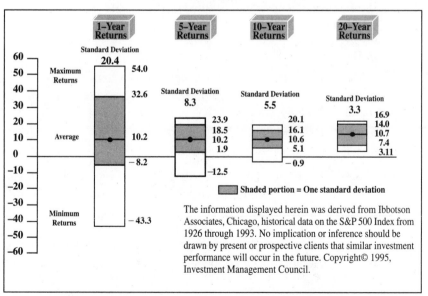

The information displayed herein was derived from Ibbotson Associates, Chicago, historical data on the S&P 500 Index from 1926 through 1993. No implication or inference should be drawn by present or prospective clients that similar investment performance will occur in the future. Copyright© 1995, Investment Management Council.

E **Expected Return**

Expected return refers to the amount by which the investor would like to increase his or her assets over a specified period of time. It is one of the primary targets of the asset allocation process. It must be realistic, which means three things:

1. It is based on realistic expectations of asset class returns.

2. If achieved, it will result in the investment portfolio meeting its specific goals (e.g., pension payouts, greatest real future asset value, large positive future pension surplus, and so on).

3. It implies an acceptable level of risk. For example, an investor cannot realistically demand 10 percent returns without incurring the risk of losing money in certain years.

The expected return should be set as either an absolute target— "I want (or need) to earn 9 percent on my portfolio"—or in relative terms —"I want to exceed the rate of inflation by 3 percent."

Optimization Models

To facilitate the decision-making process, and to assist the investor in understanding the tradeoffs between risk and return, we use software that simultaneously displays all four variables of the acronym RATE and incorporates the capital markets assumptions previously described (see Figure 4–5).*

From Figure 4–5:

Risk is labeled as the worst case and depicts a loss of -6.0.

Asset mix is shown as mostly equities with some fixed income and cash.

Time horizon is shown as five years or greater.

Expected return depicts a value of 9.3.

To take this illustration one step further, we have included in Appendix 4–3 11 portfolios representing different risk/return profiles presented in the format shown above.

Fiduciaries and investors are prone to choose asset allocation methods that are easily applied. The mean-variance model remains the most widely accepted optimization model for asset allocation and portfolio

---

*Software developed jointly by Frontier Analytics and Callan Associates Inc.

FIGURE 4–5   Sample Screen from Optimization Software

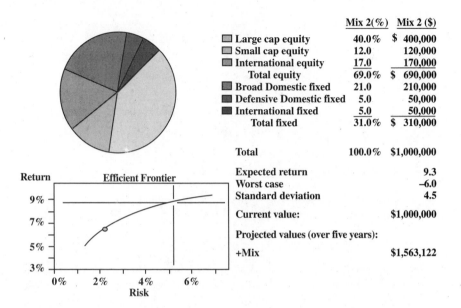

	Mix 2(%)	Mix 2 ($)
☐ Large cap equity	40.0%	$ 400,000
☐ Small cap equity	12.0	120,000
■ International equity	17.0	170,000
Total equity	69.0%	$ 690,000
■ Broad Domestic fixed	21.0	210,000
■ Defensive Domestic fixed	5.0	50,000
■ International fixed	5.0	50,000
Total fixed	31.0%	$ 310,000
Total	100.0%	$1,000,000

Expected return	9.3
Worst case	–6.0
Standard deviation	4.5
Current value:	$1,000,000
Projected values (over five years):	
+Mix	$1,563,122

investment.[13] Its quantitative asset allocation technique analyzes expected asset returns, the volatility of those returns, and the correlation of returns among asset classes in conjunction with a quantification of the investor's risk tolerance, investment objectives and time horizon.

The efficient frontier of investment possibilities generated by the mean-variance optimization model is common to all asset allocations involving the same initial universe of selected asset classes. "The uniqueness of the allocation decisions appropriate for different investors rests entirely with the assumed level of risk tolerance."[14] For example, Table 4–4 illustrates one set of optimal asset allocations generated by a mean-variance model utilizing the capital markets expectations summarized in this chapter.

[13] Markowitz, "Portfolio Selection;" Markowitz, *Portfolio Selection;* Harry M. Markowitz, *Mean-Variance Analysis in Portfolio Choice and Capital Markets* (Cambridge, MA: Basil Blackwell, 1987); and J. Tobin, "Liquidity Preference as Behavior Toward Risk," *Review of Economics and Statistics,* February 1958.

[14] W. V. Harlow and Keith C. Brown, *The Role of Risk Tolerance in the Asset Allocation Process: A New Prospective* (Charlottesville, Va: The Research Foundation of the Institute of Chartered Financial Analysts, 1990) at 3.

TABLE 4–4 Investment Alternatives

Asset Class	Mix 1	Mix 2	Mix 3	Mix 4
Large cap equity	11.0	33.0	26.0	0.0
Small cap equity	3.0	9.0	30.0	100.0
International equity	4.0	19.0	40.0	0.0
Broad Domestic fixed	0.0	31.0	0.0	0.0
Defensive Domestic fixed	70.0	0.0	0.0	0.0
Real estate	3.0	8.0	4.0	0.0
Cash	9.0	0.0	0.0	0.0
Return expectations (5 yr period)	7.5%	9.3%	10.4%	10.8%
Loss limit (worst case scenario)	− .6	− 5.4	− 10.2	− 15.4

Each of these asset allocations is optimized so that it can provide the investor with the highest expected return for the given level of risks, considering only these asset classes and subject to any constraints imposed by the investor on minimum or maximum holdings of any particular asset class. At this point, an investor would then be asked to examine the range of outcomes associated with each of the mixes and then choose the preferred mix. This would constitute the investor's strategic or policy asset allocation.

Unfortunately, many investors do not employ this methodology, and instead pick the average asset mix of similar investors or take the recommendations of market strategists. There is no reason for investors to "shoot from the hip" with respect to their asset allocation decision. While a 50/50 allocation between equities and fixed income may make sense on average for a class of investors, individual or otherwise, we have not met any average investors. Every investment services firm publishing a rough guideline (with all the common disclaimers) is motivated by one of two reasons: (1) marketing purposes (everyone else is doing it), or (2) the belief they are being helpful, since almost any allocation is better than having 100 percent of an investor's money in a money market fund, CD, or GIC (where most of the 401(k) money is invested today).

Review of Asset Allocation

The optimized asset allocation indicates the appropriate asset mix to be held under normal conditions. It also suggests the investor's long-run or average level of risk tolerance. As conditions change in either the capital markets expectations or the investor's circumstances (RATE), alterations in the asset mix should be considered. An analysis of the effect of these changes should be straightforward, following the same process used to develop the asset allocation in the first place.

One should avoid abrupt decisions made purely on the basis of quar-ter-by-quarter investment results.

> There are widespread misunderstandings about asset allocation evident in its practice in portfolio management. These conceptions lead to error in its practice which would be comical, were they not so terribly costly. [Investors] shuffle their asset mix and churn portfolios in an emotional response to the markets.[15]

Unfortunately, many investors still enter the equity markets at market highs and sell at market bottoms. They will buy the recently success-ful hot mutual fund only to see that style's performance fail to beat the averages, then sell the mutual fund just before results turn.

Summary

Asset allocation is not something an investor can choose to do or avoid. Either the investor will proactively choose an asset allocation that is right for his or her needs, or the collective activities of the investor's money managers and service vendors will determine one by default. In any event, the financial markets will modify the investor's actual allocations to different asset classes over time, so the investor must be prepared to evaluate when and how to re-adjust the portfolio.

---

[15] Robert D. Arnott, "Managing the Asset Mix: Decisions and Consequences," in *Pension Fund Investment Management: A Handbook for Sponsors and Their Advisors,* ed. Frank J. Fabozzi (Chicago: Probus Publishing Company, 1990), p. 60.

APPENDIX 4–1
SOURCES OF ASSET ALLOCATION SOFTWARE

BARRA
1995 University Ave
Berkeley, CA 94701-1058
(510) 548-5442

CDA Cadence
1355 Piccard Drive
Rockville, MD 20850-4315
(301) 975-9600

Frontier Analytics
8910 University Center
Suite 700
San Diego, CA 92122-1085
(619) 552-1268

Ibbotson Associates Inc.
225 North Michigan Ave
Suite 700
Chicago, IL 60601-7676
(312) 616-1620

Frank Russell Company
P.O. Box 1616
Tacoma, WA 98402
(206) 572-9500

Vestek Systems
388 Market Street
Suite 700
San Francisco, CA 94111-5347
(415) 398-6340

Wilshire Associates Inc.
1299 Ocean Ave
Santa Monica, CA 90401
(310) 451-3051

Wyatt Software
5335 Southwest Meadows Rd
Suite 200
Lake Oswego, OR 97035-3113
(503) 620-9800

APPENDIX 4–2
ASSET ALLOCATION SUMMARY

Allocation by Percentages	Probable Range of Annualized Returns Over a 5-Year Period[1]			Worst Case Scenario In Any Given Year[2]
	Low	*Expected*	*High*	
100 Equities	4.2	9.8	15.4	-9.1
80 Equities / 20 Bonds	4.6	9.3	14.0	-6.8
80 Equities / 10 Bonds / 10 Cash	4.5	9.1	13.7	-6.7
80 Equities / 20 Cash	4.3	8.8	13.3	-6.6
60 Equities / 40 Bonds	4.9	8.9	12.9	-4.7
60 Equities / 20 Bonds / 20 Cash	4.7	8.3	11.9	-4.3
60 Equities / 40 Cash	4.4	7.8	11.2	-4.0
40 Equities / 60 Bonds	5.1	8.4	11.7	-3.0
40 Equities / 30 Bonds / 30 Cash	4.9	7.6	10.3	-1.9
40 Equities / 60 Cash	4.5	6.8	9.1	-1.3
20 Equities / 80 Bonds	5.2	8.0	10.8	-1.9
20 Equities / 40 Bonds / 40 Cash	5.0	6.9	8.8	0.2
20 Equities / 80 Cash	4.6	5.8	7.0	1.5
100 Bonds	4.8	7.5	10.2	-1.9
100 Cash	4.4	4.8	5.2	3.5

[1]There is a 66 percent probability that the annualized return will fall between the *high* and *low* ranges indicated.
[2]There is a 95 percent probability that the annualized return will be better than the *worst case scenario.*

Source: Copyright © 1995, Investment Management Council.

Diversified Portfolio Alternative:

Sample Global Mix #1

Conservative

Asset Mix Profile

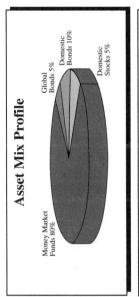

Money Market Funds 80%

Global Bonds 5%

Domestic Bonds 10%

Domestic Stocks 5%

Investor Profile

Investment Time Horizon: *Short-Term*

Appropriate for participant whose investable time horizon is less than 3 years. Achieving a long-term excess return over inflation is not a primary goal.

Investment Risk: *Low*

Participant cannot tolerate losses in any given year.

Projected Return Performance

Range of Projected Rates of Returns (Five–Year Time Horizon)

7.9% Maximum*

6.2% Expected

3.0% Minimum*

7.7%

In 2 out of 3 years, the return will likely fall within shaded area.

4.8%

Expected Asset Growth

Assuming that this portfolio achieves its expected 6.2% return each year, $1,000 would grow to $1,307 over 5 years. Returns in any year, however, will vary.

*A 5% probability exists that the maximum or minimum return in the adjacent chart will be exceeded.

Historical Return Performance[1]

Calendar Years

1994	*1993*	*1992*	*1991*	*1990*
3.26%	4.62%	4.37%	8.62%	7.74%

Time Periods Ended December 31, 1994

Last Quarter	*Last 1 Year*	*Last 3 Years*	*Last 5 Years*	*Last 10 Years*
1.07%	3.26%	4.08%	5.70%	7.26%

[1]Returns for periods of 1 year or longer are annualized. No inference should be made that this asset mix will achieve similar results in the future.

Source: Copyright© 1995, Callan Associates Inc.

Diversified Portfolio Alternative: *Sample Domestic Mix #2*

Conservative

Investor Profile

Investment Time Horizon: *Short-Term*

Appropriate for participant whose investable time horizon is less than 3 years. Achieving a long-term excess return over inflation is not a primary goal.

Investment Risk: *Low*

Participant cannot tolerate losses in any given year.

Asset Mix Profile

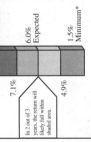

Money Market Funds 60%

Domestic Bonds 30%

Domestic Stocks 10%

Historical Return Performance[1]

Calendar Years

1994	*1993*	*1992*	*1991*	*1990*
1.68%	5.80%	5.27%	11.47%	7.13%

Time Periods Ended December 31, 1994

Last Quarter	*Last 1 Year*	*Last 3 Years*	*Last 5 Years*	*Last 10 Years*
0.82%	1.68%	4.24%	6.22%	8.14%

[1]Returns for periods of 1 year or longer are annualized. No inference should be made that this asset mix will achieve similar results in the future.

Projected Return Performance

Range of Projected Rates of Returns (Five-Year Time Horizon)

- 8.1% Maximum*
- 7.1%
- 6.0% Expected
- In 2 out of 3 years, the return will likely fall within shaded area.
- 4.9%
- 1.5% Minimum*

Expected Asset Growth

Assuming that this portfolio achieves its expected 6.0% return each year, $1,000 would grow to $1,338 over 5 years. Returns in any year, however, will vary.

*A 5% probability exists that the maximum or minimum return in the adjacent chart will be exceeded.

Diversified Portfolio Alternative:

Sample Global Mix #3

Conservative

Investor Profile

Investment Time Horizon: *Short-Term*

Appropriate for participant whose investable time horizon is less than 3 years. Achieving a long-term excess return over inflation is not a primary goal.

Investment Risk: *Low*

Participant cannot tolerate losses in any given year.

Asset Mix Profile

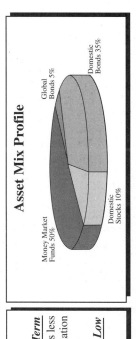

Money Market Funds 50%

Global Bonds 5%

Domestic Bonds 35%

Domestic Stocks 10%

Historical Return Performance[1]

Calendar Years

1994	*1993*	*1992*	*1991*	*1990*
1.22%	6.64%	5.58%	12.50%	7.38%

Time Periods Ended December 31, 1994

Last Quarter	*Last 1 Year*	*Last 3 Years*	*Last 5 Years*	*Last 10 Years*
0.73%	1.22%	4.45%	6.60%	8.68%

[1]Returns for periods of 1 year or longer are annualized. No inference should be made that this asset mix will achieve similar results in the future.

Projected Return Performance

Range of Projected Rates of Returns (Five–Year Time Horizon)

8.8% Maximum*

7.9%

In 2 out of 3 years, the return will likely fall within shaded area.

6.5% Expected

5.1%

1.1% Minimum*

Expected Asset Growth

Assuming that this portfolio achieves its expected 6.5% return each year, $1,000 would grow to $1,370 over 5 years. Returns in any year, however, will vary.

*A 5% probability exists that the maximum or minimum return in the adjacent chart will be exceeded.

Source: Copyright© 1995, Callan Associates Inc.

Diversified Portfolio Alternative:

Sample Domestic Mix #4

Conservative

Investor Profile

Investment Time Horizon: *Intermediate*

Appropriate for participant whose investable time horizon is 3–5 years. Achieving a long-term excess return over inflation is an important goal.

Investment Risk: *Average*

Participant can tolerate some risk and an occasional loss in any given year.

Asset Mix Profile

Money Market Funds 35%

Domestic Bonds 50%

Domestic Stocks 15%

Historical Return Performance[1]

Calendar Years

1994	*1993*	*1992*	*1991*	*1990*
0.01%	7.50%	6.29%	14.90%	6.70%

Time Periods Ended December 31, 1994

Last Quarter	*Last 1 Year*	*Last 3 Years*	*Last 5 Years*	*Last 10 Years*
0.53%	0.01%	4.55%	6.98%	9.36%

[1]Returns for periods of 1 year or longer are annualized. No inference should be made that this asset mix will achieve similar results in the future.

Projected Return Performance

Range of Projected Rates of Returns (Five–Year Time Horizon)

10.0% Maximum*

7.0% Expected

0.5% Minimum*

8.9%

5.1%

In 2 out of 3 years, the return will likely fall within shaded area.

Expected Asset Growth

Assuming that this portfolio achieves its expected 7.0% return each year, $1,000 would grow to $1,338 over 5 years. Returns in any year, however, will vary.

*A 5% probability exists that the maximum or minimum return in the adjacent chart will be exceeded.

Source: Copyright© 1995, Callan Associates Inc.

Diversified Portfolio Alternative:

Sample Global Mix #5

Moderate

Asset Mix Profile

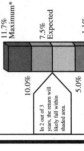

Domestic Stocks 20%
Money Market Funds 15%
Global Bonds 5%
Domestic Bonds 60%

Investor Profile

Investment Time Horizon: *Intermediate*

Appropriate for participant whose investable time horizon is 3–5 years. Achieving a long-term excess return over inflation is an important goal.

Investment Risk: *Average*

Participant can tolerate some risk and an occasional loss in any given year.

Historical Return Performance[1]

Calendar Years

1994	*1993*	*1992*	*1991*	*1990*
10.48%	10.12%	6.01%	17.69%	4.72%

Time Periods Ended December 31, 1994

Last Quarter	*Last 1 Year*	*Last 3 Years*	*Last 5 Years*	*Last 10 Years*
0.22%	10.48%	5.12%	7.44%	10.97%

[1]Returns for periods of 1 year or longer are annualized. No inference should be made that this asset mix will achieve similar results in the future.

Projected Return Performance

Range of Projected Rates of Returns (Five-Year Time Horizon)

11.7% Maximum*
10.0%
In 2 out of 3 years, the return will likely fall within shaded area.
7.5% Expected
5.0%
–1.1% Minimum*

Expected Asset Growth

Assuming that this portfolio achieves its expected 7.5% return each year, $1,000 would grow to $1,436 over 5 years. Returns in any year, however, will vary.

*A 5% probability exists that the maximum or minimum return in the adjacent chart will be exceeded.

Source: Copyright© 1995, Callan Associates Inc.

Diversified Portfolio Alternative: *Sample Domestic Mix #6*

Moderate

Asset Mix Profile

Global Bond 10%.
(no 59)

Money Market
Funds 10%

Domestic
Stocks 30%

Domestic / 50%
Bonds 60%

Investor Profile

Investment Time Horizon: *Intermediate*

Appropriate for participant whose investable time horizon is 3–5 years. Achieving a long-term excess return over inflation is an important goal.

Investment Risk: *Average*

Participant can tolerate some risk and an occasional loss in any given year.

Projected Return Performance

Expected Asset Growth

Assuming that this portfolio achieves its expected 8.0% return each year, $1,000 would grow to $1,469 over 5 years. Returns in any year, however, will vary.

*A 5% probability exists that the maximum or minimum return in the adjacent chart will be exceeded.

Range of Projected Rates of Returns (Five–Year Time Horizon)

12.6% Maximum*

10.8%

In 2 out of 3 years, the return will likely fall within shaded area.

8.0% Expected

5.2%

−1.9% Minimum*

Historical Return Performance[1]

Calendar Years

1994	*1993*	*1992*	*1991*	*1990*
−1.72%	9.63%	7.63%	20.66%	4.94%

Time Periods Ended December 31, 1994

Last Quarter	*Last 1 Year*	*Last 3 Years*	*Last 5 Years*	*Last 10 Years*
0.08%	11.72%	5.06%	7.99%	11.21%

[1]Returns for periods of 1 year or longer are annualized. No inference should be made that this asset mix will achieve similar results in the future.

Source: Copyright© 1995, Callan Associates Inc.

Diversified Portfolio Alternative:

Sample Global Mix #7

Moderate

Asset Mix Profile

Domestic Stocks 30%

International Stocks 10%

Domestic Bonds 60%

Investor Profile

Investment Time Horizon: *Intermediate*

Appropriate for participant whose investable time horizon is 3–5 years. Achieving a long-term excess return over inflation is an important goal.

Investment Risk: *Average*

Participant can tolerate some risk and an occasional loss in any given year.

Historical Return Performance[1]

Calendar Years

1994	*1993*	*1992*	*1991*	*1990*
−11.01%	12.12%	5.75%	20.82%	1.68%

Time Periods Ended December 31, 1994

Last Quarter	*Last 1 Year*	*Last 3 Years*	*Last 5 Years*	*Last 10 Years*
−10.10%	−11.01%	5.49%	7.60%	12.29%

[1]Returns for periods of 1 year or longer are annualized. No inference should be made that this asset mix will achieve similar results in the future.

Projected Return Performance

Range of Projected Rates of Returns (Five–Year Time Horizon)

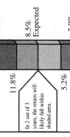

14.1% Maximum*

11.8%

In 2 out of 3 years, the return will likely fall within shaded area.

8.5% Expected

5.2%

−3.0% Minimum*

Expected Asset Growth

Assuming that this portfolio achieves its expected 8.5% return each year, $1,000 would grow to $1,504 over 5 years. Returns in any year, however, will vary.

*A 5% probability exists that the maximum or minimum return in the adjacent chart will be exceeded.

Source: Copyright© 1995, Callan Associates Inc.

Diversified Portfolio Alternative:

Sample Domestic Mix #8

Aggressive

Asset Mix Profile

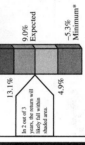

Domestic Stocks 65%

Domestic Bonds 35%

Investor Profile

Investment Time Horizon: *Long–Term*

Appropriate for participant whose investable time horizon is greater than 5 years. Achieving a long-term excess return over inflation is a primary goal.

Investment Risk: *High*

Participant can tolerate some risk and an occasional loss in any given year.

Projected Return Performance

Range of Projected Rates of Returns (Five–Year Time Horizon)

16.0% Maximum*

9.0% Expected

–5.3% Minimum*

13.1%

In 2 out of 3 years, the return will likely fall within shaded area.

4.9%

Expected Asset Growth

Assuming that this portfolio achieves its expected 9.0% return each year, $1,000 would grow to $1,539 over 5 years. Returns in any year, however, will vary.

*A 5% probability exists that the maximum or minimum return in the adjacent chart will be exceeded.

Historical Return Performance[1]

Calendar Years

1994	*1993*	*1992*	*1991*	*1990*
–11.24%	10.17%	8.19%	26.46%	0.87%

Time Periods Ended December 31, 1994

Last Quarter	*Last 1 Year*	*Last 3 Years*	*Last 5 Years*	*Last 10 Years*
–10.31%	–11.24%	5.39%	8.47%	12.63%

[1] Returns for periods of 1 year or longer are annualized. No inference should be made that this asset mix will achieve similar results in the future.

Source: Copyright© 1995, Callan Associates Inc.

Diversified Portfolio Alternative:

Sample Global Mix #9

Aggressive

Investor Profile

Investment Time Horizon: *Long-Term*
Appropriate for participant whose investable time horizon is greater than 5 years. Achieving a long-term excess return over inflation is a primary goal.

Investment Risk: *High*
Participant can tolerate a potential loss in any given year to achieve higher long-run returns.

Asset Mix Profile

Domestic Stocks 60%

International Stocks 20%

Domestic Bonds 20%

Historical Return Performance[1]

Calendar Years

1994	*1993*	*1992*	*1991*	*1990*
0.91%	14.54%	4.06%	25.61%	−15.73%

Time Periods Ended December 31, 1994

Last Quarter	*Last 1 Year*	*Last 3 Years*	*Last 5 Years*	*Last 10 Years*
−10.59%	0.91%	6.35%	7.33%	14.26%

[1]Returns for periods of 1 year or longer are annualized. No inference should be made that this asset mix will achieve similar results in the future.

Projected Return Performance

Expected Asset Growth

Assuming that this portfolio achieves its expected 9.5% return each year, $1,000 would grow to $1,574 over 5 years. Returns in any year, however, will vary.

*A 5% probability exists that the maximum or minimum return in the adjacent chart will be exceeded.

Range of Projected Rates of Returns (Five-Year Time Horizon)

17.6% Maximum*

14.3%

9.5% Expected

In 2 out of 3 years, the return will likely fall within shaded area.

4.7%

−6.7% Minimum*

Source: Copyright© 1995, Callan Associates Inc.

Diversified Portfolio Alternative:

Sample Domestic Mix #10

Aggressive

Asset Mix Profile

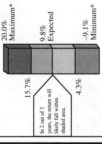

Domestic
Stocks 100%

Investor Profile

Investment Time Horizon: *Long-Term*

Appropriate for participant whose investable time horizon is greater than 5 years. Achieving a long-term excess return over inflation is a primary goal.

Investment Risk: *High*

Participant can tolerate a potential loss in any given year to achieve higher long-run returns.

Projected Return Performance

Range of Projected Rates of Returns (Five–Year Time Horizon)

20.0% Maximum*

15.7%

In 2 out of 3 years, the return will likely fall within shaded area.

9.8% Expected

4.3%

-9.1% Minimum*

Expected Asset Growth

Assuming that this portfolio achieves its expected 9.8% return each year, $1,000 would grow to $1,595 over 5 years. Returns in any year, however, will vary.

*A 5% probability exists that the maximum or minimum return in the adjacent chart will be exceeded.

Historical Return Performance[1]

Calendar Years

1994	1993	1992	1991	1990
-0.16%	10.44%	8.61%	33.53%	-4.78%

Time Periods Ended December 31, 1994

Last Quarter	Last 1 Year	Last 3 Years	Last 5 Years	Last 10 Years
-0.77%	0.16%	6.19%	8.77%	13.88%

[1]Returns for periods of 1 year or longer are annualized. No inference should be made that this asset mix will achieve similar results in the future.

Source: Copyright© 1995, Callan Associates Inc.

Diversified Portfolio Alternative: *Sample Global Mix #11*

Aggressive

Investor Profile

Investment Time Horizon: *Long-Term*

Appropriate for participant whose investable time horizon is greater than 5 years. Achieving a long-term excess return over inflation is a primary goal.

Investment Risk: *High*

Participant can tolerate a potential loss in any given year to participate in higher long-run returns.

Asset Mix Profile

International Stocks 30%

Domestic Stocks 70%

Projected Return Performance

Range of Projected Rates of Returns (Five-Year Time Horizon)

39.4% Maximum*

26.8%

In 2 out of 3 years, the return will likely fall within shaded area.

10.1% Expected

−4.3%

−8.9% Minimum*

Expected Asset Growth

Assuming that this portfolio achieves its expected 10.1% return each year, $1,000 would grow to $1,617 over 5 years. Returns in any year, however, will vary.

*A 5% probability exists that the maximum or minimum return in the adjacent chart will be exceeded.

Historical Return Performance[1]

Calendar Years

1994[2]	*1993*	*1992*	*1991*	*1990*
3.15%	16.84%	2.15%	26.89%	−10.41%

Time Periods Ended December 31, 1994

Last Quarter	*Last 1 Year*	*Last 3 Years*	*Last 5 Years*	*Last 10 Years*
3.91%	4.89%	9.46%	7.39%	15.72%

[1]Returns for periods of 1 year or longer are annualized. No inference should be made that this asset mix will achieve similar results in the future.
[2]Year-to-date ended December 31, 1994.

Source: Copyright© 1995, Callan Associates Inc.

5

STEP 3—DEVELOPING AN INVESTMENT POLICY STATEMENT

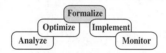

"In calm water every ship has a good captain."
Swedish Proverb

*"Long range planning does not deal with future decisions,
but with the future of present decisions."*
Peter Drucker

The most important duty of the fiduciary or trustee is the development and ongoing maintenance of an investment policy statement (IPS). A good, well-communicated IPS can go a long way in preventing disaster, provided all concerned actually read and understand it. It is not the responsibility of the fiduciary to follow every tic of the stock market, but it is his or her duty to understand everything in the IPS: *if one doesn't understand it, it shouldn't be there.*

Successful investors have many different approaches to increasing their wealth, but virtually all develop clear, unambiguous investment strategies and apply them consistently. This discipline is the key defining characteristic of all investment professionals—from currency traders to money managers. A fiduciary, charged with the responsibility of managing other people's money, needs this discipline perhaps more than anyone else.

103

Legal Requirements

The ERISA fiduciary will find that satisfaction of his or her duty requires the development of a written funding policy. The funding policy elaborates on, among other things, the type of retirement plan being established, how contributions will be calculated and made, and how investments will be managed. "Every employee benefit plan shall provide a procedure for establishing and carrying out a funding policy..."[1] Though ERISA only implies the requirement for the development of an IPS, subsequent case law, DOL releases, and practices in the industry have clearly mandated the prudence of its development.[2]

The Third Restatement, likewise, reinforces the importance of the IPS. "The trustee must give reasonably careful consideration to both the formulation and the implementation of an appropriate investment strategy, with investments to be selected and reviewed in a manner reasonably appropriate to the strategy."[3]

The investment committee for a foundation or endowment is charged with prudent management under various IRS regulations and state legislation.[4] (See Chapter 14 for more details.) The generally accepted practice of a prudent fiduciary is the development of a written investment strategy. Ordinarily, the foundation incorporates the general contents of an IPS in its spending policy. The spending policy details the sources and uses of assets and delineates the investment strategy that is adopted to meet specific objectives.

The private investor obviously has no regulated requirement to have an IPS. However, an IPS can be a valuable communication tool between family members and close professional advisers (attorney and accountant). It allows the investor to come to grips with the issues needed to make well-thought-out investment decisions.

The Need for the IPS

There are a number of important benefits to be obtained from producing and maintaining an IPS. It is a virtually indispensable tool for investment management and communication that should be used by every

---

[1] ERISA Sec. 402(b)(1).

[2] See *Brock v. Robbins,* 830 F.2d 640 (7th Cir. 1987); *Katsaros v. Cody,* 744 F.2d 270 (2nd Cir. 1984); and *Davidson v. Cook,* 567 F.2d 225 (4th Cir. 1983).

[3] Restatement Third, p. 14.

[4] Uniform Management of Institutional Funds Act; see also Chapter 14, Endowments and Foundations.

investor. Though regulations and codes exist that require or suggest the development of an IPS, most individuals like to know why they should do something, not just that they must. Among the more important benefits are

1. The IPS provides a paper trail of policies, practices, and procedures for investment decisions. The document can be critical evidence used in the defense against litigation or accusations of imprudence. It serves as an excellent example of compliance to auditors. Conversely, the absence of a well-thought-out IPS alerts litigators and auditors of a possible deficient situation.

2. The IPS negates second-guessing or Monday morning quarter-backing, and ensures continuity of the investment strategy when there is a high turnover of committee members. Nothing is as irritating to an ex-investment committee member than to learn that new board members are questioning past investment decisions or disrupting a well-thought-out but undocumented investment strategy. The vulnerability of being second-guessed is reduced when decisions are rooted in a well-written IPS.

3. The IPS reassures corporate and public contributors as well as individual donors affected by the investment performance of investment stewardship. Whether the affected party is a corporation making a contribution to the retirement fund or an individual making a donation to a local foundation, people want to be certain that their money is going to be prudently managed. [We have even suggested that a copy of the IPS be included in presentations to potential donors for charitable giving purposes.]

4. During bull markets almost any investment strategy will generate impressive results — " A high tide lifts all boats." The real value of the IPS is seen during periods of market decline. It is during these difficult times that an investor feels the need to do something. How many committees met in emergency sessions following the October Crash of 1987 and debated whether their equity positions should be sold or reduced? The IPS can have a calming effect, reminding members of why the investment strategy was structured in the first place and the risks inherent in the portfolio.

5. The IPS provides a baseline from which to monitor investment performance of the overall portfolio, as well as the performance of individual money managers. In addition, proposed changes to the investment process can be evaluated and reviewed against the strategic policy.

6. For the private investor, the IPS provides logical guidance for implementation. Often intelligent investors make the mistake of entering into periods of emotionally driven binges of buying and selling. For example, the average investor does not consider equities to be an appropriate (safe) asset class until the stock market reaches a new frenzied high. Or the investor who needs income doesn't think about total return or diversification until fixed-income securities are offering historically low yields, or inflation has wiped out the purchasing power of the income stream.

7. For the older investor who has built a successful portfolio, an IPS should be incorporated in estate documents. At the investor's demise, less sophisticated heirs and/or executors may be left to manage, and oftentimes second guess, the investment strategy of the portfolio. During the time it takes to settle the estate, the portfolio is often left unattended with the very real threat that market movement could diminish substantial gains. Consider blue-chip portfolios at the start of 1993 that had significant positions in IBM. Within months, the value of IBM fell by 50 percent.

Contents of the IPS

The IPS combines elements of planning and philosophy and should cover the five steps in the investment management process, starting with information about the assets and the portfolio, working through asset allocation and manager selection, and finishing with monitoring performance. In between, it should even address the IPS itself, spelling out maintenance procedures and review requirements (not a small point).

The IPS should not be written by money managers or product vendors who have a vested interest in writing the IPS to the specifications of their product. Nor should the IPS be written by a well-meaning adviser that is not intimately familiar with the requisite features of the invest-ment management process. (The rising popularity among attorneys and accountants of continuing education courses on this topic is evidence of their desire to learn more about the investment management process.)

We suggest six specific sections for an IPS (see Figure 5–1). A sample IPS for a defined benefit plan is provided as an appendix. It serves as an example and is not meant to be copied and rubber-stamped. Neither should it be used as a substitute for the time that decision makers should spend discussing the long term strategy of the portfolio.

Section 1. Purpose and Background

Section 1 of an IPS should contain

1. An explanation as to the purpose of the IPS, objectives of the portfolio, and the legal structure (if one exists) under which the portfolio is regulated.
2. The size of the portfolio, the likelihood and amount of future contributions, and a schedule of pending disbursements.

FIGURE 5–1   The Investment Policy Statement

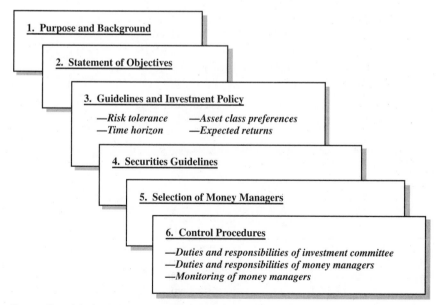

Source: Copyright © 1993, Investment Management Council.

3. The tax status of the portfolio—whether the portfolio is taxable (and its tax bracket) or tax exempt.

4. For corporate and public retirement plans that offer lump-sum benefits to terminated or retiring participants, a description of the participant demographics, particularly as they impact the timing of disbursements.

5. For corporate and public retirement plans that offer defined benefit plans, a description of the fiscal health of the sponsoring entity. Will the entity be able to maintain the current level of contributions and, in the event of poor investment performance, make up shortfalls?

Section 2. Statement of Objectives

Objectives are the desired interim and end results of the investment program. They should be set in conjunction with a comprehensive review and assessment of

- Projected financial requirements.
- Present investment allocation.
- Attitudes, expectations, and goals of the committee or decision makers.
- Investment time horizon and risk tolerance level of the portfolio *and* the committee. These may be different, and it is better to address this situation up front than to be surprised by it in a crisis.

There are a number of general investment objectives that most fiduciaries and investors should consider:

1. To take a "reasonable and prudent" amount of risk, as defined by the committee, and to maximize the return obtained at that risk level.

2. To limit risk exposure through prudent diversification.

3. To establish policies based on total return rather than current income. This provides the greatest investment flexibility, and therefore the greatest opportunity for growth of assets.

4. To control costs of administering and managing the portfolio.

There are additional objectives that are specific to the type of portfolio being managed.

For Defined Benefit Plans

Objective: To maintain a fully funded status with regard to accumulated benefit obligations (ABO), and to achieve a fully funded status with regard to the projected benefit obligation (PBO).

Note: The ABO measures the ratio of assets to liabilities for benefits accrued to date, and is based on a valuation interest rate and an expected return on investments. The ABO ratio is a measure of funding progress for an ongoing plan and would represent the coverage of liabilities if a plan was actually terminated on the given date. The objective is to keep the ratio at, or above, 100 percent.

The PBO also takes into consideration anticipated future pay increases and is considered the best ratio for comparing different plans.

Objective: To have the ability to pay all benefit and expense obligations when due.

Note: A reasonable approach is to hold 120 percent of short-term obligations in cash, unless a near-term contribution is anticipated to cover the obligations. Disbursements for the next three years must be kept in marketable securities.

Objective: To maintain a funding cushion for (1) unexpected developments, (2) possible future increases in benefit structure and expense levels, and/or (3) a reduction in the expected return on investments or interest rate assumptions.

Objective: To maintain flexibility in determining the future level of contributions.

Note: An aggressive investment policy produces lower long-term employer contributions but greater year-to-year volatility. A less aggressive investment policy may require larger contributions but produces more stable, predictable contribution requirements.

Objective: To exceed actuarial earnings assumptions.

Note: A well-funded plan can afford a more aggressive policy and has the ability to withstand interim short-term losses. Poorly funded plans have either to pursue a more aggressive policy or increase their contribution levels.

For Defined Contribution Plans

Objective: To meet the specific requirements [or meet the intent] of ERISA Section 404(c) regulations, especially concerning the provision for a range of good investment choices and employee education.

Note: 404(c) rules are provided so plan sponsors are afforded safe harbor rules when participants are permitted to direct their own investment decisions. The 404(c) rules are not mandatory. Many sponsors have elected not to formally adopt 404(c), but still elect to abide by the intent of the rules.

Objective: To have the ability to pay all benefit and expense obligations when due.

Objective: To maintain flexibility in determining the future level of contributions.

For Endowments and Foundations

Objective: Follow a spending policy based on total return.

Note: A total return based policy allows the committee (1) to map out a long-term investment strategy and (2) to employ modern investment management techniques.

Objective: Maintain the purchasing power of the fund.

Note: The objective is to maintain the level of services and programs in relation to average cost increases. This requires establishing an equilibrium spending rate of _____ percent.

Objective: Apply a smoothing rule to mitigate the effects of short-term market volatility on spending.

Note: Since investment returns may vary dramatically from year to year, spending a constant percent of the fund's market value would play havoc with spending amounts. Therefore, either of the following smoothing rules will be applied:

Moving average. The equilibrium spending rate will be applied to an average of the past several years (three to five years) of the fund's market values.

Preset increment over last year. The level of spending will be increased by _____ percent over that of the previous year's.

Judging the need for spending. The investment committee will determine the amount to be spent based on the needs of recipient organizations.

Objective: Maintain a constant funding-support ratio.

Note: The desire of the investment committee is to maintain the level of programs and services currently provided. This objective can only be met if sufficient total return is reinvested and sufficient new funds added to keep pace with cost increases and program expansions.

For Individuals

Objective: Maintain a minimum level of cash reserves to meet short-term expenditures, or to serve as an emergency cash reserve.

Note: A prudent policy is to maintain at least six months of budgetary expenses in cash, and 120% of one year's expenses in short-term fixed income.

Objective: Minimize federal and state income taxes.

Note: Investors should communicate their tax status to hired money managers, particularly if alternative minimum taxes (AMT) is a current or pending problem. On the other hand, individuals are cautioned not to automatically accept a tax-advantaged investment strategy solely because of the favorable tax consequences. Tax-advantaged strategies should be carefully compared against the after-tax projected returns of normal investment programs.

Section 3. Guidelines and Investment Policy

Guidelines are established to identify the parameters of the investment strategy. This section is the appropriate place to articulate concerns and expectations, and acknowledge the uncertainties of investing in the capital markets.

A common mistake is to set guidelines that actually impede the attainment of the objectives: for example, establishing an objective of a 5 percent real rate of return after inflation, but having guidelines that limit equity exposure to just 30 percent of the portfolio. The low equity allocation corresponds to a probable return that will not provide the desired performance objective.

The principal components of the guidelines are the very same inputs that were used to develop the optimal asset allocation. Specifically, the IPS should identify the investor or fiduciary's

R Risk tolerance

A Asset class preferences

T Time horizon

E Expected or desired rate of return

If the guidelines have been properly written, a person subsequently reviewing the portfolio, such as an auditor or litigator, should be able to reconstruct the process that was followed in structuring the portfolio. Inevitable transitory market movements should have little or no impact on determining the validity of an IPS.

The challenge in writing guidelines is to make them specific enough to clearly establish the parameters of the desired investment process, yet with enough latitude so as not to create an oversight burden. This is particularly true when establishing the rebalancing limits for the IPS. The rebalancing limits define the points when a portfolio should be reallocated to bring it back in line with the strategic asset allocation.

The process of setting an appropriate rebalancing limit is somewhat subjective. For the fiduciary that accepts the concept of strategic allocation—setting a specific policy and sticking with it—rebalancing limits of plus or minus 5 percent should keep the parameters tight enough to maintain the risk/return profile of the strategic allocation, yet require rebalancing on average twice a year. Rebalancing limits could be opened up as much as plus or minus 10 percent, but any limits above 10 percent should be set in conjunction with adopting a tactical asset allocation strategy. Rebalancing should generally be a function of a percentage change and not based on a specific time period. (See Chapter 8 for more details.)

The Problem with Broadly Written Guidelines

Consider the following common mistake: An IPS is written with the following broad guidelines:

Asset Class	Limits
Cash	0–50%
Fixed income	20–60%
Equities	30–70%

The guidelines look innocuous enough until one examines the possible outcomes:[5]

---

[5] The possible outcome returns are based on Callan's five-year projected return on each asset class. The risk is defined as the "worst case" scenario in any given year of the same projected five-year period, with a statistical confidence level of 90 percent.

Allocations	Return	Risk
Cash 50%/ Fixed 20%/ Equities 30%	6.8%	− .3%
Cash 15%/ Fixed 35%/ Equities 50%	8.3%	− 3.4%
Cash 0%/ Fixed 30%/ Equities 70%	9.1%	− 5.8%

Notice that there is a return differential of over 33 percent between the outcomes, as well as a sizable difference in risk levels.

Section 4. Securities Guidelines

Securities guidelines, like the investment guidelines, have to be specific enough to define the boundaries of the playing field for hired money managers. Yet, the securities guidelines should not be so specific that the fiduciary is, per se, retaining discretionary control over the assets. In addition, the securities guidelines should not be so restrictive that they hamper a manager's ability to produce expected returns. Fiduciary "safe harbor rules," defined in the next section, apply only when the money manager has discretionary control over assets.

The securities guidelines contained in the example IPS of the appendix are traditional investment guidelines. Most institutional money managers find these to be acceptable, workable guidelines. Note that the guidelines are modified when all or a portion of the assets is invested in mutual funds. There is a growing tendency for mutual fund investment strategies (which can be found in the fund's prospectus) to permit investments in derivatives, futures, options, and/or hedging strategies.

This section should also specifically state which securities, or activities, are not permissible. Common prohibitions might include futures and commodities (unless included as an asset class in the investment guidelines, or permitted as a limited investment strategy for a mutual fund), option writing, securities lending and margin accounts.

Fiduciaries that desire to follow a socially responsive investment strategy would also note their preferences in this section. Again, the need exists to make the restrictive list as specific as possible to a particular common cause. (See Chapter 12 for more details.) Guidelines such as "establish a sin-free portfolio" are not specific enough for a money manager. There needs to be a reference to restrictions such as: no tobacco or alcohol stocks or debt securities of such companies.

Section 5. Selection of Money Managers

A well-written IPS should be portable—that is, a total stranger should be able to take the document and implement the investment program. In the case of money manager selection, one should be able to hand the IPS to a consultant, and the consultant should be able to come back with an appropriate list of managers to implement the IPS.

A well-written IPS should also form a defensive perimeter around the investment committee or investor that is approached by prospective money managers. By establishing very specific asset allocation parameters and money manager selection criteria, it is much easier to determine whether a prospective manager fits into the general investment program. Those managers that do not fit can be easily excused by referencing the requirements of the IPS.

In establishing search criteria, the fiduciary is well advised to incorporate the requirements of ERISA's safe harbor rules. (See Chapter 6 for details.) With the number of highly qualified money managers and mutual funds available, there is little reason to deviate from the adopted standards. Keep in mind that the search conducted by a powerful large fund will be quite different from that conducted by a small investor. The large fund can demand answers to questions, while the small investor may be forced to make do with publicly available information. General search criteria should include:

1. The money manager must be a registered investment adviser (registered both in the state in which it is conducting business and with the SEC), bank, insurance company, or investment company (mutual fund). The manager should provide information on his or her firm by providing either an ADV Part II (registered investment adviser), a prospectus (investment company), or comparable information, such as an annual report from a bank or insurance company.

2. The money manager should provide at least five years of actual quarterly performance information that is time weighted, is a representative composite of all accounts, and, preferably, meets AIMR standards (see Chapter 8 for more details). Performance information should include a comparison of the performance to appropriate market indexes and peer groups, taking into consideration both risk and return.

3. The manager should provide information that depicts key investment personnel stability (e.g., have been together for at least five years) and that the firm is capable of handling the current level of new account growth.

4. The money manager should be able to clearly articulate the firm's investment strategies and philosophy. The manager should provide a statement that the strategy has been followed for at least five years and will continue to be followed for the specific account.

5. The money manager should affirm that it has not been subject to, nor does it have pending, litigation censures, or regulatory investigations, and, if such events take place during the period the funds are managed, the client will be notified.

6. The money manager should be willing to acknowledge his or her fiduciary status in writing. This is required for ERISA plans. (Mutual funds are exempted from this requirement.)

Section 6. Control Procedures

There are numerous parties involved in the investment management process. Each service provider should have its specific duties and requirements delineated in this section. In addition, the investment management process triggers a number of reviews and events that should be scheduled periodically.

Monthly. The custodian should submit an appraisal report that shows the portfolio's current holdings, market value, and transactions. The appraisal should be reviewed by the investor to ensure that the money managers are following their stated investment strategy, and that the strategy is consistent with the objectives and guidelines of the IPS. The investor should finalize strategies for handling scheduled contributions and disbursements for the upcoming month.

Quarterly. The investment consultant or custodian should prepare a performance measurement report. The investment committee should review the report to (1) ensure that assets are allocated according to the IPS, (2) compare performance of the overall portfolio to a weighted benchmark, and (3) compare the performance of individual managers or mutual funds to their peer group.

Annually. The actuarial reports should be reviewed to ensure that ABO/PBO funding objectives are being met. The IPS should be revised if there are any material changes to the investor's risk tolerance, expected or desired rate of return, asset class preference, or time horizon to major disbursements. Expenses for the management of the portfolio should also be analyzed, including transaction costs, custodial costs, and fees paid to money managers and consultants.

On an As-Needed Basis. The investment committee should meet if there have been any material changes to hired money managers, unexpected and material changes to contributions and disbursements, and/or any other event that materially impacts the committee's ability to carry out their fiduciary duties.

Performance Criteria
Specific performance criteria and objectives should be identified for each manager. The criteria should include, as a minimum, the index and the style against which the manager's performance will be compared, as well as expectations for performance net and gross of fees. When performance criteria are agreed to by the manager at the start of the engagement, there is less tendency for controversy between the investor and the manager if the manager has to be subsequently fired.

Suggested **review** guidelines for both money managers and mutual funds include

- A manager performs in the bottom quartile (75th percentile) of his or her peer group over a quarterly or annual period.

- A manager falls in the southeast quadrant of the risk/return scattergram for three- and/or five-year time periods.

- A manager has its five-year risk-adjusted return fall below that of median managers within the appropriate peer group.

Performance that may require the **replacement** of a manager includes

- A manager consistently performs below the median (50th percentile) of his or her peer group over rolling three-year periods.

- A manager performs below the top 40 percent of his or her peer group over a five-year period.

- A manager has a negative alpha for three- and/or five-year time periods.

Major organizational changes may also warrant immediate **review** of the manager, including

- Change in professionals.

- Significant account losses.

- Significant growth of new business.

- Change in ownership.

Signatures

Once the investor or investment committee has finally approved the contents of the IPS, and it has been approved by legal counsel, all of the following parties involved in the implementation of the IPS should affix their signature signifying their understanding and acceptance:

- Each investment committee member.

- Named fiduciaries and/or trustees.

- Hired money managers.

- Investment consultant and attorney.

Summary

The IPS is the most important document the fiduciary prepares. The process required to complete the IPS ensures that all bases have been covered and that all ongoing tasks and responsibilities are spelled out. All material investment facts, assumptions, and opinions should be included, as well as evaluative criteria for service providers. The IPS requires ongoing maintenance to keep up with changing circumstances, and it should not be regarded as a static or historical document, but rather a current working tool. In fact, it may be the most useful tool the investor carries.

INVESTMENT POLICY STATEMENT

for

ABC COMPANY

(Defined Benefit Plan Sample)

Prepared on February 5, 1995

CALLAN ASSOCIATES INC.

This Investment Policy Statement has been prepared for consultants to serve as an example of the information that should be included in a comprehensive IPS. Consultants, however, must ensure that every IPS be written to the specific needs and requirements of the client.

Table of Contents

Executive Summary

Type of Plan:	Defined Benefit
Current Assets:	$12,542,634
Planning Time Horizon:	Greater than five years
Expected Return:	9.4 percent (5.9 percent over CPI)
Risk Tolerance:	High, losses not to exceed −8.8 percent per year, based on a statistical confidence level of 90 percent

	Asset Allocation		
	Lower Limit	*Strategic Allocation*	*Upper Limit*
Domestic large capitalization equities:			
Value	13%	18%	23%
Growth	14	19	24
Domestic small capitalization equities	7	12	17
International equities	14	19	24
Fixed income: Active duration	27	32	37

Evaluation Benchmark: Total return to exceed performance of median plan in Callan's Balanced Fund database and a policy index based on the strategic asset allocation of the plan to various broad asset classes. Specifically, the policy index will be a weighted index comprised of:

- 37 percent S&P 500.
- 12 percent Callan Small Capitalization Equity Index.
- 19 percent MSCI EAFE Index .
- 32 percent Lehman Government/Corporate Index.

Purpose

The purpose of this investment policy statement (IPS) is to assist the Defined Benefit Board of Directors (Board) in effectively supervising, monitoring, and evaluating the investment of the Company's Retirement Plan (Plan) assets. The Plan's investment program is defined in the various sections of the IPS by

- Stating in a written document the Board's attitudes, expectations, objectives, and guidelines for the investment of all Plan assets.

- Setting forth an investment structure for managing all Plan assets. This structure includes various asset classes, investment management styles, asset allocations, and acceptable ranges that, in total, are expected to produce a sufficient level of overall diversification and total investment return over the long term.

- Providing guidelines for each investment portfolio that control the level of overall risk and liquidity assumed in that portfolio, so that all Plan assets are managed in accordance with stated objectives.

- Encouraging effective communications between the Board, the investment consultant (Consultant), and the money managers.

- Establishing formalized criteria to monitor, evaluate, and compare the performance results achieved by the money managers on a regular basis.

- Complying with all ERISA, fiduciary, prudence, and due diligence requirements that experienced investment professionals would utilize, and with all applicable laws, rules, and regulations from various local, state, federal, and international political entities that may impact Plan assets.

This IPS has been formulated based on consideration by the Board of the financial implications of a wide range of policies, and describes the prudent investment process that the Board deems appropriate.

Background

[Insert Plan Specific Information]

The Plan is a defined benefit plan established in conjunction with the spin-off of Defined Benefit in July 1985. The Plan covers the hourly employees of Defined Benefit, including those who were previously covered under the Defined Benefit Corporation Retirement Plan for Hourly Rated Employees. The Board will discharge its responsibilities under the Plan solely in the long-term interests of Plan participants and their beneficiaries.

The Plan currently covers 364 employees. The number is anticipated to [increase/decrease/remain stable] at the rate of _____ percent per year for the next _____ years. Plan size is currently $12,542,634 and annual contributions are not currently required due to the well-funded status of the Plan. Under current regulations, the Plan is not required to make any quarterly contributions for 1994.

Key Information.

Name of Plan: ABC Retirement Plan

Plan Sponsor: ABC Company

Plan IRS Tax ID: 12–3456789

Plan Board of Directors:

                _____, Chairman

                _____, Secretary

                _____, Investment Committee Member

                _____, Investment Committee Member

                _____, Investment Committee Member

                _____, Investment Committee Member

Custodian: The Bank of New York

Investment Manager(s): Sirach Capital (Domestic Large Cap Equity Growth)

                                  Palley Needelman (Domestic Large Cap Equity Value)

                                  Burridge Group (Domestic Small Cap Equity)

                                  Criterion (Active Duration Fixed Income)

Investment Consultant: Callan Associates Inc.

Legal Counsel: ERISA Attorneys Inc.

Accountant: Arthur Andersen & Co., SC

Statement of Objectives

The objectives of the Plan have been established in conjunction with a comprehensive review of the current and projected financial requirements. The objectives are:

Objective #1: To maintain a fully funded status with regard to accumulated benefit obligations (ABO), and to achieve a fully funded status with regard to the projected benefit obligation (PBO).

Objective #2: To have the ability to pay all benefit and expense obligations when due.

Objective #3: To maintain a funding cushion for (1) unexpected developments, (2) possible future increases in benefit structure and expense levels, and/or (3) a reduction in the expected return on investments or interest rate assumptions.

Objective #4: To maintain flexibility in determining the future level of contributions.

Objective #5: To exceed actuarial earnings assumptions.

Investment results are the critical element in achieving the investment objectives, while reliance on contributions is a secondary element.

Guidelines and Investment Policy

Time Horizon. The investment guidelines are based on an investment horizon of greater than five years, so interim fluctuations should be viewed with appropriate perspective. Similarly, the Plan's strategic asset allocation is based on this long-term perspective.

Short-term liquidity requirements are anticipated to be nonexistent, or at least should be covered by the annual contribution.

or

[There is a requirement to maintain sufficient liquid reserves to provide for the payment of retirement benefits. Analysis of the cash flow projections of the Plan indicates that benefit payments will exceed contributions for at least several years. The Committee's secretary will notify the investment managers well in advance of the withdraw orders to allow sufficient time to build up necessary liquid reserves.]

Risk Tolerances. The Board recognizes the difficulty of achieving the Plan's investment objectives in light of the uncertainties and complexities of contemporary investment markets. The Board also recognizes that some risk must be assumed to achieve the Plan's long-term investment objectives.

In establishing the risk tolerances of the IPS, the ability to withstand short and intermediate term variability was considered. These factors were

- ABC Company is in an industry that should experience milder fluctuations than the general economy. ABC believes that it should be able to achieve above-average growth during the next several years.

- ABC's strong financial condition enables it to adopt a long-term investment perspective.

- Demographic characteristics of participants suggest an above-average risk tolerance due to the younger-than-average work force.

- Actuarial data related to future projected benefit payments, along with future projected expenses of the Plan, are significantly less than conservative forecasted investment income projections through 1999. Therefore, liquidity requirements are immaterial over the next 10 years, which implies that a higher risk profile is acceptable.

- Current Plan assets have been accumulated to exceed the value of the Plan's total accrued benefit liability, allowing for a less aggressive risk tolerance.

In summary, ABC Company's prospects for the future, current financial condition, and several other factors suggest collectively that the Plan can tolerate some interim fluctuations in market value and rates of return in order to achieve long-term objectives.

Performance Expectations. The desired investment objective is a long-term rate of return on assets that is at least 9.4 percent, which is 5.4 percent greater than the anticipated rate of inflation as measured by the Consumer Price Index (CPI). The target rate of return for the Plan has been based on the assumption that future real returns will approximate the long-term rates of return experienced for each asset class in the IPS.

The Board realizes that market performance varies and that a 9.4 percent rate of return may not be meaningful during some periods. Accordingly, relative performance benchmarks for the managers are set forth in the "Control Procedures" section.

Over a complete business cycle, the Plan's overall annualized total return, after deducting for advisory, money management, and custodial fees, as well as total transaction costs, should perform above the median of Callan's Balanced fund universe and above a customized index comprised of market indexes weighted by the strategic asset allocation of the Plan.[6]

Asset Allocation Constraints. The Board believes that the Plan's risk and liquidity posture are, in large part, a function of asset class mix. The Board has reviewed the long-term performance characteristics of various asset classes, focusing on balancing the risks and rewards of market behavior. The following asset classes were selected:

- Domestic large capitalization equities
- Domestic small capitalization equities
- International equities
- Domestic fixed income
- Cash equivalents

Based on the Plan's time horizon, risk tolerances, performance expectations, and asset class preferences, an efficient or optimal portfolio was identified. The strategic asset allocation of the Plan is as follows:

---

[6] The strategic index is comprised of 37 percent S&P 500, 19 percent MSCI EAFE Index, 12 Percent Callan Small Cap Equity Index, and 32 percent Lehman Government/Corporate Index.

| | Strategic Asset Allocation | | |
	Lower Limit	*Strategic Allocation*	*Upper Limit*
Domestic large capitalization equities:			
Value	13%	18%	23%
Growth	14	19	24
Domestic small capitalization equities:	7	12	17
International equities:	14	19	24
Fixed income: Active duration	27	32	37

Rebalancing of Strategic Allocation. The percentage allocation to each asset class may vary as much as plus or minus 5 percent, depending on market conditions.

When necessary and/or available, cash inflows/outflows will be deployed in a manner consistent with the strategic asset allocation of the Plan. If there are no cash flows, the allocation of the Plan will be reviewed quarterly.

If the Board judges cash flows to be insufficient to bring the Plan within the strategic allocation ranges, the Board shall decide whether to effect transactions to bring the strategic allocation within the threshold ranges (strategic allocation).

Securities Guidelines

Every money manager selected to manage Plan assets must adhere to these guidelines.

The following securities and transactions are not authorized unless receiving prior Board approval:

1. Letter stock and other unregistered securities, commodities or other commodity contracts, and short sales or margin transactions.

2. Securities lending, pledging, or hypothecating securities.

3. Investments in the equity securities of any company with a record of less than three years' continuous operation, including the operation of any predecessor, and investments for the purpose of exercising control of management are all restricted.

Domestic Equities.

- Equity holdings in any one company should not exceed more than 10 percent of the market value of the Plan's equity portfolio.

- Not more than 25 percent of the market value of the portfolio should be invested in any one economic sector.

- The manager shall emphasize quality in security selection and shall avoid risk of large loss through diversification.

- The managers shall have the discretion to invest a portion of the assets in cash reserves when they deem appropriate. However, the managers will be evaluated against their peers on the performance of the total funds under their direct management.

- Holdings of individual securities shall be large enough (round lots) for easy liquidation.

Domestic Fixed Income.

- All fixed-income securities held in the portfolio shall have a Moody's, Standard & Poor's, and/or Fitch's credit quality rating of no less than "BBB". U.S. Treasury and U.S. government agencies, which are unrated securities, are qualified for inclusion in the portfolio.

- No more than 20 percent of the market value of the fixed income portfolio shall be rated less than single A quality, unless the manager has specific written authorization.

- The exposure of the portfolio to any one issuer, other than securities of the U.S. government or agencies, shall not exceed 10 percent of the market value of the fixed-income portfolio.

- Holdings of individual issues shall be large enough (round lots) for easy liquidation.

International Equities.

- Equity holdings in any one company shall not exceed more than 10 percent of the international equity portfolio.

- No more than 25 percent of the portfolio shall be invested in one industry category.

- Allocations to any specific country shall not be excessive relative to a broadly diversified international equity manager peer group. It is expected that the non–U.S. equity portfolio will have no more than 40 percent in any one country.

- The manager may enter into foreign exchange contracts on currency provided that use of such contracts is limited to hedging currency exposure existing within the manager's portfolio. There shall be no direct foreign currency speculation or any related investment activity.

Cash/Cash Equivalents.

- Cash equivalent reserves shall consist of cash instruments having a quality rating of A-1, P-1, or higher. Eurodollar certificates of deposit, time deposits, and repurchase agreements are also acceptable investment vehicles.

- Any idle cash not invested by the investment managers shall be invested daily through an automatic interest-bearing sweep vehicle managed by the custodian.

Selection of Money Managers

The Board, with the assistance of the Consultant, will select appropriate money managers to manage the Plan assets. Managers must meet the following minimum criteria:

1. Be a bank, insurance company, investment management company, or investment adviser as defined by the Registered Investment Advisers Act of 1940.
2. Provide historical quarterly performance numbers calculated on a time-weighted basis, based on a composite of all fully discretionary accounts of similar investment style, and reported net and gross of fees.
3. Provide performance evaluation reports prepared by an objective third party that illustrate the risk/return profile of the manager relative to other managers of like investment style.
4. Provide detailed information on the history of the firm, key personnel, key clients, fee schedule, and support personnel. This information can be a copy of a recent request for proposal (RFP) completed by the manager.
5. Clearly articulate the investment strategy that will be followed and document that the strategy has been successfully adhered to over time.
6. Selected firms shall have no outstanding legal judgments or past judgments that may reflect negatively on the firm.

Control Procedures

Duties and Responsibilities of the Money Managers. The duties and responsibilities of each money manager retained by the Board include

1. Managing the Plan assets under its care, custody, and/or control in accordance with the IPS objectives and guidelines set forth herein, and also expressed in separate written agreements when deviation is deemed prudent and desirable by the Board.

2. Exercising investment discretion [including holding cash equivalents as an alternative] within the IPS objectives and guidelines set forth herein.

3. Promptly informing the Board in writing regarding all significant and/or material matters and changes pertaining to the investment of Plan assets, including, but not limited to:

   a. Investment strategy.

   b. Portfolio structure.

   c. Tactical approaches.

   d. Ownership.

   e. Organizational structure.

   f. Financial condition.

   g. Professional staff.

   h. Recommendations for guideline changes.

   i. All legal material and SEC and other regulatory agency proceedings affecting the firm.

4. Promptly voting all proxies and related actions in a manner consistent with the long-term interests and objectives of the Plan set forth herein. Each manager shall keep detailed records of said voting of proxies and related actions and will comply with all regulatory obligations related thereto.

5. Utilize the same care, skill, prudence, and due diligence under the circumstances then prevailing that experienced, investment professionals acting in a like capacity and fully familiar with such matters would use in like activities for like retirement plans with like aims in accordance and compliance with ERISA and all applicable laws, rules, and regulations from local, state, federal, and international political entities as they pertain to fiduciary duties and responsibilities.

6. Acknowledge and agree in writing to their fiduciary responsibility to fully comply with the entire IPS set forth herein, and as modified in the future.

Actuarial Policy. All major liability assumptions regarding number of participants, compensation, benefit levels, and actuarial assumptions will be subject to an annual review by the Committee. This review will focus on analysis of major differences between the Plan's assumptions and actual experience.

Brokerage Policy. All transactions effected for the Plan will be "subject to the best price and execution." If a manager utilizes brokerage from the plan assets to effect soft dollar transactions, detailed records will be kept and communicated to the Board.

Performance Objectives. Investment performance will be reviewed at least annually to determine the continued feasibility of achieving the investment objectives and the appropriateness of the IPS for achieving those objectives.

It is not expected that the IPS will change frequently. In particular, short-term changes in the financial markets should not require adjustments to the IPS.

Monitoring of Money Managers. Quarterly performance will be evaluated to test progress toward the attainment of longer-term targets. It is understood that there are likely to be short-term periods during which performance deviates from market indexes. During such times, greater emphasis shall be placed on peer-performance comparisons with managers employing similar styles.

On a timely basis, but not less than four times a year, the Board will meet to focus on

- Manager's adherence to the IPS guidelines.
- Material changes in the manager's organization, investment philosophy, and/or personnel.
- Comparisons of the manager's results to appropriate indexes and peer groups, specifically:

Asset Category	Index	Peer Group Universe
Domestic large Capitalization equity:	S&P 500	Total equity database
Value	S&P 500	Value equity style
Yield	S&P 500	Yield equity style
Growth	S&P 500	Growth equity style
Core	S&P 500	Core Equity Style
Domestic small Capitalization equities	Callan Small Capitalization Index	Small capitalization Equity
International Equity: Core	MSCI EAFE	International equity
Domestic fixed income:		Total F/I database
Defensive fixed	Merrill Lynch 1–3 year	Defensive F/I style
Active duration	Lehman Government/ Corporate	Active duration style
Intermediate	Lehman Government/ Corporate Intermediate	Intermediate style
Core bond	Lehman Government/ Corporate Intermediate	Core fixed municipal bond fund database
International fixed income	Salomon Government World	Global fixed income style
Real estate	Callan Real Estate Index	Commingled real estate database

The risk associated with each manager's portfolio, as measured by the variability of quarterly returns (standard deviation), should not exceed that of the benchmark index and the peer group without a corresponding increase in performance above the benchmark and peer group.

In addition to the information covered during the quarterly reviews, the Board will meet at least annually to focus on:

- The manager's performance relative to managers of like investment style or strategy. Each manager is expected to perform in the upper half of the manager's respective style universe.
- The Plan's investment performance results compared to the manager's overall composite performance figures to determine unaccounted for dispersion between the manager's reported results and the Plan's actual results.

The Board is aware that the ongoing review and analysis of money managers is just as important as the due diligence implemented during the manager selection process. Accordingly, a thorough **review** and analysis of a money manager will be conducted if

- A manager performs in the bottom quartile (75th percentile) of his or her peer group over a quarterly or annual period.
- A manager falls in the southeast quadrant of the risk/return scattergram for three- and/or five-year time periods.
- A manager has a five-year risk-adjusted return fall below that of the median manager within the appropriate peer group.

Furthermore, performance that may require the **replacement** of a manager includes:

- A manager that consistently performs below the median (50th percentile) of his or her peer group over rolling three-year periods.
- A manager that performs below the median (50th percentile) of his or her peer group over a five-year period.
- A manager with a negative alpha for three- and/or five-year time periods.

Major organizational changes also warrant immediate **review** of the manager, including

- Change in professionals.
- Significant account losses.
- Significant growth of new business.
- Change in ownership.

The performance of the Board's investment managers will be monitored on an ongoing basis, and it is at the Board's discretion to take corrective action by replacing a manager if they deem it appropriate at any time.

STEP 4—IMPLEMENTATION: MANAGER SEARCH AND SELECTION

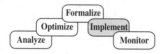

"Every man should make up his mind that if he expects to succeed, he must give an honest return for the other man's dollar."

Edward H. Harriman

"The higher you climb the flagpole, the more people see your rear end."

Don Meredith

Investment returns and risks are largely determined by asset allocation decisions. What starts out as strategy must be translated into reality with implementation. This chapter and those that follow will serve as a guide through the process of implementing an investment program once the investment policy has been formalized.

An examination of the common mistakes made during the implementation phase reveals the importance asset allocation decisions have on the success of a portfolio. If these potential problems are avoided or eliminated, successful management of the investment portfolio can be achieved. Some of the more common implementation errors follow:

• **An investment policy is not developed.** Critical asset allocation decisions may be abdicated, by default, to an outside third party
(money manager or product vendor) that may not understand or appreciate the specific risk/return objectives or unique cash flow requirements
of the funds to be invested. The third party attempts to match the investment situation to what he or she has to offer as opposed to conforming
the product to what the client needs. By analogy, this is like the producer
that holds a casting call for a new play before the script is ever written. How do you know what talent to look for? The basics must be
defined first.

• **Unrealistic performance expectations have been set.** Investment decisions can be unduly influenced by recent performance or short-
term investment results. This often results in the classic syndrome of
buying high and selling low. Chasing the latest return without understanding why it may have occurred can lead to disappointing results.
Just because international equities returned 20 percent in one year
does not mean they will do so the next year. The folly of most unedu-
cated investors is they expect the outstanding returns of a "hot" manager
to be repeated year in and year out. Unfortunately, the flow of funds to
the best performing mutual fund or money manager on an after-the-
fact basis, and the subsequent disappointing results, proves this investor
axiom time and time again.

• **Lack of style diversification within an asset class.** Fluctuations
in returns within an asset class can be reduced by employing different
investment styles. A corollary is the mistaken belief that a portfolio is
appropriately diversified because it has been divided between different
money managers—the managers could all be following the same strategy and style. Diversification helps reduce risk, whether it is applied
to the number of shares held, managers employed, or asset classes
used (within reason).

• **Money managers are interviewed and selected without following a due diligence checklist.** This can lead to a host of related mistakes:
important search criteria are omitted, performance is compared to
irrelevant indexes, peer comparisons are overlooked, or presentations
given by managers focus on what the manager wants the investor to
hear, not necessarily on what the investor needs to know. Manager selection should start as an objective undertaking and conclude with a subjective evaluation of the manager's organization. The reverse leads to
inappropriate justification of the decision that is ultimately made.

These mistakes are certainly not all inclusive. However, they do help in understanding the process that should be followed in finding and hiring managers, and what the governing laws require in this area.

Fiduciary Requirements

ERISA and the Third Restatement do not expressly require the use of money managers. However, fiduciaries are held to a similar expert standard of care, and their activities and conduct are measured against those of investment professionals.

> A fiduciary shall discharge his duties . . . with the care, skill, prudence and diligence under the circumstances then prevailing that a prudent man acting in a like capacity and familiar with such matters would use in the conduct of an enterprise of a like character and with like aims.[1]
>
> In deciding whether, to whom, and in what manner to delegate fiduciary authority in the administration of a trust, the trustee is under a duty . . . to exercise fiduciary discretion and to act as a prudent person would act in similar circumstances.[2]

Citations from ERISA case law often comment on the imprudence of the fiduciary who did not seek professional expertise with the management of investment assets. The defense that the fiduciary was a simple, honest businessperson is not sufficient to avoid liability since a fiduciary is held to a much higher standard of care than a good businessperson.[3]

Safe Harbor Rules

Further evidence of the government's desire to have investment decisions made by professionals is the inclusion of safe harbor rules governing the use of money managers. Under ERISA, these guidelines come close to providing an *exculpatory* clause for fiduciary conduct.[4] When properly implemented by the fiduciary, they provide insulation from liability claims arising from poor investment results.

---

[1] ERISA Sec. 404(a)(b)

[2] Restatement Third, Sec. 171.

[3] See *Whitfield v. Cohen,* 682 F.Supp 188 (S.D.N.Y. 1988); *Katsaros v. Cody,* 744 F.2d at 279.

[4] ERISA expressly prohibits exculpatory clauses pertaining to fiduciary conduct under ERISA Sec. 410(a). This prohibition is designed to cover both prohibited transactions and investment conduct.

ERISA safe harbor rules have very specific requirements, all of which must be met in order for the fiduciary to be afforded liability protection.[5] The Third Restatement references similar rules, but the requirements are not as specific as those under ERISA.[6] However, the rules are similar in intent, and the satisfaction of the ERISA safe harbor rules would appear to satisfy the Third Restatement requirements. ERISA requires that

> **Investment decisions are to be made by prudent experts.** The term *expert* is defined as either a registered investment adviser, investment company (mutual funds), insurance company, and/or bank. (Note the absence of stockbrokers in this list.)
>
> **A due diligence process must be followed in selecting money managers.** Managers should not be selected on an ad hoc basis, nor should they be selected solely on recent stellar performance or because everyone else at the country club uses the same manager. The details of a proper due diligence process are provided later in this chapter.
>
> **Money managers must be provided general investment direction.** The managers must be given meaningful guidelines about security selection and return expectations. The most suitable means of communication with the managers is the investment policy statement (IPS).
>
> **Money managers must acknowledge their cofiduciary status in writing.** The most appropriate action is to have the manager sign a copy of the IPS. Alternatively, the manager should acknowledge their fiduciary status by signing an acknowledgment letter to such effect. (See Appendix 6–1, Sample Portfolio Manager Appointment and Acceptance Form Letter.) Mutual funds are exempt from this requirement since each prospectus contains acknowledgment of the fund's fiduciary status.
>
> **The activities of money managers must be monitored.** Once hired, the manager cannot be left without some ongoing level of accountability for the results obtained. Results should be compared against managers with a similar style of investment management. The details necessary to perform the monitoring function are contained in Chapter 8.

---

[5] ERISA Secs. 404, 405, and 406 and regulations and interpretations thereunder.

[6] Restatement Third, Sec. 227 (page 38).

Subasset Class Style Diversification

Before the manager search process begins, it is necessary to determine the extent implementation will include the use of subasset class styles. Chapter 3 reviewed in detail the following subasset class styles:

Equity	*Fixed Income*
Core	Core
Value	Defensive
Growth	Intermediate
Yield	Extended maturity
Small cap	Active duration
	High yield

The benefit of using various subasset class styles is that short-term performance volatility of a broad asset class can be limited. As an example, the commitment of a portion of the portfolio to equities (broad asset class) may result in an allocation to both growth and value styles (subasset classes of equity management). Each style has been shown to have unique characteristics that result in one style being in favor at different times (see Figure 6–1).

Although different year-to-year results of the equity subasset classes are obtained, long-term (e.g., 10 years) performance of each style has a tendency to converge over time and result in returns consistent with equities as a whole. The advantages of limiting interim volatility for different pools of money are as follows:

Individuals may be more concerned about the limitation of fluctuations in their portfolio than with performance relative to an index. The less volatility a portfolio exhibits, the less worried an individual investor becomes.

Qualified plans that make (or allow) lump-sum distributions to terminated participants would not want to unnecessarily penalize these participants by having them roll out when the plan assets are committed to an out-of-favor style of management. Fiduciaries can limit the interim fluctuations by diversifying across subasset classes.

FIGURE 6–1   **Benefits of Investment Style Diversification**

Relative Performance
Callan Equity Manager Styles v. S&P 500

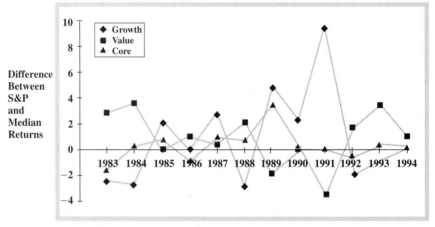

Source: Copyright ©1994, Investment Management Council.

Investment committees in general want to reduce boardroom risk, or the criticism members fear will result from interim subpar performance. Not placing all of the eggs in one basket helps avoid criticism that is based on "20–20 hindsight."

One hurdle for the investor is identifying the style of management a particular manager is following. Most databases on money managers label managers on the basis of a statistical analysis of the manager's returns, portfolio characteristics, and/or information compiled from the prospectus (for a mutual fund) or the responses made by the manager to a questionnaire. Appendix 6–2 contains sources for money manager databases for both mutual funds and separate account managers.

Practically speaking, there is also the issue of when subasset class diversification becomes overkill. Size of the portfolio is a major determinant. With the abundance of excellent mutual funds, it is arguable that no account is too small. However, tax considerations, cost, rebalancing, and monitoring ease may impact the desire to limit the style diversification of a portfolio. For accounts utilizing separately managed portfolios, three primary factors also come into play:

1. *Transaction costs.* Trading costs consume total return. Whatever value added came from diversification can just as easily be taken away if custody and brokerage charges become exorbitant relative to the account size.

2. *Manager's fee schedule.* Most all managers have tiered fee schedules (breakpoints) that result in lower incremental management fees for larger accounts. This equally applies to load mutual funds that have sales charge breakpoints. However, the fee savings (usually 50 basis points at the most) must be evaluated against the performance differential of a multi-style approach. Growth versus value equity styles have been shown to have an average annual performance differential of over 400 basis points (see Figure 6–5).

   Take for example the investor who decides to hire a single equity manager in order to save 25 basis points on fees. If the hired manager happens to be employing a growth style (or any style for that matter), the investor will likely see the annual performance of the growth manager varying by as much as 400 basis points from managers in other styles. The savings of 25 basis points now begins to pale in comparison to the performance differential that may have been reduced by hiring a value manager to complement the growth manager.

3. *Account size minimums.* These are set by the money managers. This may limit the ability of an investor to diversify the portfolio by using multiple managers. If an account is not large enough to diversify between money managers with different management styles, then it may be more appropriate to consider mutual funds.

Once it has been determined whether implementation will include a multi-style approach across the broad- and subasset classes, the search process for the specific managers is ready to begin.

Due Diligence Process for Selecting Money Managers

The previous chapter emphasized that a well-written IPS should include the specific process that is to be followed in selecting money managers. In addition, it was noted that ERISA's safe harbor rules require a due diligence process.

FIGURE 6–2   Due Diligence for Selecting Money Managers

1. Performance numbers	Time weighted, composite of actual results, quarterly returns, and net and gross of fees
2. Performance relative to assumed risk	Sharpe ratio and/or Alpha
3. Performance among peers	Third-party objective evaluations, long-term upper median performance
4. Performance of manager's adherence to stated investment style	Articulates investment strategy and demonstrates discipline to maintain strategy over time
5. Performance in both rising and falling markets	Clear defensive strategies and sell disciplines
6. Performance of key decision makers and their organizations	Growth in assets, track record attributed to same decision makers

Source: Copyright © 1993, Investment Management Council.

When the discussion turns to the selection of money managers, the most frequently asked question is: "What is the manager's performance?" Typically, the investor is asking about the most recent investment returns of the manager. This myopic focus on short-term performance can be flawed and counterproductive. However, since investors respond to performance criteria, we have expanded it to be a broad catch-all for each of the components of a comprehensive due diligence process (see Figure 6–2).

1. Performance Numbers

Statistics have shown that a manager's prior performance is of limited value in determining future performance. The primary benefit of looking at prior performance is that it enables one to narrow the list of potential candidates so that other quantitative and qualitative criteria can be applied.

Consistency of Prior Performance.   One reason prior performance numbers are examined is to ascertain whether the returns are consistent—the result of luck or brains. Whether or not 5 (even 10) years' worth of

TABLE 6–1 Ranking of Mutual Funds 1985–1994

Fund	Ranking During the Period 1985–1989 *(out of 326 Funds)*	Ranking During the Period 1990–1994 *(out of 326 Funds)*
20th Century Giftrust	1	2
Fidelity OTC	2	51
Fidelity Magellan	3	40
Transam Capital Growth	4	294
Flag Inv. Telephone Income	5	239
AIM Weingarten	6	139
IAI Regional	7	150
Putnam Voyager	8	20
Scudder Capital Growth	9	265
AIM Constellation	10	10
Fidelity Strat Opp	11	185
New York Venture	12	47
Fidelity Adv Inst Equity Growth	13	7
Federated Growth Trust	14	282
United Income	15	123
Lexington Corp Leaders	16	210
Smith Barney Aggressive Growth	17	84
IDS New Dimensions	18	27
Dodge & Cox Stock	19	103
20th Century Growth	20	105
Average Ranking		119 37th percentile
S&P 500	39	29

Mutual fund rankings were calculated by Callan Associates Inc. using returns reported by Lipper. No implication or inference should be drawn by present or prospective clients that similar investment performance will occur in the future.

Source: Copyright © 1995, Investment Management Council.

performance data will answer the question is subject to debate. To have any statistical confidence in analyzing performance, an estimated 25 years of quarterly performance data are necessary just to determine whether a manager has the ability to produce long-term above-average results.[7]

[7] John Bogle, *On Mutual Funds,* (Burr Ridge, IL: Irwin Professional Publishing, 1993), p. 177.

TABLE 6–2   **Top Ranked Mutual Funds 1985–1994**

Top 10 Funds *For Ten Year* *Period 1985–1994*	Highest Annual Ranking Out of 326 Funds For 10 Years Ending 12/94		Lowest Annual Ranking Out of 326 Funds For 10 Years Ending 12/94		Average Annual Ranking Out of 326 Funds For 10 Years Ending 12/94	
	Numeric	*Percentile*	*Numeric*	*Percentile*	*Numeric*	*Percentile*
1. 20th Century Giftrust	2	1	301	92	62	19
2. AIM Constellation	2	1	160	49	84	26
3. Fidelity Adv Inst Equity Growth	6	2	216	66	94	29
4. CGM Capital Development	1	1	320	98	100	31
5. Berger 100	3	1	312	96	126	39
6. 20th Century Ultra	3	1	285	87	129	40
7. PIMCO Adv Opportunity	2	1	306	94	125	38
8. Fidelity Contrafund	9	3	240	74	101	31
9. FPA Capital	4	1	287	88	108	33
10. Fidelity OTC	1	1	245	75	126	39
Average for Top 10 Funds	3	1	267	82	106	32
S&P 500	69	21	213	65	125	38

Mutual fund rankings were calculated by Callan Associates Inc. using returns reported by Lipper. No implication or inference should be drawn by present or prospective clients that similar investment performance will occur in the future.

Source: Copyright © 1995, Investment Management Council.

Two studies illustrate why performance numbers alone may not be helpful in selecting a money manager. Table 6–1 summarizes a study of equity mutual funds for the period 1985–1994. The left-hand column shows the top 20 funds for the first 5 years (1985–1989) of the 10-year period. The right-hand column shows the performance of the same funds over the subsequent 5-year period (1990–1994). The average performance of the top funds during the first 5 years of the study fell to the 37th percentile over the next five years.

Table 6–2 is a study of equity funds for the same time period, 1985–1994, and shows the top 10 funds for the entire 10-year period. The left-hand column is the best **annual** ranking of each of the funds. Unsurprisingly, each of the funds had at least one year when they were in the top 10 percent. The middle column shows the worst **annual** ranking. Some of the same funds also had at least one annual period when performance fell to the bottom 10 percent. How many investors would have fired their manager following the poor performance? The right-hand column shows the average annual performance for each fund. The average was the 32nd percentile for each of these top performing funds.

Important conclusions can be made from these studies: (1) superior five year performance does not guarantee long-term success; and, (2) superior long term performance does not require top quartile performance every year.

Even though superior long-term performance is no guarantee of future performance, historical performance cannot be dismissed completely. Studies have also determined that managers who rank in the top quartile for one three-year period have a statistically significant probability that they will rank in the top quartile the next subsequent three-year period.[8] In a similar study, it was also found that managers who rank in the bottom quartile for a given three-year period have a very low probability of reaching above median performance over the five-year period that includes the three-year observation.[9] The inferior three-year performance has too great an impact on the overall returns to allow for the five-year average returns to be above average.

With the adoption of voluntary performance reporting standards for money managers, gathering performance information has become easier. To ensure that a fair comparison is made between appropriate managers, performance should be (1) reported time weighted and on a quarterly basis, (2) a composite of the manager's actual portfolios, and (3) preferably audited or verified by an independent third-party, such as an accounting firm or investment consulting firm.

---

[8] Scott M. Elliott, "Tracking Down the Value of Active Management: The Good News and the Bad," *The Journal of Investing,* Winter 1993.

[9] Paul Troup and Paul Erlendson of Callan Associates Inc., "Performance Standards for Fund Managers," February 1991.

FIGURE 6–3   Endpoint Sensitivity Test

Performance vs. core equity style for periods ended December 31, 1993

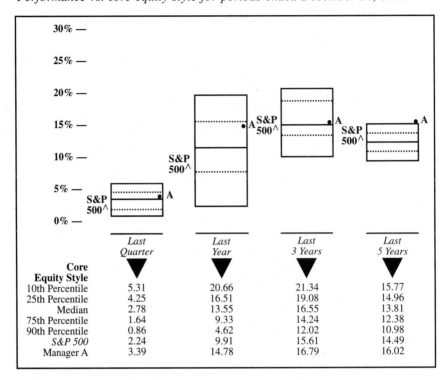

Core Equity Style	Last Quarter	Last Year	Last 3 Years	Last 5 Years
10th Percentile	5.31	20.66	21.34	15.77
25th Percentile	4.25	16.51	19.08	14.96
Median	2.78	13.55	16.55	13.81
75th Percentile	1.64	9.33	14.24	12.38
90th Percentile	0.86	4.62	12.02	10.98
S&P 500	2.24	9.91	15.61	14.49
Manager A	3.39	14.78	16.79	16.02

Source: Copyright © 1994, Callan Associates Inc.

End Point Sensitivity. Even if performance numbers are accurate and complete, they may still be misleading, depending on when they start and end. This is termed *end point sensitivity.* A manager's performance is typically analyzed on quarterly, annual, and cumulative 3-, 5- and 10-year rolling time periods. As new information is gathered, the procedure is to drop the oldest quarter of data and add the latest quarter's results.

Figure 6–3 shows the performance of a core equity manager. (For information regarding the reading of floating bar charts, also known as dancing diamond charts, see Chapter 8.) If you applied a search criterion that required the manager to be in the upper median of his or her peer group for three- and five-year cumulative periods, this manager would pass the screen.

FIGURE 6–4 Endpoint Sensitivity Test
Performance vs. value equity style for periods ended June 30, 1994

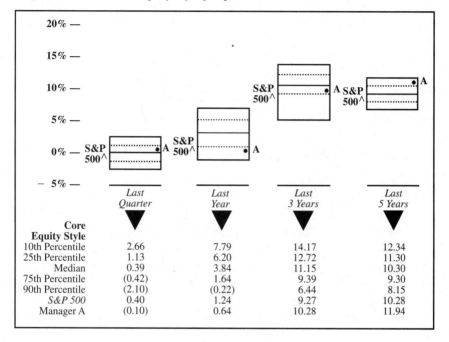

Core Equity Style	Last Quarter	Last Year	Last 3 Years	Last 5 Years
10th Percentile	2.66	7.79	14.17	12.34
25th Percentile	1.13	6.20	12.72	11.30
Median	0.39	3.84	11.15	10.30
75th Percentile	(0.42)	1.64	9.39	9.30
90th Percentile	(2.10)	(0.22)	6.44	8.15
S&P 500	0.40	1.24	9.27	10.28
Manager A	(0.10)	0.64	10.28	11.94

Source: Copyright © 1994, Callan Associates Inc.

Figure 6–4 shows the performance of the same manager two quarters later. Note the manager no longer meets the upper median for the three-year cumulative period search criterion. The selection of end points determined what information was considered. Using this information as an example, is it proper to say that the manager is no longer worthy of consideration? The analysis must include various beginning and ending periods. Looking at one ending period is not sufficient.

"In" and "Out" of Favor Style Analysis. The engagement of a manager based on short-term performance results also creates the problem of chasing styles of management that may have been in favor during the period examined. (This issue was addressed earlier in the discussion of subasset class diversification, the prime example comparing value to growth equity managers.)

If a short-term observation is used, the manager that was managing an in-favor style may be selected—this in spite of the fact the style will be moving out of favor at some future point in time. Likewise, an excellent manager may be terminated after a short period of poor performance only because the manager's style is out of favor relative to a broad market index. For these reasons, it is critical to understand what style the manager candidates or hired managers are following so they can be compared or monitored against appropriate peer groups. (Chapter 8 covers the topic of monitoring managers in more detail.)

2. Performance Relative to Assumed Risk

The absolute return of a manager reveals only part of a manager's performance. The amount of investment risk the money manager undertook to achieve the returns should also be considered. All things being equal, if two managers of the same style had comparable returns, and one manager achieved the returns with less volatility or risk than the other manager, then one would want to choose the manager who took less risk.

There are four widely used investment-related statistical terms that measure a manager's risk or risk-adjusted return: standard deviation, alpha, beta and Sharpe ratio.

Standard deviation is the most commonly referenced term and is defined as the degree of variation in a manager's returns compared to the manager's median return. In other words, if one was to graph the manager's performance results, would the graph produce a tight grouping (small standard deviation) or broad dispersion (large standard deviation). A common perception is that the greater the manager's standard deviation, the riskier the manager (less desirable). A major shortcoming of this thinking is that the variation of returns can also be a result of a manager's positive outperformance. That is, the manager may have a large standard deviation merely because of a number of positive exceptional years, a consequence all investors would agree is not bad.

Alpha measures the manager's return in excess of market return and adjusted for risk. It is a good measure of the manager's ability to select securities that have outperformed the manager's index. A positive alpha indicates that the manager has provided a return above that which the investor would have received had the investor been passively invested in the index.

Beta measures the volatility, or sensitivity, of a manager's returns in comparison to a market index. The returns of a manager that track or correlate directly with those of the market would have a beta of 1.0. A manager who has greater volatility than the market would have a beta greater than 1.0. A shortcoming of using beta as the sole risk indicator is that the manager can "game" the results. That is, the manager could be buying risky stocks, but then hold a portion of the portfolio in cash to dampen the overall volatility of the portfolio. The unsuspecting investor would think the portfolio is comprised of securities of average risk, but in reality the securities are quite risky.

Sharpe ratio is commonly used to measure a manager's risk-adjusted return relative to a benchmark. It is calculated by subtracting the risk-free return (usually the return of three-month Treasury bills) from the manager's return and dividing the result by the portfolio's standard deviation. The result is a measure of return gained per unit of risk taken. When comparing two managers of the same style, the manager with the higher Sharpe ratio would be preferred. (The Sharpe ratio is not an accurate measure when comparing managers of dissimilar styles.)

When comparing managers, there is no single perfect risk measure. Ideally, the investor should examine all four measures to ensure there is a consistent message. If, however, the investor chooses to rely on just one measurement tool, we would suggest focusing on the manager's alpha. A positive alpha indicates returns that were higher (than one would expect) given the level of portfolio risk. On the other hand, a negative alpha indicates that the investor did not receive returns that were commensurate with the level of risk taken.

3. Performance Among Peers

Earlier in the chapter, the benefits of style diversification were discussed. By diversifying between and among asset classes, performance volatility can be reduced. Peer or style groups facilitate the identification of managers who specialize in each of the broad asset classes and subasset classes. Within the broad equity universe, the more common subasset classes are growth, value, and core. (See Figure 6–5.)

When conducting a search for an equity manager, it is much more relevant to compare managers against their peer group, as opposed to comparing the manager against the equity universe as a whole or against a market index such as the S&P 500.

FIGURE 6–5   Comparison of Manager Styles* (1984–1994)

1984		
	Return	
Value	7.2%	S&P 6.2%
Core	3.9%	
Growth	0.8%	
Differential	6.4%	

1985		
	Return	
Growth	32.0%	S&P 31.8%
Core	30.9%	
Value	29.9%	
Differential	2.1%	

1986		
	Return	S&P 18.6%
Value	17.4%	
Growth	16.4%	
Core	15.5%	
Differential	1.9%	

1987		
	Return	
Growth	6.0%	S&P 5.2%
Core	4.2%	
Value	3.6%	
Differential	2.4%	

1988		
	Return	
Value	17.6%	S&P 16.8%
Core	16.2%	
Growth	12.6%	
Differential	5.0%	

1989		
	Return	
Growth	31.8%	S&P 31.5%
Core	30.3%	
Value	24.9%	
Differential	6.9%	

1990		
	Return	
Growth	−0.9%	
Core	−3.0%	S&P -3.2%
Value	−3.2%	
Differential	2.3%	

1991		
	Return	
Growth	41.9%	
Core	31.2%	S&P 30.6%
Value	28.7%	
Differential	13.2%	

1992		
	Return	
Value	9.1%	
Core	6.8%	
Growth	5.9%	S&P 7.7%
Differential	3.2%	

1993		
	Return	
Value	13.5%	
Core	10.2%	S&P 9.9%
Growth	9.1%	
Differential	4.4%	

1994		
	Return	
Value	1.1%	
Core	0.2%	S&P 1.27%
Growth	−0.2%	
Differential	1.3%	

Average style differential	4.6%

*Median returns from each style.

Source: Callan Associates Inc. Copyright © 1994, Investment Management Council.

4. Performance of the Manager's Adherence to Stated Investment Style

The selection of a manager is based on the assumption that the manager will adhere to a specific strategy or style—to do otherwise renders the search process useless. The manager should be able to clearly articulate the investment strategy that has been and will be followed. This should include not only the buy strategy, but also the sell discipline.

As part of the due diligence process, you must confirm that the manager has consistently followed the same style and does not show tendencies to chase the latest Wall Street fad in an attempt to obtain superior performance. This may occur if a manager has had a period of lagging performance. If the market has not rewarded the manager's style, there may be a temptation for the manager to alter the security selection process to increase the chances of obtaining better performance. This creates unwarranted risk.

5. Performance in Both Rising and Falling Markets

Bull markets can cover up mistakes a manager may make in his or her security selection. Cumulative performance figures, even annual figures during bull markets, can shelter even the most inept managers as they ride the momentum of an up market. By studying the manager's quarterly returns, one develops much more realistic expectations and a sense of the manager's true capabilities.

But even superior equity management firms experience negative quarterly returns 30 percent of the time. It is a statistical improbability that a manager is going to grow the portfolio from day one. Even in a bull market there is a better than 1-in-4 chance that the portfolio will actually go down before it begins to go up.

An understanding of the downside potential is critical for an investor. Individuals are typically more concerned about absolute performance, not relative performance. Individuals typically want all of the upside potential of the market and none of the downside movement. This is contrasted with institutional portfolios (e.g., pension plans, profit-sharing plans, or foundations) that are usually examining performance relative to the market or relative to that of other managers or portfolios. Educating the individual investor about the manager's falling market performance is critical in preparing that investor for the periodic reduction in portfolio value that will inevitably occur.

6. Performance of Key Decision Makers and Their Organizations

A common characteristic of quality money management firms is that the decision makers have the ability to "observe subtleties, make judgments and weigh thousands of facts and observations in a powerful, analytical and intuitive way."[10] Even firms that state they rely on a quantitative model (black box) still need professionals to interpret and implement the output.

The best and the brightest decision makers need a good home. Although not true in every case, there are some general observations that can be made about solid investment organizations.

Ownership. Decision makers who are owners of the investment firms tend to outperform those that are employees. The vested interest in

---

[10] Frank J. Fabozzi, ed., *Pension Fund Investment Management 1: A Handbook for Sponsors and Their Advisors* (Chicago: Probus Publishing Company, 1990), p. 91.

performance (as it translates to additional revenues and more assets under management) makes employee-owned firms a general plus.

Size of Firm.   Smaller organizations tend to be more focused and concentrated in one investment style. As a result, performance is more volatile—when they're hot, they're very hot, but when they're cold, they freeze up.

Assets Under Management.   This is a close corollary to the size of a firm. One should ensure that the firm can properly invest the dollars being placed. As a rule of thumb, never give a manager more than 10 percent of the manager's current asset base. (For example, if a manager has $200 million under management, one would not want to give the manager more than $20 million.) Also, one should be cautious of management firms that have had explosive asset growth. Many times tremendous growth is a precursor to lagging performance or regulatory problems since, administratively, the firm is unable to practically handle and absorb the increased number of accounts and/or assets.

Change in Personnel.   When there has been a change in personnel, or when a decision maker has left one firm to join another, prudence dictates that the firm be placed on hold until sufficient time (two years) has passed in order to determine the impact the change may have on performance.

Trading Capability.   Execution costs have a great impact on performance. (See Chapter 9 for more details.) One should analyze the firm's in-house trading capability, as well as how the firm ensures the investor is receiving favorable or best execution of trades and transactions.

Research.   This requires determination of the percentage of investment research that is generated in-house. The firm that is purchasing all its research from Wall Street is accessing the same investment data and reviewing the same investment ideas as other investment managers. The data may be too widely disseminated to make the management decisions truly unique.

Soft Dollars.   Managers who purchase street research usually pay for the information from commissions generated from client transactions. (For an example of soft dollars, see Chapter 9.) Under such a scenario, the investor should understand that part of the manager's costs is paid for by transactions generated from the investor's account.

Conflicts of Interest. Firms that are affiliated with broker dealers, banks, insurance companies, or investment companies (mutual funds) need to affirm that their money management operations are completely independent of other corporate activities. Ethical walls may exist in theory, but they can be hard to carry out in practice.

Other Manager Search Issues

Overlapping Styles

During the search process, one must be mindful of the portfolio characteristics of the different managers being screened. Although two managers may have different styles, they may still have overlapping or similar portfolio characteristics. The selection of a manager in one style may eliminate a manager candidate in another style if the two managers have a tendency to hold similar securities.

As an example, the selection of core and value equity managers may be redundant if both managers hold large capitalization, low price/earning ratio, high-dividend-paying stocks. These overlaps are evident in Figure 6–6.

FIGURE 6–6   Equity Style Matrix

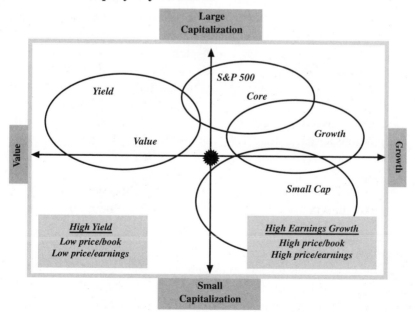

Balanced Managers

If the investor has made an asset allocation decision, is there a place for a balanced manager in the management of the portfolio? There are at least two reasons why a balanced manager may still be appropriate. First, investors with small-to medium-size portfolios may wish to have a separately managed account. There may not be sufficient assets to have a separate account manager for both the equity and fixed income. One solution is to hire a balanced manager for a significant portion of the portfolio, and then use mutual funds to round out the desired asset allocation.

The second reason to hire a balanced manager would be to use the manager as a swing manager that follows a tactical rather than strategic rebalancing strategy. Separate from their style of management (e.g., value equity and intermediate fixed income), balanced managers can also be categorized into strategic or tactical strategies.

- *Strategic.*   The balanced manager typically maintains an allocation of equity within the range of 40–60 percent. When analyzing strategic managers, it is useful to determine if the manager's strength lies with equity or fixed-income security selection. Over the long run, managers tend to tilt the portfolio towards their strong suit.

- *Tactical.*   The balanced manager maintains a broader allocation between equities, fixed income, and cash. The equity range typically falls between 15–85 percent. The manager looks for transitory imbalances between the relative returns of the different asset classes, and over-exposes an asset class that is currently underperforming or beginning to overperform other asset classes. [Tactical managers differ from market timers in that a tactical manager will not make big bets when changing the allocations—i.e., they will not shift from 100 percent equities to cash and back again. When tactical managers make shifts between asset classes, they are usually done over extended periods of time and in small increments.]

Cash Management

One overlooked area in the search process is giving consideration to how uninvested cash will be managed. Virtually every portfolio has at least a portion of its assets invested in cash. Even portfolios that are 100 percent invested with an equity manager will have a cash account for dividend sweeps and a holding depository for executing buy and sell trades. Many times, by default, the portfolio will use the custodian's cash or money market vehicle. This should not be viewed as the only alternative.

With recent changes to SEC regulations, there is now uniformity in the way money market funds report their yields. However, there are still marked differences between money market funds.

- *Fees.* There is a large disparity in the annual expenses charged by money market accounts. Average fees can range between 10 and 80 basis points, with higher-priced funds charging over 100 basis points.[11] Most large financial and brokerage institutions have different money market products with multiple pricing structures, so it is imperative to inquire about the cost differences.

- *Quality.* To boost yields, firms will invest in cash instruments of lower quality, defined as ratings of A-2, P-2, or lower. In addition, some money market funds have come perilously close to "breaking the buck" by using higher risk derivatives.[12] Inquiry must be made about the use of such strategies and the financial wherewithal to make contributions to the fund when problems do arise.

The Selection Process

When all of the due diligence principles are applied, definitive search criteria are developed. However, the ability to develop uniform search criteria that can be applied to each and every asset class is difficult. Sample search criteria are provided in Appendix 6–3.

---

[11] Susan E. Kuhn, "Raise Your Return without Raising Your Risk," *Fortune,* 1994 Investor's Guide, p. 44.

[12] In fact, during the time that this book was being edited, Community Bankers U.S. Government Money Market Fund became the first money market fund since 1976 to break the buck by lowering its NAV below $1. Derivative instruments were to blame for this problem. The derivative debacle also extended into money market funds that held Orange County, California, securities. The sponsors of these funds either bought these securities out of the funds or pledged letters of credit to secure their value to maintain the $1 NAV.

Consideration must also be given as to whether or not the portfolio is to be separately managed, or if the search is for a mutual fund. More subjective criteria can typically be used in the search process for a separate account manager than for a mutual fund since both the investigation and discussion can be manager specific.

Request for Proposal (RFP)

As the due diligence criteria are applied, the field of potential managers should be narrowed down to a select few that satisfy the criteria. The selection process then continues with the manager candidates completing a request for proposal (RFP) or the investor using the RFP as a checklist for gathering information on each of the managers. The RFP contains a specific listing of questions and documents necessary to fully evaluate each candidate. (RFPs are not usually sent to mutual fund sponsors. However, information such as the prospectus, the latest annual report for the fund, and the Statement of Additional Information filed with the SEC should be requested.) As a reminder, safe harbor rules require that a fiduciary follow a due diligence process in selecting prudent experts. This process must be logical and consistently applied for it to be useful. The RFP helps maintain this consistency. (A sample RFP is provided as Appendix 6–4.)

RFPs are at once both a boon and a bust to money managers (and investment consultants). Often, a manager is not even aware of an opportunity to work with a prospect until an RFP is received at the manager's office. The fact that an RFP has been issued is a good sign that the manager will have a fair shot at competing for the business. Public funds, in particular, are sensitive to the use of an RFP to ensure a formal, open search process is undertaken to avoid even the suspicion of cronyism.

On the other hand, RFPs have become so complex and lengthy that most firms have had to hire full-time staff members just to prepare answers. Clearly, it is imperative that the investor limit inquiries to reflect the most critical issues so a meaningful conclusion can be drawn. A manager may not feel it is worth the time and effort to complete an extensive RFP if the amount to be managed is small. Usually, a manager has taken this into consideration when publishing their minimum acceptable account size. If a manager has established a certain minimum, the manager should be willing to fill out a questionnaire that contemplates the management of funds at that minimum level.

Final Selection

Once the RFPs have been returned and confirmation of the criteria is obtained, the next step is the actual selection of the manager. For a committee, this can be an arduous task unless a standardized process is followed. One of the most democratic approaches is to utilize a scoring system. This system begins with an agreement of the weights to be applied to each search criterion.

As an example:

Criterion	*Weight*
Organization: • Type • Professionals • Depth	10%
Philosophy/strategy: • Characteristics • Turnover • Sell discipline	10%
Return performance • Consistency • Relative • Results	40%
Risk performance • Control • Alpha • Sharpe ratio	30%
Fit with overall strategy of plan	10%
Total	100%

Each manager is then scored by committee members on a scale of 1 to 10 (10 being the best) for each criterion. The score is then multiplied by the percentage weight for each criterion. The weighted numbers are then summed, resulting in a final score for the manager. This process is applied until every manager is fully evaluated. A sample matrix that can be used for this process is presented as Appendix 6–5. This process documents both the procedures utilized and the results obtained. This is important in understanding and supporting why a particular manager was selected. Appendix 6–6 contains a sample agreement that could be used with the selected manager.

In the next chapter we will continue with topics pertinent to the implementation decisions that an investor has to make.

APPENDIX 6–1
Sample Portfolio Manager Appointment and Acceptance Letter

Anywhere Asset Management, Inc. (the Portfolio Manager) hereby acknowledges receipt of the Investment Policy Statement for the ABC Company Retirement Plan (the Client). Client appoints Portfolio Manager of Client's designated account and Portfolio Manager accepts such appointment.

Portfolio Manager agrees to manage the investment and reinvestment of Client's account assets in accordance with the investment objectives and guidelines set forth in Client's Investment Policy Statement, receipt of which is hereby acknowledged.

Client is a qualified plan under ERISA. Portfolio Manager acknowledges that it is a fiduciary with respect to Client in accordance with Section (3)(21)(A) of ERISA and an Investment Manager as defined in Section 3(38) of ERISA. No other fiduciary of Client shall be liable for the acts or omissions of the Portfolio Manager or be under any obligation to invest or otherwise manage any of Client's assets that are subject to the management of the undersigned Portfolio Manager.

Client acknowledges that it has received a current copy of the Portfolio Manager's Form ADV Part II.

Anywhere Asset Management, Inc.:	*Client:*
Signature:_____	Signature:_____
Name:_____	Name:_____
Title:_____	Title:_____
Date:_____	Date:_____

APPENDIX 6–2
Sources of Information on Money Managers

To assemble information on potential managers, it is necessary to utilize various databases that contain information on either mutual funds or separate account managers. Some of the more commonly used sources of information include the following:

Mutual Funds

CDA Wiesenberger
1355 Piccard Dr.
Rockville, MD 20850
(800) 232-2285

Lipper Analytical Services
74 Trinity Place
New York, NY 10006
(212) 393-1300

Morningstar Reports
Morningstar, Inc.
225 West Wacker Drive
Chicago, IL 60606
(800) 876-5005

Steele Systems Inc.
Alexander Steele's Mutual Fund
12021 Wilshire Blvd., Suite 407
Los Angeles, CA 90025
(800) 237-8400 ext. 767

Value Line Mutual Fund Survey
220 East 42nd Street
New York, NY 10017-5891
(800) 824-7607

Separately Managed Accounts

Becker, Burke Associates
221 North LaSalle Street
Suite 1000
Chicago, IL 60601
(312) 782-5665

Buck Investment Consulting Group
Two Pennsylvania Plaza
New York, NY 10121-0047
(212) 330-1000

Callan Associates Inc
71 Stevenson Street Suite 1300
San Francisco, CA 95105
(415) 974-5060

DeMarche Associates, Inc.
6320 Lamar Ave
Overland Park, KS 66202
(913) 384-4994

Effron Enterprises, Inc.
363 Westchester Ave
Port Chester, NY 10573-3809
(914) 939-0200

Evaluation Associates, Inc.
200 Connecticut Ave.
Norwalk, CT 06854
(203) 855-2200

Frank Russell Company
P.O. Box 1616
Tacoma, WA 98401
(206) 572-9500

Hewitt Associates LLC
100 Half Day Road
Lincolnshire, IL 60069
(708) 295-5000

LCG Associates, Inc.
100 Galleria Parkway
Suite 1200
Atlanta, GA 30339
(404) 644-0100

William M. Mercer
1417 Lake Cook Road
Deerfield, IL 60015
(708) 317-7418

Mobius Group
68 T.W. Alexander Drive
Research Triangle Park, NC 27709
(919) 549-0444

PIPER
85 Old Kings Highway N.
Darien, CT 06820-4733
(203) 656-5930

SEI
680 East Swedesford Road
Wayne, Pa 19087
(800) 407-2275

Wilshire Associates Incorporated
1299 Ocean Ave
Santa Monica, CA 90401
(310) 451-3051

Wyatt Investment Consulting
345 California Street
Suite 1400
San Francisco, CA 94104
(415) 986-6568

APPENDIX 6–3
Sample Manager Search Criteria

Specific Search Criteria

1. Manager Styles.
Search #1—Core Equity Manager
Managers whose portfolio characteristics are similar to that of the S&P 500 with the objective of adding value over and above the index, typically from sector or issue selection. Managers that deviate from the industry weights of the S&P 500 are acceptable as well as those that exhibit growth-like portfolio characteristics.

Search #2—Growth
Managers who invest in companies that are expected to have above average prospects for long-term growth in earnings and profitability. Cap ranges from mid (cap range $1–$6 billion) to large (cap range over $6 billion).

Search #3—Value/Yield/Contrarian
Value managers who invest in companies believed to be undervalued or possessing lower-than-average price/earnings ratios based on their potential for capital appreciation. Yield managers whose primary objective is a higher than average dividend yield. Contrarian managers who invest in stocks that are out of favor or have little current market interest, on the premise that gain will be realized when they return to favor.

Search #4—Tactical Balanced
Managers who try to capitalize on the cyclical behavior of the economy and market price trends by moving in and out of the equity market in anticipation of these cycles, using tactical asset allocation.

Search #5—Strategic Balanced
Managers who maintain, on average, a fully discretionary, balanced portfolio with equity ranges between 40 and 60 percent.

Search #6—Defensive/Intermediate Fixed Income
Managers whose objective is to minimize interest rate risk by investing only in short- to intermediate-term securities. The average portfolio maturity is typically two to five years. Appropriate benchmarks include the Merrill 1–3 Year Treasury Index or the Lehman Government/Corporate Intermediate Index.

Search #7—Core Bond
Managers who construct portfolios to approximate the investment results of the Lehman Government/Corporate Bond Index or the Lehman Aggregate Index with a modest amount of variability in duration around the index.

Search #8—Active Duration
Managers who employ either interest rate anticipation or business cycle timing. Portfolios are actively managed so wide changes in duration are made in anticipation of interest rate changes and/or business cycle movements.

Search #9—Global Fixed Income
Managers who incorporate both domestic and international regions into their asset allocation using, generally, the Salomon World Government Bond Index as the benchmark.

2. Type of Manager. Managers must be appropriate for taxable and tax-exempt accounts: bonded, appropriately registered, and willing to acknowledge cofiduciary status in writing.

3. Assets under Management. There must be a minimum of $100 million in the asset class under management. [Exceptions to this screen have been made for a few of the style groups (i.e., global fixed income) due to the limited number of managers in the universe. The decision as to whether the manager is appropriate in spite of not meeting this screen will be made by the investment committee.]

4. Employee Turnover. Stable organizations are sought. There must not have been any substantive change in key decision makers or owners of the firm over the past four years. For those managers that have experienced a loss of key investment professionals over the last four years, organizational and portfolio management stability must have been demonstrated over at least the last several years.

5. Investment Process. The decision-making body must have followed the same investment process for at least four years, and that process should be easily understood.

6. Minimum Track Record. The decision-making body must have a verifiable real track record of four years or more. [Exceptions to this screen have been made for a few of the style groups (i.e., global fixed income) due to the limited number of managers in the universe. The decision as to whether the manager is appropriate in spite of not meeting this screen will be made by the investment committee.]

7. Performance Criteria. Managers should pass three out of three (two out of three for a few styles) of the following performance screens versus the 50th percentile of the relevant style group:
  1. Pass 1/2 of available cumulative periods (1, 3, 5, 7, 10 years).
  2. Pass 1/2 of available annual periods.
  3. Pass 1/2 of available rolling three-year periods.

8. Risk. The manager should have positive risk-adjusted performance versus the appropriate peer group over various time periods. The manager's standard deviation should be no higher than 125 percent of the relevant market's standard deviation for the four years ending December 31, 1994.

9. Trading. Managers must have a demonstrated process of ensuring that client accounts are traded at best execution.

10. Use of Cash. For managers that hold more than 15 percent in cash, the manager must demonstrate that the cash is held in reserve for buying opportunities as opposed to market timing.

11. Fees. The firm must be willing to negotiate fees and account size minimums.

12. References. Finalist firms will be asked to provide a list of accounts gained and lost over the past five years with explanations for account terminations.

13. Business Plan. The firm should be well managed and have a long-range business plan. Candidates should be able to demonstrate a high probability of a continuing commitment to the investment management of comparable funds and have the financial resources to weather a poor business environment. A willingness to share ownership in the firm would be a strong indication of an ability to attract and retain talented professionals. A controlled growth policy should be in place that will provide assurance that the firm will be able to absorb additional asset growth without altering its investment philosophy and strategy.

General Search Criteria

The following criteria should be used by the investment committee to aid in discriminating between managers who meet all of the specific search criteria.

1. The firms should operate independently with key decision makers having compensation tied to the success of the firm.
2. The selection of managers should have diverse geographic representation.
3. The firm should have experience in working with taxable and tax-exempt clients.
4. The manager should have a demonstrated history of low portfolio turnover in order to control transaction costs.
5. Equity managers should be trading in listed securities, and fixed-income managers should be investing in investment-grade securities.

APPENDIX 6–4
Money Management Services Request
for Proposal (RFP)

I. Identity and Address of Principals

A. Name of firm(s).

B. Name, address, and telephone numbers of key contact.

C. Ownership structure of firm(s).

1. Is your firm (1) independently owned and operated, (2) a limited or master partnership, (3) part of a publicly traded company, (4) affiliated with an insurance company, (5) affiliated with a bank, or (6) affiliated with a brokerage firm?

2. Are you registered with the SEC? If so, please provide a copy of your ADV Parts I and II.

3. For insurance company and bank affiliates, please provide a copy of your annual report.

D. How many full-time staff are employed by your firm?

E. Brief biographies of key decision makers.

1. Are decisions made by committee, or does each portfolio manager have independent discretion over the assets?

2. How many key professionals have been added and/or deleted from the staff over the last three years?

3. What percentage of the key decision makers have ownership in the firm?

II. Business Focus

A. What is your firm's average account size?

B. How many portfolios do you currently manage?

C. What is your stated minimum account size for separately managed accounts?

D. Do you offer commingled accounts? If so, what is the minimum account size?

E. What is your client turnover (gains and losses) for the last three years?

F. What percentage of your clients are taxable versus tax exempt?

G. Do you manage other clients who are similar to us in size and investment profile?

III. Management Style

A. What investment strategies or styles does your firm offer? If more than one style, what is your best style?

B. How long have you been managing each style?
C. Is any portion of your performance record carried over from another firm? If so, what was the name of the other firm?
D. Have any independent investment consulting firms analyzed your style(s)? If so, what were their findings?

IV. Security Selection

A. What percentage of your research is generated in-house versus purchased from other sources?
    1. What percentage of the purchased research is paid for with soft dollars?
B. Please describe in detail the process you would go through in selecting securities for our portfolio.
C. Please describe in detail the process you would go through to monitor our portfolio, and how decisions would be reached to sell a security in the portfolio.
D. For equity styles:
    1. Will you hold cash if there are no buying opportunities? If so, what is the most cash you will hold?
    2. What capitalization range do you favor?
    3. Do you have a bias for or against any sectors?
    4. How many securities do you normally buy for a portfolio of our size?
    5. What has been the average turnover of securities for a portfolio of our size?
E. For fixed income styles:
    1. How active is your style in anticipating interest rate changes?
    2. What sectors do you favor?
    3. How many different securities would you buy for a portfolio of our size?
    4. What percentage of your portfolios are invested in below investment grade portfolios? Were these client-directed purchases?
F. For balanced managers:
    1. How do you determine the mix between equity and fixed income?
    2. What has been the average mix between equity and fixed income?
    3. What have been the lowest and highest equity exposures?
    4. When you change the mix, how large a percentage change will you make at one time?

5. What is the average length of time you have taken to move a portfolio from one extreme of the asset mix to the other?
G. For international/global managers:
   1. Is there a bias for or against any countries or geographic areas?
   2. Would you view your style as being active or passive in selecting countries? In selecting securities?
H. Do you offer socially responsive screens? If so, what types of socially responsive portfolios do you manage?
I. Do you have in-house traders? If so, what has been their experience?
   1. What top three brokerage firms do you favor for trading?

V. Performance

A. Do you calculate performance according to AIMR standards? If so, Level I or Level II? If no, please state why.
B. Please state your performance for each style being considered for this RFP. Performance must be (1) reported on a time-weighted basis (dollar weighted if a commingled account), (2) reflective of actual performance (not simulated), and (3) a representation of all clients within each style. We would prefer performance reported on a net and gross of fees basis; however, either one is acceptable. If available, performance exhibits should include (1) quarterly results, (2) annual results, (3) cumulative results for three- and five-year periods, and (4) risk-adjusted returns.
C. Against what benchmark should your performance be compared for each style?
D. What has been the standard deviation and alpha for each style being considered for this RFP?

VI. Fees

A. What is your stated fee for an account of our size?
B. Does your fee include anticipated costs for client meetings? If so, how many meetings per year?
C. What percentage of the portfolio's transactions are you anticipating to use for soft dollars?

Final Selection Criteria

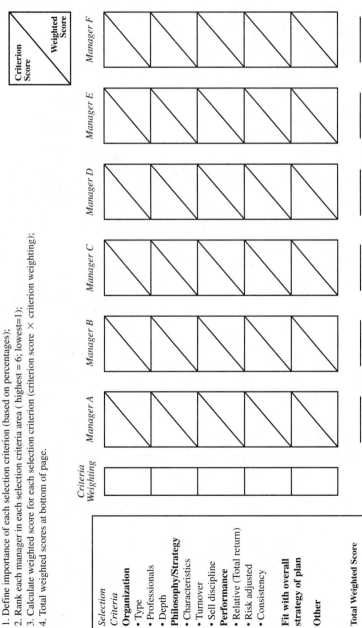

Manager Selection Worksheet

1. Define importance of each selection criterion (based on percentages);
2. Rank each manager in each selection criteria area (highest = 6; lowest=1);
3. Calculate weighted score for each selection criterion (criterion score × criterion weighting);
4. Total weighted scores at bottom of page.

	Criterion Score / Weighted Score

Criteria Weighting | Manager A | Manager B | Manager C | Manager D | Manager E | Manager F

Selection
Criteria
Organization
 • Type
 • Professionals
 • Depth
Philosophy/Strategy
 • Characteristics
 • Turnover
 • Sell discipline
Performance
 • Relative (Total return)
 • Risk adjusted
 • Consistency

**Fit with overall
strategy of plan**

Other

Total Weighted Score

Manager Selection Worksheet

1. Define importance of each selection criterion (based on percentages);
2. Rank each manager in each selection criteria area (highest = 6; lowest=1);
3. Calculate weighted score for each selection criterion (criterion score × criterion weighting);
4. Total weighted scores at bottom of page.

SAMPLE

Legend: Criterion Score (lower) / Weighted Score (upper)

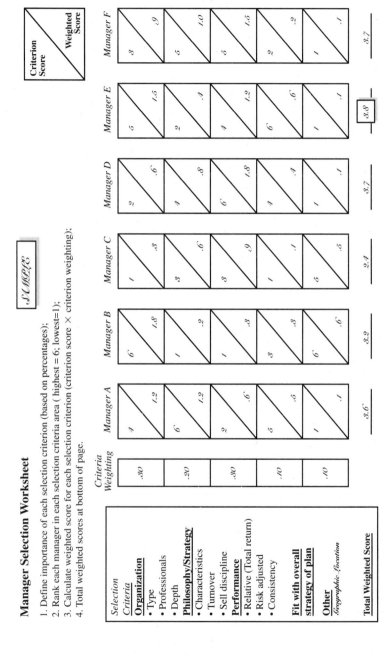

Selection Criteria	Criteria Weighting	Manager A	Manager B	Manager C	Manager D	Manager E	Manager F
Organization · Type · Professionals · Depth	.80	4 / 1.2	6 / 1.8	1 / .8	3 / .6	5 / 1.5	3 / .9
Philosophy/Strategy · Characteristics · Turnover · Sell discipline	.20	6 / 1.2	1 / .2	3 / .6	4 / .8	2 / .4	5 / 1.0
Performance · Relative (Total return) · Risk adjusted · Consistency	.80	2 / .6	1 / .3	3 / .9	6 / 1.8	4 / 1.2	5 / 1.5
Fit with overall strategy of plan	.10	5 / .5	3 / .3	1 / .1	4 / .4	6 / .6	2 / .2
Other *Geographic Location*	.10	1 / .1	6 / .6	5 / .5	1 / .1	1 / .1	1 / .1
Total Weighted Score		3.6	3.2	2.4	3.7	3.8	3.7

164

APPENDIX 6–6
Uniform Investment Management Agreement

THIS AGREEMENT is made by and between _____

_____ (**"Client"**) and _____

(**"Advisor"**), whose principal office is located in the state of _____ ,

and county of _____ , for _____
investment style.

Client has entered into a Consulting Services Agreement with _____

_____ , a registered
investment adviser under the Investment Advisers Act of 1940, (**"Consultant"**). Pursuant
to the Consulting Services Agreement, **Client** has informed **Consultant** of **Client's**
financial circumstances and investment objectives, and **Consultant** has assisted
Client in developing an investment policy statement and making an informed decision
about the suitability of **Advisor** for **Client.**

Client has entered into a Custodial Services Agreement with _____

_____ (**"Custodian"**) to act as a
custodian of **Client's** assets.

In consideration of the premises contained herein, **Client** and **Advisor** hereby agree as
follows:

1. Retention as Manager.
Must check one and initial:

—   [   ] **Client** hereby appoints and retains **Advisor** to act as investment
manager with respect to the assets placed under management of the **Advisor**
from time to time (individually and collectively, the "Account") and **Advisor**
hereby accepts such appointment.

OR
For ERISA accounts only; check if appropriate and initial:

—   [   ] The **Named Fiduciary** hereby appoints and retains **Advisor** to
act as investment manager with respect to the Account and **Advisor** hereby
accepts such appointment.

2. Management of Assets. Advisor shall have sole discretionary authority
to invest and reinvest the securities, property, cash and other investments
("Assets") in the Account at such time and in such manner as **Advisor** deems
advisable in accordance with **Advisor's** Investment Strategy set forth in Exhibit
A as it may be amended and **Client's** Investment Policy Statement as it may
be amended in writing from time to time. In providing all services hereunder,
Advisor is entitled to rely on the financial and other information provided by
Client, including Exhibit B, without any duty or obligation to investigate the
accuracy or completeness of the information. **Advisor** does not guarantee the
investment performance of any of the Assets.

Check if appropriate and initial:

___   [   ] **Advisor** shall have sole discretionary authority to invest and reinvest in derivative products including, without limitation, options, financial futures contracts, forwards, swaps and similar instruments. **Client** and **Advisor** may, from time to time, enter into such additional agreements as may be necessary to fulfill the purpose of this Agreement.

___   [   ] **Advisor** may hold all or a portion of the Account Assets in mutual funds including those for which the **Advisor**, or any of its subsidiaries, acts as investment advisor, provided, however, that the Account Assets upon which **Advisor's** fee shall be based shall exclude any Account Assets which are invested in such mutual funds.

3. **Additions and Withdrawals.** **Client** may make additions to, or cause withdrawals to be made from, the Assets of at least $10,000, at such times and in such amounts as **Client** shall determine. **Client** shall notify **Advisor** in writing of any additions to the Assets, including the amount thereof. **Client** shall notify **Advisor** in writing at least seven business days prior to a withdrawal, including the amount thereof.

4. **Execution Services.** **Advisor** shall place all orders for the purchase and/or sale of Assets for the Account with broker-dealers subject to **Advisor's** duty to seek best execution. All transaction costs shall be borne by the Account. **Advisor** shall not be liable to **Client** for any act, conduct or omission of any broker. When **Advisor** determines that the purchase or sale of a security or other investment is in the best interest of the Account, as well as **Advisor's** other clients, **Advisor,** to the extent permitted by law, may aggregate the securities or investments to be purchased or sold for the Account with those of its other clients in order to obtain a favorable execution and favorable brokerage commissions. In such event, allocation of the securities or investments to be purchased or sold, as well as the expenses incurred in the transactions, will be made by **Advisor** in a manner **Advisor** considers equitable and consistent with its obligations to **Client** and to its other clients.

5. **Custodial Services.** The Account Assets shall be held for safekeeping with **Custodian**. **Advisor** shall not act as custodian for the Account Assets and shall not be liable to **Client** for any act, conduct or omission of **Custodian**. **Advisor** is hereby authorized and empowered to issue instructions to **Custodian**.

6. **Confidential Relationship.** All information and advice furnished by either party to the other shall be treated as confidential and shall not be disclosed to third parties except as required by law.

7. **Proxies.** **Advisor** is hereby appointed **Client's** agent and attorney-in-fact to vote proxies in connection with the Account Assets. **Advisor** shall not incur any liability to **Client** by reason of any action, or failure to act, with respect to the foregoing.

8. **Fees.** **Client** hereby authorizes that **Advisor's** fees set forth in Exhibit A, be paid by **Custodian** directly from the Account based upon a statement sent by

Advisor to **Custodian** with a copy sent simultaneously to **Client.** Such fees shall be paid quarterly in arrears, and shall be prorated for periods of less than three months. **Client** represents that the agreement with **Custodian** provides that **Custodian** will send to **Client,** at least quarterly, a statement showing all amounts disbursed from the Account, including **Advisor's** fees.

9. **Standard of Care.** It is agreed that **Advisor** shall discharge its duties under this Agreement with the care, skill, prudence and diligence under the circumstances then prevailing that a prudent person acting in a like capacity and familiar with such matters would use in the conduct of an enterprise of a like character and with like aims. **Client** recognizes that the opinions, recommendations, and actions of **Advisor** will be based on advice and information deemed to be reliable, but not guaranteed by or to **Advisor.** The federal securities laws impose liability under certain circumstances on persons who act in good faith, and therefore nothing herein shall in any way constitute a waiver or limitation of any rights which the undersigned may have under any federal securities laws which cannot be modified in advance by contract.

10. **Services to Other Clients.** **Client** acknowledges that **Advisor** (and its affiliates) provide(s) investment management and other advisory services to various other clients. **Client** acknowledges and agrees that **Advisor** (and its affiliates) may hold or deal in securities, property or other assets which may be the same or different from the securities, property or other assets recommended for sale, purchase or retention in the Account, and that **Advisor** (and its affiliates) may give advice, and take action, with respect to any of those clients that may differ from the advice given, or the time or nature of action taken, with respect to the Account, so long as it is **Advisor's** policy, to the extent practical, to allocate investment opportunities to the Account over a period of time on a fair and equitable basis relative to other clients. **Advisor** shall have no obligation to recommend for purchase or sale by the Account, or to order transactions for the Account with respect to, any security, property or other asset recommended, purchased or sold for **Advisor,** its officers, directors or employees, its affiliates or for clients of **Advisor** or its affiliates.

11. **Termination of Agreement.** This Agreement shall continue in effect until terminated by either party. This Agreement may be terminated at any time by **Client** effective immediately upon receipt of written notice from **Client** to **Advisor,** and this Agreement may be terminated at any time by **Advisor** upon at least thirty (30) days' written notice from **Advisor** to **Client.** Such termination will not affect the liabilities or the obligations of the parties under this Agreement arising from transactions initiated prior to such termination. In the event of termination of this Agreement, **Advisor** shall have no obligation whatsoever to recommend any action with respect to, or to liquidate, the securities, property or other assets in the Account. The authority of **Advisor** under this Agreement shall continue until receipt of written notice of the death or incapacity of **Client,** and any action taken by **Advisor** prior to receipt of written notice of such event in reliance upon this Agreement shall be binding upon **Client** and **Client's** legal representatives, heirs and assigns.

12. **Representations.** **Advisor** represents that it is (1) registered as an investment advisor under the Investment Advisers Act of 1940 ("Advisers Act") and that such registration is currently effective, or (2) a bank, as such term is defined in Section 202(a) (2) of the Advisers Act.

Advisor represents that it will render individualized investment advice with respect to the Account.

If the Account is subject to the Employee Retirement Income Security Act of 1974 ("ERISA"), **Advisor** acknowledges that (1) it is a fiduciary under ERISA with respect to the Account, and (2) **Advisor** shall carry out its investment management responsibilities in accordance with all applicable provisions of ERISA including those set forth in Section 404(a) of ERISA.

Client represents that no one except **Client** has any interest, directly or indirectly (except for the beneficial interest of the participants in a qualified plan or trust) in the Account Assets.

The undersigned, on behalf of **Client**, represents that the execution of this Agreement by **Client** has been duly authorized by all appropriate action and represents a valid and binding obligation of **Client**, enforceable in accordance with its terms, and does not violate any regulations, agreements or instruments by which the Account is bound.

Check if appropriate and initial:

___   [   ] Exhibit B identifies those individuals that have authority to act on behalf of **Client.**

13. **Fidelity Bonding.**

If regulated by ERISA, check and initial:

___   [   ] **Client** agrees to obtain and maintain a bond satisfying the requirements of Section 412 of ERISA, and to include **Advisor**, and its agents, among those insured under that bond.

14. **Assignability.**   **Client** may not assign this Agreement without the consent of **Advisor.** No assignment, as that term is defined in the Investment Advisers Act of 1940, of this Agreement shall be made by **Advisor** without the consent of **Client.**

15. **Change in Management or Ownership.**   **Advisor** shall promptly notify **Client** if (A) any change occurs in the directors, officers or partners of **Advisor** who are (1) members of **Advisor's** investment committee which makes investment decisions for the Account, (2) responsible for investment decisions for the Account, or (3) supervisors of the person(s) responsible for investment decisions for the Account; or (B) more than 5 percent of **Advisor's** equity capital is sold. If **Advisor** is a partnership, **Advisor** shall promptly notify **Client** of a change in the ownership of **Advisor.**

16. **Governing Law; Successors and Assigns.**   This Agreement shall be governed by and construed under the laws of the state in which the principal office of **Advisor** is located, without giving effect to its principles of conflicts

of law. This Agreement shall be binding upon the successors and assigns of the parties.

17. **Severability.** If any provision of this Agreement shall be held invalid by a statute, rule, regulation, decision of a tribunal or otherwise, the remainder of this Agreement shall not be affected, and, to such extent, the provisions of this Agreement shall be severable.

18. **Communications.** Instructions with respect to securities transactions may be given orally and shall be confirmed in writing as soon as practicable.

    Any written notice required by or pertaining to the Agreement shall be delivered by U.S. mail or facsimile transmission. Any written notice to **Client** required by or pertaining to the Agreement shall be delivered to **Client** at address stated below.

    If to **Client**:   Name: _____

    Address: _____

    _____

    Attention of: _____

    Telecopy: _____

    If to **Advisor**:   Name:

    Address: _____

    _____

    Attention of: _____

    Telecopy: _____

    If to **Consultant**: Name:

    Address: _____

    _____

    Attention of: _____

    Telecopy: _____

19. **Appraisal Reports.** **Custodian** will prepare and deliver to **Client** a monthly appraisal report containing information on **Client's** holdings and transactions. If Advisor is a bank, **Client** hereby directs **Advisor** to send quarterly appraisals, based on what **Advisor** believes is held in **Client's** custody account, to **Consultant** on behalf of **Client.**

Check if appropriate and initial:

_____   [   ] **Consultant** will deliver to **Client** a quarterly performance measurement report on **Advisor.**

20. **Acknowledgement of Receipt of Documents.** **Client** acknowledges receipt from **Consultant** of (1) Part II of **Advisor's** Form ADV or Advisers Act Rule 204-3 brochure more than 48 hours prior to entering into this Agreement, or

(2) if **Advisor** is a bank, organizational and investment-related information about **Advisor.**

21. **Arbitration.** Unless unenforceable due to federal or state law, any controversy or claim, including, but not limited to, errors and omissions arising out of or relating to this Agreement or the breach thereof, shall be settled by arbitration in accordance with the rules, then in effect, of the American Arbitration Association ("AAA") or, if AAA shall refuse to arbitrate any such controversy, by such arbitrators as the parties shall mutually agree upon. Judgment upon any award rendered by the arbitrators may be entered in any court having jurisdiction thereof. Any arbitration shall be held in the state and county in which the principal office of **Advisor** is located. Nothing in this Agreement shall constitute a waiver or limitation of any right that **Client** may have under any provision of the federal securities laws, including the right to choose the forum, whether arbitration or adjudication, in which to seek dispute resolution.

22. **Entire Agreement.** This Agreement constitutes the entire agreement between the parties and can be amended only by a written document signed by both parties.

Agreed to effective as of this _____ **day of** _____ **199** _____ **by:**

_____

Typed Name and Title, if any, of Signatory

_____

Name of Client

_____

Client's Address

Agreed and Accepted by:

_____   _____

Name   Title   Date

_____

Name of Advisor

_____

Advisor's Address

EXHIBIT A Sample Uniform Investment Management Agreement

Account Size Minimum:	*Fee Schedule:*
$500,000	.40 percent on the first $500,000.
	.35 percent on the next $1.5 million
	.30 percent over $2 million

The **Advisor** will be paid in arrears quarterly. Quarterly fees shall be based on the Account's market value as of the close of business on the last business day of the quarter. Accounts opened or closed during the quarter shall be charged a prorated fee. Any unearned fees which have been prepaid at the date of termination will be refunded.

Advisor's Investment Strategy: Growth Equity

Manager A's investment process is based on identifying companies which have a projected growth rate greater than the market, significant product niche, stable management team and strong financials.

Research is conducted internally while relying on "street" research for information only, not opinions. The firm does not visit with company management, believing that company information flows directly to "street" analysts. In-house efforts focus on annual reports and in-depth conversations with brokers.

Screening a universe of 400 companies, analysis focuses on the management record; its products, markets and competition; its costs and cash flows. The firm employs 8 growth screens focusing on the internal cash flow of the company, projected earnings growth rate over a three and five-year time period, and trading volume. The resulting universe of approximately 120 names typically has an average market capitalization in excess of $500 million.

The firm's 10 research analysts, divided by industry, concentrate on the resulting companies and compile in-depth reports on up to 10 new names within their industry to present to the Investment Committee. The Committee meets formally on a bi-weekly basis to discuss the current holdings and the analysts' reports on any new names; typically 30 new companies are presented or revisited on a weekly basis. The Committee ranks the names, including current holdings and any new names, based on several growth-oriented and valuation screens. Those companies that remain in the bottom 10th percentile of the ranking for three consecutive weeks are sold out of all portfolios. Average annual portfolio turnover is 65%.

Portfolios hold 20-30 issues. Average market capitalization of the portfolios is $5.2 billion; 10% of the portfolio typically represents an average market capitalization of less than $3 billion.

EXHIBIT B   Authorization to Act on Behalf of Client

Must check one:

     [   ]   Trustees of Plan

     [   ]   ERISA: Named Fiduciary

     [   ]   Other, please identify _____

Authority to appoint an investment manager is contained in the document entitled

_____.

Evidence of signatory authority is attached. A copy of the entire Plan/Trust documents is maintained at: _____.

As described in the above document, appointment of an investment manager is the specific responsibility of _____.

     Current Members are:

     _____

     _____

     _____

     _____

     _____

     _____

     _____

     The Named Fiduciary within the meaning of ERISA is:

     _____

     Current Members are:

     _____

     _____

STEP 4 CONT.— IMPLEMENTATION: STRUCTURE AND ALTERNATIVE INVESTMENTS

"A winner ... knows how much he still has to learn, even when he is considered an expert by others; A loser ... wants to be considered an expert by others, before he has even learned how little he knows."

Sydney Harris

"There are two times in a man's life when he should not speculate in stocks: when he can't afford it, and when he can."

Mark Twain

This chapter continues with the general topic of the decision-making process involved in implementing the investment policy statement (IPS). It specifically addresses some of the theoretical issues typically debated during the implementation phase of the investment management process, some of which may affect the manager selection process detailed in the previous chapter. These include

- Passive (indexing) versus active money management strategies.

173

- Mutual funds versus separately managed portfolios.
- Structuring international or global investments in a portfolio.
- Market timing and tactical asset allocation.
- Dollar cost averaging and value averaging versus lump sum investing.
- Guaranteed investment contracts (GICs) and synthetic GICs.
- The use of alternative investments.

Passive versus Active Investment Strategies

One of the first decisions to make when implementing an investment allocation is whether passive and/or active management strategies will be employed in whole or in part. Passive investing, also referred to as *indexing,* involves buying an investment product that contains the entire basket of stocks that make up the index, or asset class, the investor has chosen as an appropriate performance objective. For example, if the asset allocation calls for 60 percent of the portfolio to be allocated to core equities, and the S&P 500 is selected as the appropriate benchmark, then the passive strategy would be to invest 60 percent of the portfolio in an S&P 500 index fund. This is contrasted with active management, where a money manager is hired to sort through the universe of stocks and bonds and to select only those that are appropriate for the account's investment objectives or the manager's investment strategy.

Indexing has been around for a long time but gained significant popularity in the late 80s as well-known and respected academicians and practitioners advanced the premise that it was not worth the risk to try to beat the index. They cited as evidence the performance results of equity money managers through the 80s that showed that well over 60 percent of the managers underperformed the indexes. The underperformance, coupled with higher fees and transaction costs for the active management, convinced many institutional investors to switch from active to passive management strategies.

A common flaw in this research was that all equity managers were lumped together and compared against the S&P 500. The research did not isolate money managers into investment styles (value, growth), nor did it look at managers based on average portfolio capitalization weightings. These factors would have resulted in a different conclusion. Today, the average active equity manager builds a portfolio that holds stocks that are not as large (relative to cap weighting) as those of the S&P 500. When large cap stocks are in favor, as was the case in the mid-to-late 80s, the index will outperform active managers. When small-to-mid cap stocks are in favor, as has been the case in the 90s, active managers will tend to outperform the common indexes.[1]

Indexing versus active management can best be decided by comparing groups of managers to their proper indexes. In the case of core equities, the proper index would be the S&P 500. Value and growth indexes, such as BARRA and Wilshire, are becoming more accessible in financial publications due to their acceptance and use in the marketplace. Style-specific index mutual funds are also becoming more readily available at index-like expense ratios.

Advantages of Indexing

- The passive strategy seeks to avoid both stock selection decisions and the timing of purchases and sales.
- Securities are purchased across all sectors of the market that the index replicates. This results in increased diversification and avoids money manager risk. (The manager concentrates in only certain sectors.)
- Indexing results in lower implementation costs since the purchase is executed with mutual or pooled funds where transaction and administrative costs are shared among all investors (shareholders).
- There is certainty in matching the risk/reward profile and performance measurement standards established in the IPS.

Disadvantages of Indexing

- Indexing requires an efficient market, whereas active management seeks to exploit mispricing in the marketplace.
- Improved technology has made the development of indexing possible. The same technology has also made it possible to discover inefficiencies in the market that make indexing an imperfect practice.

---

[1] Scott M. Elliot, "Tracking Down the Value of Active Management: The Good News and the Bad," *The Journal of Investing,* Winter 1993.

- Indexing can be erroneously interpreted to mean only the S&P 500 index. This can expose a portfolio to the large cap bias inherent in the S&P 500.
- Some active managers will begin to build cash when securities become, in their opinion, overpriced. If a correction does occur, the cash portion should cushion the portfolio from losses that would have been incurred had the portfolio been fully invested.
- An index fund will always vary from the actual index performance due to execution costs (the actual index does not take into consideration commission costs), cash awaiting investment or raised to meet redemptions, and management fees. These are collectively referred to as the tracking error of the fund.

Mutual Funds versus Separate Account Portfolios

Over the long term, research has not shown any significant difference in performance between mutual funds[2] and separate accounts. Both can be used to effectively implement an investment strategy. The differences are primarily a matter of the investor's personal preference.

A smaller portfolio may be limited to mutual funds because of minimum account size restrictions. Most no-load mutual funds have an initial minimum account size of about $2,500. As technology in trading no-load funds has improved, account minimums have decreased. An investor that allocates a portfolio between asset (and subasset) classes should not have any difficulty finding suitable no-load mutual funds with accessible minimums.

A separate account manager with an established track record will generally have an account size minimum around $5 million. Some managers may command minimums as high as $50 million. As a manager's reputation and track record increase, it is not unusual for the manager to begin to increase the account minimum. Several managers who normally have higher minimums have, however, agreed to accept accounts as low as $100,000 when an outside organization, such as a brokerage or consulting firm, has agreed to assume responsibility for sales, marketing, and client servicing.

---

[2] Included within the general discussion of mutual funds are commingled funds that are offered by banks and insurance companies. However, they lack the disclosure requirements of mutual funds and may not have the same level of regulatory oversight as mutual funds due to the lack of SEC jurisdiction.

At what account size should an investor begin to consider using separate account managers instead of mutual funds? There are a number of variables to be considered, but the asset class selection will have the primary influence on the answer. It is easier to establish a lower minimum separate account for a large cap domestic equity portfolio than for an international portfolio, particularly one invested in emerging markets.

As a general rule, most upper retail and middle market accounts (size $500,000 to $50 million) will use a combination of mutual funds and separate account managers to implement their investment strategies. Large cap domestic equity and core fixed-income portfolios may be established with separate account managers. Small cap and international asset classes would be implemented with mutual funds. Institutional accounts (accounts larger than $100 million) usually use separate account managers rather than mutual funds due to cost efficiency. Many institutional accounts do use funds, however, to provide short-term market exposure with cash positions so that the portfolio is always fully invested according to stated investment guidelines. For example, an equity mutual fund would be used as a sweep vehicle for dividend payments until sufficient dollars were accumulated to be reallocated to separate account managers.

The following is a summary of some of the differences that exist between separately managed accounts and mutual (or pooled) funds.

Costs. Mutual funds spread their costs across all shareholders, and unless there are different classes of shares for larger shareholders, larger shareholders end up subsidizing a larger percentage of costs. For this reason, most institutional investors use separate accounts.

Audits. Mutual funds are required to be audited by independent accounting firms. Money managers are encouraged to have performance results audited, but this is not required. (AIMR Standards have taken steps to cure this deficiency. See Chapter 8.) Access to information and performance data is more readily available for mutual funds than for separate account managers.

Tax Planning Opportunities. With a separately managed account, a taxable investor has some degree of tax-planning flexibility. At year end the money manager could be instructed to sell off investment losses to offset investment gains, and the sold stocks could be repurchased again after

30 days to effect a tax swap. This paper loss may be used to offset other gains recognized during the tax year. In addition, short-term capital gains from mutual funds are taxed as dividend income. They are reported on an investor's 1099-DIV each year. Only mutual fund long-term capital gains are reported as a separate line item to be added with the taxpayer's other long-term capital gains. In a separately managed account, short-term gains are netted against long-term losses (if they exist). This can benefit the taxpayer because of the tax rate differential between dividend income and capital gains. It also provides the individual investor with the ability to utilize losses to offset both long- and short-term capital gains.

Phantom Tax Gain. When an investor buys into a mutual fund, there may exist unrealized capital gains tax liabilities in the portfolio. For example, if a mutual fund purchased ABC stock for $30, held it for several years, and then sold it for $75, all mutual fund shareholders in the fund would be hit with the same capital gain—even if the shareholder had just bought into the fund the day before the capital gains distribution was declared.

Short Short Rule. In order for a mutual fund to be able to pass through gain and income to its shareholders, it must satisfy certain stringent tax rules. If these rules are violated, a fund can find itself being taxed as a corporation with the distributions to shareholders being dividends (and subject to tax again). One of the rules that must be followed is the short short rule.[3] This rule requires the fund to hold stock or securities that have been purchased for at least 90 days prior to sale. If more than 30 percent of a fund's annual gross income comes from disposition of stock or securities held less than 90 days, the fund has failed one of the tests. With a professionally managed account, no such restrictions exist. The ability to quickly buy and sell can be of great economic value to a managed account, especially in volatile markets.

Fund Liquidation and Purchases. Besides managing the securities portfolio of the mutual fund, the mutual fund manager must also contend with purchases and liquidations within the fund from new or existing shareholders. This can become a problem when major market movements occur and investors begin to follow the herd. In a down market

---

[3] Internal Revenue Code Sec. 815(b)(3).

the manager may be forced to sell securities at fire sale rates, further depressing the net asset value of the mutual fund. Managers may also be faced with having to hold more cash than they would like because of the possible need to meet liquidations.

Diversification.   Most mutual funds hold 80–120 different securities. In a separately managed account, the number of securities is usually half that amount. For an investor who is willing to accept greater performance volatility, with anticipated greater returns, a more concentrated portfolio (fewer securities) may be more appropriate.

Tax Deductible Management Fee.   With a mutual fund, an individual investor cannot deduct the management and transaction fees for the fund. The net asset value of the fund takes into account these deductions. However, an individual can deduct the fees paid to a money manager of a separately managed account. The fee is part of the individual's miscellaneous itemized deductions taken each year.[4]

Brokerage Expenses.   Mutual fund expense ratios do not include the brokerage costs incurred to buy and sell securities in and out of the fund. Many funds turn over their portfolios quite frequently. The trading activity from new contributions and redemptions being made can increase this expense. The total costs for the average mutual fund can be very similar to those of a separately managed account if these additional costs are added to the total expenses of investment management.[5]

Investment Education.   Separately managed account investors receive annual and quarterly reports from the companies in which they hold shares. For many investors, this is an excellent way to understand the process the manager is following in analyzing and selecting the stocks for the portfolio. Mutual funds also send annual and quarterly reports to their shareholders detailing the security positions held by the fund. However, very little information is usually provided about the specific companies, their financial condition, or their products/services.

Specific Identification of Securities.   With a separately managed account, the investor is kept up-to-date with trading activity through receipt of either confirmations on trades or a monthly custodial statement showing

---

[4] Internal Revenue Code Sec. 212.

[5] Brokerage expenses can be found in the Statement of Additional Information requested from the mutual fund organization.

all transactions. The investor knows exactly what securities are in the portfolio. With a mutual fund, the shareholder receives less frequent reports showing total fund holdings.

In addition, a separately managed account can avoid illiquid securities or inappropriate securities being purchased. As an example, if a derivative security is to be permissible in a separately managed account, it would have been specified in the securities guidelines for the IPS. Investments allowed in a mutual fund (disclosed in the prospectus) may be defined so broadly that an investor is unaware that these types of securities are utilized until after the market has already significantly depressed their value.

Control over Asset Allocation. Because separately managed portfolios can be examined on a daily basis, it is easier to monitor the account's commitment to appropriate or different asset classes. It is not unusual for equity mutual funds to hold high percentages of cash or for a perceived domestic equity or balanced fund to hold international securities. The mutual fund manager may be betting his fund assets on market segments not previously utilized but permissible under the prospectus. Again, manager discretion may be overly broad in a mutual fund setting but capable of being controlled in a separately managed account.

Performance. Mutual funds report performance on a net-asset-value basis, representing performance after all recurring fees have been deducted. On the other hand, separate account managers typically report performance on a gross-of-fees basis.

Fees and Compensation. There may be circumstances when certain investment fees are desired to be paid separately, such as a company that wants to pay all pension plan management expenses. In a mutual fund, these fees cannot be separately paid since they are incurred at the fund level, not the investor level.

Also, employment contracts for mutual fund managers tend to be structured so the manager is provided with a bonus for outperforming his or her peer group. While there is little opposition to such an incentive, it does create the possibility of undue risk or major sector bets (such as technology stocks). This is one of the reasons it is so hard to find out exactly what positions a mutual fund manager may be holding on a current basis. This clouds the portfolio in secrecy since the manager does not want competitors to know the fund's holdings. The SEC does not require that portfolio positions be disclosed to a shareholder on a current basis.

Structuring International Portfolios

For purposes of the following discussion, international and global investing are limited to the decision-making process that must be managed and to the identification of the primary issues to be considered in implementing this asset class. There are unique attributes and challenges of investing in international asset classes that must be considered.

A distinction must be made between international and global investment strategies. International investing involves constructing portfolios with non–U.S. securities. Global portfolio managers, on the other hand, consider securities from *both* non–U.S. and U.S. financial markets. The tendency is for smaller separate accounts to go global because they are not large enough to maintain distinct international and domestic portfolios. More and more investment decisions are made with a global perspective through the use of money management firms that are equally comfortable and confident in investing in any of the world's financial markets.

Depending on the risk tolerance level and return objective of the portfolio, step 2 of the investment management process will typically include an examination of international investment class alternatives. Most investment consulting firms and academicians agree that it is worthwhile to add international asset classes to an optimization model that includes a commitment to equities. When as little as 10 percent, but not more than 40 percent, of the equity portfolio is allocated to international equities, expected returns are greater with a corresponding decrease in risk. See Table 7–1.

An allocation to international capital markets, whether it be fixed income or equity, will provide some diversification benefits to most portfolios. Most investors, however, make their first international allocation into equities (equity markets are relatively more efficient than fixed income) and later add fixed income. The addition of the second international asset class (typically fixed income) does not add as much benefit to the total optimization equation as the first.

TABLE 7–1   The Impact of Adding International Equities

Equity Mix	Expected Return	Worst Case Scenario
100% Domestic/ 0% International	9.8%	− 9.1%
90% Domestic/ 10% International	9.9%	− 8.8%
80% Domestic/ 20% International	10.0%	− 8.8%
70% Domestic/ 30% International	10.1%	− 8.9%
60% Domestic/ 40% International	10.2%	− 9.3%
50% Domestic/ 50% International	10.3%	− 9.9%
40% Domestic/ 60% International	10.4%	− 10.7%
20% Domestic/ 80% International	10.5%	− 12.6%
0% Domestic/100% International	10.7%	− 14.9%

Source: Derived from the 1994 capital markets model developed by Callan Associates Inc.

If international investing has not been previously utilized in a portfolio, the IPS, prepared in step 3, should be rewritten to reflect not only the new risk-and-reward profile, but also new performance benchmarks, monitoring procedures, currency hedging policies, and securities guidelines. Of critical importance is the decision whether the international equity portfolio will be invested in developed nations only (Japan, Germany, Great Britain, and so on), or whether it will also have an allocation to emerging markets. The suggested approach is an allocation to both since country allocation decisions (i.e., investing in Mexico and avoiding Hong Kong) have had far more impact on performance returns than stock selection.

A relevant performance benchmark must also be identified in the IPS. This can be challenging. The industry standard, Morgan Stanley Capital International European, Australia and Far East (MSCI EAFE) Index, covers only 22 countries and is cap weighted. The cap weighting is heavily influenced by the larger Japanese market. A second index, the Financial Times Actuaries Index (FT-A) captures slightly more of the market, including a small cap component. Active international managers can minimize exposure to underperforming markets and easily beat the index if the index is too broad. The best known benchmark for international fixed income is the Salomon Brothers World Government Bond Index (WGBI).

The move into international securities exposes the investor to currency risks which may be reduced by various hedging and futures alternatives. U.S. dollars that are invested overseas (the act of buying and selling foreign securities) must, at some point, be converted to local currency. If the price of the U.S. dollar rises after the investment, the investor will suffer in return performance. For example, if the portfolio is invested in Japanese equities that have earned a 4 percent return in yen, an increase in the value of the U.S. dollar versus the yen may wipe out the gain.

To mitigate or avoid currency market risk, some managers will buy futures in the specific foreign currency to lock in all or a substantial portion of the value of the invested U.S. dollar. In general, money managers can be categorized three different ways, depending on the currency strategy they employ:

Opportunistic managers hedge currencies in an overt move to add value to the existing investment. In essence, the manager is treating futures as an additional asset class and has allocated more than is necessary to adequately hedge the position.

Defensive managers hedge in an effort to protect existing investments against unfavorable changes in the exchange rate.

Passive managers choose not to hedge.

Some large institutional investors have chosen to divide the currency hedging decisions from the security selection process. In those cases, a separate currency overlay manager is chosen. This manager's specific job is to position futures contracts and hedging strategies so that the entire portfolio stays monetarily neutral. The intended purpose is to remove the impact of foreign currency fluctuations from the portfolio.

To implement an international allocation, the decision to follow a passive versus active management strategy is similar to the discussion at the beginning of this chapter regarding passive versus active strategies (see Table 7–2). The primary difference with international implementation is that the passive strategy is fully allocated across all international markets. As mentioned in the discussion about benchmarks, active managers have been able to weight country allocations sufficiently to be able to outperform the passive index.

If the decision is made to implement the allocation to international asset classes through an active strategy, the next decision is whether to use a separately managed account or a mutual fund. The pros and cons are summarized in Table 7–3 with the key difference being the substantial cost differential between the two for portfolios of less than $10 million ($25 million for emerging markets). The separate account should only be considered by larger institutional investors that need the custom-built portfolio. The exception may be hiring a U.S. manager that utilizes ADRs to obtain foreign market participation. Although not a perfect proxy for international investing, the benefits of a separately managed portfolio may overcompensate for the differences.

TABLE 7–2 International Portfolios: Active versus Passive

	Pros	*Cons*
International passive	Highly liquid	Fully invested
	Unhedged	Market inefficiencies
	Easy to assemble	Country weighted (e.g., Japan)
	Accommodates large	Large cap bias
	allocations	Inflexible short term
	Lower fees	Limited number of players
	Assures diversification	Currency risk
International active	Global overview	Higher costs
	Currency management	Large minimum account sizes
	Leverage market	
	inefficiencies	
	Multiple styles/strategies	

TABLE 7–3 International: Separate Accounts versus Mutual Funds

	Pros	*Cons*
International separate accounts	Customized reporting	Need global custodian
	Education benefits	Increased costs:
	Access to managers	• Trading
	Ability to impose guidelines	• Custody
		• Money managers
International mutual funds	Low maintenance	Client servicing may be less
	Low minimum account size	attentive
	Global custodian in place	Tied to investment approach
	Reduced administrative costs	Possible entry/exit fees
	Diversification of securities	Trustee-imposed limitations

Assuming an active strategy has been selected and separate account management will be used, the next critical decision is the selection of a custodian. The trading, settlement, and custody of international assets are extremely complex and challenging for even the largest of master trustees around the world. A brilliantly conceived investment strategy developed by a money manager can be easily rendered average by an ineffective global custodian that cannot adequately execute trades. The money manager selected may be the first choice for a discussion about a qualified custodian if the current custodial relationship will not adequately serve the needs of the investor. Points that must be considered in selecting a global custodian include

Does the custodian have an effective global network of subcustodians?

What are the trade processing capabilities of the custodian?

What are the foreign exchange (FX) capabilities of the custodian, and what has been the traditional markup or spread on the exchange? (For many global custodians, this trading function generates their greatest profits.)

How quickly can the custodian settle trades? (This question underscores the importance of the subcustodian network.)

How does the custodian handle proxy voting, dividend collection, and foreign tax reclamation?

How will ERISA jurisdiction issues be dealt with if a qualified plan is in place?

The Pitfalls of Market Timing

There are many investment management topics where fiduciaries, investors, and consultants have widely different opinions about the same subject. The topic of market timing, however, is not one of them. Though attempts at market timing exist, the overwhelming consensus is that market timing is a fool's game since it is statistically improbable that some system or someone can consistently *time* when to be in or out of the market. There are differences between strategic asset allocation, tactical asset allocation, and market timing, albeit a discussion of one inevitably leads to another.

Strategic asset allocation involves setting a specific asset allocation and rather tight rebalancing limits, such as $+/-$ 5 percent. The
logic is that each investor has specific risk/return objectives and cash
flow requirements. Once the unique attributes of a portfolio have been
determined, the strategy that carries the least investment risk for the
investor is the optimal mix of assets derived from the asset allocation
study (step 2 of the process).

Tactical asset allocation is one step removed from strategic asset
allocation. Tactical planning attempts to improve investment returns
by taking advantage of obvious transitory imbalances between historical and current returns of the different asset classes. It involves a contrarian view of the markets—that when everyone is buying, the tactical
allocator is selling because markets are overpriced relative to historical
norms. By definition, the tactical allocator begins with the strategic asset
allocation and sells off small percentages (5 percent) at a time of the
perceived overvalued asset class and buys the undervalued asset class.

FIGURE 7–1   **Tactical Asset Allocation**

PURPOSE:	Active management of strategic asset allocation

STRATEGY:	Taking advantage of transitory imbalances between historical risk and return expectations

Execution:
1. **Set band around strategic asset allocation.**
   Example:

Strategic Allocation		Tactical Bands of 10%	
40%	Equity	30–50%	Equities
50%	Fixed Income	40–60%	Fixed Income
10%	Cash	0–20%	Cash

2. **Appoint specialists for equity, fixed income, and a Swing Manager (tactical allocator) to manage asset bands.**

30%	Core equity manager
40%	Core fixed-income manager
30%	Swing manager to allocate between equity, fixed income, and cash

Source: Copyright © 1993, Investment Management Council.

There are a number of balanced money managers that state they follow a tactical balanced philosophy. Figure 7–1 shows how they would be used in concert with traditional equity and fixed income managers.

Market timing involves total or large-scale shifts in the portfolio's allocation between stocks, bonds, and cash. When the market timer is bullish, 100 percent of the portfolio is invested in stocks. Conversely, when the timer anticipates a market correction, 100 percent of the portfolio is invested in cash. For a timer to add value above the returns that can be achieved following a strategic asset allocation strategy, the timer has to correctly implement the following steps:

1. Identify the relative position of the current economy to a full market cycle.
2. Identify the factors that will impact the value of securities within each asset class.

FIGURE 7–2   Market Timing Study

Summary:
One must consider the "risks" associated with being out of the market.

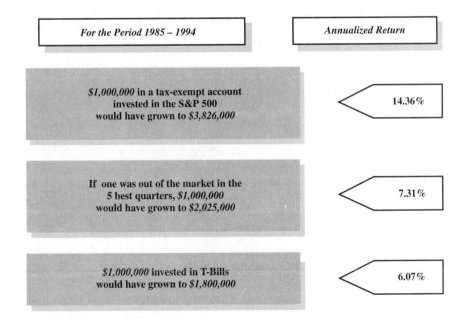

For the Period 1985 – 1994	Annualized Return
$1,000,000 in a tax-exempt account invested in the S&P 500 would have grown to *$3,826,000*	14.36%
If one was out of the market in the 5 best quarters, *$1,000,000* would have grown to *$2,025,000*	7.31%
$1,000,000 invested in T-Bills would have grown to *$1,800,000*	6.07%

Source: Copyright© 1995, Investment Management Council.

3. Identify the asset class that will benefit from evolving price scenarios.

4. Weigh the exposure to each asset class.

5. Liquidate current holdings to realize accumulated gains.

6. Redeploy the assets to exploit the succeeding economic scenario.

7. Effectively control transaction costs to minimize impact on performance.

It is worth repeating that, in order for timing to work, *all* of the above steps have to be correctly executed. It doesn't help the long-term investor to be pulled out of the market before a crash, only to miss the inevitable bull market that follows, as Figure 7–2 illustrates.

Dollar-Cost and Value Averaging versus Lump-Sum Investing

When money managers (mutual funds) have been selected, the final decision is the timing of the funding of the account. There are two alternatives: *dollar-cost averaging (*and its cousin *value averaging)* or *lump-sum investing.* Neither strategy has a clear-cut advantage from a cost and performance standpoint.

Dollar-cost averaging involves making equal weighted deposits over a given period of time. The goal is to reduce the risks of a sudden downturn in the markets by slowly buying into a particular asset class. Dollar-cost averaging has been particularly successful during periods of volatile markets, defined as either a rapidly rising or falling market. There is no magical formula defining an appropriate deposit schedule, but transaction costs should be considered. For this reason, mutual funds are generally a more appropriate vehicle for dollar cost averaging than separately managed accounts. One strategy would be to space implementation over the course of a year with quarterly purchases (sells). A second strategy would be to space the implementation over six months with monthly purchases (sells). Whichever strategy is adopted, it is important to maintain the adopted implementation schedule.

Value averaging is similar to dollar-cost averaging except that instead of investing a fixed amount at each time period, the ending value of the portfolio is determined and an amount is either added to or taken away from the account. This way, the total value of the portfolio is increased only by the amount of the intended periodic investment. With value averaging the period and ending values are known, but the amount to invest each period is unknown. With dollar-cost averaging, the amount to invest each period is known, but the period and ending values are unknown. As an example:

		Dollar Cost Averaging ($100 invested per period)		Value Averaging ($100 increment per period)	
Period	Unit Value	Units	Value	Units	Value
1	$10	10.00	$100.00	10.00	$100.00
2	9	11.11	$190.00	12.22	$200.00
3	12	8.33	$353.32	2.78	$300.00
4	8	12.50	$335.52	25.00	$400.00
5	$11	9.09	$561.34	(4.55)	$500.00
Total		51.03		45.45	

Although dollar-cost averaging can result in a greater ending amount, in many instances value averaging has actually been shown to produce a higher internal rate of return.[6] This is because one is selling when values rise dramatically and allocating more funds when values fall.

Lump-sum investing calls for the strategic asset allocation to be implemented over a relatively short period of time—a matter of weeks. Purists stoically defend this strategy as the most prudent course of action. The argument is made that once an appropriate asset allocation has been determined, delays in implementation can be viewed as attempts to market time (lost opportunity risk). Arguably, the initial short-term fluctuations will have minimal impact on the long-term performance of the portfolio if the long-term time horizon is kept in focus.

Guaranteed Investment Contracts (GICs)

Over the last several decades, a popular investment vehicle for retirement plans has been the guaranteed investment contract (GIC), also known as the guaranteed insurance contract. GICs are issued by insurance

---

[6] John Markese, "Starting an Investment Program with Dollar Cost Averaging," *AAII Journal* 14, No. 8 (September 1992), p. 29.

companies that assume the risk of the return of principal as well as an agreed upon interest rate. A retirement plan sponsor can enter into a contract with an insurance company that would guarantee that on a specified date the amount invested with the insurance carrier would be returned with interest, much like a CD. The agreed-upon interest rate is typically a rate set between what short and intermediate fixed-income portfolios are yielding at the time of the negotiations.

GIC funds are deposited and commingled in the insurance company's general account. Retirement plans that had a defined obligation at some future date, such as a defined benefit plan, and entered into GICs prior to March 20, 1992, enjoyed the fact that the GIC could be carried at book value, thus avoiding interim fluctuations in asset values. Financial Accounting Standards Board (FASB) Statement 110 now requires defined benefit plans to carry GICs at fair market value. Defined contribution plans, however, can continue to carry GICs at book value. Some retirement plans that are risk adverse find the GICs attractive because the principal and interest are guaranteed.

Problems arose with GICs in the 90s when three major insurance carriers—Executive Life, Mutual Benefit, and Confederation Life—required government rehabilitation, leaving GIC holders in a lurch. Fiduciaries of retirement plans that had invested with these insurance carriers found themselves accountable to the Department of Labor (DOL) and their plan participants for the due diligence that went into the selection of the insurance carriers and the selection of GICs as an appropriate investment option.

As a result of these problems, the insurance industry has responded by providing an alternative solution—separate accounts and synthetic GICs. Separate account GICs, also known as asset-backed GICs, have been around since the 60s. The assets are held outside the general account of the carrier. Therefore, if the carrier fails, the GIC policyholder is not waiting in line with the carrier's other creditors.[7]

---

[7] Separate account designation to avoid seizure of these assets is still a function of state jurisdiction. In the case of Mutual Benefit, the New Jersey Insurance Commissioner was not successful in seizing the assets of these separate GIC accounts. The insurance regulations in New York, however, suggest that the assets in these separate accounts belong to the insurance company and may be chargeable against the general liabilities of the insurance company in the event the insurance company fails.

With a separate account, the retirement plan sponsor generally must structure the portfolio characteristics: for example, developing an investment policy statement which would state what would be acceptable as an average maturity, duration, and credit rating for the portfolios underlying fixed-income securities. Like a traditional GIC, the insurance carrier assumes the risk of the difference between market and book value. Unlike a traditional GIC, the interest rate is restated on a more frequent basis, such as every six months. The advantage of the separate account is that it is easier for the retirement plan fiduciary to perform due diligence on the underlying securities and to monitor the activities of the portfolio manager. This overcomes one of the major disadvantages of the traditional GIC, in that the fiduciary was left in the blind in understanding in what the GIC was invested, or what the portfolio manager's strategy was going to be.

In response to the concerns about separate account GICs, synthetic GICs were also made available in the marketplace. Synthetic GICs provide for two contracts. One contract is with a bond manager. The other contract is with a financial institution that wraps the bond portfolio by agreeing to make up any difference between market value and book value for all participant withdrawals. The yields for synthetic GICs are typically lower than for traditional GICs.

In conducting due diligence on insurance carriers offering traditional GICs, separate account GICs, or synthetic GICs, the following should be observed:

- What is the carrier's rating according to A. M. Best, Moody's, and/or Standard & Poor's? A carrier should, at least, have a top rating from two out of the three carriers.

- Does the carrier adhere to stated investment strategies?

- Are the carrier's portfolios properly diversified?

- What are the benefit-paying obligations of the carrier across all product lines?

- Does the carrier have enough liquidity to pay benefits when due?

Alternative Investments [8]

Alternative investments can be defined as institutional blind pool limited
partnerships that make private debt and equity investments in privately
held companies or direct asset investments. Neither the partnerships nor
the investments they make are registered with the SEC. The most common
examples are venture capital and leveraged buyout funds, but other preva-
lent strategies include subordinated debt, bankruptcy investing, and oil
and gas partnerships. Some investors consider hedge funds and other
publicly traded derivative–based strategies also as alternative investments.

Because of the large dollar denomination of the partnerships, they
typically require a significant commitment of $20 to $30 million to begin
building a diversified portfolio. Most institutional partnership minimums
are in the $1 to $5 million range, with a minimum of six partnerships
needed to properly diversify a portfolio for geography, industry, and
strategy. At present, most retirement plans commit only 1 percent to 5
percent of their assets to this asset class.

For the more adventurous investor, a fund-of-funds can provide a
diversified approach to venture capital and occasionally other types
of alternative investment strategies. A fund-of-funds is a commingled
blind pool that in turn invests in other limited partnership or direct
placement offerings. A benefit of these vehicles is having a single
reporting relationship for a diversity of funds. Partnerships that
invest in other partnerships still typically require minimums in the
$1 to $5 million range.

Procedural Due Diligence

There are two aspects to creating or managing an alternative investment program for a portfolio. The first is strategic planning and establishing an administrative process, and the second involves selecting
the actual investments.

Security or partnership due diligence is akin to the stock and bond
research performed by security analysts in the publicly traded arena, the
difference being that partnership analysis is more qualitative in nature
because partnerships are blind pools and have no specified assets at
the outset. There are three areas to examine in any partnership opportunity. The first is whether the investment strategy and expected outcome

---

[8] This section was prepared by Gary Robertson, Callan Associates Inc..

are viable and realistic. The second is whether the partnership management team has the knowledge and skill to properly execute the investment plan. The third is whether the terms and conditions of the limited partnership are fair, do not contain material conflicts of interest, and properly align the interests of all parties involved.

Is the Investment Strategy Realistic? Most investment partnerships have a strong element of "sizzle" that is alluring. Exotic investments in oil and gas partnerships, leasing partnerships, venture capital, or buyout funds must be evaluated as part of the strategic appropriateness for the retirement plan. Partnerships typically base the promise of future success on past performance. However, the state of the capital market is constantly changing, and a successful business plan or investment style at one point in time may quickly become outdated. The proposed business plan must fit with the perceived economic, business, and competitive environments of the ensuing investment period.

Are the General Partners Qualified? As many of the partnerships are blind pools, one is essentially investing in the resume of the general partner (GP). To the extent the investment does not already have specified assets, one must make determinations about the GP's ability to execute the proposed investment plan and manage all of the rather complex aspects of fund management: deal flow, investment evaluation, decision process, negotiation and closing, monitoring, adding value, and exiting to maximize value. The ability to accurately make these determinations will have a major effect on whether private investing will have positive results. Partnerships are very long lived and once the documents are signed, the investment decision will have to be maintained for a long time. Over the past 20 years, a due diligence framework for evaluating partnerships has been established and an overview of the key areas to be explored are provided in the appendix to this chapter.

Partnership Structure. Partnership terms cannot change a bad investment into a good one, but can make a superior investment of a good one. The terms and provisions in alternative investment partnership agreements are becoming more standardized as competition for investment dollars has increased. In pure institutional partnerships, the terms and conditions are negotiated between the GP and the limited partners (LPs). One or two LPs who take the lead in the investment usually set the terms the smaller or later investors must accept. In retail partnerships, there may not be any room for improvement or for customization of requirements.

It cannot be assumed that the business plan will unfold as expected. It is important for LPs to build in protective covenants, so that positive action can be taken if investments do not perform to reasonable standards. Legally, limited partnership agreements give almost absolute powers to the GPs, except for those LP rights and provisions that are explicitly written into the agreement. A list of structural elements to examine is included in the checklist in the chapter appendix.

There are very few disclosure requirements and little active regulatory oversight in the private placements arena. The history of institutional private limited partnerships is relatively short, on the order of 20 years for venture capital and less for other strategies such as buyouts or subordinated debt funds. Meaningful quantitative information is scant. Investing in this asset class requires substantial investment analysis.

APPENDIX
ALTERNATIVE INVESTMENTS DUE DILIGENCE CHECKLIST[9]

Due Diligence Questions for Investments in Venture Capital Partnerships

The evaluation of the general partners themselves is intended to determine their level of (1) integrity; (2) experience and prior achievement, ideally in both venture investing and with an operating company; (3) intelligence and creativity; (4) overall investment management skills; and (5) the ability of the partners to work as a team.

A. Evaluation of General Partners.
  1. What is their level of integrity?
  2. Experience.
    a. How many years of venture experience do they have?
    b. Have they been through a full venture portfolio cycle?
    c. Have they experienced economic downturns?
    d. How many years of other related experience do they have?
    e. Do they have operating company experience?
    f. How many deals have the individual partners done?
    g. How extensive is their exit knowledge and experience?
  3. Intelligence.
    a. How solid is their judgment?
    b. How creative are they?
  4. Investment management capability/skills.
    a. What returns were achieved on earlier funds (verify IRR)?
    b. What is their reputation in the venture community?
    c. Can the partners work together as a team?
      (1) How many years have they been working together?
      (2) Is there joint ownership of investments?
      (3) Does their organization promote teamwork?
    d. How many dollars will be under management per general partner?
    e. Is there the capacity to add more dollars given the maturity of portfolio companies?
    f. How many board seats will there be per general manager?
    g. Is there the capacity to add more seats given the maturity of portfolio companies?
    h. How extensive is their network of contacts in accounting, legal, banking, and public relations circles?

---

[9] Special thanks to Gary Robertson for the preparation of this checklist.

    i. What is their philosophy about working with limited partners?

    j. Is there a limited partner advisory board?

    k. What is the relationship with such board?

    l. Is there a technical advisory board?

    m. What is the relationship with such board?

    n. How many offices are there?

    o. Are multiple locations manageable?

    p. Does special industry experience exist (if fund is specialized)?

5. Source of references.

    a. Limited partners of the fund or prior funds.

    b. Other private equity general partners who are familiar with them.

    c. Former employers.

    d. Portfolio companies and board members of portfolio companies.

    e. Entrepreneurs.

    f. Financing sources (banks, insurance companies).

B. Assessment of the Partnership's Investment Strategy. This portion of the evaluation will focus on (1) the reasonableness of the partnership's objectives and the likelihood that they can be achieved and (2) whether the skills of the partners are matched with the type of investments they plan to make.

1. Does the fund have a special focus?

    a. Geographic focus?

    b. Industry focus?

    c. Stage focus?

2. How many dollars will be invested per year?

3. How many deals will be done per year?

4. What will be the minimum/maximum deal size?

5. Does the fund have a co-investment policy?

6. Will the fund share deals with limited partners?

7. What is the fund's follow-on investment strategy?

8. Is investment strategy internally consistent with the background and capabilities of the general partners?

9. What competitive forces are there in the geographic area, industry focus, and so on?

10. What is the preferred deal structure of the fund (debt, preferred stock, warrants, equity, and so on)?

11. How able are the partners to buy public securities?

12. How able are the partners to do leverage buyouts?

13. Do the partners have a technology or nontechnology orientation?

14. Do the partners have a current return or capital gains orientation?

C. Evaluation of the Partnership's Due Diligence Process. The evaluation will determine the quality of the due diligence performed by the partnership when it investigates potential portfolio companies. The evaluation will focus on the partnership's ability to (1) ask key questions of appropriate sources and (2) be very thorough.

1. Management assessment of potential portfolio companies.
    a. What key management qualities are sought?
    b. How are objective references obtained?
    c. What questions are references asked?
2. Product/service/concept evaluation.
    a. How are products/services evaluated?
    b. Do the partners have special industry expertise?
3. Market research and evaluation.
    a. What sources are used to evaluate market potential?
    b. How extensive is the market analysis?
    c. In what situations is a consultant hired to perform a market analysis?
4. Financial analysis.
    a. How is the prior performance of potential portfolio companies analyzed?
    b. How are pro forma projections for potential portfolio companies analyzed?
    c. How is the rate of return analyzed for a potential portfolio of a company?
    d. Is an IPO always assumed?
    e. How are potential investments valued (multiples, cash flow, and so on)?
5. Investment decision-making process.
    a. What internal review process is used to screen potential investments?
    b. Who makes the final decision to invest?
    c. How long does the review take?
6. Due diligence documentation.
    a. How is the due diligence process documented?
    b. Is file documentation organized and current?

D. Evaluation of the Partnership's Monitoring Process. This evaluation will look at the partnership's monitoring process to determine the (1) importance placed on monitoring, (2) partners' philosophy about how they will work with portfolio companies, (3) ability of the partners to add value to portfolio companies, and (4) ability of the partners to turn around failing companies.

1. Is the partnership structured to give proper emphasis to monitoring or does it seem to be an afterthought?

2. Board observation/participation.
   a. What observer/directorship rights does the partnership have in a typical investment?
3. Performance information supplied by portfolio companies.
   a. What information is required to be reported by portfolio companies?
   b. How regularly is it reported?
   c. What is the process for review of this information?
4. Nature of working relationships with portfolio companies.
   a. How do the partners characterize their relationship with portfolio companies?
   b. How do portfolio companies characterize their relationship with the venture capital partnership?
5. Sophistication of financial analysis.
   a. What key financial performance measures does the partnership use to evaluate the financial statements of portfolio companies?
   b. Does the partnership use a computer model to analyze the financial statements of portfolio companies? If so, what analysis will the model perform?
6. Services that add value.
   a. What post-investment services does the partnership routinely provide to its portfolio companies?
   b. What special expertise do the partners have that enables them to help portfolio companies?
   c. How do the partners use their network to put the management of their portfolio companies together with special expertise when needed?
   d. Under what circumstances are consultants hired?
7. Capacity to handle turnarounds.
   a. What experience do the partners have with turnarounds?
   b. Generally speaking, what strategies have the partners used to turn failing companies around?
8. Dealing with management problems.
   a. How are management problems resolved?
   b. In what situation(s) is the management of a company replaced?

E. Assessment of the Partnership's Ability to Generate a Deal Flow. This portion of the evaluation will determine how the partners find out about potential investments. Specifically, it will attempt to answer (1) whether the partners are able to originate investments using their reputation and network or whether they tend to be included in investments originated by someone else, and (2) whether they are able to generate a flow of quality investments.

1. How do the partners find out about potential investments?
2. Do the partners generally originate their investments or do they tend to co-invest in deals generated by others?
3. How extensive is the partnership's network of contacts that serves as a source of potential investments?
4. How many deals does the partnership look at in a year?
5. What is the quality of the partnership's deal flow?

F. Assessment of the Partnership's Ability to Structure, Negotiate, and Liquidate Investments.   This portion of the due diligence effort will examine the partners' ability to (1) negotiate the price and structure of an investment so it is consistent with the risk taken and (2) achieve a timely and profitable liquidation of investments.

1. Ability to structure and negotiate investments.
    a. Is the rate of return consistent with the risk taken?
    b. Is the price paid for prior investments appropriate?
    c. What is the level of the general partner's negotiating skills?
2. Ability to successfully and profitably liquidate investments.
    a. Have the partners demonstrated an ability to successfully liquidate venture capital investments?
3. Quality of legal documents.
    a. What is the reputation of the legal firm used by the partnership to prepare its investment documents?
    b. Are the legal documents appropriate and of high quality?

8

STEP 5—MONITORING THE PORTFOLIO

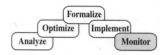

*"It is not the return on my investment that I am concerned about;
it is the return of my investment."*
Will Rogers

*A young banker asked an eighty year old banker
what the secret of success was in banking.*
Old Banker: *"Good judgment."*
Rookie: *"How do you get good judgment?"*
Old Banker: *"Experience."*
Rookie: *"How do you get experience?"*
Old Banker: *"Bad judgment."* [1]

Once the optimal portfolio has been designed and the investment policy
statement (IPS) prepared and implemented, the final critical step is the
ongoing monitoring and supervision of the investment process. The
monitoring function extends beyond a strict examination of performance;
by definition, monitoring occurs across all policy and procedural
issues previously addressed.

---

[1] Joe Griffith, *Speaker's Library of Business Stories, Anecdotes and Humor,* (Englewood
Cliffs, NJ: Prentice Hall, 1990), p. 184.

Fiduciary Requirements to Monitor and Supervise

A common fiduciary breach is the failure to monitor the activities of a money manager once the manager has been hired. It is not enough for the fiduciary to develop strategic long-term investment objectives and hire competent professionals to manage the strategy; the fiduciary must be diligent in fulfilling the oversight responsibility. Both ERISA and the Third Restatement make specific reference to this duty.

> [I]n addition to any liability which he may have under any other provision of this part, a fiduciary with respect to a plan shall be liable for a breach of fiduciary responsibility of another fiduciary with respect to the same plan . . .[2]
>
> A trustee has a duty personally to perform the responsibilities of trusteeship . . . to delegate fiduciary authority . . . and thereafter in supervising agents . . .[3]

Procedures mandated by ERISA and proposed by the Third Restatement have practical application to all fiduciaries and serious investors. The process and procedures involved in monitoring a portfolio are no exception.

Performance Attribution Analysis

Performance attribution analysis is comprised of two overlapping and sequential procedures—performance measurement, the science, and performance evaluation, the art.

Performance measurement consists of calculating portfolio rates of return, characteristics, and sector commitments. The source and handling of data may have an impact on the calculations. Whenever possible, calculated time-weighted rates of return from the custodian should be reconciled against those reported by the money manager.[4] Larger institutional clients often hire an independent third party, such as an investment consultant, to provide yet another source of comparison.

---

[2] ERISA Sec. 405(a).

[3] Restatement Third, Sec. 171.

[4] Of course, some smaller plans use a broker dealer as custodian and money manager, which limits the possibilities for comparisons.

For an additional fee, the custodian should be able to calculate the portfolio characteristics for each asset class represented in the account. For equity portfolios, the relevant characteristics include the portfolio's average price/earnings ratio, price/book ratio, yield, market capitalization weighting (large cap or small cap companies), industry and sector concentrations, trading costs, and turnover. For fixed-income portfolios, the investor should request the computation of the portfolio's average duration, maturity, quality ratings, and sector weights (percentage invested in government, mortgage-backed, and agency bonds).

Performance evaluation consists of a top down approach to the factors that contributed to the returns of the portfolio.

Step 1.   Analyze the current macroeconomic environment and the returns on all major asset classes and subclasses, measured by indexes and groups of style managers. For example, are we in a period of rising interest rates, and has that had a negative impact on fixed income? Did an investment category get bloodied in the press (junk bonds and derivatives in the 90s) and impact returns? Try to stick to macroeconomic facts and clear relationships (e.g., rising long-term rates caused bond portfolios to suffer losses) and avoid superficial market talk (e.g., expectations of another Fed tightening hurt the stock market this year). Earnings, analysts' earnings forecasts, interest rates, Fed policy, tax policies, inflation—these are observable facts that affect markets and expectations for the future.

Step 2.   Review the investment policy statement and become reacquainted with the strategic asset allocation and security guidelines.

Step 3.   Review the stated investment strategies of each of the money managers or mutual funds.

Step 4.   Compare the performance of the money managers or funds with those of other managers following the same strategy or style, and compare their portfolio characteristics (calculated in the performance measurement phase) as well. By so doing, one can check two important things:

    1. The manager is not deviating from stated strategy. Experience has shown that just evaluating a manager's returns will not always reveal a shift in investment strategy, whereas an

examination of the manager's portfolio characteristics will provide timely insight to such changes.

2. If a manager's performance has significantly deviated—either positively or negatively—from the peer group, an examination of the portfolio's characteristics should reveal the source(s) of the difference.

Step 5. Evaluate the performance of the money manager against benchmarks and security guidelines agreed upon in the IPS, and determine whether performance complies with guidelines.

Terminating a Money Manager

The decision to terminate a manager should not be taken lightly, as there are a number of costs associated with changing managers. The following questions have been assembled as a guide to relevant questions.

- Has there been any change in the manager's investment style?

- Have there been any organizational changes?

- Has the manager experienced any large increase/decrease in assets or accounts?

- Has there been any personnel turnover, or has a new portfolio manager been assigned?

- Has the manager consistently underperformed relative to the peer group?

- Is the manager still properly registered with the SEC and state regulators?

- Is the manager still adhering to the securities, asset allocation, and procedural guidelines established in the IPS?

- Has the manager been involved in any litigation claims, assessments, or regulatory investigations?

- Has the manager correctly calculated fees?

- Has the manager's reporting been timely and accurate?

One would think that money managers are usually fired for poor performance, but in reality managers are often fired for poor servicing or communications with the client. Managers may get the account by overemphasizing past stellar performance—setting unreasonably high expectations. A meaningful and realistic relationship between investor and manager requires a basis other than past performance; when performance slips, as it will from time to time, it is important that the manager actually increase the level of communications with a client. Without this communication, the manager will surely be fired for what may be a temporary downturn.

When poor performance does become an issue, it is important that the investor approach the evaluation process with realistic standards. The performance should be evaluated against the benchmarks established in the IPS. Committees should not be lulled into rethinking their manager lineup simply because of the reported success of other money managers. A review of the IPS and a reminder of the benefits of long-term strategic planning should help the committee stay the course.

Since performance will be compared against the IPS, it is important that realistic benchmarks be set. For example, setting a benchmark that the money manager's annual performance fall within the upper quartile (top 25 percent) of the manager's peer group is not realistic and would result in high unnecessary manager turnover. Figure 8–1 shows the performance of equity and fixed-income managers for the period 1985–1994. Note that not a single fixed-income manager was able to sustain top quartile performance in 10 out of 10 years, and only four equity managers were able to reach the lofty goal. Even setting a threshold of top quartile performance 7 out of 10 years results in only 2 percent of the equity managers and 8 percent of the fixed income managers meeting the benchmark.

Conversely, setting too low a performance benchmark may result in a money manager being retained beyond the point that performance can reasonably recover. A reasonable performance expectation is for the manager to fall in the upper 40 percent of the manager's peer group over a five year period. If a manager's performance is below the median for the peer group for a three year period, the statistical odds are that the manager will not be able to improve performance to meet the 40 percent objective within the given five-year period.[5]

---

[5] Paul Troup and Paul Erlendson of Callan Associates Inc., "Performance Standards for Fund Managers" February 1991.

FIGURE 8–1   Manager Performance: Consistency in Top Quartile
(1985–1994)

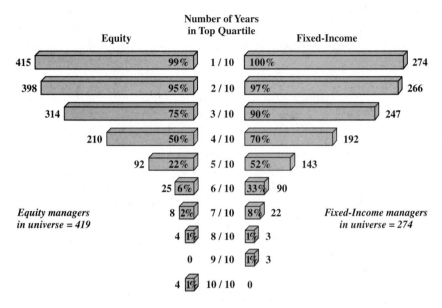

Source: Callan Associates Inc. Copyright © 1995, Investment Management Council.

Measuring Money Manager Performance

As various managers are being considered and/or evaluated, it is important that a standardized review of performance be adopted so that an apples-to-apples comparison can be made. In the past, managers had fairly broad discretion on how they reported performance information. However, a standardized reporting format has been instituted by the Association for Investment Management & Research (AIMR). Additional reporting standards have been adopted by the Investment Management Consultants Association (IMCA) that expand upon the AIMR standards and make certain adjustments that are consistent with investment consulting procedures. In addition to these two standards, the SEC has issued guidelines on advertising and reporting performance results. The combined effect of these three standards makes for complementary disclosure requirements.

AIMR Standards

The AIMR standards were effective January 1, 1993, and require the following of managers when reporting performance in compliance with AIMR standards:[6]

1. A composite return figure must be calculated that includes all fee-paying discretionary portfolios that represent a specific asset class or a similar strategy or investment objective.[7]

2. Firm composites must include only actual assets under management. Model portfolios may be presented as supplementary information provided they are so identified.

3. Performance results for accounts are to be asset weighted, not equal weighted. Equal-weighted results are also recommended, but are not required.

   For an example of asset-weighted versus equal-weighted results, assume that a money manager has a total of $100 million with two accounts. One account is equal to $90 million and provides a return of 15 percent. The other account is $10 million and provides a return of 10 percent. Under the equal-weighting method, each portfolio's return would be summed and divided by two to present the composite return figure of 12.5 percent. Under the asset-weighted method, 90 percent of the composite return would be made up of the return generated from the $90 million account and 10 percent of the return would come from the smaller $10 million account. This results in a composite return figure of 14.5 percent.

4. Performance results should be presented by asset class (e.g., stocks) and include cash equivalents and any other securities held by the manager in place of that asset class (e.g., convertible securities in a stock portfolio). Performance results should also be shown excluding cash. (Asset only and asset plus cash are not to be mixed in the same composite).

5. Retroactive compliance is encouraged for at least 10 years.

---

[6] For more details, see the appendix at the end of the chapter.

[7] If investment restrictions hinder or prohibit the application of an intended investment strategy, the portfolio may be considered nondiscretionary. Nondiscretionary results are also encouraged to be presented.

6. The composite return results belong to the money management firm and not the individual manager that produced the return. (This is controversial—Peter Lynch, for example, cannot promote his Magellan track record since it remains the property of Fidelity.)

7. Results should be presented before fees (and in compliance with SEC rules on advertising). Performance net of fees is permitted. In either case, an appropriate fee schedule should be presented so clients can determine performance on a pre- and post-fee basis.

8. The number of portfolios in the composite should be disclosed along with the total composite assets and the composite assets as a percentage of the firm assets.

9. Total return is to include accrued income (cash-basis accounting is unacceptable) and capital appreciation. Portfolios should be valued at least quarterly (monthly is preferred).

10. External risk measurements, such as alpha, beta, and standard deviation, should be used for composite results. Also, internal risk measurement (dispersion) among specific accounts should be provided. This reflects disparity among results of accounts managed, even though they may have the same style and objective.

The standards encourage verification of the composite results and performance figures. Verification may take the form of what has been referred to as Level I or Level II verification. Inquiry with the money manager should be made regarding which level of verification exists.

Level I Verification. This is verification that all of a firm's actual, discretionary, fee-paying portfolios are included in at least one composite. Examination procedures include spot checking the accuracy of the (1) linkage of performance numbers, (2) number of clients, (3) size of assets, (4) standard deviation of returns, and (5) dispersion of results.

Level II Verification. Level II is the preferred verification process and includes a review of both the investment management process and performance measurement. In addition to the items verified in Level I, the review should include (1) verification of prices, (2) tests on income stream, (3) recalculation of performance figures, and (4) an independent audit confirming all of the AIMR compliance procedures.

IMCA Adjustments

The IMCA standards were developed to provide guidelines for investment consultants on presenting individual portfolio and money manager performance results to clients. They differ from the AIMR standards in that money manager composites are to be depicted as equal weighted versus size or asset weighted. Each group does, however, recommend that the other type of measurement be included.

SEC Rules and Regulations

Guidelines from the SEC have been provided to the industry based on a series of no-action letters beginning in 1986.[8]

Performance information must be presented net of management fees (after the deduction of management fees), although it is permissible in one-on-one presentations to present performance information without the deduction of an advisory fee. In presenting results before the deduction of fees, additional requirements must be met:

1. Disclosure that the performance figures do not reflect the deduction of investment advisory fees.
2. Disclosure that the client's returns will be reduced by the advisory fees and any other expenses that may be incurred in the management of its advisory account.
3. Disclosure that the investment advisory fees are described in Part II of the Advisor's Form ADV.
4. A representative example by way of table, chart, graph, or narrative that shows the effect an investment advisory fee, compounded over a period of years, would have on the total value of a client's portfolio.

Performance Calculations

Performance measurement results can be very confusing unless certain standards are followed. The money management industry has adopted certain standards that should be followed in preparing performance

---

[8] See Clover Capital Management Inc. (October 28, 1986); Investment Company Institute (August 24, 1987); Securities Industry Association (November 27, 1989).

information for an investment account. Additional industry standards for calculating, measuring, and evaluating portfolio performance follow.

• *Standard deviation,* the most common statistical measure of risk, is defined as volatility. It is a statistical measure of the degree to which individual returns vary from the mean (average) over a specified period of time. In comparing two managers (or two portfolios), the manager with the larger standard deviation would be viewed as the riskier manager. That is, if one plotted the riskier manager's returns, one would see that they were not as concentrated around the manager's mean return as would be the less-risky manager's. A problem with using standard deviation as the sole measure of risk is that the dispersion of returns may have been a result of significant positive performance, a problem most investors could live with.

• R^2, the coefficient of determination, tells one about the quality of the other statistical measures. It ranges from 0 to 1, where 1 indicates that the alpha and beta are valuable and 0 indicates there is no fit to the data at all. The R from which R^2 is calculated is the coefficient of correlation, which ranges from -1 to 1 and indicates whether the portfolio or stock and the market benchmark (e.g., S&P 500) are positively correlated, negatively correlated, or uncorrelated.

• *Alpha* is a risk-adjusted measure of how an equity portfolio performed relative to the market—that is, the S&P 500. The risk measure is beta (see the next item). A positive alpha implies the manager delivered more return than one would expect given the level of risk to which the portfolio was exposed. Conversely, a negative alpha implies the investor was not adequately rewarded for the risk the portfolio took.

• *Beta* is a measure of performance volatility and correlation relative to the S&P 500; it measures how much impact movement in the S&P 500 has on a stock or portfolio. For example, a beta of .80 would indicate that a 2 percent gain in the S&P 500 would result in a 1.6 percent gain in the portfolio or stock. Keep in mind, however, that the portfolio may have other sources of risk not related to the S&P 500, and these are not measured by beta. Beta measures how much market risk—not total risk—the portfolio has. In the extreme case, a portfolio or stock could be quite risky but have a beta of 0.00 percent because its returns are unrelated to the S&P 500—a portfolio of lottery tickets, for example. The R^2 tells you how much of the portfolio's total risk is explained by beta.

• The *Sharpe ratio* measures return per unit of risk (standard deviation), a higher number indicating more return for risk taken—generally considered a positive indicator. The Sharpe ratio can be a useful measure of value added when comparing managers of like style or strategy. It is not as good a measure when comparing managers of dissimilar styles, because the mathematical formula favors managers who hold less volatile assets. For example, a fixed-income manager might have a better Sharpe ratio than an international equity manager, but that is not a useful comparison. The managers may be equally good (or bad) compared to their respective peer groups.

• *Geometric returns,* as opposed to *arithmetic returns,* should be calculated for performance measurement over multi-year periods. Arithmetic returns are simple averages of annual returns, but they do not reflect the compounding effect of linked returns. Geometric returns are determined by linking portfolio returns period to period and taking the root, as follows:

$$\text{Geometric mean return} = [(1 + r_1) \times (1 + r_2) \times (1 + r_3) \times \ldots (1 + r_n)]^{1/n} - 1$$

$$\text{where } r_n = \text{annual return.}$$
$$n = \text{number of years.}$$

Instead of averaging the annual return, you take the nth root of the actual multi-period total return, which accounts for compounding. For a portfolio that made 25 percent one year and lost 20 percent the next, the calculation would be

$$[(1+.25) \times (1-.2)]^{1/2} - 1 = (1.25 \times .8)^{1/2} - 1 = 1^{1/2} - 1 = 0$$

The portfolio did indeed break even. Note that the arithmetic average return (2.5 percent) would be positive, which is incorrect:

$$(25\% - 20\%)/2 = 5\%/2 = 2.5\%$$

• Performance results must be based on total return, including realized and unrealized gains/losses and all income. This is depicted by the following formula:

$$\frac{\text{Ending market value} - \text{Beginning market value}}{\text{Beginning market value}}$$

The beginning and ending market values include accrued income.

• *Time-weighted returns* should be used instead of *dollar-weighted returns*. A time-weighted return links the period returns geometrically, with equal weight. A dollar-weighted return weights the return of each period by the asset size. If a portfolio had more assets in period 2 than in period 1, a dollar-weighted return would be more influenced by the second-period results, whereas the time-weighted return would ignore the assets and treat the period returns equally.

• Quarterly valuations of the portfolio are required, but more frequent valuations are desirable. Monthly portfolio valuations are acceptable as long as consideration is given to additions and withdrawals; cash or securities moving in and out of a portfolio between valuations will distort the return calculation unless they are taken into account. The standards suggest three alternative methods for calculating monthly performance results. Each of these is an approximation; the only way to calculate time-weighted returns accurately is to revalue the portfolio every time there is a contribution or withdrawal.

Method 1, the modified Dietz method, is determined using the formula

$$\frac{\text{Ending market value} - \text{Beginning market value} - \text{Net flow}}{\text{Beginning market value} + \text{Flow weighted}}$$

The net flow is the sum of additions to and withdrawals from the portfolio. The flow weighted is the net flow with each item weighted for the time it spent in the portfolio. The market values include accrued income.

Method 2, the modified Bank Administration Institute (BAI) method, is an internal rate of return (IRR) calculation. It assumes that the gain or loss achieved by the portfolio in the period was achieved in a linear fashion, and does the iterative IRR calculation to arrive at a result close to what the Dietz method calculates.

Method 3, liquidation value method, assumes that the accrued income is part of the capital at work and is therefore included in the denominator of the basic formula. It is determined by

$$\frac{\text{Ending market value} + \text{Ending accrual} - \text{Flow}}{\text{Beginning market value} + \text{Beginning accrual} + \text{Flow weighted}}$$

The flow does *not* include reinvested income. This is a more complicated formula that is not utilized as much as the other two. The standards are specific in stating that if a contribution or withdrawal is significant (e.g., over 10 percent of the latest market value), the portfolio should be revalued on the date of the contribution or withdrawal to reduce the chances of distorting the portfolio return.

• Accrual-basis accounting should be utilized instead of cash-basis accounting. Accrued interest income should be included in both the beginning and ending market values. Accrual accounting for dividends as of the ex-dividend date (not declaration date) should be utilized.

Performance Measurement Reports

Investment consulting firms will often produce measurement reports and graphs for clients to help communicate performance—a picture is worth a thousand words. There are no industry standards on the format of these reports; however, there are several graphs that are more commonly used.

The first are floating bar charts, also known as dancing diamond charts, which comes from the diamond on the chart that depicts the actual performance being evaluated. (See Figure 8–2.) These charts are used to depict annual and cumulative performance and to compare common portfolio characteristics. With regards to performance presentations, managers will often disclose the time periods they were top quartile.

Another commonly used chart is the scattergram (see Figure 8–3). The scattergram plots return on the vertical axis and risk (standard deviation) on the horizontal axis. Superimposed as crosshairs on the graph are the median return and risk for the comparative benchmark. The grid divides the chart into quadrants. The upper left hand portion of the chart, referred to as the northwest quadrant, represents the best returns with the least amount of risk. Conversely, the lower right hand corner, referred to as the southeast quadrant, represents the worst returns with the most risk. The manager's specific return and risk are then plotted on the chart. Naturally, a money manager wants to earn more return with less risk than his peers, which results in the manager being plotted in the northwest quadrant. You will often hear a manager refer to his performance as being in the northwest quadrant.

FIGURE 8–2   Sample Floating Bar Chart

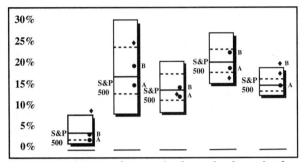

How to Read a Bar Chart

The top line of the bar indicates the top 10th percentile of the universe. The middle solid line is the median, which has a percent rank of 50. The 75th percentile is indicated by the lower dotted line and the 90th percentile is indicated by the bottom line.

	Last Quarter	Last Year	Last 2 Years	Last 3 Years	Last 5 Years
Total Equity Database	▼	▼	▼	▼	▼
10th Percentile	7.58	30.17	19.91	25.73	18.84
25th Percentile	5.38	22.34	16.16	22.00	15.89
Median	3.69	15.91	13.17	19.21	14.44
75th Percentile	2.52	12.37	11.02	17.12	13.01
90th Percentile	1.50	7.96	8.76	15.33	11.79
S&P 500	2.57	12.99	12.01	18.09	14.69
Manager A	2.52	12.79	11.81	17.82	14.47
Manager B	3.30	18.30	13.32	20.87	19.58
Your Fund	9.34	23.78	12.55	16.36	17.16

	10th Percentile
- - - - -	25th Percentile
◆	◆ Fund Return
▬▬▬	50th Percentile —*Median*
- - - - -	75th Percentile
	90th Percentile

Source: Copyright © 1994, Callan Associates Inc.

FIGURE 8–3   How to Read a Scattergram

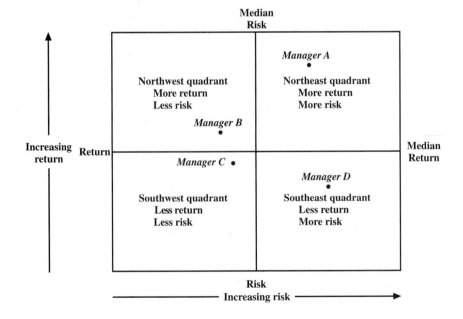

Rebalancing the Portfolio

The final topic we consider under monitoring is periodically rebalancing the portfolio to the strategic asset allocation formalized in the investment policy statement (IPS). Studies have shown that disciplined rebalancing can increase returns as much as minor asset mix changes. For example, changing the IPS equity allocation from 50 percent to 60 percent may have less impact on long-term performance than the decision on when and how to rebalance the portfolio.[9]

The asset mix changes as a result of price fluctuations in the portfolio; when the asset mix falls outside the limits established in the IPS, it is time to rebalance. For example, if the IPS calls for an allocation of 60 percent to equities with a limit of $+/-$ 5 percent, then the portfolio should be rebalanced to 60 percent when the equity portion drifts outside the permissible portfolio ranges of 65 percent or 55 percent.

The discipline of rebalancing, in essence, controls risk and forces the portfolio to move along a predetermined course. It automatically takes gains from stellar performers or favored asset classes and reallocates them to lagging styles or asset classes that are out of favor with the capital markets, thus forcing the investor to sell high and buy low.

The objective of rebalancing is to manage a portfolio to a specific risk/reward profile. Recalling the discussion in Chapter 4 on setting asset allocation, the optimal asset mix was determined after analyzing the investor's

R Risk tolerance
A Asset class preference
T Time horizon
E Expected return

By rebalancing, the investment portfolio is pulled back within the optimal allocation that was set to the investor's specific requirements. Failure to rebalance lets the investor's asset mix float, taking on risk/return characteristics that may be inappropriate for the investor.

Rebalancing limits for the IPS should be set so they do not trigger continuous readjustment of the portfolio. An optimal limit would require readjustments twice a year on average—more than twice a year and the benefits may be eroded by transaction costs in buying and selling into different asset classes.

---

[9] Robert D. Arnott and Robert M. Lovell, "Rebalancing: Why? When? How Often?", The Journal of Investing, Spring 1993, pp. 5–7.

Summary

The fifth and final step of the prudent investment process calls for an ongoing monitoring effort. Performance of money managers must be evaluated over the appropriate time periods to ensure they are doing the job well and staying within the set guidelines. The asset allocation needs to be maintained and adjusted for changes in circumstance. Finally, the IPS needs to be kept up to date, reflecting the current needs of the portfolio and the board and all changes undertaken. As always, time horizon is a critical factor—the fiduciary must regularly conduct the necessary review steps, but must avoid hasty or premature decisions regarding performance.

APPENDIX
Performance Measurement Checklist

At Least Monthly

❑ Review custodian's appraisal report for

Current holdings consistent with money manager's investment strategy.

Asset mix within guidelines, particularly cash component of an equity manager's portfolio.

Trading costs and custodial transactions.

Compare performance against relevant industry indexes for outlying performance (extreme over- or underperformance).

At Least Quarterly

❑ Review the portfolio for compliance with investment guidelines, particularly asset mix and securities guidelines. If rebalancing is required, consider the impact that forthcoming contributions and withdrawals will have on the asset mix.

❑ Determine if there are anticipated withdrawals over the forthcoming quarter and ensure that there is adequate cash to meet disbursements. If securities have to be liquidated to raise cash, determine which money managers should be notified. (Check to see if rebalancing is required.)

❑ Determine if contributions are going to be made to the portfolio over the forthcoming quarter, and decide how the contribution is to be invested. (Check to see if rebalancing is required.)

❑ Review the market values of all securities held in the portfolio, especially those with limited marketability. If the money manager is providing the market values, conduct periodic audits of the valuations to ensure accuracy.

❑ Resolve any discrepancies that exist between the money manager's report of holdings and transactions and those contained in the custodian's appraisal report.

❑ Compute the portfolio's rate of return:

By asset class.
By style of strategy (peer group comparison).
On a composite basis.

❑ Compare each manager's results against an appropriate benchmark, and against a performance universe of the manager's style or peer group.

❑ Verify each money manager's and vendor's fee computation.

At Least Annually

❑ Review the plan's short-term investment procedures, including cash management.

❑ Determine performance results for short-term investments and cash management.

❑ Review the manager's proxy voting policy and results/issues.

❑ Review the manager's brokerage and trading activities, including
   Use of soft dollars.
   Clearing arrangements and brokerage firms utilized.
   Quality of the trade execution.
   Portfolio turnover.
   Commission costs.

❑ Review the money manager's organizational structure to determine if significant changes have occurred in corporate or capital structure, investment style, brokerage affiliation or practices, investment process and professional staff.

Monitoring the Custodian

Custodial or brokerage statements should be reviewed at least annually to verify

❑ That expenses are as specified and determined in accordance with the custodial or brokerage agreement.

❑ Cash management procedures are examined to verify that sweeps and other appropriate accounting methodologies are utilized.

❑ The custody or brokerage statements are examined to determine credits, execution, brokerage costs, and uses of commission dollars.

❑ Where appropriate, proxy voting policies and procedures should be determined, particularly if assets are in a third-party custodian's name.

❑ Asset valuation is credible and where appropriate has been independently verified (e.g., pricing service for thinly traded securities such as municipal bonds).

❑ Income accruals are in place and are valid (e.g., accrued interest on bonds).

❑ The account reconciles—there are no suppressed trades. (See Table 8A–1 for a typical reconciliation.)

TABLE 8A–1 Reconciling the Account

	Year to Date	Change from Prior Month
Value as of December 31, 1994/prior month	$2,952,071	$3,263,678
Dividend income	66,557	5,757
Interest income received	71,664	5,271
Accrued interest purchased	(5,530)	(431)
Accrued interest (12/31/94 = $15,783)	2,733	1,478
Long-term gain (loss)	28,566	5,398
Short-term gain (loss)	57	0
Unrealized gain (12/31/94 = $98,433)	162,403	(24,862)
Management fees	(11,878)	0
Custody and consulting fees	(12,481)	(2,127)
November 30, 1995, value	$3,254,162	$3,254,162

This process allows for verification of the custody statement if the numbers utilized are taken from the individual transactions listed on the custody statement.

Details of AIMR Performance Reporting Standards Enacted for Money Manager on January 1993

1. A composite return figure must be calculated that includes all fee-paying discretionary portfolios that represent a specific asset class or a similar strategy or investment objective. (More than one composite may be necessary if multiple asset classes or strategies are utilized. Mutual funds, commingled funds, or unit trusts may be treated as separate composites or be combined with other portfolios or assets of similar strategy.) Selected portfolios should not be excluded. Non–fee-paying portfolios may be included, provided they are disclosed as such.

2. Portfolios no longer under management must be included for the periods they were under management. (Survivor bias performance results are to be avoided.) New portfolios must not be added to a composite until the start of the next performance measurement period (month or quarter) or according to reasonable and consistently applied manager guidelines. Portfolios must not be switched from one composite to another unless documented changes in client guidelines make this necessary.

3. Performance results should be presented by asset class (e.g., stocks) and include cash equivalents and any other securities held by the manager in place of that asset class (e.g., convertible securities in a stock portfolio). Performance results should also be shown excluding cash. (Asset only and asset plus cash are not mixed in the composite.) For portfolios containing multiple asset classes (e.g., balanced accounts), the total return of the entire portfolio is required for purposes of the multi-asset composite whenever the manager has discretion over changes from one asset class to another. If the client has set limits, the asset class should be divided and the return for each separate asset class included in its respective composite. Appropriate indexes should be used that are similar in risk and return to the portfolio (e.g., S&P 500 Index).

4. Retroactive compliance is encouraged for at least 10 years. The composite return results belong to the money management firm and not the individual manager that produced the return. (This is controversial, since arguably Peter Lynch cannot individually promote his Magellan track record because it remains the property of Fidelity.) Results should be presented before fees (and in compliance with SEC rules on advertising). Performance net of fees is permitted. In either case, an appropriate fee schedule should be presented so clients can determine performance on a pre- and post-fee basis. The number of portfolios in the composite should be disclosed along with the total composite assets and the composite assets as a percentage of the firm assets.

5. Total return is to include accrued income (cash-basis accounting is unacceptable) and capital appreciation. Portfolios should be valued at least quarterly (monthly is preferred). Although cash flow impact can be adjusted in accordance with certain accepted methods (see time-weighted discussion contained in Chapter 10), if a contribution or withdrawal is greater than 10 percent, the portfolio should be revalued on the date of the flow to minimize distortion. Compound annualized returns (time weighted) should be utilized. Trade date valuation (versus settlement date) should be utilized.

6. External risk measurements, such as alpha, beta, and standard deviation, should be used for composite results. Also, internal risk measurement (dispersion) among specific accounts should be provided. This reflects disparity among results of accounts managed, even though they may have the same style and objective.

The AIMR standards encourage verification of the composite results and performance figures. These may take the form of what has been referred to as Level I and Level II verification. Inquiry should be made regarding what level of verification exists.

Level I Verification.   This is verification that all of a firm's actual, discretionary, fee-paying portfolios are included in at least one composite. Examination procedures include

1. Each portfolio, including those no longer under management, is in fact either included in a composite or has been documented as excluded for valid reasons. A complete list of all accounts managed since inception is obtained and compared against the composite results.
2. All portfolios sharing the same guidelines are included in the same composite, and shifts from one composite to another are based on documented client guidelines. Restrictions on accounts included and not included are verified.
3. Portfolio returns in the composite are size weighted and randomly verified for deletion or addition to the composite.
4. Performance is calculated using a time-weighted rate of return, with a minimum of quarterly valuations and accrual of income. Geometric linkage of results is spot checked.
5. Disclosures are provided that are necessary to ensure full and fair presentations.

Level II Verification. This examines both the investment management process and the performance measurement and verifies that

1. All actual, discretionary, fee-paying portfolios are included in at least one composite.
2. Performance is calculated using a time-weighted rate of return, with a minimum of quarterly valuations and accrual of income. Geometric linkage of results is spot checked.
3. Verification of period-end asset pricing is obtained through independent sources such as *Barron's* or *The Wall Street Journal.*
4. Trades on a sample basis should be examined and tracked/traced for appropriate inclusion in the respective accounts.
5. Sample income streams, gains, cash flows, and fees are examined and spot checked.
6. Independent confirmation is made of account valuations and balances.
7. Disclosures are reviewed for compliance with the standards to provide a full and fair presentation.

9

CONTROLLING
INVESTMENT EXPENSES

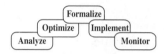

*"A man would do nothing if he waited until he could
do it so well that no one could find fault."*
John Henry Newman

*"If you want to make decisions, then eliminate all the alternatives
with the power of factual data. If you do not want to make
decisions, then do us all a favor by staying out of the way."*
John Mott

For investors with an existing asset allocation policy, it is important that
they revisit their strategies because of the probability that investment
returns in the 90s will not equal those of the 80s. Single-digit returns
for balanced portfolios may once again become the norm, and fiduciaries and investors will have to make excellent investment decisions to
meet return targets of even 9 percent.

In this environment, cost control will play an increasingly important role in helping investors achieve their targeted net returns. For the
investment committees of pension plans, foundations, and endowments,
controlling investment expenses is a key fiduciary duty in addition to
being a necessity for maximizing returns. Having a good understanding
of *all* investment-related expenses can be as difficult as it is important.

223

This chapter provides a general overview of all expenses incurred by an investor and a framework for evaluating them not strictly by themselves but in light of the function they play in the process. Apparent economies achieved in one step often result in higher costs or suboptimal results in another. Only by looking at the whole process can this inadvertent trade-off be avoided.

1. **Analyze.** Investors are often understandably surprised by the total of their investment management costs. For example, they fail to account for transaction fees for custodial services, trading costs charged in addition to published mutual fund expenses, the spreads on principal trades, and/or the fees paid to vendors with soft dollars.

2. **Optimize.** The investor's asset allocation will affect the cost structure of the portfolio. Different asset classes will have different manager fees, account size minimums, and custodial and transaction costs.

3. **Formalize.** It is undisputed that the preparation of an investment policy statement is an absolutely essential part of the prudent investment process and a key fiduciary responsibility. The issue is, what is the most cost-effective way to develop a quality statement?

4. **Implement.** This step includes the evaluation and hiring of managers and a custodian and the establishment of brokerage relationships. There is disparity between published fees and actual fees that may be disclosed during negotiation.

5. **Monitor.** Periodic reviews should cover compliance with the investment policy and an evaluation of performance versus benchmarks for money managers and the portfolio as a whole. The review should also include an analysis of all current costs involved in the management of the portfolio.

The first three crucial steps of the investment management process determine the quality of the rest of the process. These steps have internal and external costs that have to be recognized and understood if the portfolio is to perform efficiently. A key mistake is to underestimate the importance and/or difficulty of these steps. Another mistake is to allow brokers or money managers to be the guide through the process because their advice is free. Either the investor has the internal capacity—time and expertise—to do this well, or one needs to get help—

professional, objective help. Either alternative incurs an expense, but cutting corners in this area of portfolio management can turn out to be more expensive in the long run.

Investment Expenses

Portfolio management costs and expenses can be broken down into four categories:

1. Money manager fees and/or annual expenses of mutual funds.
2. Trading costs, including commission charges and execution expenses.
3. Custodial charges, including custodial fees, transaction charges, and cash management fees.
4. Consulting and administrative costs and fees, including costs for activities that may be done internally or externally.

Before describing each cost and expense in detail, realize that these costs can be obscured or moved from one category to another to create an apparent savings. A low custodial fee may be subsidized by high transaction and/or commission costs. This often occurs across what is known as the *line*. Above-the-line expenses are invoiced or appear as line item expenses, while below-the-line expenses are netted out of the performance of the portfolio. Reduced above-the-line expenses may be offered to entice the unwary into a suboptimal below-the-line structure. Great diligence and care need be taken to ensure that all costs are disclosed and understood.

Also, a larger pool of assets to be managed equates to more negotiating power. There are substantial differences between retail and institutional fee schedules (see Figure 9–1).

Money Manager Fees

Money manager fees vary widely depending on the asset class to be managed, the size of the account, and whether the funds are managed separately or placed into a commingled or mutual fund. Fees are usually charged as a percentage of assets under management, and often decline significantly with increasing asset size. A 1993 fee study reflected

FIGURE 9-1   Total Portfolio Management Costs: Retail versus
              Institutional Pricing

	Brokerage Commissions	
RETAIL		**INSTITUTIONAL**
☐ Stocks trade at $0.30 - $0.40 per share. ☐ Bonds trade on a spread between the bid and ask prices plus a brokerage commission. ☐ Use of retail money market funds to hold uninvested cash. ☐ Wrap Fees - Penalize low turnover periods/managers and may discourage efficient execution of trades.		☐ Stocks trade at $0.06 – $0.08 per share. ☐ Bonds trade on a spread between the bid and ask prices with no brokerage commission. ☐ Use of institutional money market funds to hold uninvested cash.

	Custody Charges	
☐ Very difficult to calculate. ☐ Banks normally charge a flat fee plus transaction fees to post income and dividends. ☐ Lost interest earnings when institutions do not sweep cash daily.		☐ Negotiated flat fee covers all services. ☐ Cash swept daily.

	Money Manager Fees	
☐ Manager's normal fee schedule.		☐ Manager's normal fee schedule discounted to reflect the size of the account and/or the negotiating leverage of the investor.

	Consulting Fees	
☐ Based on directed brokerage commissions or included in a wrap fee.		☐ Bundled fees based on assets under advisement or separate fees for specific services rendered.

a wide range of fees for domestic equity, balanced fixed-income, and international managers.[1] (See Table 9–1.)

Money managers (conducting business as registered investment advisors) are required to publish their fee schedules in ADV Part II filed with the SEC. This schedule is many times subject to variation depending on the client relationship, size, and servicing requirements.

Mutual fund annual charges (expense ratios) also vary widely—see Table 9–2. Expense ratios, as commonly defined, include custody fees, shareholder servicing fees, administrative expenses (postage, printing, overhead, accounting, and legal), money management fees, and, in

---

[1] The money manager fee study was conducted by Callan Associates Inc. and reported fees charged by money managers during the year 1992.

TABLE 9–1   Investment Expenses
Published Investment Management Fees for Investment Managers

	Size of Accounts ($Mil)					
	$1 M	*$5 M*	*$10 M*	*$25 M*	*$50 M*	*$100 M*
Active equity	0.89%	0.87%	0.76%	0.66%	0.57%	0.52%
Active fixed income	0.67	0.61	0.46	0.42	0.36	0.33
Balanced	0.81	0.70	0.67	0.58	0.50	0.42
Active international equity	N/A	N/A	0.82	0.74	0.67	0.60

Source: Copyright © 1994, Callan Associates Inc.

TABLE 9–2   No-Load Mutual Fund Expense Ratios

	Domestic Equity	*Domestic Fixed Income*	*International Equity*	*Global Fixed Income*
High	2.90%	1.54%	2.69%	1.50%
Median	.96	.67	1.43	.93
Low	.07	.05	.32	.42

some cases, 12b-1 fees.[2] Some funds also charge front-end, annual, or exit fees called loads. Front-end loads may be as high as 8 percent. Alternatively, exit fees, also known as contingent deferred sales charges (or CDSC), may also be quite large. This can act as a substantial disincentive to prudent investment management due to the cost of change. There is wide availability of excellent no-load funds, publicly available research on these funds, and fee-based consultants who can objectively evaluate and recommend their use. A cost-conscious fiduciary may find this avenue more appealing.

---

[2] 12b-1 fees are paid to outside third parties who are involved in the sales or marketing of the fund. The fee has become controversial because it is often charged as an alternative to a sales load, thereby avoiding the stigma associated with load funds. Fiduciaries should also be aware that many funds charge 12b-1 fees even where no services are provided by an outside third party.

Performance-Based Fees

A minority of managers and their clients have agreed to performance-based fees. Under these arrangements, managers receive a higher fee if they are able to exceed a predesignated benchmark over a specified time period (e.g., annually). These arrangements may only be utilized by entities with assets in excess of $1 million, sophisticated investors, or registered investment companies.[3] They are not permitted in all states and principalities. (Appendix 9–1 contains a survey of states that do and do not permit performance-based fee arrangements.)

Performance-based fees may be appropriate under limited circumstances. Until the mid-80s they were prohibited altogether; however, today SEC Rule 205-3 permits the fees under certain conditions. The SEC remains concerned about the potential for investment managers to take on significantly more and different risk than anticipated by the client. Performance-based fees, as commonly structured, can be quite attractive for managers. The fee structures generally limit the manager's downside (often 20 basis points) while offering significant upside, similar to an option. The manager can't lose, and may win big.

The manager may also have a strong incentive to make trading decisions that are not in the investor's best interests. Remember, while the manager's downside is limited, *the investor's is not!* A large cap manager, measured against the S&P 500, may buy some small cap growth stocks in the portfolio, hoping the small cap will outperform the large cap *sometimes*. The manager only has to be right now and then to make a substantial fee. Meanwhile, the investor ends up with a different asset allocation than originally planned.

It is not the manager's ability to select securities or even asset classes that is rewarded. It is the selection of assets that will not track the manager's benchmark that makes money! Also, if the manager has been underperforming, the manager may be tempted to take more risk (i.e., to swing for the fences) hoping to get lucky. Bottom line: if the activities of the manager cannot be closely monitored, performance-based fees should be avoided.

---

[3] See sections 205(b), and 206A of the Investment Advisors Act of 1940, and rules and regulations promulgated thereunder. See also Rule 205-3 for specifics regarding sophisticated investors.

Trading Costs

Fees paid to money managers and/or selected mutual funds do not include trading costs. Trading costs have two components: commissions and execution costs. This large and important area of cost control, often overlooked by investors, has a major impact on investment return. One way a money manager can improve portfolio return (save money for the investor) is by buying and selling securities at a low commission and effecting a low transaction cost through skillful trading.

The more familiar and easily determined cost is the commission. Until the mid-70s, commissions were fixed by mutual agreement by the members of the New York Stock Exchange. In May 1975, the securities industry instituted negotiated commission rate schedules, and two distinct tiers of customers took shape: institutional and retail.

Commissions at the retail level primarily support the sales and research efforts of the brokerage firms. Most retail brokerage concerns will provide an individual with a listing of the formula or schedule used to arrive at the cost. Commission costs are negotiable, but the issue must usually be initiated by the client. The brokerage industry has evolved to create a competitive environment among brokerage houses, as evidenced by the success of investment services firms such as Charles Schwab & Co. and Jack White & Co.

From an institutional viewpoint, commission costs paid by professional money managers and major institutions range between 3 and 6 cents per share. The commission charge is calculated as a function of

1. The number of shares to be traded.
2. The price per share.
3. The degree of difficulty in executing the trade. For example, the commission costs for trading 1,000 shares of IBM should be less than the commission costs of trading 1,000 shares of a smaller company with a much lower trading volume.
4. The money manager's (or investor's) relationship with the broker.

Commission costs are also affected by whether the trades are executed as either an agency or principal trade. With an agency trade, the brokerage firm acts as an agent for the investor and never takes title to the stock. In other words, the brokerage firm buys/sells the securities for the investor on the open market and seeks to find the best available price.

A principal trade occurs when the security is purchased from or sold to the broker's own inventory of stocks and bonds. Such a trade is indicated on the confirmation ticket with the notation "We make a market in this security." In a principal trade, the investor knows only the execution or strike price—the spread received by the broker may not be disclosed. The broker is on the other side of the trade from the investor; the broker's gain is the investor's loss, and vice versa. It is important to realize that when a broker is engaged in principal trading, there may be more revenue flowing to the broker than initially indicated. The investor should make an inquiry to determine how large this markup may be.[4]

Commission-related costs also become an issue when a manager cannot seek the lowest commission and best execution on trade. This lack of freedom can result in higher portfolio costs. One example is when a manager (or the investor) has agreed to direct trades to a broker in exchange for soft dollar benefits (see below). It may also occur when a manager or mutual fund executes trades through its own brokerage firm. The income generated from high commissions and principal trading in such an arrangement can dwarf all other costs and fees *combined.* This cost is rarely disclosed and may only show up over time in underperformance by the portfolio. A portfolio bearing such a burden cannot be expected to keep up with the market.

Execution Costs

Besides the commission costs, there are execution costs, which are much more difficult to calculate. The execution cost is defined as the difference between the strike price (price at which the investor actually buys or sells the stock) and the fair market price. The fair market price is determined by analyzing the behavior of the stock price immediately after the trade is placed.

Fiduciaries are charged with seeking best execution, which has been defined in several technical publications.[5] These guidelines state that

---

[4] See Article III, Sections 1 and 4 of the National Association of Securities Dealers, Inc. Rules of Fair Practice, where a liberal 5 percent markup policy is discussed. Markups are appropriate or inappropriate based on the facts and circumstances surrounding the trade. Whether the percentage markup is fair is determined by several factors: (1) type of security, (2) availability of the security in the market, (3) price of the security, (4) amount of money involved, (5) disclosure to the customer, (6) pattern of markups, and (7) nature of the firm's business.

[5] See Technical Release 86-1 in Prohibitive Transaction Exemption 86-128, *Securities Transactions Involving Employee Benefit Plans,* November 18, 1986.

best execution goes beyond analyzing the commission costs and includes an analysis of the actual strike price of the security and the quality and reliability of the trade. As an example:

Calculating Execution Costs

A buy order is placed for 1,000 shares of XYZ (at the market).

Strike price (what the investor paid)	$62 1/8
Subsequent trade	<u>62</u>
Difference	1/8, or $.125 per share
Execution cost:	$.125 × 1,000 = $125

If the trade was at a negotiated commission cost of 6 cents a share, the $60 ($.06 × 1,000) commission would have been over-shadowed by the $125 execution cost. The total cost of this trade would be $185.

The requirement to seek best execution raises the issue of whether it is prudent for a fiduciary (or hired money manager) to place all trades through one brokerage firm in order to benefit from reduced commission costs, or to receive ancillary services, such as investment consulting. To the uninformed fiduciary whose familiarity with brokerage firms is limited to paying traditional retail commission costs, such arrangements may appear to offer a significant cost advantage. However, closer examination may reveal higher trading costs compared to money managers that could shop for "best execution."

For an equity portfolio, hidden execution costs can be discovered since stock quotes and prices are easily obtainable for specific points in time. However, hidden execution costs are generally harder to discover when trading bonds or thinly traded securities, which are bought and sold in a negotiated marketplace. The fact the bid/ask spreads of these securities are neither standard nor disclosed means that a broker may buy and resell an issue with a very large markup. Therefore, when buying a bond, it may be advantageous to have these securities competitively bid through various brokerage houses to shop for the best price.

Another form of this hidden cost for bond investors occurs when they are selling. With no central exchange, the price one broker bids on an investor's bond can differ significantly from the bid of another, and the variability of bids can be substantial. For example, one major money manager of fixed income portfolios has found that the difference among the prices bid by brokers on a block of municipal bonds can be as much as 3 percent, or even more. The variability of the bid prices on a 100 bond trade would have the potential to limit the investor's proceeds by up to $3,000 or more.[6]

The Money Manager's Selection of Brokers

Money managers have a vested interest in trying to secure the lowest commission cost and best execution since, ultimately, trading costs will impact the account's performance and their composite performance in managing portfolios. Typically, an investor grants full investment discretion to its money manager(s). The manager(s), under these circumstances, become responsible for directing transactions to brokers they select and negotiating the commissions.

It is impossible to make a future determination that the best price can be obtained by the use of one broker over another. However, if a broker continually underperforms or appears to be less than professional in its operations and procedures, questions should be raised regarding the manager's choice. Managers usually select brokers to handle trades based on the following criteria:

- The broker has position trading capability.
- The broker either has in-house investment research capability or subscribes to investment research on behalf of the manager. (This is referred to as third-party, soft-dollar research, as described below.) Managers will purchase the research to aid in their analysis of securities they may wish to buy or sell for the investor.
- The broker has execution capability in the auction market.
- The broker is a buyer or seller of the stock issue the manager is transacting.
- The broker is active in the new issue (IPO) market where the manager must maintain good working relationships.
- The investment committee has requested that commissions be directed to a specific broker (referred to as directed brokerage) for the purchase of certain services that would normally be the financial obligation of the investment committee.

---

[6] Based on two studies conducted by Weiss, Peck & Greer of all municipal bonds sold for their clients on July 15, 1992 and on January 19–20, 1994.

Use of Commission Dollars

Since commission costs paid to a broker constitute payment for both research and execution services, directed brokerage arrangements assign a portion of the commission cost towards specific research benefits for the portfolio or its money managers. The balance of the commission cost is then retained by the broker as payment for execution. Excess commissions for research benefits are normally only available to the midsize and institutional investor. (Portfolios of less than $50 million generally do not generate sufficient trading activities to warrant the implementation of a directed brokerage program.)

The fiduciary has an ongoing responsibility to monitor the direction of commissions and execution capability of brokers to the portfolio. When an investor desires to direct commissions for its own benefit, the decision should be discussed in advance with hired money managers. The money managers will indicate the percentage of the portfolio's commissions they are willing to allocate to pay for some of the investor's expenses. Industry experience has been that most managers are willing to have between 25 to 50 percent of the portfolio's commissions directed in this manner. The fiduciary should not be giving direction to the money manager that could interfere with the manager's investment process, nor should the fiduciary direct the manager to use a broker the manager feels is not professional or competitive.

Types of Directed Brokerage Arrangements

Brokers have developed three directed brokerage options: soft dollars, discount brokerage, and commission recapture.

Soft-dollar arrangements are typically quoted on a conversion ratio such as $1.00 for every $2.00 in commission costs. The $1.00 could be applied towards the purchase of investment consulting services, investment research, custodial services, rating or technical analysis, quote machines, subscriptions to investment periodicals, or investment-related training programs.[7]

Soft-dollar arrangements have received DOL and SEC scrutiny and negative publicity because they, at times, have not operated in the best interests of plan beneficiaries and have been subject to abuse.[8]

---

[7] For more information on soft-dollar arrangements, see SEC Circular 28e and Release No. 23170 (April 23, 1986).

[8] See "A Hard Look at Soft Dollars," *Barron's,* June 21, 1993, p. 13.

Questionable soft-dollar practices exist where it is hard to see the connection between commissions paid and actual benefit to the pension plan (investor), or when the fiduciary unknowingly leaves soft-dollar decisions to other parties. The latter occurs when the fiduciary remains silent on the subject of brokerage direction, allowing discretion to unscrupulous consultants or money managers.

A common fiduciary breach involving soft-dollar arrangements is the inability of the fiduciary to account for all dollars paid to service vendors. The fiduciary is charged with ensuring that reasonable fees are paid to service vendors and that no party is unduly compensated. This requires the fiduciary to account for all dollars spent for services, whether those dollars are paid directly from the account or through soft-dollar arrangements. Often a lapse occurs when the fiduciary is offered bundled investment services in exchange for having brokerage directed through a specified broker. To the uninformed, the appearance is that the services are free, after all the portfolio has to execute trades somewhere—why not with this particular brokerage firm? Unfortunately, such arrangements may result in higher commission costs and poor execution.

Discount brokerage refers to trades that are charged a negotiated, low commission rate, often one-half the normal commission. The discount rate is quoted net—that is, the broker retains the entire commission and does not apply any of it for research purposes.

Commission recapture is an arrangement between the fiduciary (investor) and the broker whereby the broker agrees to refund a portion of the commission it receives directly, or indirectly, back to the portfolio. This has the same economic effect as discount brokerage, yet is far more popular. The reason for the popularity is that managers typically execute large block trades and allocate the completed trade among a number of clients. It would be unfair to the manager's other clients to have the broker charge a lower rate to the directing client than to the other clients. Therefore, recapture allows the manager to negotiate the same commission rate for all the clients. The refund takes place between the broker and the fiduciary and is transparent to the money manager.

Directed Brokerage Policies

For those fiduciaries that desire to implement a directed brokerage policy, the following guidelines should be established:

1. A determination should be made with regard to the allocation of the portfolio's commissions between manager uses (research) and the portfolio's needs.
2. The hired money manager's opinion about directed brokerage should be incorporated into the policy.
3. The policy should afford the money manager enough flexibility to use a portion of the commissions to purchase the research and block trading services that are needed to effectively manage the assets.
4. Commissions not required by the manager should be directed by the fiduciary (investor) for its own use.
5. The fiduciary has an ongoing responsibility to monitor the direction of commissions and the execution capability of brokers used by the managers.
6. A determination should be made regarding directed commissions, discount brokerage, and commission recapture arrangements.
7. A fiduciary's decision to direct brokerage must be made prudently and solely in the interest of plan participants and beneficiaries.

Regulatory Scrutiny

Periodically, the SEC and DOL indicate that they would like to see an end to directed brokerage programs. Admittedly, there are abuses; however, there are a number of fiduciaries that are dependent on these programs to help defray their investment management costs. The debate for and against directed brokerage can be summarized as follows:

Arguments *for* the Allowance of Directed Brokerage

- Many large institutional funds are sensitive to the fact that above-the-line expenses for investment services may draw the ire of plan sponsors, donors, and/or recipients. By allocating soft dollars to the payment of investment services, the investment committees are provided the support and resources they need without appearing to pay for them. For example, the cost of consulting work on asset allocation may be paid as a fee or buried in higher commission costs.

- High commissions/soft dollars often pay for research. If these expenses were known and explicit, then less research might be purchased. If that research helped performance, then performance may be adversely affected.

Arguments *against* the Use of Directed Brokerage

- It may be more difficult to equate precisely the value of services received to the dollars spent, something not conducive to standard auditing practices.

- It is an expense that is inevitably paid by the investor or plan participant that may not be adequately disclosed. It may be much larger than an explicit fee and may compromise the fiduciary's ability to get best execution, incurring further large but hard-to-quantify expenses. The overall result will likely be underperformance.

- It may be an attempt to hide expenses and avoid constraints. The better approach, if possible, is to acknowledge all needs and costs and then meet those needs in a cost-effective fashion. This approach will achieve the best results for beneficiaries and acceptable accounting for (and control of) costs.

Custodial Charges

In the management of assets, a custodian is selected to (1) hold custody of securities, (2) report on the holdings and transactions, (3) collect interest and dividends, and (4) if required, effectuate trades. In essence, the custodian serves as guardian of the investor's assets and as an independent third-party intermediary between the money manager and the investor.

At the retail level, the custodian is typically a brokerage firm. Most individual accounts are held in street name, with the assets commingled with those of the brokerage firm. To protect the assets, brokerage firms are required to obtain insurance from Securities and Investor Protection Corp. (SIPC). Client coverage is typically $100,000 for cash and $500,000 for securities. Several brokerage firms offer substantially higher coverage through the use of blanket umbrella coverage. SIPC covers theft, fraud, or improper conversion of securities but does not cover the loss of principal due to market risk.

Most mid-size and institutional investors choose to use trust companies as custodians. The primary benefit is that the assets are held in a separate account and are not commingled with other assets of the institution. In addition, the trust custodian is often viewed as offering better reporting on portfolio holdings and transactions.

In selecting a custodian, critical cost containment issues revolve around fees, the efficiency of posting transactions, and procedures for collecting income and dividends.

1. Annual account charges for midsize and institutional accounts should be negotiated below 10 basis points. Retail accounts can expect to pay up to 30 basis points.
2. Dividend and interest payments should be swept daily into an interest-bearing account. Dividends should be posted on the declaration date as accrued income.
3. The costs for ancillary services should be compared to other institutions that compete for business in the same market. These include costs for providing checks to either beneficiaries or service providers, trade posting charges, annual account charges, and so on.
4. Idle cash should be placed in a competitive money market or cash management account. Annual expenses for a money market account should be less than 40 basis points.

Competition among custodians, coupled with improved technology in record keeping, has resulted in dramatically reduced fees. Investors that have not conducted a search for a new custodian in the past three years will almost certainly discover significant savings. A sample letter that can be used to determine the fees and expenses in a custodial relationship is provided as Appendix 9–2.

Other Cost-Related Considerations

Administrative Costs. Costs associated with the administration of investment decisions vary widely from investor to investor, depending on the nature of the portfolio and the quality of the services. A large investor may have the expertise and in-house staff to perform most administrative functions. While it may appear tempting to forgo the expense of a consultant, there are reasons (even aside from the quality of the result) that make using a consultant an option worth considering.

- A good consultant will help an investor move quickly and thoughtfully through the investment process, greatly reducing the time spent on different activities.

- An experienced consultant can often negotiate lower fees from money managers, custodians, and brokers; total explicit costs may very well be *lower* using a consultant than not.

Rebalancing Expenses. Periodic rebalancing of a portfolio creates additional transaction expenses. However, the expense of rebalancing is outweighed by the economic benefit of setting a long-term strategic asset allocation and sticking with it. In general, if rebalancing limits are set to trigger a reallocation about twice a year, transaction costs should be minimal. (See rebalancing discussion in Chapter 8.)

Breakpoints on Money Manager and Mutual Fund Fee Schedules. Typically, the more money placed with a manager, the lower the fee charges on incremental dollars managed. Managers encourage this by publishing fee schedules with fees that decline as managed assets increase. However, straying far from the optimal asset allocation is not justified by fee savings. Having fewer managers, particularly active managers, increases risk. Should the investor decide to concentrate some money for this purpose, a passive manager may provide less risk and even lower fees.

Termination Costs. There are three costs associated with terminating a manager. First is the internal work (and strain) of having to fire the manager and hire someone else. Second, the portfolio may sit idle while awaiting the selection of a new manager. Third, the new manager will probably want to purchase new securities for the portfolio. Transaction costs will be incurred in both selling the old portfolio and buying the new.

The first cost—firing and hiring—cannot be helped, but the other two costs can be controlled for larger accounts. For example, a large index manager with major equity trading volume can be hired on an interim basis to liquidate the portfolio at the lowest possible cost, and then place the proceeds into an appropriate stock index fund (e.g., S&P 500) while the investor decides on a new manager. Thus, equity exposure can be inexpensively maintained while minimizing trading costs.

Summary

The responsibility to control all investment-related expenses of a portfolio can be rewarding. Becoming familiar with all of the costs involved in managing an investment program, and the source of these costs, is, however, a significant activity.

Every service provider should properly disclose all fees and sources of compensation. At least once every three years, each service provider's contract should be reviewed and renegotiated to ensure that the portfolio is paying no more than is necessary—and no less. Above all, costs must be evaluated in the proper context—needs and total costs—including internal and hidden costs.

Consultants can frequently help in this analysis and can often more than cover their fees with savings to the portfolio. Failure to consider all costs in the overall portfolio context can result in significant opportunity costs, such as achieving inadequate returns from having too little equity exposure. A good process will result in the right asset allocation and cost-effective implementation, which in turn will certainly produce the best results.

APPENDIX 9–1
Performance-Based Fees

State laws will dictate whether performance-based fee arrangements are permissible for individually managed portfolios. Not all states have approved the use of performance-based fees. States where such arrangements are permitted include

Arizona	Iowa	Rhode Island
Colorado	Louisiana	Tennessee
District of	Maine	Texas
Columbia	Massachusetts	Vermont
Florida	Nevada	Wyoming
Georgia	New York	
Indiana	Ohio	

States that restrict the use of performance-based fee arrangements, and so such arrangements may not be available, include

California	Minnesota	Oregon
Connecticut	Missouri	Pennsylvania
Idaho	Nebraska	South Dakota
Illinois	New Jersey	Virginia
Kansas	New Mexico	Washington
Kentucky	North Carolina	Wisconsin
Maryland	Oklahoma	

States, or territories, that prohibit the use of performance-based fee arrangements include

Alabama	Hawaii	North Dakota
Alaska	Michigan	Puerto Rico
Arkansas	Mississippi	South Carolina
Delaware	Montana	Utah
Guam	New Hampshire	West Virginia

APPENDIX 9–2
Controlling Investment Expenses

ABC RETIREMENT PLAN
Administrative Committee
1313 Mockingbird Lane
Anywhere, USA

May 10, 1995

Mrs. J. Fuller
XYZ Bank Trust Department
P.O. Box 7610
Anywhere, USA

Re: ABC Retirement Plan

Dear Mrs. Fuller:

Under ERISA Section 404(a), we are required to control the expenses incurred by the ABC Company Retirement Plan. In order to fulfill this requirement, this letter is to request confirmation and detail regarding certain Plan expenses incurred with your institution on our Plan assets.

Enclosed is a **Fee Analysis** that requires your attention. Please provide me with confirmation that the **Fee and Expense Schedule** is correct. If any discrepancies are in place, please note them on the Schedule. Please also provide me with an explanation and detail of the additional items listed on this Analysis.

If you have any questions regarding these requested items, please do not hesitate to contact me. Your attention to this request is appreciated.

Sincerely yours,

ABC Retirement Plan

cc: Consultant

Enclosure to Letter

ABC Retirement Plan
FEE ANALYSIS

SERVICE PROVIDER: XYZ Bank

CAPACITY: Named Fiduciary—Trustee

FEE AND
EXPENSE SCHEDULE: .25% per year first $5,000,000
                             .15% thereafter
                             (billed quarterly in arrears)

Additional fees are:

$750 per year for each GIC
$500 per year for each subaccount
$10.00 per distribution check
$25.00 per transaction charge

Provide any other fees or expenses in addition to the above charges

FUNDS INQUIRY:

What is the management fee and/or transaction expense charged internally against the following funds?

Funds

XYZ Money Market Trust (Common Trust Pooled Fund)
XYZ America Income Trust (Common Trust Pooled Fund)

Also, please provide any:

annual reports,
annual asset statements,
description of funds,
investment guideline descriptions,
historical return information, and/or
other relevant information for these funds.

If commission or transaction compensation is received by XYZ or any XYZ affiliates or related parties, please provide a detail of these costs and expenses.

INVESTMENT MANAGEMENT CONSULTANT

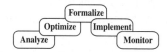

"A consultant is an ordinary man away from home giving advice."
Oscar Wilde

"It used to be that a guy went into the Army when everything else failed; now he goes into the consulting business."
Blackie Sherrod, *sportswriter*

The role of the investment consultant is to *manage*, not to *make* investment decisions. At first blush there may appear to be little variance between the two alternatives, but the subtle differences are the primary means of distinguishing a true consultant from other professionals in the financial services industry. With increases in fiduciary liability and the complexities of our global capital markets, the need for consulting services provided by objective, independent third parties has never been greater.

For fiduciaries and trustees, one important notion that is anchored by ERISA statutes, proposed in the Third Restatement, and reinforced by case-law is that the fiduciary's activities will be judged by the investment process that was followed, not the ultimate investment results. Furthermore, experience has shown that investors that develop and

243

remain committed to following an intelligent, long-term investment strategy achieve far greater success than those who acquiesce to the latest Wall Street fad. Herein lies the true role of the consultant and what is referred to as *the management of investment decisions*. Specifically, the consultant is charged with

- Assisting in the development of an asset allocation strategy that meets the specific risk/reward requirements of the investor.
- Assisting in the preparation of written investment policy statements and assisting in the documentation of all investment decisions.
- Assisting in the selection of "prudent experts" (money managers) who, in turn, are charged with *making* investment decisions that are consistent with the investment policy statement.
- Assisting in the control of investment expenses; including helping to negotiate fees paid to money managers and custodians, and to ensure that brokerage is transacted at "best execution". When soft dollars or commission recapture is deemed appropriate by the client, ensuring that the program is properly executed.
- Monitoring the activities of hired money managers and service vendors. [If the consultant is also managing the money, how can the consultant objectively evaluate the performance of the portfolio? Is it not an example of "asking the fox to count the chickens"?]
- Educating board or committee members on their fiduciary responsibilities, or the investor on the fundamentals of investment management.
- Assisting fiduciaries and trustees in avoiding conflicts of interest.

Consulting has become one of the growth industries of the 90s, and there are many individuals that call themselves investment consultants. Unfortunately, there are few that truly measure up to the role outlined above. The rest use guises of the investment consulting process merely to sell investment product.

Background

As long as there has been a system of barter, there have also been experts offering their opinion on how goods and products perform, and how they should be reallocated to improve performance. The growth of investment consulting, as it is practiced today, can be traced to the late 60s with real momentum gained when fiduciary standards were codified under ERISA.

Until recently, consulting was the private domain of the largest pension plans, wealthiest families, and highly endowed foundations. There were three major hurdles that kept smaller portfolios from accessing qualified consultants. First, there were few professional consultants available in the marketplace. Consultants had to be home grown and self-taught. There were no formal or self-study training programs specific to investment consulting.

Second, most consulting fees were project-based. That is, there was a fixed cost for performing services, regardless of the portfolio size. For the largest of pension funds, the fee was minuscule compared to the total assets. To a smaller portfolio, the fee was perceived to be astronomical and could not be cost-justified. Smaller plans were economically locked out of accessing the same scope and level of services that benefited institutional plans.

The third hurdle was implementation. Even if a smaller plan could justify the costs of investment consulting, it was difficult to actually implement the strategies that were developed. Money manager fees and account size minimums made it impractical to obtain the same degree of diversification as larger plans.

Today, any fiduciary or investor, regardless of portfolio size, should be able to secure the services of an objective investment consultant who can follow the investment management process detailed in this book. There are now formal training programs specifically designed for consultants, and several professional associations have emerged.[1]

Within the last five years, basic consulting functions that once required the use of a mainframe computer can now be run on the PC. Technology has dramatically improved the accessibility of asset optimization software, databases on money managers, and performance measurement software.

---

[1] At least two professional associations offer certification programs on investment consulting: Investment Management Consultants Association (IMCA), Denver (303-770-3377); and the Institute for Investment Management Consultants (IIMC), Phoenix (602-265-6114). In addition, the Association for Investment Management and Research, the College for Financial Planning, and the American College offer courses in investment management and planning.

Additionally, with the tremendous growth of no-load mutual funds, discount brokerage firms, and small fee-based independent consulting firms, even smaller portfolios can implement sophisticated investment strategies. Portfolio management software is now available that links money managers, custodians, and consultants together. The result is a reduction of redundant services, with money managers and custodians willing to lower fees and minimums. When brought together with no-load mutual funds, implementation of sophisticated investment strategies is now possible for any account size.

Both the fiduciary and the investor have an incentive to hire the consultant to improve performance. The improvement may be the result of (1) identifying more appropriate money managers, (2) fine tuning an optimal asset allocation, (3) lowering costs and expenses for money managers and security transactions, or (4) saving time in the development and maintenance of an investment strategy.

Investment Consulting Alternatives

One way investment firms are differentiated is by the size of their average client portfolio. Figure 10-1 shows the approximate division between the three major market segments defined by asset size. Naturally, there are no absolute boundaries between each of the markets, and one firm could actually service clients in several different markets.

The retail market is normally defined as accounts below $5 million and is serviced, for the most part, by small independent fee-based investment planners, stockbrokers, accounting firms, banks, and insurance companies.

The middle market, with accounts between $5 and $500 million, is serviced by regional investment consulting firms and divisions of actuarial and benefits consulting firms. Though the firms are typically independently owned and operated, they often form alliances or associations to achieve economies of scale and to share research.

The institutional market is defined as portfolios above $500 million, serviced by a handful of consulting firms with any appreciable market share: Callan Associates Inc., Cambridge Associates, Evaluation Associates, Frank Russell Company, Mercer Meninger, SEI, and Wilshire Associates. Most of these institutional firms have augmented their traditional project-based fee services by offering their own mutual funds,

FIGURE 10–1 Markets

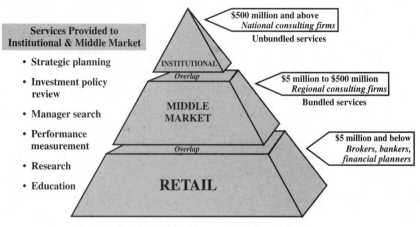

Services Provided to Institutional & Middle Market

- Strategic planning
- Investment policy review
- Manager search
- Performance measurement
- Research
- Education

INSTITUTIONAL
Overlap
MIDDLE MARKET
Overlap
RETAIL

$500 million and above
National consulting firms
Unbundled services

$5 million to $500 million
Regional consulting firms
Bundled services

$5 million and below
Brokers, bankers, financial planners

Source: Copyright © 1994, Investment Management Council.

TABLE 10–1 Investment Advisory Alternatives

| | Registered Representatives | | | Registered Investment Advisers | |
	Stockbrokers	Financial Planners (Product-Based)	Bank Trust Officers	Money Managers	Investment Management Consultants
• Primary responsibilities	• Brokerage transactions (stocks, bonds, options, etc.)	• Packaged product sales (funds, partnership annuities, insurance, etc.)	• Fiduciary services • Asset management • Asset custody services	• Asset management disciplines • Generalists versus specialists	• Portfolio planning disciplines • Money manager selection • Performance monitoring and reporting • Fiduciary counsel
Compensation	Commissions & mark-ups on transactions	Commissions built into products	Fees	Fees	Fees
Required client disclosure	Product prospectuses	Product prospectuses	None	Form ADV (SEC)	Form ADV (SEC)

which provide the firms with asset-based fees and much higher profit margins. For the institutional firms that sell mutual funds, the challenge is to maintain objectivity in the delivery of their consulting services.

Other ways to differentiate between firms are by their regulatory requirements and structure. (See Table 10–1.)

Registered Representatives

Registered representatives include stockbrokers and most financial planners. These individuals are subject to supervision from the National Association of Securities Dealers (NASD) and possibly rules of the New York Stock Exchange (NYSE). Compensation is typically derived from commissions or markups on security transactions. It is important that the ERISA fiduciary understand that the safe harbor rules (see Chapter 6 for more details), which provide insulation for investment decisions, do not list registered representatives as a source for discretionary investment advisory services. If a fiduciary is using a stockbroker or financial planner as the primary source of investment advice, the fiduciary may still be directly liable for those investment decisions. Conversely, NASD firms that permit registered representatives to advise ERISA fiduciaries may be exposed to cofiduciary liability.

Stockbrokers.   With the advent of wrap-fee programs (discussed in more detail later), a large number of stockbrokers have begun offering consulting services to investors. The wrap-fee product can be a viable alternative for smaller portfolios when (1) it is properly implemented, (2) the fee has been substantially negotiated downward, and (3) the investor has eliminated no-load mutual funds as alternatives. The investor should insist that each of the components of the investment management process be provided in conjunction with the wrap-fee product. Anything short of the full delivery of comprehensive services should be avoided.

Financial Planners.   In the 80s, the term *financial planning* was abused by a number of individuals and organizations that used the term as a front, when all they were doing was selling investment products. Too often financial plans were written to enhance the particular product the planner wanted to sell and did not address what the client actually needed. Today, most financial planners are highly trained, conscientious professionals. Unfortunately, some product peddlers still exist, except now they use fancy looking asset allocation models, instead of financial plans, to snare their customers. As before, the client's optimal solution just happens to be the product sitting on the planner's shelf.

One way an investor can ensure that the planner's interests are aligned with those of the investor's is to insist that the only compensation be fee or retainer-based.

Bank Trust Officers

Bank trust officers are regulated by the Office of the Comptroller at both the state and federal levels. A number of banks have put together very successful money management divisions that offer extremely competitive investment returns and services in the industry. However, most banks still struggle with an image problem of being too stodgy. One explanation may be that they are still perceived as lacking the ability to deliver the sophisticated investment management services covered in this book, such as designing client-specific investment strategies, or to implement those strategies with multiple styles and specialists.

Registered Investment Advisers

Registered investment advisers (RIAs) are regulated by the Securities and Exchange Commission (SEC) at the federal level and comparable state regulatory agencies at the state level. Registration with the SEC does not guarantee or imply a specific level of adviser competence. Therefore, it is imperative that the investor carefully read the adviser's ADV Parts I and II (registration documents filed with the SEC) to learn of the adviser's experience, services offered, and the adviser's method of compensation.[2]

Registration with the SEC is the same for money managers, investment advisers, and investment consultants, which causes confusion in the marketplace.[3]

Money managers. Of the 18,000 firms registered with the SEC, an estimated 2,000 are money managers. Money management firms are in the primary business of managing portfolios under a well-defined investment discipline and strategy. They take discretionary control of the investor's assets and make buy and sell decisions on specific

---

[2] ADV Form Part II is required to be delivered to a customer. Part I is not, but it should also be requested.

[3] The distinction between a money manager and a consultant is critical. The SEC should consider imposing separate registration requirements for the two, with a third registration category for the hybrid between a money manager and a consultant, such as "counselor managers," broker/consultants, and financial planners.

securities. The role of the money manager is *not* to develop and manage an in-depth, client-specific investment strategy, but rather to make investment decisions for the portfolio that are consistent with the investor's investment policy.

Investment Consultants. There are relatively few (probably less than 500) true investment consulting firms that provide investment planning and management services to investors. These firms do not sell investment products, nor do they take discretionary control of an investor's assets. By comparison to money managers, they do not effectuate trades or transactions.[4]

Investment Advisers. These make up the balance of registered firms. The adviser is composed of elements of both the money manager and the consultant. They may take discretionary control of a client's portfolio and actually buy and sell securities for the portfolio. Or they may develop a specific investment strategy for an investor and then offer to implement the strategy with appropriate money managers or mutual funds.

Consultant Search Criteria

With the closely paralleled and sometimes overlapping business strategies of the above professionals, it is difficult for the uninformed to distinguish between service providers. In searching for a consultant, the criteria are similar to those used in looking for a money manager. Review the firm's five Ps: People, Processes, Procedures, Policies, and sources of Payment. The following questions are provided as a quick screening tool. A more detailed questionnaire, in the form of a request for proposal (RFP), is provided in the appendix at the end of this chapter.

1. *Does the firm provide, as a minimum, the following services?*
   - Analysis of current investment needs and objectives.
   - Asset allocation studies.
   - Preparation of investment policy statements.
   - Money manager structure analysis.
   - Money manager searches.
   - Performance measurement.
   - Research and education.

---

[4] See NASD Notice 94-44.

2. *Does the firm have the professional staff with technical experitise to integrate an interdisciplinary approach between all service providers?* A competent staff should be able to coordinate information provided by the actuary, accountant, attorney, administrator, trust officer, and/or money manager(s).

3. *Can the firm demonstrate or affirm independent advocacy?* This is particularly necessary during the implementation phase of the investment management process. The firm that conducts an asset allocation study and then reports that the appropriate solution happens to be a selection of mutual funds manufactured by the consulting firm may not be working in the best interests of the investor.

4. *What are the training, experience, and depth of staff?* As mentioned previously, there are no formal degree programs in investment consulting, nor are there any special educational requirements to be a registered investment adviser. However, there are several excellent educational programs offered through professional associations and selective courses offered through traditional educational programs. None of these courses, though, are prerequisites for a person to call themselves an investment consultant.

5. *What are the firm's sources of data and research on money managers?* Larger consulting firms gather their own statistics on money managers. A follow-on question for the larger firms is whether or not money managers have to pay a fee to have their information included in the database. Obviously, firms that do not charge money managers tend to have a purer database. Smaller firms often purchase their data from commercial sources. A possible drawback is that the information may lack the depth of qualitative information that a larger firm would maintain on both a formal and informal basis.

6. *What are the firm's sources of background universes for performance measurement?* Background universes that are compiled from the measurement of actual client portfolios tend to offer better comparisons than background universes compiled from returns supplied by money managers. Managers that have large dispersions in performance results (differences between top and bottom performing portfolios) are more easily identified. The investor should check to see if the background universes are composed of mutual funds only, separately managed accounts only, or money manager-provided rates of return.

7. *What are the firm's sources of compensation?* The response to this question will probably reveal the greatest differences between firms.

Investment performance may be impacted by how the consultant is compensated. At one end of the spectrum are the product sellers, who are compensated from the commissions generated by the products sold to the investor. Typically, the investor's implementation choices are limited, and determining actual consultant compensation is difficult. At the other end of the spectrum are consultants that are compensated by a flat retainer, hourly fee, or asset-based fee. The consultant's compensation is not dependent on asset mix or implementation solutions and is easily determined. However, an asset based fee approach may be biased if the consultant receives a greater percentage for equity allocations as opposed to fixed income. Arguably, this creates an incentive for the consultant to recommend equity asset classes.

There can be significant differences among the fees charged by different consulting firms. One reason for this is that some firms, especially those affiliated with broker dealers, receive compensation other than their fee. These low fees should be carefully examined for hidden costs and arrangements not in the investor's best interests. Another reason for fee differences is that there are substantially different levels or quality of consulting services. A very small consulting firm may provide only advice, a canned approach, or a limited menu of services. Their resources may be quite limited, which reflects what the market will pay for their services. A large firm, on the other hand, may be able to deliver the full range of investment consulting services, calling upon vast internal resources, research, and knowledge. A careful needs assessment will tell a fiduciary which way to go.

In summary, the attributes of a good consultant mandate that he or she must (1) be willing and capable of educating the investor, (2) have equal access to all types of managers and product structure, (3) be free of conflicts of interest, and (4) be able to improve performance by either reducing expenses and costs or increasing returns.

The Consultant as a Cofiduciary

Generally, anytime a consultant has discretion over a client's assets, the consultant will be considered a fiduciary under common law and ERISA. A good consultant should always adhere to the standards of a fiduciary and conduct themselves accordingly, whether or not he or she is deemed to be a fiduciary.

Specific to ERISA, the following guidelines define the fiduciary status of consultants and other professional advisors:[5]

- Renders advice to the plan as to the value of securities or other property or makes recommendations as to the advisability of investing in, purchasing, or selling securities or other property.

-and-

- Either directly or indirectly (e.g., through or together with an affiliate):

Has discretionary authority or control with respect to purchasing or selling securities or other property for the plan

-or-

Renders investment advice on a regular basis to a plan pursuant to a written or oral mutual agreement, arrangement, or understanding with the plan or a plan fiduciary that such services will serve as the primary basis for investment decisions with respect to plan assets and the investment advice rendered to the plan will be individualized advice based on the particular needs of the plan regarding such matters as investment policies or strategy, overall portfolio composition, or diversification of plan investments.

But what about the consultant that does not have discretionary control, or does not fall within the formal ERISA definition? Are there circumstances when the consultant could still be considered a fiduciary? Final determination is ultimately made by the courts; however, three tests can be used to measure the likelihood of whether the consultant will be deemed a fiduciary, and therefore liable for cofiduciary breaches.[6]

1. *How sophisticated is the fiduciary or investment committee?* The consultant who provides services to a fiduciary that is sophisticated and knowledgeable about investments is less likely to be deemed a cofiduciary. On the other hand, the consultant who serves a committee that is totally dependent on the consultant's advice and suggestions is more likely to be considered a cofiduciary.

---

[5] ERISA Sec. 3(21); 29 U.S.C. Sec. 1002(21).

[6] White paper prepared by Tim Patterson, Esq. of the law firm Cooley Godward Castro Huddleson & Tatum, San Francisco, October, 1, 1993.

2. *How specific are the consultant's recommendations?* The consultant who provides an investment committee with specific implementation recommendations, such as submitting the name of one money manager for the committee to consider, is more likely to be deemed a fiduciary. The consultant who provides a lengthy list of appropriate and suitable solutions or options is less likely to be considered a cofiduciary.

3. *What is the scope of services provided?* The consultant who is hired for a single engagement, such as a money manager search, is less likely to be deemed a cofiduciary than the consultant who is providing full retainer services.

Wrap-Fee Programs

Wrap-fee programs have become increasingly popular with broker-consultants. The term *wrap fee* refers to a host of different brokered products that incorporate elements of traditional consulting services. The quality of the product varies dramatically between sponsoring broker-age firms and between the actual brokers who service the accounts. The following is a guide to the pros and cons of wrap fees, and questions to ask to help avoid costly mistakes.

> In short, wrap accounts probably aren't as bad as their critics claim, nor as good as their proponents argue. But it's a stretch to say they work as well as mutual funds for people with only $100,000 or so to invest.[7]

Wrap Fees—Pros

Wrap-fee programs were started by brokerage firms in the mid-80s to service clients who wanted access to professional money managers. Initially, costs under these programs for money management and transactions were typically 3.0 percent (300 basis points) for equity accounts. This resulted in a savings for the investor who was paying an average of 4.0 percent each year for commissioned products. Touted benefits of the wrap-fee programs include the following:

---

[7] Russ Wiles, "Picking a Strategy for Diversifying Investments," *Los Angeles Times,* August 9, 1993, p. D5.

1. **The client is provided a portfolio of individually managed securities.** The client's account is not commingled, as it is with a mutual fund, and is therefore insulated from the redemption activity of other investors. This is a particularly attractive feature for the long-term investor who knows the imprudence of selling-out in the middle of a crisis. Mutual funds must hold a certain percentage of a portfolio in cash to meet shareholder redemptions. If a large number of shareholders panic at once, the mutual fund is forced to sell securities in a down market at exactly the time the manager might prefer to be a purchaser rather than a seller. This decline may depress the value of the overall mutual fund portfolio. The long-term investor that stays with the fund is penalized by the flight of less-sophisticated investors.

2. **The client only has to a pay a single, all-inclusive fee that is negotiated and disclosed up front.** This is true, although in some cases there can still be hidden costs. For example, the sponsoring brokerage firm may earn additional revenue from the spread on fixed-income securities. The brokerage firm may be marking up bonds that it purchased for its own account and then reselling the bonds to the wrap-fee accounts at a substantial profit. The spread is never revealed in confirmations or monthly statements. Also, annual account fees, SEC trading fees, and wire charges may still apply.

3. **The client has the opportunity to employ personalized, tax-related investment strategies.** The taxable investor may be able to direct the money manager to sell securities to generate investment losses/gains for a particular tax year.

4. **The client is provided assistance in selecting the appropriate money manager.** This depends on the skills and objectivity of the broker-consultant.

Wrap Fees—Cons

As with many good ideas from Wall Street, there is the propensity for a product to be oversold and client expectations never to be met. Wrap fees are no exception. The following are some of the criticisms of wrap fee programs.

1. **Brokers are not trained to be consultants—they're trained to sell product.** It is very easy to distinguish brokers from consultants— one uses the mouth, the other the ears. Good consultants ask questions, lots of questions. Fortunately, brokerage firms are beginning to require

brokers to go through formal training programs on investment consulting before the broker is allowed to sell wrap-fee products. This is a step in the right direction.

2. **The fee is excessive, particularly if the client is serviced by a broker who has not been trained.** If, however, the broker is trained, and provides the client with (1) an asset allocation study, (2) assistance in writing an investment policy statement, (3) comprehensive information on a number of suitable managers, (4) performance measurement reports, and (5) education, then the fee is quite reasonable for portfolios below $500,000. Portfolios of greater value should be negotiating substantial discounts off the 3.0 percent.

3. **The client may not be receiving *best execution* in security transactions.** Some brokerage firms require money managers to place all, or a substantial portion, of their transactions with the brokerage firm. The client is at a disadvantage because the money manager is unable to trade away or seek the best price on each transaction. In some cases, the client may be paying substantially more (a hidden cost) for certain securities. As mentioned previously, potential abuse is highest with fixed-income portfolios where the price of a bond may be marked up by the brokerage firm. For fiduciaries who are charged with monitoring best execution, wrap-fee programs can potentially be viewed as contrary to this requirement.

4. **The strike price of securities purchased for wrap-fee clients may be at a disadvantage compared to institutional clients with the same money manager.** When a money manager has made a determination to either buy or sell a security, the manager places its trades with selected brokers. The trades for institutional clients are normally blocked—all the trades may be lumped and traded at once. For wrap-fee clients, the manager may have to segregate the trades and place them with the sponsoring brokerage firm. By the time the brokerage firm executes the same trade, the market may have been impacted by the larger institutional trade. [Since the performance of wrap-fee clients has not been made public by brokerage firms, it has been impossible to calculate the performance impact.]

5. **Smaller investors may be lulled into the glamorous appeal of having an individually managed wrap-fee account before carefully examining the option of implementing an investment strategy with no-load mutual funds.** As espoused throughout this book, asset allocation decisions have far more impact on long-term performance than

money manager selection. The investor that has only $100,000 will be better off diversifying the portfolio between four or five no-load mutual funds than one wrap-fee manager. In addition, the total costs of implementing the no-load mutual fund strategy should be substantially less.

6. **Turnover rates may be reduced and the number of security positions limited.** Brokerage firms typically do not like high-turnover managers or managers that hold a large number of positions in accounts. These features will eat into a brokerage house's profitability. For these reasons, some accounts may not be managed in the same manner as the manager's institutional clients.

Fund Wraps

A new twist to wrap-fee products are fund wraps. These products use no-load mutual funds as opposed to separately managed accounts. The investor, as always, is cautioned to examine and compare expenses. The brokerage firm will quote an advisory fee between 1.0 and 1.5 percent. On the surface this seems more appealing than the traditional wrap fee. But the broker has not included the total operating expenses of the funds, which when added to the advisory fee can easily push the total investment expense well above the 3 percent wrap. The following are specific questions that should be directed to providers of the fund wrap.

1. *How much is the wrap fee, and what do I receive in the way of personalized services?* Reasonable fund-wrap fees should be 1 percent with breakpoints for every $100,000. You should receive a personalized asset allocation study, detailed information on the funds from which you may select, ongoing comparative performance information, and assurance that your broker knows what he or she is doing.

2. *What are the total operating expenses of the funds?* Reasonable total operating expenses should range between 50 bp and 80 bp for fixed income and between 75 bp and 140 bp for equity accounts (including small cap and international). Remember, these fees are going to be in addition to the advisory fee.

3. *What have been the historical returns of the funds?* The funds should have a track record of at least five years. If the fund is new, ask if the money manager has at least a five-year track record managing a similar fund. In all cases compare the returns to other no-load funds with similar investment strategies.

4. *Will I receive ongoing performance measurement reports on my account?* If the answer is no, move on—there are plenty of firms who will provide the service.

5. *How will the portfolio be rebalanced (realigned to the original asset mix between equity and fixed-income funds)?* The mix between equity and fixed income funds should not be left to drift with the market. A specific strategy and mechanism should be provided in order to rebalance the portfolio.

Summary

A good consultant should more than earn his or her fee—a bad one can cost an investor much more than the fees paid. An excellent consulting relationship empowers the investor to make more intelligent decisions, informed by the theory, tools, and wisdom of experts. Thus, as curious investors learn more about the power of the prudent process, they turn to professional consultants to facilitate their commitment to an intelligent, long-term investment strategy and to ensure they gain maximum benefit from its thoughtful implementation. This can be even more compelling for fiduciaries when they realize they will be judged by the process they followed and not by the investment results ultimately achieved.

Of course, each individual investor must ask what value consultants might add to his or her own specific investment process. Does the consultant have the right tools to address one's portfolio needs? Are the consultant's services entirely objective? Can one distinguish the truly superior consultant from the one who merely mouths the right words?

As we've seen in the first nine chapters of this book, there is a lot more to a good investment process than the average investor or fiduciary realizes, and there are many ways to go wrong by skipping or shortchanging a step. A good consultant can be an enormous help in executing a prudent process and protecting the fiduciary from liability, not to mention achieving excellent long-term investment results. The icing on the cake is that the consultant's ability to negotiate with other service providers may actually save an investor more than the sum of the consultant's fee.

APPENDIX
INVESTMENT CONSULTING SERVICES (RFP)

I. Identity and Address of Principals

A. Name of firm(s).

B. Name, address, and telephone numbers of key contact.

C. Ownership structure of firm(s).

D. Brief biographies of individuals to be assigned.

E. Business focus/client base.

    1. What is the primary business focus of your firm? Is your firm affiliated with any organization(s), specifically a brokerage firm? If yes, describe the relationship in full.

    2. What is your firm's targeted market in terms of plan size?

    3. How many consulting clients do you currently have? What is the average plan size of your clientele?

    4. What is the client turnover (gains and losses) of your firm over the last three years?

    5. How many full-time staff are employed by your firm?

II. Investment Management Process

A. Asset allocation methodology.

    1. Describe in detail how your capital markets projections are derived.

    2. Describe your asset allocation software. Is it developed in-house? If purchased externally, who is the vendor?

    3. Do you have a full-time staff committed to the development of your modeling capabilities? If so, briefly describe their qualifications.

B. Investment policy statements.

    1. Describe in detail the process you go through to prepare an investment policy statement.

    2. Include a copy of an investment policy statement that would be appropriate for a plan of this size.

C. Money manager structure and search process.

    1. Do you maintain a database of money management organizations? If so, is the database compiled internally or purchased from an outside source? If purchased externally, who is the vendor?

    2. How many money managers do you currently track?

    3. What is the method for gathering information on the investment managers? How often are the data updated?

    4. Are managers required to pay a fee for inclusion in your database?

5. Describe, in step-by-step detail, your due diligence/search process for selecting managers.
6. What are the guidelines you give a client with respect to the possible termination of a money manager?
7. How many full-time staff do you employ who are professionally trained in due diligence?
8. How often does your staff visit with money managers, both in-house and on-site?

D. Performance measurement.
1. Describe your firm's process of monitoring money managers for a client. Relate the process to a client's goals, objectives, and investment policy.
2. List comparisons, including databases, used to analyze the performance of portfolios. If a firm's own database is utilized, describe its derivation.
3. Are the various databases your firm uses developed in-house or are they purchased from another source? If purchased, please provide the source of the database and describe your ability to monitor and/or control the contents of the database and any alternative resources if the database was no longer available to you.
4. Does your firm maintain style groups for comparative purposes? Briefly describe how the style groups are derived.
5. How soon after the quarter-end are your reports available?
6. Please provide a sample performance measurement report.

III. Trustee Training

A. Does your organization offer training of trustees as it relates to their fiduciary responsibilities?
B. Describe the materials available to facilitate the training.
C. Describe the qualifications of the individuals assigned to conduct the training.

IV. Fee Schedule

A. Please outline your fee structure for this plan. Please indicate all services you propose to provide and their associated fees. Specifically, detail in terms of retainer, manager searches, performance monitoring on a quarterly basis, and other functions.
B. The stated fee schedule must include all charges associated with your service provisions; the above fees must reflect your costs in their entirety.

C. Does your firm accept soft dollars as a method of payment for services provided? If so, how do you prevent conflicts of interest? Please list the advantages and disadvantages you see in the use of soft dollars.

D. If hired, will your firm receive any other form of compensation from working with this account that has not yet been revealed? If yes, what is the form of compensation?

LEGAL INVESTMENT PRINCIPLES AND COMMON FIDUCIARY BREACHES

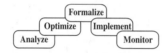

*"Some people are like dirty clothes.
They only come clean when they're in hot water."*
J. W. Sullivan

*"If you don't know where you are going,
you might wind up someplace else."*
Yogi Berra

The legal and practical scrutiny a fiduciary undergoes is tremendous. It comes from multiple directions and for various reasons. Over the last several years, this scrutiny has increased the liability placed on fiduciaries for making investment decisions. The following are some general reasons why fiduciaries have seen their liability increase.

General Investment Truisms

- The 90s will probably not see the same spectacular investment returns as the 80s. Investors today tend to have unrealistically high return expectations, and litigation is likely to ensue when

263

those expectations are not met. Returns from traditional
investment classes will likely be closer to their lower
historical averages.

- There is a higher propensity for investor litigation because of
  the failure of so many financial institutions and Wall Street
  investment products. Dissatisfied investors are vocal and more
  visible, as evidenced by widespread increases in investor
  litigation and arbitration.

Retirement Plan Arena

- There are increased enforcement efforts by the government
  to ferret out fraud, prohibited transactions, and the mismanagement of investments. While other government agencies
  are experiencing funding cuts, the DOL and IRS are receiving
  additional resources to properly police the management of
  retirement plan assets.[1]

- The government is concerned that it will not be able to sustain
  the current level of social security system retirement payments.
  It is estimated that within twenty years disbursements for social
  security payments will exceed contributions. If no alterations
  are made to the system's collection and payment policies,
  social security will be bankrupt by the year 2029. Pressure on
  the social security system can only be relieved if the private
  sector assumes more responsibility for the management of their
  retirement funding sources.

- Public retirement funds have become the latest target of the
  political agenda. Charges of investment mismanagement levied
  against investment committee members are easy to make and
  difficult for the investment committee to defend. Ensuing
  investigations make sensational headlines that are exploited
  by disenfranchised politicians.

---

[1] The 1989 Omnibus Reconciliation Act implemented a 20 percent penalty against fiduciaries
for detected violations of their responsibilities owed to retirement plan participants. The act
also provided for 100 new Department of Labor compliance officers and 33 new Department
of Labor attorneys. In 1990, the Department of Labor released its Enforcement Strategy
Implementation Plan that targeted service providers, financial institutions, and high-risk plans.

- Retirement plan participants have become more sophisticated and knowledgeable and are demanding and expecting a higher level of fiduciary conduct from trustees.

Trust Arena

- In family trusts, as the succession of wealth is made from one generation to the next, there sometimes exists a presumptive attitude by the next generation that they have a right to their inheritance without encumbrance. Charges of mismanagement against current trustees is a typical avenue beneficiaries have used to terminate trust documents.
- Estate planning and other documents that created trusts are continuing to spring into life as settlors and individuals die or become disabled or incompetent. With medical advances allowing the body to outlive the mind, trusts and guardianship proceedings are becoming more commonplace. The proliferation of living trusts has also created an area of the law that has not matured as extensively as the interpretative law of will provisions.
- Bank trust administrations have come under intense examination due to today's age of instant information. Advancements have fostered a degree of accountability and have increased performance pressure due to the ability to obtain quick comparative results.
- Charitable trusts and foundations are experiencing a demand for a higher level of accountability from donors prior to, or in conjunction with, the making of gifts. Poor investment results or the inability to articulate investment objectives will cause donors to rethink their gifting strategies and make gifts to charities that are more accountable.
- Even investments made under the Uniform Gift to Minors Act and the Uniform Transfers to Minors Act have subjected individuals to fiduciary scrutiny.[2]

---

[2] One case involved a spouse being found to have violated the prudent person rule where speculation, and not preservation of capital, was undertaken. This premise has been used following a divorce as a source of recoupment of losses and removal of an ex-spouse as custodian. *Buder v. Sartore,* 759 P.2d 785 (Colo. Ct. App. 1988), *aff'd,* 774 P.2d 1383 (Colo. 1989).

The growth of these pressures can best be examined against the backdrop of the evolution of prudent investment practices. The following discussion analyzes and addresses the current principles that have sprung from this topic.

Historical Perspective

The concept of prudent fiduciary conduct is rooted in the 1830 case of *Harvard College* v. *Armory* that described the duty owed by a trustee to beneficiaries:

> All that can be required of a trustee to invest is, that he shall conduct himself faithfully and exercise sound discretion. He is to observe how men of prudence, discretion, and intelligence manage their own affairs, not in regard to speculation, but in regard to the permanent disposition of their funds, considering the probable income, as well as the probable safety of the capital to be invested.[3]

On its face, this classic expression of prudence was flexible and open-ended to adjust for changing economic circumstances. Of primary importance, the court established a process standard—the trustee should govern affairs according to the prevailing standard of "how men of prudence, discretion and intelligence managed their own affairs." The court also realized that absolute safety was impossible, but the trustee was to acquire investments subject to a substantive standard of safety— appropriate for permanent disposition of one's own funds, not for speculation.

Thereafter, however, the courts and legislators traced a circuitous route in giving guidance to fiduciaries, over time diminishing the flexibility of the *Harvard College* standard. At first, perhaps driven by the desire for certainty, states abandoned the workable notion of prudence found in the *Harvard College* test and adopted all sorts of legal lists of investments that were considered absolutely safe and prudent (mostly government bonds) and those that were per se imprudent (common stock and just about everything else). When the capital markets collapsed in the Great Depression, the legal community was understandably less enamored with the legal lists of so-called prudent investments.

---

[3] *Harvard College* v. *Armory,* 26 Mass. (9 Pick) 446, 461 (1830), hereinafter, *Harvard College.*

By 1940, most of the legal list statutes were replaced with some form of what is now known as the *prudent man rule.* While the rule was meant to release the fiduciary from the constraints of the legal lists, the rule became nearly as inflexible as the legal lists it replaced. What the state statutes gave with one hand, case law took away with the other.

The prudent man rule did not allow fiduciaries full investment freedom according to money management principles current at the time of investment. Rather, it again drew a distinction between prudent and imprudent investments. Case law generally required that the prudence of each investment or security be judged in isolation, without regard to its intended purpose in the overall design of the investment portfolio. In addition, fiduciaries were expected to preserve the nominal value of their funds, but did not have to strive to increase the value of the portfolio even in the face of inflation. This became an impediment to successful investing.

> Prohibitions that developed under the traditional prudent man rule have been potential sources of unjustified liability for trustees generally and, more practically, of inhibitions limiting the exercise of sound judgment by skilled trustees.[4]

In the last decade, a new standard of prudence has been advanced (the Third Restatement) through the efforts of numerous academicians, investment experts, lawyers, and judges. Rooted in modern portfolio theory, the Third Restatement emphasizes that the portfolio should be examined in its totality and that the results of a single investment can only be meaningfully evaluated against this macro framework. Losses may be acceptable if they were the result of the desire to obtain appropriate diversification that maximized return of the overall portfolio while limiting overall portfolio risk.

The Third Restatement bears a strong resemblance to ERISA fiduciary standards, which embraces the original process test of the *Harvard College* language. A fiduciary must consider "the circumstances then prevailing" and the "character" and "aims" of the "enterprise." Without following a process, the fiduciary can be deemed to have breached his or her duties, regardless of whether the decisions ultimately proved to be correct. Furthermore, *no fiduciary has been held to a standard of reading tomorrow's* Wall Street Journal *today.*

---

[4]Restatement Third, p. 4.

The Third Restatement plays on this same process theme by acknowledging that it "seeks to modernize trust investment law."[5] It is also designed to be a general and flexible doctrine that gives consideration to changes in the financial world. It is not to be a rigid and harsh doctrine that creates prohibitions that become potential sources of unjustifiable liability for trustees or inhibitors of sound investment judgment. "The trustee must give reasonably careful consideration to both the formulation and the implementation of an appropriate investment strategy, with investments to be selected and reviewed in a manner reasonably appropriate to that strategy."[6]

The Third Restatement promotes the following general principles:

1. Sound diversification is fundamental to risk management and is therefore ordinarily required of trustees.

2. Risk and return are so directly related that trustees have a duty to analyze and make conscious decisions concerning the levels of risk appropriate for the purposes, distribution requirements, and other circumstances of the trusts they administer.

3. Trustees have a duty to avoid fees, transaction costs, and other expenses that are not justified by needs and realistic objectives of the trust's investment program.

4. The fiduciary duty of impartiality requires a balancing of the elements of return between production of current income and the protection of purchasing power.

5. Trustees may have a duty as well as having the authority to delegate as prudent investors would.[7]

The Third Restatement, like ERISA, realizes that the test of prudence is one of conduct, not one of performance.[8] Consequently, the broad outlines of a fiduciary's duty of prudent investing are substantially the same regardless of whether one is a director of a foundation, a college or pension fund trustee, the trustee of a private trust, or the serious investor that merely desires successful investment results.

---

[5] Ibid., Introduction, page 5.
[6] Ibid., p. 14.
[7] Ibid., pp. 5–6.
[8] Ibid., p. 23.

Process Standard

Process is the key to the approach required of fiduciaries by today's prudence standard. Of course, the purpose of the process standard is to best assure well-reasoned decisions leading to long-term positive investment performance, taking advantage of the best information and practices available.

Today's standards shift the focus from the investments themselves to the fiduciary, the portfolio, and its purpose. A fiduciary will be found to have met the standard by examining the process by which investment choices were decided. In essence, did the actions resemble those of prudent men and women engaged in the real world of investments? How were investment strategies developed, adopted, implemented, and monitored in light of the purposes of the investment funds?

A fiduciary demonstrates prudence by the process through which investment decisions were managed, rather than by a showing that investment products and techniques were chosen because they were prelabeled as "prudent." No investments are imprudent on their face. It is the way in which they are used, and how decisions as to their use are made, that will be examined to determine whether the prudence standard has been met. Even the most aggressive and unconventional investment can meet that standard if arrived at through a sound process, while the most conservative and traditional one may not measure up if a sound process is lacking.

The process standard incorporates the traditional duty of caution to address the need for limits on risk taking as well as value judgments about the soundness of the fiduciary's economic assumptions. But it does so by considering the suitability of an investment in light of the portfolio's resources, cash flow needs, and risk tolerance, not by mandating the choice of securities.

Common Problem Areas

An examination of case law dealing with breaches of fiduciary conduct center around several themes. These can be classified into the following general categories:

1. Failure to follow a structured investment process.

2. Ignoring of investment provisions in plan/trust documents governing the investable funds.
3. Selection of inappropriate asset classes.
4. Failure to properly diversify the portfolio.
5. Failure to avoid prohibited transactions and/or involvement in improper conduct.

Failure to Follow a Structured Investment Process

Most litigation dealing with breaches of fiduciary conduct start because someone lost money or did not receive what they thought they were owed or promised. Where there has been a loss, there has been a tendency to closely scrutinize the conduct of the fiduciary in the hopes of finding some mistake, fraud, or error to help justify a decision that the fiduciary should be held liable. Many times it is not a single error, but rather the cumulative and compound effect of sloppy conduct that gives rise to the finding of liability. That is why this book has stressed the importance of conduct and process and not performance in order to protect the fiduciary from criticism and liability.

ERISA, the Third Restatement and other statutes and case law require the fiduciary to "investigate the merits of the investment."[9] This is not so much an examination and research of specific stocks or bonds, especially if delegation of investment decisions has been made to an appropriate money manager.[10] Rather, this focus is tied closely with the fiduciary's actions. Under ERISA, inappropriate conduct typically hinges on the lack of appropriate energy, effort, and analysis of the activity that led to the subsequent investment loss.[11] Or the lax monitoring by the fiduciary of investment activities failed to detect and avoid the losses that may have subsequently occurred. A finding of fiduciary breach is often coupled with inappropriate initial conduct and ongoing failure to take corrective measures.

---

[9] *Donovan* v. *Mazzola,* 716 F.2d 1226, 1232 (9th Cir. 1983).

[10] Delegation is permissible under ERISA Sec. 405(d)(1). However, some state statutes dealing with public pension plans still require that the trustees approve each trade made by a money manager. (See Texas Local Firefighters Retirement Act, Article 6243e—see legislative history.)

[11] See *GIW Industries, Inc.,* v. *Trevor, Stewart, Burton & Jacobsen, Inc.,* 895 F.2d 729 (11th Cir. 1990), dealing with mismatching of benefits potentially payable to long-term U.S. government bonds purchased by the plan; *Marshall* v. *Glass/Metal Association & Glazers & Glassworkers Pension Plan,* 507 F.Supp. 378 (D. Hi. 1980), dealing with inappropriate procedures that a prudent lender would follow; and *Donovan* v. *Tricario,* 5 EBC 2057 (S.D. Fla. 1984), dealing with life insurance.

The Third Restatement recognizes that investment losses are inevitable, but may be acceptable if the portfolio has been properly invested to accomplish the objectives of the trust. "The test of prudence is one of conduct and not of performance."[12] Losses may occur, but prudence should have prevailed in anticipating these losses. [This would seem to repeal existing anti-netting provisions under common trust law. However, the Third Restatement does not go this far and still suggests the isolation of breaches of trust and does not permit the reduction of a loss by the gain obtained from a separate investment activity.[13]]

Ignoring Investment Provisions of Plan/Trust Documents

Chapter 3 provided an extensive discussion on the fact-finding process required of a person making investment decisions. Part of this process is the examination of the document(s) governing the invested portfolio. For a trust or pension plan, this entails a detailed examination of the trust agreement or plan document for provisions that restrict or mandate the use of certain asset classes or securities (for example, provisions that call for investments in government bonds only, or restrict investments in futures or derivatives). Some of these restrictive or mandated provisions may not be readily apparent or may not be contained in one specific area of the document. For this reason, there is no substitute for reading the entire document in order to see if hidden provisions exist.

ERISA requires a fiduciary to act "in accordance with the documents and instruments governing the plan insofar as such documents and instruments are consistent with the provisions of this title (I) or Title IV."[14] Although this provision has been used primarily to enforce benefit claims, it has also been used when there were obvious violations of investment provisions contained in the plan document. Even though this would seem like an easy requirement to satisfy, there are cases where there has been a finding of a breach of fiduciary duty simply because investments violated the plan document provisions. Examples include (1) the failure to annually provide the fair market value of plan assets as required under the plan document;[15] (2) the failure to follow the plan's written investment guidelines deemed to be part of the "documents

---

[12] Restatement Third, Sec. 227, Comment e, *General requirement of caution,* p. 23.

[13] Ibid., Sec. 213.

[14] ERISA Sec. 404(a)(1)(D).

[15] *Brock* v. *Self,* 632 F.Supp. 1509 (W.D. La. 1988).

and instruments governing the plan;" [16] and (3) exceeding a specified plan limitation against investing more than a specified percentage of plan assets in one investment unless certain procedures were followed.[17]

The Third Restatement has likewise addressed this common breach.[18] Trustees are required to invest funds according to the terms of the trust.

One area of potential difficulty is the situation where the trust document includes instructions that investments should be made in accordance with the Third Restatement, but state law governing the trust has not yet adopted the Third Restatement provisions. If the law of the particular jurisdiction does not permit the overriding of its more restrictive policy, then a trustee following the document language (and intent) might unwittingly adopt an investment strategy that is legally imprudent. For this reason, it must also be determined if appropriate state law allows the language or desired intent. Inquiry about this potential problem should be made to competent legal counsel. It is advisable to obtain a brief legal opinion on whether a proposed investment policy statement contravenes or violates any applicable statutes before it is implemented. [This is an expense that may be appropriately charged to trust assets.]

Even if broadly worded trust investment provisions are expressly followed, there still exists a requirement that the fiduciary understand the exact purpose and circumstances surrounding the original intent of the trust, its goals, and the needs of the beneficiaries. Most trust documents have been prepared from standard boilerplate forms that address only the basic trust provisions (e.g., who is the trustee, when will trust distributions be made, when will the trust terminate, and so on). These documents typically do not contain language that provides sufficient information from which to build an investment management program.

As an example, a simple trust document provides for payment of all income to a grandchild. This trust may have been funded because the settlor was concerned about that grandchild's inability or inexperience to manage investments or because the grandchild is a spendthrift. If it is because the grandchild has no investment experience, then the trustee

---

[16] *Dardaginis v. Grace Capital, Inc.,* 644 F.Supp 105 (S.D.N.Y. 1989), *aff'd,* 889 F.2d 1237 (2nd Cir. 1989).

[17] *Marshall v. Teamsters Local 282 Pension Trust Fund,* 458 F.Supp. 986 (E.D.N.Y. 1978).

[18] Restatement Third, Secs. 228 and 210.

should encourage the grandchild to develop an investment program of his or her own and to incorporate this into the investment decisions made with the trust assets. If, however, the purpose of the trust is to avoid a spendthrift problem, then the trustee has a duty to monitor the beneficiary's spending habits and adjust the level of income accordingly. Involvement in the total facts and circumstances of each particular case goes a long way in diffusing potential claims of breach of fiduciary conduct.[19]

It is incumbent on a fiduciary to assess the provisions dealing with restrictions or procedures that must be followed under plan documents in order to comply with such provisions. It is both embarrassing and expensive to miss basic provisions that can create this type of liability.

Selection of Inappropriate Asset Classes

Investment decisions of a fiduciary may be measured against the then-prevailing standards or practices of similar fiduciaries in like circumstances. Therefore, it is incumbent on the fiduciary to be aware of the consensus thoughts and practices in the industry. For example, there are few in the investment consulting industry that would suggest the use of commodity trading in other than a hedging technique.[20]

One aspect of the adoption of modern portfolio theory by the Third Restatement and ERISA is the potential breach that can occur even if safe investments are utilized. Since these standards incorporate the requirement to at least preserve the portfolio against the ravages of inflation, allocating all the assets into safe investments, such as CDs, government securities, and GICs (guaranteed investment contracts), may run afoul of the intent of these standards.

On a related matter, the asset class may be entirely appropriate but considering the circumstances, the subasset class or implementation approach is wrong. Fiduciary liability can also result from investments in securities that have marginal liquidity or collateral.[21] An example would be the appropriate allocation to fixed income, but the inappropriate purchase of thinly traded, hard-to-price collateralized loan pools.

---

[19] Example and premise used by permission from May 1993 presentation of William Hoisington entitled "Modern Investment Principles and the Prudent California Trustee" at the UCLA-CEB Estate Planning Institute.

[20] See *Matter of Hyde Trust,* 458 N.W.2d 802 (S.D. 1990), where commodities were considered imprudent per se.

[21] See *Katsaros* v. *Cody,* 744 F.2d 270 (2nd Cir. 1984); *Martin* v. *Daugherty,* No. C89-3780 (N.D. Cal.); and *Whitfield* v. *Tomasso,* 682 F.Supp. 1287 (E.D.N.Y. 1988).

Finally, the fiduciary must also give consideration to the investment vehicles utilized to implement the strategy. A widely held belief is that the decision to make a commitment to a particular asset class will be impacted by the size of the entire portfolio. International investments may be appropriate for a portfolio containing equities but should only be obtained through mutual funds if there are size constraints. As another example, it may be wholly appropriate for a $100 million retirement plan to make an allocation of 5 percent to alternative investments, however, the $1 million plan should not be so inclined.

Failure to Properly Diversify the Portfolio

Certain investment risks can be diversified away, and the lack of diversification should be cause for frustration. The $400,000 stock portfolio that only contains 8 to 10 issues relies too much on the performance of those individual securities. Clearly, diversifying the portfolio among more issues will uncouple the portfolio from being so dependent on so few securities.

ERISA and the Third Restatement are very specific about the requirement for diversification:

> [A fiduciary shall discharge his duties with respect to a plan solely in the interest of the participants and beneficiaries . . .]:
>
> > (C) by diversifying the investments of the plan so as to minimize the risk of large losses, unless under the circumstances it is clearly prudent not to do so.[22]
>
> In making and implementing investment decisions, the trustee has a duty to diversify the investments of the trust unless, under the circumstances, it is prudent not to do so."[23]

A claim against a fiduciary for lack of diversification is particularly troublesome since, once the plaintiff proves a failure to diversify, the burden shifts to the fiduciary to prove that under the circumstances the lack of diversification was appropriate.[24] Breaches of fiduciary duty

---

[22] ERISA Sec. 404(a)(1)(C).

[23] Restatement Third, Sec. 227(b).

[24] See the Conference Report on ERISA, H.R. 93-1280; *Freund* v. *Marshall & Ilsley Bank,* 485 F.Supp. 629 (W.D. Wisc. 1979); and *Marshall* v. *Glass/Metal Association & Glazers & Glassworkers Pension Plan, supra* note 12, but see *Jones* v. *O'Higgins,* 11 EBC 1660 (N.D.N.Y. 1989); *DeBruyne* v. *Equitable Life Assurance Society of U.S.* 720 F.Supp. 1342 (N.D. Ill. 1989), *aff'd,* 920 F.2d 457 (7th Cir. 1990); and *Etter* v. *J. Pease Construction Co.,* 963 F.2d 1005 (7th Cir. 1992), where large percentages of plan assets into specific asset classes did not violate ERISA diversification requirement. Under Third Restatement, see discussion of Illustration 11 contained on page 22, where it may be appropriate to have entire trust assets invested in secure, short-term debt instruments.

due to the lack of diversification have typically fallen into three general areas: (1) geography, (2) capital markets, and (3) industry. No specific percentage has been stated as to what constitutes lack of diversification, although the DOL has informally adopted a threshold level of 20 percent.[25] A breach will be dependent on the facts and circumstances of each case.

Geographical Lack of Diversification. Liability for the concentration of investments into a limited geographic region has usually included mortgages secured by real estate and/or direct real estate investments. To date, case law has primarily involved ERISA fiduciaries.[26] The concentration of assets into one economic region subjects the portfolio to too much reliance on the health of the local economy. As an example, an allocation to real estate may be more appropriately implemented by using a real estate sector mutual fund, REITs, or an investment pool. An inappropriate choice would be the purchase of a single apartment complex.

A similar argument could be made in the selection of service vendors, particularly money managers. Fiduciaries who have purposefully limited money manager searches to only those managers that reside in a particular geographic area may not be fulfilling their responsibilities. This myopic selection criterion, while noble in order to retain revenues within a geographic area, is completely unwarranted in today's competitive marketplace.

Lack of Diversification within Capital Markets. The placement of assets into only one asset class is contrary to the benefits obtained from asset allocation. The courts have found liability in situations where there has been an overcommitment to certain asset classes, such as risky loans and even government bonds.[27]

Under the Third Restatement, there exists an overriding duty to make trust property productive (including the preservation of the purchasing power of the trust) and to balance the trust portfolio between the needs

---

[25] See discussion of this lack of the ability to specify percentages contained in the Conference Report on ERISA, H.R. 93-1280 at 304. The informal DOL percentage is based on discussions with certain DOL and U.S. attorneys litigating ERISA cases against fiduciaries for lack of diversification. Plan assets in excess of this percentage are initially determined based on the answer to question 27d and 31 on the IRS Form 5500.

[26] *Brock* v. *Citizens Bank of Clovis*, 841 F.2d 344 (10th Cir. 1988); and *Donovan* v. *Guaranty National Bank*, 4 EBC 1686 (S.D. W. Va. 1983).

[27] See *GIW Industries, Inc.*, v. *Trevor, Stewart, Burton & Jacobsen, Inc.*, *supra* note 12.

of beneficiaries. Where a trustee has assumed responsibility for an undiversified portfolio (e.g., a large block of a single publicly traded stock), the trustee may be required to either adopt appropriate accounting practices or sell some or all of the property within a reasonable period of time.[28] Appropriate accounting practices include the establishment of reserve, amortization, or depreciation accounts to take into consideration the current and future needs of beneficiaries. Where an asset once was productive but subsequently becomes unproductive, the trustee is under an obligation to sell the property. This again stresses the importance of the monitoring function.

Too Much Industry Concentration.   Even though the portfolio may be diversified between different asset classes, the placement of a large percentage of assets in one specific industry sector will subject the portfolio to too much reliance on the economic viability of that industry. As an example, a balanced manager that utilizes a value style of management may decide to make a large commitment to the perceived undervalued oil industry. On the fixed-income side of the portfolio, the manager may also be buying bonds issued by utilities tied to oil consumption. In this situation, the portfolio may appear to be diversified, but in reality the portfolio has too much riding on the price per barrel of oil.

Failure to Avoid Prohibited Transactions and/or Involvement in Improper Conduct

Claims of imprudent conduct arise where the fiduciary has not dealt with the beneficiaries/participants impartially or has utilized the assets for purposes other than for the primary benefit of the beneficiaries/participants. ERISA requires plan fiduciaries to act solely in the interest of plan participants and beneficiaries.[29] The Third Restatement also requires the trustee to "conform to fundamental fiduciary duties of loyalty (Sec. 170) and impartiality (Sec. 183)."[30]

ERISA case law includes instances where action was brought against fiduciaries that (1) treated plan assets as if they were their own

---

[28] Restatement Third, Secs. 239 and 240.

[29] ERISA Sec. 404(a)(1)(A).

[30] Restatement Third, Sec. 227.

property,[31] (2) made loans to a related corporation,[32] (3) kept plan assets in a bank that lent money to the company president,[33] (4) did not pursue collection of loans made to a related entity,[34] (5) structured the trustee provisions for continued job security,[35] and (6) received various gifts, including the use of a vacation condominium, from the plan's principal service provider.[36] Fiduciary breaches of conduct also include instances when the fiduciary may not have benefited personally, but some related third party did. Examples include payments to a widow of a former trustee[37] and favorable loan terms to a friend of a trustee.[38]

Any activity that does not provide an exclusive benefit for plan participants or trust beneficiaries will cause problems. It is paramount that the plan assets be treated with respect and that no one receives any benefit simply by being the trustee or fiduciary, friend of the trustee or employer, or a relative of any of the trustees or employer. Prohibited transaction rules address similar issues and are discussed below.

The Third Restatement expressly requires loyalty and impartiality of the trustee. Loyalty prohibits the trustee from investing or managing the trust assets in such a way that there arises either a personal conflict of interest or a benefit to someone other than the beneficiaries or for purposes of the settlor. The trustee must at all times have a sense of undivided loyalty to all beneficiaries so the intended purposes of the trust can be accomplished. The trustee cannot use the trust assets to advance his or her own personal agenda, whether it be for social or political causes.

The duty of impartiality is far more difficult to satisfy than the duty of loyalty. The most difficult aspect in dealing with impartiality is the competing or, as the Third Restatement terms it, the "divergent economic interests" of trust beneficiaries.[39]

---

[31] *Wright* v. *Nimmons,* 641 F.Supp. 1391 (S.D. Tex. 1986).

[32] *Marshall* v. *Kelly,* 465 F.Supp. 341 (W.D. Okla. 1978).

[33] *Marshall* v. *Carroll,* 2 EBC 2491 (N.D. Cal. 1980), *aff'd without op.,* 673 F.2d 1337 (9th Cir. 1981).

[34] *Marshall* v. *Mercer,* 4 EBC 1523 (N.D. Tex. 1983).

[35] *Teamsters Local No. 145* v. *Kuba,* 631 F.Supp. 1063 (D. Conn. 1986).

[36] *Brink* v. *DeLesio,* 496 F.Supp. 1350 (D. Md. 1980), *aff'd,* 667 F.2d 420 (4th Cir. 1981).

[37] *Marshall* v. *Cuevas,* 1 EBC 1580 (D. P.R. 1979).

[38] *Marshall* v. *Kelly,* 465 F.Supp. 341 (W.D. Okla. 1978).

[39] Restatement Third, Comment c, p. 13.

When there are two or more beneficiaries of a trust, the trustee is under a duty to deal impartially with them.[40]

If a trust is created for beneficiaries in succession, the trustee is under a duty to the successive beneficiaries to act with due regard to their respective interests.[41]

Potential conflicts are in place where the interests of a life income beneficiary must be delicately balanced with the interests of the remainder beneficiaries. The balance requires an examination and awareness of inflation and tax considerations (portfolio preservation) along with the issue of the generation of income to the detriment of principal growth. An attempt to achieve a respectable total return may ignore the needs of the income beneficiary. The generation of too much income is inevitably at the expense of the remainder beneficiary. For this reason a Schedule of Cash Flows and Projection of Principal Growth will need to be prepared and made a part of the investment policy statement.

Illustration.   John is successor trustee of a living trust established and previously administered by Bob, who recently died. The trust is now designed to pay its net income to Bob's spouse, Betty, for life, with remainder thereafter to pass to the then-living children of Betty and Bob.

Like the typical individual investor dealing with personal funds, Bob was in a position during his life to concentrate on total return without having to consider the principal or income ingredients of that return. Following his death, two new factors come into the picture. First, implicit in the terms of the trust, now there is a significant distinction between income and principal. Second, there is now a fiduciary duty of impartiality between the successive beneficial interests of Betty and those of the children. These factors combine to impose a duty on John to make the trust estate productive of income in the trust accounting sense.[42]

In this example, the trust's investment objectives have gone through a metamorphosis and are now going to require the reallocation of the trust assets to income-producing assets while giving consideration to the remainder beneficiaries (children). This would require an evaluation

---

[40] Ibid., Sec. 183.
[41] Ibid., Sec. 232.
[42] Ibid., Illustration 16, p. 35.

of the life expectancy and the income requirements of Betty. Betty's children have an expectation of reasonable principal growth so their future receipt of assets is at least inflation protected. If all these factors are not taken into consideration, John has breached the fiduciary duty of impartiality to one of the trust beneficiaries. This is a tightrope walk that must be documented in order to protect John from future liability.

Prohibited Transactions. ERISA expressly contains language dealing with plan transactions that are prohibited:

(1) A fiduciary with respect to a plan shall not cause the plan to engage in a transaction, if he knows or should know that such transaction constitutes a direct or indirect:
  (a) sale or exchange, or leasing, of any property between the plan and a party in interest
  (b) lending money or other extension of credit between the plan and a party in interest
  (c) furnishing goods, services, or facilities between the plan and a party in interest
  (d) transfer to, or use by or for the benefit of, a party in interest
  (e) cause a plan to acquire and to retain employer securities or employer real property in violation of Section 407(a)." [43]

A common prohibited transaction is the sale or exchange of real property between the fiduciary/owner and the plan. For example, a professional buys his or her own office condominium with qualified plan assets and then leases the office space back to the business. Another example would occur when the company uses retirement plan assets to purchase new land or buildings for expansion. Besides the ERISA cases cited above, other prohibited transactions have included (1) a loan being made to a party in interest,[44] (2) fiduciaries investing plan

---

[43] ERISA Sec. 406(a)(1)(A)–(E). The first four categories are also prohibited transactions under I.R.C. Sec. 4975. In addition to these five specific prohibited transactions, Sec. 406(b) prohibits fiduciaries from engaging in various acts of self-dealing or conflicts of interest: a fiduciary may not (1) deal with plan assets in its own interest (Sec. 406(b)(1)), (2) act in a transaction involving a plan on behalf of a person whose interests are adverse to the interests of a plan, participant, or beneficiary (Sec. 406(b)(2)), or (3) receive any consideration for the fiduciary's personal account from any party dealing in connection with a transaction involving the plan's assets (Sec. 406(b)(3)).

[44] *M&R Investment Company* v. *Fitzsimmons,* 685 F.2d 283 (9th Cir. 1982). At the time of loan commitment, the borrower was a party in interest. Severance of the party-in-interest relationship prior to funding did not avoid finding a violation.

assets to help the plan sponsor in takeover activities,[45] and (3) a loan being negotiated between two plans with common trustees.[46]

A two-part test is applied against a fiduciary's conduct to answer the question of whether there was a prohibited transaction. The fiduciary must either (1) prove by a preponderance of the evidence that an exemption applies or (2) prove by clear and convincing evidence that the consideration received is not "in connection with a transaction involving the assets of the plan."[47]

For smaller plans, a common prohibited transaction is the use of collectibles as investments. Since 1982, plans that hire an independent corporate trustee have been permitted to invest in collectibles (cars, stamps, art, coins, and so on) as long as the collectibles are held by a third party for investment reasons only. For example, a corporation could invest a portion of its qualified plan assets in coins, but it cannot display the coins in its headquarters (the corporation would derive a current benefit). If a determination is made that a plan is deriving a current benefit, then a premature distribution of plan assets has occurred and the plan will be required to pay both income and excise taxes.[48]

Loans from qualified plans to participants, fiduciaries, and other parties in interest are a frequent target of examination because of their potential for abuse or inconsistent treatment. Specific guidelines are in place that specify the requirements for valid plan loans to participants:

1. Plan documents must permit the loans.
2. Loans must be available to all participants on an equivalent basis.
3. Loans must not be available for highly compensated employees in greater amounts than the amount made available to other employees.
4. Loans must bear a reasonable rate of interest.
5. Loans must be adequately secured.[49]

ERISA also restricts the investment of plan assets into certain assets. Section 404(a)(2) prohibits the investing of any plan assets outside the jurisdiction of the U.S. district courts. Therefore, foreign plan investments

---

[45] *Leigh* v. *Engle,* 669 F.Supp. 1390 (N.D. Ill. 1987), *aff'd,* 858 F.2d 361 (7th Cir. 1988).

[46] *Cutaiar* v. *Marshall,* 590 F.2d 523 (3rd Cir. 1979) (interest of borrower and lender are legally opposed).

[47] *Lowen* v. *Tower Asset Management,* 829 F.2d 1209 (2nd Cir. 1987).

[48] ERISA Sec. 501.

[49] DOL Reg. § 2550.408(b)-1.

must be held by a U.S. intermediary so the assets remain within the purview of our justice system. This allows the government to be able to seize the assets if, in its determination, it is in the best interests of the plan participants.

ERISA also limits the amount of employer stock that can be owned by a defined benefit plan to 10 percent of the plan assets.[50] This does not apply to profit-sharing plans, stock bonus plans, or ESOPs.

The IRS, which has the responsibility of monitoring the tax-exempt qualifications of ERISA plans, also has specific rules and regulations that specify prohibited transactions (IRC Sec. 4975). These are similar to, and under some provisions harsher than, ERISA provisions dealing with the same conduct.[51]

Liability, Remedies, and Damages

In the event of a breach of fiduciary conduct, there are numerous curative (and creative) measures that will be pursued along with the imposition of trustee liability. The following discussion breaks these into the broad general categories of liability, remedies and damages.

Liability

The acceptance of the role of the trustee or fiduciary carries with it the acceptance of personal liability in the event of a determined breach of fiduciary conduct. ERISA imposes liability on a fiduciary that has committed a breach to

1. Make restitution to the plan for losses resulting from the breach.

2. Disgorge the profits obtained by the fiduciary because of the breach.

3. Be subjected to such other remedial or equitable relief deemed appropriate, including removal (see below).[52]

---

[50] ERISA Sec. 407(a)(2).
[51] *Alden M. Lieb*, 88 T.C. 83 (1987).
[52] ERISA Sec. 409(a).

The Third Restatement contains a similar provision; however, unlike ERISA, the beneficiaries have the option of affirming the activity and retaining the profit.[53] Contrast this with ERISA, where even profitable investments that are the result of a breach may still result in liability to the fiduciary.

Remedies

To correct the wrong that was done and to ensure that a similar type of mistake does not happen again, there are several remedies that are available in the event a breach of fiduciary conduct has occurred. Both ERISA and the Third Restatement provide for

1. Recoupment of investment losses.[54]
2. Disgorgement of profits.[55]
3. Payment of the differences between actual investment returns and the returns that could have been achieved from reasonably prudent investment alternatives.[56]
4. Preliminary and permanent injunctive relief.[57]
5. Removal of a fiduciary and appointment of a receiver or successor.[58]
6. For qualified plans, disqualification of the tax-deferred status of the plan.[59]

Penalties and Damages

ERISA makes no provision for punitive damages, but it does provide for the assessment of a penalty against a fiduciary of 20 percent for

---

[53] Restatement Third, Sec. 205.

[54] ERISA: *Donovan* v. *Bierwirth,* 680 F.2d 263 (2d Cir. 1982). Restatement Third, Sec. 205(b).

[55] ERISA: *Leigh* v. *Engle,* 727 F.2d 113 (7th Cir. 1984); and *Lowen* v. *Tower Asset Management, Inc.,* 829 F.2d 1209 (2d Cir. 1987). Restatement Third, Sec. 205(a).

[56] ERISA: *Leigh* v. *Engle,* 858 F.2d 361 (7th Cir. 1988) (*Leigh III*); and *Lowen* v. *Tower Asset Management, Inc.,* 829 F.2d 1209 (2d Cir. 1987). Restatement Third, Secs. 205 and 208–211, and *Taylor* v. *Croker National Bank,* 205 Cal.App.3d 459, 252 Cal. Rep. 388 (1988).

[57] *Brock* v. *Robbins,* 830 F.2d 640 (7th Cir. 1986); *Marshall* v. *Teamsters Local 282 Pension Trust Fund,* 458 F.Supp. 986 (E.D. NY 1978); and *Fink* v. *National Savings & Trust Co.,* 772 F.2d 951 (D.C. Cir. 1985).

[58] ERISA: *Marshall* v. *Snyder,* 572 F.2d 894 (2d Cir. 1978). Restatement Third, Sec. 107 (denial of fees and removal from office) and Comments under Sec. 205.

[59] Through failure to satisfy ERISA Sec. 401.

any amount recovered as a result of an ERISA violation.[60] Trust law generally allows for the imposition of punitive and exemplary damages, depending on the jurisdiction and the application of tort law principles.[61] In addition, some state jurisdictions may have treble damage statutes similar to the Texas Deceptive Trade Practices Act that can apply against corporate trustees for misrepresentations. Because of federal jurisdiction, ERISA plan trustees may also be faced with treble damages under the Racketeer Influenced and Corrupt Organizations Act (RICO).[62] ERISA even allows the imposition of a jail sentence if the assets of the plan have been grossly mishandled.[63]

Conclusion

Lawsuits alleging fiduciary misconduct will increase. Some of these breaches may be entirely justified. Most, however, could have been (or will be) avoided had the fiduciary followed the principles of investment process and conduct specified in this book, for it is the process, not investment performance, that determines liability.

---

[60] ERISA Sec. 502(1). See also "Report to the Secretary of the Tax Force on Enforcement," September 1990, relating to the ERISA Enforcement Strategy Implementation Plan.

[61] As an example, see *InterFirst Bank Dallas, N.A.* v. *Risser,* 739 S.W.2d 882 (Tex. App., Texarkana 1987); but see *Dabney* v. *Chase National Bank of City of New York,* 196 F.2d 668 (2nd Cir. 1952), *cert. dism'd,* 346 U.S. 863 (1954).

[62] *Crawford* v. *La Broucherie Bernard, Ltd.,* 815 F.2d 117 (D.C. Cir. 1987).

[63] ERISA Sec. 501. The Comprehensive Crime Control Act of 1984 clarified the DOL criminal investigative authority to detect, investigate, and refer criminal violations of ERISA to the U.S. attorney general's office.

12

MANAGING A SOCIALLY RESPONSIBLE INVESTMENT AGENDA

"The superior man seeks what is right;
the inferior one, what is profitable."
Confucius

"The quality of your work will have a great
deal to do with the quality of your life."
Orison Swett Marden

The management of socially responsible investing involves "the systematic incorporation of ethical values and objectives in the investment decision-making process."[1] Included within the context of this broad definition are three subsets: (1) social investing, or the construction of sin-free portfolios; (2) minority and women-owned business enterprises (MWBEs); and (3) economically targeted investments (ETI).

This is an area of ongoing contention that has been the subject of legislation and litigation for several decades. It is not our purpose here to enter the debate or to predict future directions, but rather to focus

---

[1] "Social Investing's Strength Lies in Readiness to Deal with World's Tough Questions," *Pension World*, April 1993.

on the role of the fiduciary in dealing with these issues. Indeed, issues such as South Africa have become management challenges for many fiduciaries; at one point, 30 states, 109 cities, and 39 counties had some form of South Africa–free investment restrictions.[2] Fiduciaries may find themselves bound to observe restrictions such as South Africa–free or may find themselves under political pressure to do so. They may even wish to initiate such policies themselves. The fiduciary must remember his or her primary responsibility is to the beneficiaries/participants of the assets and the law governing their conduct.

Fiduciary Issues

Regardless of one's personal views of the merits of social investing, *a prudent fiduciary must recognize that any restriction on an investment program has the potential to reduce the portfolio's total return.* Consequently, when social restrictions are adopted, the fiduciary must be willing to accept the potential for lower returns and plan accordingly. It is wishful thinking to imagine that such portfolio constraints will have no impact on performance.

ERISA fiduciaries, in particular, are cautioned that the DOL has taken the firm position that the returns of retirement portfolios cannot be sacrificed, and that social investing cannot be set as a *primary* investment objective. What is acceptable to the DOL is to first evaluate all investment options according to objective economic criteria, and, if there are equally attractive investments, social factors may be considered to tip the balance in favor of one or more of the prudent investment options.[3]

For the fiduciary of private trusts, the strict duty of loyalty in trust law ordinarily prohibits the fiduciary from pursuing investment objectives that will give rise to a personal conflict of interest.[4] Therefore, the fiduciary is prohibited from using trust assets to further the fiduciary's own personal views of social or political issues.

Investment committees of foundations and endowments, in particular, should review stated investment objectives of endowed assets before

---

[2] Ibid.

[3] Marc Gertner, "Fiduciary Standards of Real Estate Investments," in *Employee Benefit Issues: The Multiemployer Perspective,* vol. 31 (Brookfield, WI: International Foundation of Employee Benefit Plans, 1989), p. 280.

[4] Restatement Third, Sec. 227, p. 8.

unilaterally pursuing social investing. For example, if a university has established an endowment to provide scholarships to indigent students, and the trust documents do not include specific language permitting social investing, the investment committee should be cautious about establishing restricted portfolios. It could be easily argued that the committee has violated their fiduciary duties since the endowed assets were set aside for the benefit of indigent students and were not set aside for the committee to advance their own social agendas.

One notable exception on the private trust side are charitable remainder trusts. The Third Restatement suggests: "In addition, social considerations may be taken into account in investing the funds of charitable trusts to the extent the charitable purposes would justify an expenditure of trust funds for the social issue or cause in question or to the extent the investment decision can be justified on grounds of advancing, financially or operationally, a charitable activity conducted by the trust."[5]

Social Investing

Socially responsible investors attempt to look beyond a company's financial statements and consider how a company serves society as a whole. There are two approaches used by social investors to influence corporate policies: (1) avoid investing in targeted companies—for example, avoid buying stock in companies that market alcoholic products; and (2) buy the stock of socially irresponsible companies and attempt to force change through corporate governance action—for example, voting in a new board of directors.

Naturally, what constitutes socially responsible management is a matter of controversy, and change in the agenda is a regular thing. There is nothing approaching a consensus on these issues. The following is a fairly typical list of some of the causes, compiled by the Investor Responsibility Research Center (IRRC).[6]

Alcohol: Avoid investments in the alcohol industry, particularly those companies whose major source of revenue comes from the manufacture or distribution of alcohol.

---

[5] Ibid., p 13.
[6] The IRRC compiles and analyzes data on the actions of businesses in society.

Animal testing: Federal law still requires pharmaceutical and chemical companies to test their products on animals. However, there are other companies, such as cosmetic firms, that are encouraged but not required to test on animals. A significant screen under this criterion would be the painful use of animals and those companies that subject animals to extreme pain for research, teaching, surgery, or tests.

Defense contracting: Avoid companies that rely heavily on the manufacture of weapons, particularly nuclear weapons.

Environment: Environmental initiatives are not easily classified, however the more common screens are the number of (1) National Priority List sites (sites the government believes pose the greatest threat to human life) for which a company has been responsible, (2) permit denials a company has received for operating a storage or disposal site for hazardous waste, (3) toxic chemical releases a company has caused, (4) oil and chemical spills a company has caused, and (5) environmental penalties a company has had to pay.

Firearms: Avoid companies that manufacture or distribute firearms or ammunition to nonmilitary markets.

Gambling: Avoid companies that are involved in the gaming industry.

Northern Ireland: U.S. corporations provide employment to 10 percent of the workforce in Ireland. Some investors are attempting to pressure U.S. companies into adopting the MacBride Principles, which are a set of opportunity/affirmative action principles aimed at fighting employment discrimination in Northern Ireland. The British government is opposed to the MacBride Principles.

Nuclear power: Avoid investments in publicly owned utilities that generate or purchase nuclear power, or companies that provide goods and services to nuclear power plants.

South Africa: Though international sanctions have been lifted, Arthur D. Little Inc. monitors and rates U.S. companies doing business in South Africa and their adherence to the Sullivan Principles, which are policy guidelines for companies operating there.

Tobacco: Avoid companies whose primary source of revenue is the manufacture or distribution of tobacco products.

Because of the broad diversity of investments in socially responsible portfolios, it is difficult to make a direct comparison of their performance to the S&P 500. However, one measure, the Domini Social Index, comprises 400 companies, 260 of which are S&P 500 firms that do not exhibit substantial involvement in: alcohol, gambling, tobacco, military contracting, nuclear power, environmental and employer relations.[7]

	For the period ending December 31, 1994		
	Last Year	*Last 3 Years*	*Last 5 Years*
S&P 500	1.27	6.23	8.67
Domini Social Index	.17	6.81	9.85

Minority and Women-Owned Business Enterprises (MWBEs)

A movement began in the 80s that reflected the desire of large corporate and public retirement funds to invest assets with emerging minority and women-owned money management firms. Interest in MWBEs was driven by several factors:

- There was the notion that emerging firms would have a higher probability of uncovering new investment ideas and strategies that larger, mainstream firms would consider too risky. Emerging firms, however, would still be accountable for delivering competitive investment returns.

- The makeup of pension committees was changing to reflect the demographics of fund participants. In turn, committee members were interested in providing MWBEs an opportunity to manage a portion of the assets.

- State and local governments, and corporations doing business with the federal government, were encouraged to award a greater percentage of their service contracts to minority and

---

[7] The Domini Social Index is maintained by Kinder, Lyndenberg, Domini & Co., Boston, MA (617) 547-7479.

women-owned businesses. Procurement practices were
extended to include money management services.

• There was an interest and awareness on the part of minority
and women investors to support MWBEs.

It has been very challenging for the fiduciary to find MWBEs
that could meet traditional screening criteria for money managers.
Either the firms were new and did not have a five-year track record,
or they had a track record but were too small to absorb a large placement of assets from an institutional pension fund. The first hurdle was
easily overcome, since most of the MWBEs were started by principals who had sterling track records at other more-established money
management firms. The second hurdle was cleared by either pooling
the investment talents of several MWBEs into a commingled trust or
setting up a "farm team," where the assets are allocated among a
number of different MWBEs.

Today there are an estimated 80 MWBEs, yet they still only manage
a tiny fraction of the country's investable assets. Several firms have
grown in size and stature and are now considered institutional money
management firms. Still others are nearing the magical five-year business marker and have sufficient assets under management to warrant
inclusion in traditional money manager searches.

Economically Targeted Investments

Economically targeted investments (ETIs) occur when investments are
structured to produce corollary economic benefits, such as jobs, housing loans, venture capital, and public assistance loans, in addition to
providing competitive risk-adjusted returns.

Taft-Hartley plans (see Chapter 17) were some of the first
investors in ETIs. The plans would invest in real estate projects that
promised to hire union members. Unfortunately, some plans carried
the initiative to the extreme and committed exorbitant amounts of their
total plan assets to geographically concentrated real estate projects.[8]

---

[8] Stephen M. Saxon, "Fiduciary Standards for Real Estate Investments by Employee
Benefit Plans," in *Employee Benefit Issues: The Multiemployer Perspective*, vol. 31
(Brookfield, WI: International Foundation of Employee Benefit Plans, 1989), p. 268.

Fiduciaries for one plan in Florida were charged with the imprudent management of retirement plan assets when 95 percent of the plan assets were invested in projects in Florida. The real estate projects failed, leaving the plan and the participants penniless. DOL officials have been particularly watchful for abuses with ETIs, and in fact have added specific questions to IRS Form 5500 to identify abuse.

To date, ETIs have not received widespread acceptance. A recent survey by the Institute for Fiduciary Education and The Ford Foundation found that roughly a third of the largest 119 public pension plans had investments in ETIs, and there has been little increase in this percentage since 1989.

For plans that have invested in ETIs, the allocation is, on average, 5 percent of the plan's total assets. Investments have been made to promote employment within a geographic area, to encourage business development, or to create partnerships with organizations that are taxpayer supported, such as the Office of Economic Development and the Housing Bureau. The investments allow the pension plan to provide needed capital to these organizations while still receiving a market rate of return.

Fiduciary Considerations. The challenge for fiduciaries is not to let short-term benefits or political pressures for investing in an ETI cloud their judgment or alter long-term investment strategies.

> Large pension funds, particularly public funds, are highly visible. Given the economic difficulties being experienced in many regions, governmental budget shortfalls, and increased conservatism on the part of traditional providers of capital, such as insurers, the large pension pools are guaranteed to be viewed as the solution to many problems. Pension funds will attract an increasing number of suitors with economically targeted investment ideas.[9]

As with all fiduciary conduct, the courts will evaluate the process followed in making the investment decisions, not the ultimate investment results. The investment policy statement must reflect the review and selection criteria and outline the established monitoring procedures used to detect potential shortcomings in the investment of an ETI. Specific policy considerations should include

---

[9] Gary Robinson, "Economically Targeted Investments Require a Proactive Policy," Callan Associates Inc., April 1994.

- The kinds of investments the plan is comfortable making, from a risk-return standpoint.

- The desired collateral benefits to be obtained from the investments.

- The procedures that will be followed in considering proposals from firms structuring ETIs.

- Allocation limits compared against total plan assets.

- Investment committee and/or staff responsibilities for monitoring and supervising the investments, including consideration for hiring an outside manager to provide independent oversight.

- The benchmarks against which performance will be measured.

Before an investment committee embarks upon an ETI investment, however, several potential pitfalls must be considered:

1. The ETI will, inevitably, require more staff time and greater due diligence than virtually any other investment. Therefore, the ETI that produces a comparable market return has cost the plan more.

2. ETIs are typically long-term investments and are often illiquid. Changing political agendas and investment committee members creates the risk that an ETI will be derailed before market returns are realized.

3. Allegations of influence peddling and pork barreling will follow on the coattails of any investment decisions. ETIs will come under public scrutiny, increasing the likelihood of charges of imprudent management.

4. It is difficult to diversify the risks associated with ETIs. There are usually only a small number of reasonable investment opportunities managed by qualified individuals.

5. Interim valuations or appraisals of ETIs are difficult. As with real estate and other hard assets, the value is hard to determine until it is sold in the marketplace.

Summary

The growth of socially responsible investing is a serious challenge to fiduciaries, who are responsible, first and foremost, for the prudent management of the assets entrusted to them. Boards will come under pressure from various groups to (1) invest in publicly traded companies according to preferred social criteria, (2) hire managers who meet a certain demographic makeup, and/or (3) invest in projects for their corollary value. Fiduciaries need to assess carefully the regulations governing their conduct, and ensure that any social investing they initiate or contemplate does not violate their governing regulations or their fiduciary responsibilities.

CHAPTER

13

HIGH NET WORTH FAMILIES

"Reservoirs of wealth in the hands of individuals are just as necessary as in the hands of banks and insurance companies, because individuals can take risks and undertake enterprises which such institutions cannot."

James Duke, *Founder of Duke University*

"About half of all shares of stock outstanding are still owned by individual investors. Many of them continue to manage their affairs as they always have—and as their fathers did. Their portfolios are badly diversified, they seize on the latest market gossip, and they have no idea how to measure whether they are doing well or poorly at the game; they are the noisiest of the noise traders. Others, perhaps out of inertia, fear, or stubborn unwillingness to pay capital gain taxes on old holdings, sit tight and do nothing."

Peter L. Bernstein[1]

This book has emphasized the fact that the fundamentals of the investment management process are the same whether one is making decisions for a pension plan or foundation or managing one's own money.

---

[1] Peter L. Bernstein, *Capital Ideas and the Improbable Origins of Modern Wall Street* (New York, NY: Free Press, 1992), p. 303.

TABLE 13-1 Family Wealth

Net Worth (excluding primary residence)	Number of Families
$1 million	2,300,000
5 million	182,000
10 million	29,000
50 million	4,800
100 million	2,560
250 million	700
1 billion	60

Sources: Sara Hamilton, in a presentation to the Family Office Forum, January 19, 1994; Sally Kleberg, "The Family Office: Hot Button of the '90s," *Private Asset Management,* vol. 1, no. 1 (April 25, 1994.)

This chapter will focus on those unique attributes that differentiate the individual investor from the corporate or institutional investor, and the alternative ways wealthy families have structured their investment programs.[2] While we recognize the critical importance of financial planning—cash flow, insurance, estate, and tax planning—all of which have serious implications on the investment process, our focus will remain on the management of investment decisions.

Total liquid investable assets (i.e., excluding primary residences) in the hands of wealthy individuals now exceed $4 trillion. There is as much money invested by individuals as there is by all the retirement plans (corporate and public) and foundations/endowments combined. The vast majority of the wealth remains in the hands of a relatively few, but the number of millionaires continues to rise, tripling in the last 15 years alone.[3] (See Table 13–1.)

Another demographic factor that will impact the management of family wealth is the forthcoming inheritance boom. Inheritance issues and challenges were once the concern of less than 10 percent of the population. Since World War II, however, there has been a tremendous redistribution of wealth and the number of families that have created significant estates to bequeath to children has more than doubled.[4]

---

[2] The authors are grateful to the contributions, ideas, and suggestions provided by Sally Kleberg; Sara Hamilton, founder and president of the Family Office Exchange; and Charlotte B. Beyer, founder and director of the Institute for Private Investors.

[3] Everett Mattlin, "Rich Pickings," *Institutional Investor,* June 1993, pp. 55–67.

[4] "The New Way to Get Rich," *U.S. News and World Report,* May 7, 1990, p. 29.

Differences between Individual and Institutional Investors

Many investment organizations (banks, money managers, consultants, and so on) make the mistake of treating all investors alike—corporate as well as individual. "The pool of wealth might resemble institutional mass but differs markedly in its personal focus."[5] There are, however, six notable differences between individual investors and institutions.

1. For most individuals, there will be a point in time when there is no longer additional cash being added to the portfolio. An institution, such as a pension plan or foundation, can usually count on contributions being added to the portfolio that can provide some relief against inflation or market reversals. Individuals, especially those retired, don't have the luxury of receiving additional contributions, and preservation of principal is paramount to their investment strategies.

2. Individual investors do not benefit from the tax-exempt status that qualified retirement plans and most foundations and endowments enjoy. The total return on an individual's portfolio is reduced by the capital gains and income taxes that must be paid. As discussed later in the chapter, it is important that the individual investor select advisers and money managers experienced in working with taxable portfolios.

3. Individual investors buy services, not products. The individual investor's relationship with his or her advisers (including money managers and consultants) is generally more important than it is to most institutions. Relative investment performance is not as critical as the overall servicing of the account by the adviser. Absolute performance is the primary focus.

4. Individual investors are less likely than their corporate peers of comparable portfolio size to hire professional advisers or consultants. Most individuals prefer to make their own investment decisions, utilizing outside advisers only when significant life events occur (e.g., the selling of a business), or to rely on the brokerage community for current Wall Street thoughts or ideas.

---

[5] Kleberg, "The Family Office."

5. Individual investors pay more for the same investment services as institutional investors of comparable size (discussed in more detail later in the chapter).

6. Unless the family wealth is tied to trusts or private foundations, the individual investor is not encumbered with regulatory oversight. Personal trusts are subject to the governing document and (by default) may be regulated by respective state statutes. Most states are expected to adopt in substantive form the Third Restatement provisions governing fiduciary investment activities. But, for the individual investor there are no statutory rules with which to be concerned. More than once a consultant has been told by clients, "Prudence be damned. It's my money and I'll do with it as I please."

The Family Office

To one extent or another, every family has (or should have) someone responsible for planning the budget, paying the bills, and making investment decisions. Many wealthier families have formalized the process and have created what is referred to as the *family office*. There are no set standards on what constitutes a family office, or how much money a family should have before it warrants the creation of its own family office; however, experts believe that it begins when investable assets exceed $50 million.[6]

As family groups began selling or recapitalizing their closely held businesses, the concept of the family office began to take shape for three reasons. First, the family office was needed to centralize the management of investable assets and to provide record keeping, tax planning, and other personal services to the family members. Second, families began to anticipate the need to serve more than one or two generations, which required a more formal structure to be put in place. Finally, families wanted to coordinate their philanthropic services, interests and activities through one entity.[7]

Ownership Structures
The typical family office has a full-time staff that often includes at least one attorney and/or accountant and administrative support. The structure

---

[6] Sara Hamilton and Sally Kleberg.

[7] Sara Hamilton in a presentation to the Family Office Forum, January 19, 1994.

of the office, or the ownership of the assets, often takes the form of either a trust, corporation, or partnership.[8]

Trusts	51%
Own outright	23
Corporations	16
Partnerships	8
Other	2

• The formation of a trust by one or more senior members of the family provides continuity of ownership and control and has the advantage of having only one legal entity. In some cases, it can also provide an effective means for the avoidance or deferral of estate and generation-skipping taxes. Some families have gone one step further by actually starting their own limited power trust company, and even selling their trust services to other family offices. The trust company acts as a fiduciary or cofiduciary of the family trusts, and as with the corporate structure, provides perpetual management and an organized structure.

• The corporate structure often includes the full-time office staff as officers and employees of the corporation, and the family members serve as directors and shareholders. This form of ownership offers the traditional advantages of a corporation in terms of an orderly structure for management and succession, limits the liability of family decision makers, and provides opportunities to establish corporate employee benefits. A potential problem is the diffusion of control—shares being distributed upon death to family members who do not share the same interests, loyalties, and objectives of the founding family members.

• The formation of a partnership is one of the easiest structures to establish, but it does not provide many of the same benefits of a trust or corporation. There may be nonexistent or inappropriate succession when a partner dies. If a limited partnership is formed, family members that are not general partners may not be able to exercise control or formally participate in the investment decision-making process. On the other hand, the drawbacks to a partnership may have an offsetting

---

[8] Ibid.

benefit—specifically, the ability for the estate attorney to argue that the value of a partnership interest left in an estate should be reduced in value to reflect this same lack of control. [9]

• A major component of the "other" category is the private foundation. (See the next chapter for a more extensive discussion on foundations and endowments.) As a general rule, foundations are formed to provide a centralized source for the philanthropic interests of the family. Private foundations are regulated by Section 4944 of the Internal Revenue Code, which requires an annual payout of at least 5 percent of the assets and prohibits the use of the funds for self-dealing (i.e., political lobbying or using funds to leverage a buyout of a company). The fiduciary standards of the foundation's trustees are those of the prudent person or prudent investor for those states that have adopted the provisions of the Third Restatement.

The Impact of Technology

Technology is beginning to have a major impact on the way family wealth is managed, much the same way it has changed the investment services world. At first, family assets were commingled to facilitate ease in administration and to take advantage of lower money management fees through breakpoints. Today, with the advances that have been made in portfolio management and accounting software, fewer families are commingling their assets; instead these families are coordinating the investment activities of each individual family unit. (A family unit may include a surviving spouse as one unit and each of the children with their spouses as additional units.)

The desired effect is to decentralize the decision-making process down to the individual family unit, whereby each family unit has the capacity to (1) design an optimal portfolio capturing their specific risk/return profile, (2) structure and maintain their own investment policy statement, (3) implement the policy with their own selection of approved money managers (approved by the family office), and (4) receive monthly account statements and quarterly appraisals that are specific to their own account. To implement a more decentralized investment management strategy, the family office would need to have in place

---

[9] Correspondence with Sally Kleberg.

- Portfolio management software that segregates and individually accounts for the assets of each family unit. Many of these packages have also been integrated with tax accounting software to facilitate the implementation of year-end tax strategies and reporting.
- An electronic link to a central custodial bank. This is a key component because without it many of the desired cost-efficiencies will be lost. For example, a family can negotiate a much more favorable fee with a money manager if the manager knows that all family units that choose to work with the manager will have settlement and custody at one specific place. This electronic interface also gives the family office the capacity to monitor the activities of hired money managers and to watch cash balances for budgeting purposes.
- Asset allocation software that enables family units to design their optimal asset mix that takes into account the specific risk-return profile of the family unit. This is a critical capability, especially when you are managing family assets across several generations or family lines. The elderly family members may not have the same investment objectives as younger family members, who may just be starting to build their own businesses.
- Performance measurement software. The central custodian should be able to provide each family unit a monthly appraisal statement of individual holdings and transactions. This information should, in turn, be downloaded (another reason for the electronic interface with the custodian) so that quarterly performance measurement reports can be produced. The reports would be used to show the comparative performance of hired managers and whether the desired investment objectives outlined in the investment policy statement are being met.

Asset Allocation[10]

As previously mentioned, one of the major differences between the individual and the institutional investor is that the individual will likely reach a point in time when there are no longer contributions being made

---

[10] This and the following sections are applicable to all investors, not just family offices.

to the portfolio. Investment losses, when they do occur, are particularly painful and, as a result, individuals often overcompensate for perceived market risks.

More often than not, when investment objectives are compared against the investor's actual asset allocation, there is not enough equity exposure to obtain the expected returns. Asset allocation modeling, as described in Chapter 4, is important in allowing the investor to structure the asset mix that will generate the needed expected return, while preparing the investor for the possible worst case scenario associated with the mix. Experience has shown that by quantifying or attaching a worst case scenario (i.e., a loss of 10 percent of the portfolio in any given year) to an asset mix, most investors are able to comfortably migrate to a greater percentage in equities. The process of addressing the worst case scenario reduces the anxiety of dealing with an unknown— possible market outcomes.

There are a number of firms in the investment services industry that suggest that an individual's asset allocation should be driven by the investor's age, often referred to as life cycle scenarios. The basic concept is that the younger an individual is, the more equities that individual should hold in his/her portfolio. Some reputable firms actually advise their clients to subtract their age from 100 percent to determine the percentage of the portfolio that should be in equities. For example, a sixty-year-old investor should hold 40 percent of his/her portfolio in equities. Though any advice to diversify into equities is better than no diversification at all (and as a general rule, a younger investor has the advantage of time to withstand periodic market volatility), studies by noted psychologists who specialize in the psychology of money management and investing have found no correlation between an investor's age and his/her ability to stay committed to a particular asset mix.[11] There are many elderly investors who wouldn't think of holding a bond, giving preference to an all-equity portfolio. Conversely, there are young intelligent professionals that have no desire to hold anything riskier than short-term government securities or certificates of deposit.

Another fad within the investment services industry is the use of questionnaires to pigeonhole investors into preset asset mixes. The shortcomings of the questionnaires are that they presuppose that the respondent possesses investment experience to understand the tradeoffs between

---

[11] Kathleen Gurney, *Your Money Personality,* (New York: Doubleday, 1988).

TABLE 13–2 Asset Allocation by Market Segment

	Families	Pension Plans	Foundations/ Endowments
Equities	48%	55%	43%
Fixed income	22	35	37
Alternative	25	7	3
Cash	5	3	17

Sources: Sarah Hamilton, Family Office Forum, January 19, 1994; and John W. Guy, *How to Invest Someone Else's Money* (Burr Ridge, IL: Irwin Professional Publishing, 1994), p. 53.

risk and return. Again, our experience has shown just the opposite. Most investors do not understand the subtleties of asset allocation until they are shown different asset mixes with the corresponding expected returns and worst case scenarios.

Finally, there are those firms that couch the risks associated with a particular preset asset mix in difficult to understand terms. Some define risk using indistinguishable terms, such as standard deviation, that most investors cannot appreciate unless they have taken a graduate level course in statistics. Others use subjective terms, such as medium risk, that mean different things to different people. What exactly is medium risk? Does it mean I am willing to lose 5 percent or as much as 10 percent? Risk has to be quantified in terms that investors understand, or the strategies that are developed will likely be abandoned during the first market upheaval.

With these nuances of the investment process by different organizations and individuals in mind, see the comparative study of the average asset allocation of wealthy families versus institutional investors shown in Table 13.2.

The most striking difference between the three market segments is the percentage invested by wealthy families in alternative investments. This can be explained in part by (1) the fact that the alternative investments category would include closely held assets of family-run businesses and (2) the number of entrepreneurs who have joined the ranks of the wealthy during the last 20 years. The self-made millionaire often feels the urge to continue to invest in new opportunities. A corollary is the sex appeal of investing in an opportunity to which other investors do not have access. Unfortunately, experience has also shown that there is a third reason why wealthy families have made investments into alternative investments—because their friends have. A recent front page article in *The Wall Street Journal* reported on the billions of dollars that were lost by individual investors when several hedge funds were pounded by rising interest rates.

> There are various lessons in a debacle like this, but among them is one about gullibility. Wealthy people can become so nonchalant when it comes to investing that a social introduction can be more compelling than a coherent strategy.[12]

Implementation Issues

Most individuals report they manage their own investment decisions. But when they do need advice, often as a result of a significant life change (i.e., retirement, divorce, or inheritance), they prefer to turn to their accountants and attorneys. Surprisingly, advisers who report they do not have investment experience (the CPA), and therefore feel they are not qualified to give investment advice, are sought after more often than those advisers who purport to be experts. One study asked investors how they chose their investment advisers. The results were[13]

Personal referral	55%
Through a consultant	21
Reputation of adviser	10
Advertising or media	8
Direct solicitation by adviser	6

The results of the survey and the preferences shown by individual investors confirm that trust and confidence in one's adviser is more important than reported performance. Or, stated differently—*what matters is the process, not performance.* Success or failure of a fiduciary is

---

[12] Laura Jereski, "Good Connections Put Hedge Fund in Business but a Bad Bet Sank It," *The Wall Street Journal,* September 29, 1994, p. 1.

[13] Charlotte Beyer, "1994 Institute Research Survey," Institute for Private Investors, August 1994.

judged by the process the fiduciary follows, not the ultimate investment results. Likewise, individual investors intuitively place greater value with the procedural process that an accountant and/or an attorney provides than they do in the hot performing products offered by salespeople.

Money Manager Searches

Regrettably, most individual investors that have hired a professional money manager have done just that—hired one money manager. The manager is typically charged with managing a balanced portfolio for the investor with one clear mandate—"Don't lose any money." The result is often less than satisfactory for both the investor and the manager. The investor abdicates the critical asset allocation decision to the money manager, who sets the allocation to that with which the manager is comfortable, and not necessarily with what is appropriate to meet the investor's investment objectives. The manager, who is initially thrilled with winning a new client, soon tires of trying to manage across investment classes or styles with which the manager may not be familiar, all the while being constantly reminded by the client to be sensitive to the client's tax situation.

A more appropriate approach is to search for money manager specialists in each of the different asset classes that make up the investor's specific asset allocation. The approach is to field a team of all-stars and not a team consisting of one franchise player. In the high net worth setting, managers should be questioned as to

- Whether they are managing portfolios for other taxable clients.
- Whether they follow the same investment process for tax-exempt as well as taxable clients.
- The manager's average portfolio turnover. A manager's after-tax performance will be impacted by capital gains, and managers with lower turnover may provide better after-tax returns.[14] That is, given two managers with identical returns, the individual is better off with the manager with the lower portfolio turnover.

---

[14] Joel M. Dickson and John B. Shoven, "Ranking Mutual Funds on an After-Tax Basis," National Bureau of Economic Research, Inc., Working Paper No. 4393.

- Whether they are properly registered with state officials. Most states do not require money managers to register as an investment adviser if their only accounts are large institutional clients. States, however, do have registration requirements (with exceptions) for managers offering services to individuals. (See the appendix on state-by-state registration requirements.)
- When applicable, whether they have alternative strategies to assist clients in exiting from low-basis stocks the client might be holding. (Two popular strategies involve covered-call option writing and short sales against the box.)

The search process is not an easy task because, until recently, conventional wisdom was that all portfolios should be managed the same. Less than 20 percent of surveyed money management firms have different portfolio management teams for taxable clients.[15] Clearly, the taxable client suffers in performance returns when a manager is not sensitive to the tax consequences of the investor. "When capital gains are realized and taxed, the portfolio loses the opportunity of investing deferred taxes. Even low turnover costs the portfolio."[16]

Investment Expenses

Individual investors pay more for investment services than their institutional peers of comparable size (see Table 13–3). The fee disparity may be easily explained as a function of one or more of the following factors: (1) individual portfolios can be more challenging to manage because of tax implications, and therefore managers are less willing to negotiate lower fees; (2) individuals generally require more servicing (hand holding); and (3) individuals rarely turn to professionals who could assist them in negotiating lower overall costs.

Another cost component that is often overlooked by individuals is trading costs and associated soft-dollar expenses. The average high-net-worth family pays an average of 9.8 cents per share compared to 6 cents per share for institutions.[17] The difference between paying 6, 9, or even 12 cents per share doesn't seem much until the total commission costs are calculated (see Table 13–4).

---

[15] Beyer, "1994 Institute Research Survey."

[16] Robert H. Jeffrey and Robert D. Arnott, "Is Your Alpha Big Enough to Cover Its Taxes?", *Journal of Portfolio Management,* Spring 1993, pp. 15–25.

[17] Beyer, "1994 Institute Research Survey."

TABLE 13–3 Expenses for Manager Fees
(Median Fees in Basis Points)

	Account Size		
	Below $5 million	*$5–10 million*	*Over $10–25 million*
Equity			
Family office	100	75	50
Institutional	85	75	53

TABLE 13–4 Comparison of Commission Costs*

Portfolio Size	*6 cents/share*	*9 cents/share*	*12 cents/share*
$ 1 million	$ 1,500	$ 2,250	$ 3,000
5 million	7,500	11,250	15,000
20 million	30,000	45,000	60,000

*Assuming $40/share—the approximate average price per share on the New York Stock Exchange.

Individuals who have hired money managers and do not give the manager specific trading instructions usually leave an average of five basis points of negotiating clout on the table. If no trading directions are given to a manager, the manager may direct trades to a particular brokerage house to pay for investment research (an example of a soft-dollar activity). The trading activity has value to the manager because the manager is otherwise forced to pay hard dollars for the same research. For example, if a client was able to negotiate a manager's fee down to 75 basis points, the next discussion would deal with directed brokerage. If the manager desires a free hand in directing brokerage, then it is reasonable to ask the manager to lower the fee an additional five basis points. If the manager is indifferent to trading direction, then the investor should consider directing brokerage through a commission recapture program and arrange to pay for some of the investor's investment management expenses from the trading commissions.

A number of wealthy individuals have tried to lower their investment expenses and increase the securities diversification of their portfolios by participating in limited partnerships or pooled funds, such as hedge funds. The downside to limited partnerships is that there is very little accountability to regulatory organizations (such as the SEC). Risk may be masked with the use of margins and other forms of leverage, and high-risk instruments, such as futures contracts, may be utilized, making the partnership difficult to monitor and evaluate.

Future Needs

There is a clear mandate from wealthy individuals for increased education and training on the investment management process. The demand is driven in part from changes in the prudent person rules that fiduciaries and trustees are required to follow, and also from the desire to ensure that younger generations and surviving spouses are properly prepared to assume responsibility for investment decisions.

Investment services firms that are anxious to market services to wealthy individuals will need to offer technology to link investors to their accounts, and to provide ready access to information and pricing on the firm's products. Larger institutional money management firms will need to recognize the different investment requirements that an individual requires versus an institution. And consulting firms will need to develop money manager and performance measurement databases that break out investment results for both taxable and tax-exempt portfolios.

APPENDIX
STATE REGISTRATION REQUIREMENTS

Forty-six states and territories now require registration of registered investment advisers (RIAs) that maintain an office and conduct business in the state. Thirty-six states have *de minimis* exemptions for those out-of-state RIAs who have clients in that state, and/or are prospecting to clients.

Jurisdiction	De Minimis Exemption
Alabama	Not more than 5 clients
Alaska	Not more than 5 clients
Arizona	Not more than 5 present or prospective clients
Arkansas	Not more than 5 clients
California	Not more than 5 clients; exemption applies only to RIA registered with SEC
Colorado	No requirements
Connecticut	Not more than 5 clients, provided RIA does not hold self out to the public as an RIA
Delaware	No exemptions
District of Columbia	Not more than 10 clients
Florida	Not more than 15 clients, provided RIA does not hold self out as RIA *anywhere*
Georgia	Not more than 15 clients, none of which are registered investment companies
Guam	Not more than 5 clients
Hawaii	Not more than 5 clients
Idaho	Not more than 5 clients
Illinois	Not more than 5 clients, provided RIA does not advertise or solicit
Indiana	Not more than 5 clients
Iowa	No requirement
Kansas	Not more than 5 clients
Kentucky	Not more than 5 clients
Louisiana	Not more than 15 clients
Maine	Not more than 5 clients, and RIA registered with SEC

Jurisdiction	De Minimis Exemption
Maryland	Not more than 5 clients
Massachusetts	No exemptions
Michigan	Not more than 5 clients
Minnesota	No exemptions
Mississippi	Not more than 5 clients
Missouri	Not more than 5 clients
Montana	Not more than 5 clients or prospective clients
Nebraska	Not more than 5 clients
Nevada	Not more than 5 clients or prospective clients
New Hampshire	No exemptions
New Jersey	Not more than 5 clients
New Mexico	Not more than 5 clients or prospective clients and RIA is registered with SEC
New York	Not more than 15 clients with exceptions
North Carolina	Not more than 10 clients
North Dakota	No exemptions
Ohio	No requirements
Oklahoma	Not more than 5 clients, but not available if client is a pension plan or government agency
Pennsylvania	Not more than 5 clients if registered with SEC
Puerto Rico	Not more than 5 clients
Rhode Island	No exemptions
South Carolina	Not more than 5 clients
South Dakota	Not more than 5 clients
Tennessee	Not more than 5 clients
Texas	No exemptions
Utah	Not more than 5 clients
Vermont	No exemptions
Virginia	No exemptions
Washington	Not more than 5 clients
West Virginia	Not more than 5 clients
Wisconsin	No exemptions
Wyoming	No requirements

Source: "State Registration—The De Minimis Exemption—Threshold and Pitfalls," The Investment Adviser's Counsel, (The Advisory Press, Inc. [413-734-1555], Summer 1994).

ENDOWMENTS AND FOUNDATIONS

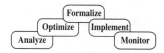

"Surplus wealth is a sacred trust which its possessor is bound to administer for the good of the community."

Andrew Carnegie

"All of us are born for a reason, but all of us don't discover why. Success in life has nothing to do with what you gain in life or accomplish for yourself. It's what you do for others."

Danny Thomas

Endowments and foundations are pools of investment assets created for charitable, social, and other public purposes. These funds allow many educational and social institutions, ideas, and interests to be promoted and sustained without either the funding or the prevailing influence of government. In most cases, the continuing vitality as well as importance of these institutions and activities significantly depends on the institutions' success in managing their investments, which provides a strong incentive for good investment management.[1]

---

[1]Arthur H. Parker, "Endowments and Their Management," in *The Challenges of Investing for Endowment Funds,* The Institute of Chartered Financial Analysts (Homewood, IL: Dow Jones-Irwin, 1987) p. 6.

311

The biggest challenge for trustees and fiduciaries is managing the usually delicate trade-off between long-term requirements (the level of support the funds will provide future generations) and current needs (spending rates and grant-making programs). The community purpose and charitable nature of these activities make resource allocations all the more difficult.

Definitions

Endowments and foundations are organized either as trusts or corporations under state law and are exempt from federal taxation, with the exception of private, non-operating foundations (described below). The titles of many foundations contain synonyms such as *fund, endowment,* and *trust,* while many others, including some of the largest, use no such identifier at all. The fundamental distinction between foundations and pension funds is that foundations frequently have no predictable cash sources and no corporate parent to ensure the financial health of the institution.

> A foundation [is] a nongovernmental, nonprofit organization with its own funds (usually from a single source, either an individual, family, or corporation) and program managed by its own trustees and directors, which was established to maintain or aid educational, social, charitable, religious, or other activities serving the common welfare primarily by making grants to other nonprofit organizations.[2]

Private Foundations

Private foundations are typically distinguished by the single private family or corporate source of the funds. They are required by law to spend or pay out 5 percent of their assets annually or face penalty taxes on the undistributed portion. On balance, tax considerations are not a major constraint for the investment committee, but the 5 percent distribution requirement is.

The vast majority of private foundations are classified as *private nonoperating* or *grantmaking foundations.*[3] Investment income of a private nonoperating foundation is currently taxed at a rate of 1 percent,

---

[2] David F. Freeman, *The Handbook on Private Foundations,* rev. ed. (New York City: The Foundation Center, 1991), p. 2.

[3] Ibid., pp. 2–4.

provided certain distribution requirements are met; otherwise a 2 percent rate applies. (Investment management and custodial expenses are deductible from investment income before taxes are applied.)

An *operating foundation* is a private foundation that primarily conducts its own charitable programs, rather than making grants to others. Operating foundations receive more favorable tax status under the Internal Revenue Code (IRC) than primarily grantmaking foundations.

Corporate foundations are private foundations established by business corporations as a means of carrying out systematic programs of charitable giving. Few corporate foundations have large endowments; most receive and distribute funds each year from current profits of the parent company.

Community foundations are classified as public charities under the IRC and are subject to fewer and different regulations than private foundations. Charitable contributions to community foundations qualify for maximum income tax deduction. They have multiple sources of funding and a local or regional focus in their giving, and typically administer investments and charitable distributions separately.

Endowments

Though *endowment* and *foundation* are often used interchangeably, charitable endowments are normally thought of as those organizations specifically excepted from the IRC's private foundation classification: principally, schools, churches, hospitals, and organizations receiving substantial support from the public.[4] Endowments are usually classified as one of two types:[5]

> *True endowments* are funds with provisions that prohibit spending principal. The restrictions on investment methods and expenditures from capital appreciation may result from either trust documents or general endowment law. The only sources of investment funds are gifts and bequests.

---

[4] IRC Secs. 509(a)(1) and 501(c)(3). The code refers to all such excluded organizations as *public charities*. Private foundations are subject to further tax rules and possible penalties.

[5] According to a 1988 National Association of College and University Business Officer's (NACUBO) study on endowments, on average about 66 percent of total collegiate endowment dollars were *true* endowment and 31 percent were *quasi*-endowment. NACUBO, 1989, p. 7. 1989 NACUBA Endowment Study, National Association of College and University Business Offices (Washington, D.C.: Cambridge Associates, Inc.).

Quasi-endowments are funds not subject to any legal prohibitions against spending. Quasi-endowments may originate from gifts or from surplus operating funds so designated by the institution's governing board.

Scope of Foundation and Endowment Funds

Benefactors have long recognized the value of segregating funds earmarked to sustain their varied social and charitable goals. In the Middle Ages, various religious groups received financial support in the form of rental income from land donated by wealthy owners. When Henry VIII unilaterally resolved his dispute with the Catholic Church by confiscating its lands, he gave substantial land to both Oxford and Cambridge Universities. In doing so, he established two of the most successful endowment funds in the world. Today endowments seem to play a very small role in England and Europe; charitable contributions and the establishment of endowments and foundations are largely American experiences.

TABLE 14–1   **Total Assets and Number of Foundation/ Endowment Funds**
(As of December 1993)

	1988		1993	
	Number	*Assets ($ billions)*	*Number*	*Assets ($ billions)*
Endowment Funds				
College, private school, museum, and hospital endowments over $1 million	520	$ 66	829	$118
Foundation Funds				
Charitable organizations with over $1 million	608	67	1,424	127
Total	1,128	$133	2,253	$245

Source: Money Market Directory of Pension Funds and Their Investment Managers, Charlottesville, VA (1988 and 1993).

At the end of 1993, combined foundation and endowment funds held more than $245 billion in assets, up sharply from $133 billion in 1988. In the last five years, the role and number of private foundations (with assets over $1 million) have increased even more dramatically, from 608 to over 1,424 funds and from $67 billion to over $127 billion in total assets. (See Table 14–1.)

Spending and Accumulation Policies

The expected perpetual nature of endowments and foundations (hereafter referred to as funds) requires trustees to take an integrated approach to investment and spending policies—considering contemplated grants and operating expenses as well as estimated future contributions. The investment policy can only be designed with an understanding of how much of the fund will be spent on an annual basis. Historically, this determination was much simpler to make since trust documents stipulated that only current income (dividends and interest) was available for spending; the principal was intended to be saved, not spent.

Today, trustees may have far more discretion under the law to determine their spending policies and to administer them consistent with a prudent investment process. Moreover, the rise in inflation rates and cost increases above and beyond those fueled by inflation have forced attention on what it truly means to support in perpetuity any individual fund.

> The interpretation that drives most modern spending policies is that the entire function for which the endowed support originally was provided should be supported indefinitely, regardless of increases in cost.[6]

Thus, it is the trustees' responsibility to determine just what costs apply to their circumstances and to ensure that these assumptions are incorporated in their spending and investment policies. Other important decisions (discussed below) that impact the fund's spending policies include the following: When is it more prudent to spend the fund than to preserve it? What kind of spending rule should be adopted? How should we manage the funding-support ratio?

---

[6] William F. Massy, *Endowment: Perspectives, Policies, & Management* (Washington, D.C.: Association of Governing Boards of Universities and Colleges, 1990), p. 22.

These questions highlight the interplay of investment policy and spending and accumulation policies. They should be resolved through a balanced decision-making process—a process involving a combination of subjective and objective decisions, analogous in many ways to the asset allocation process we discussed in Chapter 4.

We first turn to the issues of how much of the fund to spend and how much surplus operating income to channel back to the fund. Once the broad outline of the fund's resources, constraints, and goals has been determined, the pivotal question can be phrased simply: Will this year's level of spending or grants negatively impact the fund's ability to accomplish similar goals in the future? Obviously, a fund's spending rate can have a major impact on its accumulation of investment assets and ultimately its ability to fund future needs. However, this straightforward expression belies the complexity of the underlying decision-making process. In general, spending rules may be divided into two categories: (1) those based on an *income-only policy* and (2) those based on a *total-return spending strategy*.

Income-Only Policies

The historical method of spending income only does provide for the automatic reinvestment of capital gains, and therefore some growth to offset cost increases. (Most funds estimate their long-term annual cost increases to be 5.0 percent—comprising both an estimated inflation rate of 3.5 percent, and a general cost of goods and services increase of an additional 1.5 percent.). Grant recipients and directors of recipient organizations tend to favor objectives that disburse either a fixed dollar amount or all of the portfolio income.

However, the income-only method has two very serious shortcomings. The amount of reinvestment may bear no relation to the amount needed by the fund to offset inflation or other cost increases. More importantly, it severely limits the investment strategies that can be pursued. This, of course, often results in asset allocations that are heavily oriented to fixed income, forgoing the known benefits of a more broadly diversified portfolio.[7]

Larger funds recognized long ago the inadequacy of this method, and other institutions are moving rapidly to adopt more prudent

---

[7] Ibid., p. 30.

approaches. Less than 11 percent of surveyed college and university endowments are still following an income-only policy.[8]

Total-Return Policies

Experienced trustees have realized that investment decisions should be based on total portfolio return, not just investment income or yield. Thus, funds should establish a *spending rate* that sets aside a percentage of the fund's total value (principal *plus* income *plus* appreciation, or gains) for expenditure each year. This projected annual distribution of the investment assets is then taken into account in designing a thoughtful, long-term investment strategy.

Determining the criteria that should be used to decide just how much should be spent each year (the spending rate) is the difficult part. The decision should not be made in an arbitrary fashion. Some funds have set a rate of 5 percent (corresponding to the minimum spending rate required by the IRC for private foundations) instead of estimating the real costs they are trying to offset. However, going to the opposite extreme and spending the total return is also not prudent if the fund hopes to accomplish any notion of longevity.

As with the overall investment process, trustees should start with the fund's goals and investment objectives. Most foundations and endowments desire to fund in perpetuity the same expenses, inflated by real and inflationary cost increases. However, this goal can only be accomplished if the growth rate of the fund and the growth rate of the expenses are equal. The spending rate required to produce this result is called the *equilibrium spending rate.*

In general terms, we can approximate the equilibrium spending rate as the difference between the portfolio's expected total return (based on the fund's asset allocation) and the fund's total rise in costs (inflation plus cost increases above the rate of inflation). For example, if the expected rate of return on the portfolio is 9 percent, inflation is estimated to be 3.5 percent, and an institution's real cost increases are expected to be 1.5 percent, the equilibrium spending rate is 4 percent.

$$9.0\% \; - \; 3.5\% \; - \; 1.5\% \; = \; 4.0\%$$
$$(\text{Return}) - (\text{Inflation}) - (\text{Real rise}) = (\text{Equilibrium spending rate})$$

---

[8] NACUBO, 1994 NACUBA Endowment Study, National Association of College and University Business Officers (Washington, D.C.: Cambridge Associates, Inc.).

However, it is not a simple matter to apply this rate to the overall fund each and every year. As Table 14–2 shows, applying this equilibrium spending rate—or any other constant spending rate—to fluctuating fund values (as a result of volatile market returns) will likely result in unacceptable swings in the fund's distributions.

In year 1, the fund distributed 4 percent of its $30 million, or $1.2 million. In year 2, the amount the fund was able to distribute was dependent on the previous year's results. When the expected rate of return of 9 percent was achieved, the fund realized both a real growth in assets (5 percent), as well as a 5 percent increase in its grants. On the other hand, when returns were −3.0%, the size of the fund decreased and consequently when the 4 percent equilibrium spending rate was applied, the amount that was distributed was reduced from $1.2 million to $1.12 million (a 7 percent reduction).

The fact that actual portfolio returns will vary from their expected returns has prompted the need for investment committees to develop smoothing approaches to even out year-to-year spending fluctuations. Three of the more common approaches include

1. *Moving average.* The most common smoothing method is to apply the equilibrium spending rate (4.0 percent) to an average of several past years (3–5) of the fund's market values. Greater smoothing is achieved by using more years but results in greater divergence between actual and targeted spending rates. Another problem is that the effect of any

TABLE 14–2 **Returns and the Impact on Spending Using a 4 percent Equilibrium Spending Rate ($ millions)**

Total Return*	Year 1		Year 2		Percent Change in Spending
	Endowment	Spending	Endowment	Spending	
−3.0%	$30	$1.2	$27.9	$1.12	−7%
9.0	30	1.2	31.5	1.26	5
21.0	30	1.2	35.1	1.40	17

*The three cases are the 9 percent expected case and one standard deviation of returns in either direction.

year's large deviation in total return will stay in the moving average with undiminished weight until it is dropped, producing undesirable jerkiness in the smoothing procedure.

2. *Preset increment over last year.*   This method escalates the level of spending by a preset amount over that of the previous year. Using the above example, the expected growth rate is 5 percent, the difference between the expected total return (9 percent) and the equilibrium spending rate (4 percent). This 5 percent escalation factor would be multiplied by the previous year's spending level ($1.2 million) to produce a spending increment of $60,000, or a total spending level of $1.26 million in year 2.

3. *Judging the need for spending.*   Some institutions still rely on the collective judgment of the investment committee for smoothing the level of spending.

These basic smoothing techniques can all be augmented with ceilings and floors to mitigate anomalies in market values. For instance, a fund might decide to "spend *x* percent of a five-year moving average, but no less than the prior year's spending amount." However, care should be taken to dodge the ad hoc flavor of these constraints. The potential to change the limits whenever some new problem arises can undermine the value of following disciplined spending rules.

Funding-Support Ratio

The *funding-support ratio* is the fraction of an activity supported by the fund, and is the key strategic variable used by experienced investment committees to track and manage contributions to a recipient's annual budget. For example, a community foundation may make a grant to the local symphony that represents 10 percent of the symphony's annual budget. The desire of the investment committee should be to maintain this 10 percent ratio over time. If, however, the symphony's expenses increase faster than the value of the fund, the spending rate of the fund would have to be increased to maintain the 10 percent funding ratio. Obviously this means less reinvestment for the fund and, all other things being equal, lower spending amounts in the future, (a good illustration of the challenge of balancing current and future needs). The investment committee should consciously monitor funding-support ratios, rather than allow them to change by default.

Legal Considerations

Endowment and foundation funds are subject to the duties imposed by the common law of trusts, except as otherwise varied by terms and restrictions imposed by donors or by statute. Other than tax rules, they are subject to few federal regulations. Funds are thought of as institutional trusts, defined as having their money permanently bestowed, "the income of which is to be used in the administration of a proposed work."[9] Unlike individual trusts, they rarely involve remaindermen with any substantive rights to receive trust assets.

For these reasons, state laws treat funds differently from individual trusts. Most states have adopted the Uniform Management of Institutional Funds Act (UMIFA), which requires that investment decisions be exercised with "ordinary *business* skill and care."[10] A leading authority on the subject has suggested that

> In most cases, that standard probably demands either the skill and care of a professional or high level of skill and care in the selection of a professional.[11]

Thus, with respect to funds, UMIFA has raised the prudent man rule of the law of trusts to a higher standard that mirrors the ERISA prudent expert and the proposed prudent investor rule of the Third Restatement.

In most states, only the attorney general, cotrustees, and successor trustees can challenge the decisions of the trustees of a fund.[12] In addition, as New York's attorney general observed, funds enjoy insulation from marketplace discipline for mismanagement: "The stock will not plummet; the organization will not report a decline in earnings or sales— there is no easy way to measure or control the quality of performance."[13]

UMIFA, as does the Third Restatement, specifically authorizes the delegation of investment management to professional experts to "act in place of the board in investment and reinvestment of institution funds."[14] In this regard, UMIFA encourages trustees to seek professional investment management services whenever and wherever appropriate.

---

[9] See *Saint Joseph's Hosp.* v. *Bennett,* 281 N.Y. 115, 188, 22 N.E.2d 305, 306 (1939).

[10] UMIFA (7 U.L.A.), Secs. 2, 5, 6 (Supp. 1971–1976).

[11] Harvey E. Bines, *The Law of Investment Management,* (Boston, MA: Warren, Gorham & Lamont, 1978; with Supp., 1991), ¶ 2.02(1) at note 13.

[12] The Restatement Third, Sec. 391 (concerning charitable trusts); Christie, "Legal Aspects of Changing University Investment Strategies," 58 *N.C.L. Rev.* 189, 209 (1980).

[13] Abrams, "Regulating Charity—The State's Role," 35 *Rec. A.V. City N.Y.* 481, 486 (1980).

[14] UMIFA, Sec. 5.

CHAPTER

15

DEFINED BENEFIT AND DEFINED CONTRIBUTION PLANS

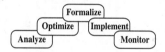

"If you simply take all that we know about retirement planning and extrapolate future retiree income based on current investment patterns, you quickly realize many workers will not be able to afford a comfortable retirement. When you shift from defined benefit to defined contribution plans, you shift from professionals to individuals who often are ill-equipped to make these decisions."

SEC Commissioner J. Carter Beese[1]

"I just got old and couldn't help it."

Jean Louise Calment, age 117, listed by the
Guiness Book of World Records as the world's oldest person.

Over the last decade, there has been a dramatic shift from defined benefit (DB) to defined contribution (DC) plans. The change is a reflection of the advantages that DC plans offer plan sponsors coupled with the portable appeal DC plans have to a mobile workforce.

---

[1] SEC Commissioner J. Carter Beese, Comments at Callan Investment Institute's 1993 National Conference.

An important aspect of this shift, however, is that investment risk has now been placed on the shoulders of plan participants. After several decades of learning how to properly manage money in DB plans, plan sponsors are turning the responsibility for investment decisions over to participants that may be the least able party to make prudent long-term investment decisions.

In a DB plan, the portfolio is used to pay for a predefined monthly retirement payment. The investment performance of the DB plan only impacts the contribution obligation of the plan sponsor—a successful investment program translates to lower contributions. It does not impact the payment made to the retiree.

This is contrasted with the DC plan, where investment performance has a direct bearing on the participant's account value and ultimately the funds available for retirement. When the individual participant selects his or her own investments (as in the case of a self-directed 401(k) plan), investment results are entirely borne by the participant. These investment decisions will ultimately define their financial independence, and the long-term impact of these decisions is tremendous.

The Impact of Improved Performance

The 25-year-old DC participant that can improve the performance of his or her account by 1 percent can obtain an additional 30 percent in retirement assets at age 65. Improving performance by 2 percent can provide the same individual with increased retirement benefits of 70 percent.

Assumptions:
  25-year-old individual.
  $1,500 per year set aside for retirement.
  Forty years later:

7% annual compounded returns	$299,452
Improving Performance by 1%	
8% annual compounded returns	$388,584
Improving Performance by 2%	
9% annual compounded returns	$506,823

Overview

Prior to a discussion of the investment decisions and characteristics of retirement plans, the section below will briefly describe the important features of different types of retirement plans.

Defined Contribution (DC) Plans

401(k) Plan. The most popular DC plan, the 401(k) plan allows participants to elect to defer a portion of their salary into a retirement plan. The plan sponsor can make an annual decision about the level of contribution it will make, if any. Typically, companies match a portion of the participants' contribution in order to create an incentive for participants to save and more employees to participate. Because of the predominate role 401(k) plans play in today's retirement community, they are addressed in detail later in the chapter.

Profit-Sharing Plan. A profit-sharing plan allows a company to make annual contributions of up to 15 percent of eligible salary (the total salary of employees that meets certain plan participation requirements) or $30,000 per participant, whichever is less. The amount of the annual contribution can be decided every year by the company and allows the flexibility to contribute in profitable years but not in loss years. Participant vesting schedules vary, but the typical schedule would be 20 percent per year.

Age-Weighted Profit-Sharing Plan. Similar to the profit sharing plan, an age-weighted plan allows a contribution of up to 15 percent of eligible salary or $30,000 per participant, whichever is less, each year. The contribution is, however, allocated among participants based on each participant's age. Older participants receive a higher contribution than younger participants. There is still the ability to decide how much of a contribution the company may make on an annual basis. Vesting, again, varies according to a specified schedule.

Money Purchase Pension Plan. This type of plan allows a company to make contributions of up to 25 percent of each participant's salary or $30,000, whichever is less. Although higher than the 15 percent limit under a profit-sharing plan, once the formula for determining the amount of the contribution is made, it must be utilized each year. Exceptions to the contribution amount are available only if the plan is amended or terminated or a waiver of funding is received from the IRS.

Target Benefit Plan. This plan is a mix of both a DC and a DB plan. Similar to a DB plan, a determination is made regarding the benefit a participant will receive at retirement, and the amount of contribution necessary to fund this obligation. As in a DC plan, the maximum annual contribution that can be made is 25 percent of salary or $30,000 per participant, whichever is less. The annual contributions to a target benefit plan are established at the time the plan is adopted. This is in contrast to a DB plan, where the annual contribution is recalculated every year to adjust for the differences between the assumed and actual earnings of the plan. The value at retirement is not an exact amount—it is only a target.

Defined Benefit (DB) Plans

The defined benefit plan provides the participant with predetermined retirement benefits for as long as the participant (and possibly a spouse) is alive. Typically, the benefit is based on years of service and salary level. The plan sponsor is required to make periodic contributions to ensure that this future payment obligation is met. Although declining in popularity, DB plans continue to be the predominate mainstay of retirement benefits with over 55 percent of all retirees receiving income from DB plans.[2]

The determination of the contribution to the DB plan that must be made each year by the plan sponsor is performed by an enrolled actuary (EA). The EA uses complex calculations to project future retirement obligations and then discounts them back to present-day dollars. The calculations are dependent on two important variables: (1) the discount rate used to arrive at the present value of the obligations and (2) the expected return on plan assets. A change to either of these variables results in significant swings in the estimated obligations of the plan sponsor.

The total of these obligations determines the accumulated benefit obligation (ABO). In essence, the ABO *assumes* the immediate termination of the plan and lump-sum payments being made to all current and retired participants. When additional assumptions are made regarding future wage increases, an alternative projected benefit obligation (PBO) is determined.

---

[2] American Bankers Association Trust and Investment Management Division, Participant Benefits Services Committee, Position Paper, Winter 1993.

The difference between the ABO and PBO narrows as the workforce ages, assuming a constant employment base. The ABO or PBO is then compared to the current or discounted future values of the plan assets to determine the funding ratio. The funding ratio is the ratio of plan assets to obligations and is measured as either a surplus or shortfall.

The Underfunding Crisis. Underfunded DB plans have received a great deal of publicity, some of which is unjustified. From the period 1987 to 1993, the underfunded liability of plans doubled from $27 billion to $53 billion.[3] Did plan sponsors abscond with the money? Did they invest the assets poorly? No, for the most part, liabilities increased significantly because they were being accounted for under different assumptions.

As previously mentioned, there are two variables (interest rate and expected return assumptions) that have a dramatic impact on the calculations of benefit obligations. There is an inverse relationship between these variables and the funding obligation. Increase the interest rate assumption and obligations decrease; decrease the expected return and funding obligations increase.

The decrease in interest rates in the early 90s resulted in the increase in the amount of funding obligations. A survey by a leading consulting firm determined that the average rate for 1994 was between 7.0 and 7.5 percent. This is down from an average of 8.00 to 8.25 percent in 1992.[4] Although this may not seem like much of a decline, this has a significant impact on the total dollar amount of the present liability. In fact, a 1 percent decline in interest rate assumptions can cause a 15 percent increase in the obligation.[5]

During the 80s, the expected return on retirement assets was ratcheted up as the bull market produced returns higher than their historical averages. So far through the 90s, plan sponsors have had to lower their return expectations to account for the regression of returns to their historical means. As the rate declines, the obligation increases. Couple the decline in the interest rate assumptions with a lower expected return assumption and one can readily understand the increase in unfunded liabilities.

---

[3] "Future of Participant Benefits Debated," *Journal of Accountancy,* May 1994, p. 20.
[4] "Why All the Fuss?", *Pension World,* July 1994, p. 33.
[5] Ibid.

As interest rates increase, the assumed discount rate will slowly begin to move up, causing the obligation to decrease. These increased interest rates may help bail out some of the perceived problems. The more likely result, however, will be proffered from Congress. In the 1994 legislative session, several bills were introduced that addressed the underfunding problem. The most accepted bill was one that focused specifically on the small minority of plans that were truly underfunded. The bill proposes an increase in the Pension Benefit Guarantee Corporation's (PBGC) compliance authority, tightens the band of permissible rates of return assumptions that can be used, increases the PBGC premium, and requires increased communication to plan participants.[6]

401(k) Plans

The most common DC plan is the 401(k) plan, named after the IRC section that enacted it. (See Appendix 15–1 for a checklist of key 401(k) items that an advisor should cover with an investment committee during the initial fact-finding sessions.) Section 401(k) permits participants to contribute pretax salary dollars through salary reduction arrangements. Participants can choose between receiving current compensation as taxable wages or deferring it into the plan on a pretax basis. The contribution made by the participant is still subject to FICA and Medicare taxes but is excluded for federal income tax purposes in the year that it is made. The amount deferred by the participant is immediately vested, and the amount contributed by the plan sponsor vests according to a specified schedule.

A participant can contribute up to 20 percent of his or her salary, or total compensation if plan documents allow. The total amount a participant can defer is indexed annually based on the Consumer Price Index. The 1994 and 1995 contribution limits equaled $9,240. (Under discrimination testing rules, this limit can be reduced on a plan-by-plan basis.) If the company contributes to a 401(k) plan, the total participant and plan sponsor contributions cannot exceed 25 percent of a participant's salary or $30,000, whichever is less. Also, the total contributions to the plan cannot exceed 15 percent of eligible payroll.

---

[6] "Future of Participant Benefits Debated," p. 20, discussing the Retirement Protection Act (HR 3396 and S 1780).

401(k) plans have strict nondiscrimination rules. These limit the amount of contributions that can be made by highly compensated participants to a multiple of the average amount contributed by non-highly compensated participants.

The plan sponsor's contributions—referred to as the plan sponsor's *match*—are determined either on a discretionary basis or with reference to profits.[7] Plan sponsor contributions are subject to a vesting schedule chosen by the sponsor within ERISA-imposed limits.

Significant features of 401(k) plans include

- Plan sponsors often match all or some part of the contributions made by participants, utilizing a wide variety of formulas and limits for doing so.

- Plan sponsors have considerable discretion to change their matching policies.

- Under certain circumstances, plan sponsors can offer company stock as an investment option. These plans are called stock bonus plans.

- Participation is voluntary; each participant has complete discretion to decide the size of the contributions within specific minimums and maximums set by the plan.

- Aftertax participant contributions may be permitted by the plan.

- Investments may be either participant directed or managed by an investment committee of the company.

- Vested benefits are distributed on termination of employment, subject to a mandatory 20 percent federal income tax withholding, unless the proceeds are transferred to another qualified DC plan or IRA.

Unique Aspects of the DC Investment Process

DC plan assets are managed in one of two different ways: (1) investment committee directed or (2) participant directed.

---

[7] Section 401(k) also covers the less common cash option profit-sharing plan, where the plan sponsor makes a substantial discretionary contribution and gives the participant the option of taking it in cash or deferring it into the plan on a pretax basis.

Investment Committee Directed

A minority of DC plans have kept the investment decisions in the hands of a designated investment committee. The assets are allocated to participants on a pro rata basis, giving consideration to contributions, investment returns, vesting, and possible forfeitures from former participants.

In this context, the investment decision process is very similar to the management of a DB plan, with the important exception that the DC plan sponsor will not suffer from the poor performance of the investment markets. This may have a significant impact on terminating or retiring participants if they happen to withdraw from the plan at a time when the capital markets have experienced poor results. For this reason, a diversified investment management approach is critical. The committee should be especially sensitive to following all aspects of the procedural process since it will both limit the committee's liability and increase the chances of the participants receiving deserved hard-earned retirement benefits.

Participant Directed

With participant-directed DC plans, plan sponsors select the investment options to be made available to participants. The participants then individually decide the amount to be invested in each investment option.

The shift of investment responsibilities to participants should be well understood by the plan sponsor. There are some responsibilities and risks that are retained by the plan sponsor—the same broad fiduciary responsibilities the sponsor had with the DB plan. Equally important, the lessons learned managing the DB plan must now be passed on to new committee members chosen to administer the DC plan. Unfortunately, the DC committee is often comprised of staff (typically from the Human Resource Department) that have never been involved in investment decisions. They are more familiar with the administrative functions of the retirement plan than investment management procedures.

The assistance that a participant-directed plan requires from an investment consultant is also somewhat different from the services that a consultant would provide a DB plan. A sample engagement letter for an investment consultant is included as Appendix 15–2. The letter addresses the more important aspects of the duties that should be performed by the consultant for this type of situation. Also included as Appendix 15–3 is a sample IPS for a participant-directed program.

The differences between areas of responsibility for DB plans versus DC plans (both investment committee directed and participant directed) are summarized in Table 15–1.

TABLE 15–1 Comparison of Investment Management Responsibility

Activity	DB Plan	DC Plan: Committee Directed	DC Plan: Participant Directed
Understanding current situation	EMP must understand plan needs and resources.	EMP must estimate overall needs of PARs.	PAR determines own goals.
Asset allocation	EMP determines asset allocation.	EMP determines asset allocation.	PAR determines own asset allocation.
Investment policy	EMP sets goals and investment policy.	EMP sets goals and investment policy.	EMP sets search criteria for options; PAR determines own strategy.
Money manager selection	EMP chooses money managers.	EMP chooses money managers.	EMP provides options; PAR chooses among options.
Performance evaluation	EMP evaluates ongoing performance of the money managers and compares to policy/goals.	EMP evaluates ongoing performance of the money managers and compares to policy/goals.	EMP evaluates ongoing performance of options; PAR has no control over EMP's hiring and firing of options.

Note: Key responsibility: Plan sponsor (EMP); Participant (PAR).

ERISA Sec. 404(c)

In the 80s, plan sponsors appealed to the DOL to interpret the safe harbor rules for DC plans. In 1992, the DOL issued regulations interpreting ERISA Section 404(c). These are *voluntary* provisions that offer plan sponsors and other fiduciaries exemption from liability for participant-directed investment results. For Section 404(c) to apply, a plan must

1. Provide an opportunity for participants to choose from at least three investment options, each of which must have a unique risk/return profile. For example, a plan that offered as investment options a money market, small cap, and an

international fund would probably not satisfy the requirement because of the common risk/return characteristics of the two equity funds. A plan sponsor that offers its own stock as an investment option must still offer three additional investment options.

2. Provide an opportunity for participants to exercise control over the assets in their individual accounts—this is defined as the opportunity to change investment options at least quarterly. (There are those that believe that the volatility of the equity markets warrants the ability for participants to make changes more frequently.)

3. Provide participants education so they can make an intelligent choice between and among investment options. This education component should include, as a minimum,

   • Information on investment fundamentals, including the importance of diversification and the asset allocation decision.

   • The relationship between risk and return.

   • The impact of the investment time horizon and the effect of inflation on investment growth.

   • Instruction on the time value of money, particularly the effects of compounding.

   • Discussion of the securities that make up each of the different investment options.

One proven solution that helps plan sponsors meet their 404(c) requirements is to build pre-allocated portfolios and offer them as investment options. Each structured option is designed to meet a specific risk/return profile. For example, the conservative option might be structured so that the worst case scenario in a given year would be a loss of no more than 0 percent. The moderate option might be structured to achieve an expected return of 8 percent, and the aggressive option might be set with a return objective of 10 percent. Figure 15–1 gives an example of such a portfolio.

The advantages to this approach are fourfold.

1. The plan sponsor knows that every participant is going to have, as a minimum, a well-diversified portfolio.

FIGURE 15–1 Sample Diversified Portfolio—Moderate

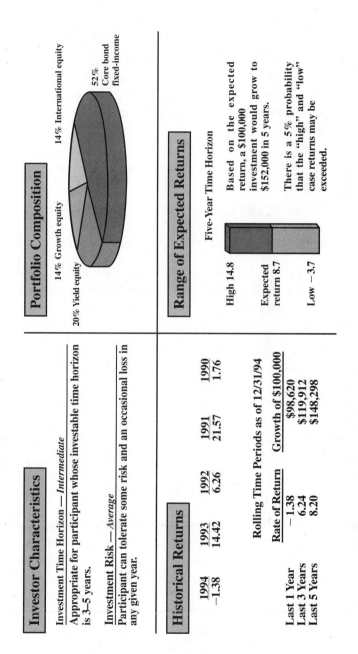

Investor Characteristics

Investment Time Horizon — *Intermediate*
Appropriate for participant whose investable time horizon is 3–5 years.

Investment Risk — *Average*
Participant can tolerate some risk and an occasional loss in any given year.

Portfolio Composition

20% Yield equity
14% Growth equity
14% International equity
52% Core bond fixed-income

Range of Expected Returns

Five-Year Time Horizon

High 14.8
Expected return 8.7
Low −3.7

Based on the expected return, a $100,000 investment would grow to $152,000 in 5 years.

There is a 5% probability that the "high" and "low" case returns may be exceeded.

Historical Returns

1994	1993	1992	1991	1990
−1.38	14.42	6.26	21.57	1.76

Rolling Time Periods as of 12/31/94

	Rate of Return	Growth of $100,000
Last 1 Year	−1.38	$98,620
Last 3 Years	6.24	$119,912
Last 5 Years	8.20	$148,298

Source: Copyright © Investment Management Council, 1995.

331

2. It is easier for the plan sponsor to replace underperforming funds that make up the structured options. The participant has selected and associates with the option, not the individual funds.

3. It is much easier to educate the participants on the risk and reward characteristics of structured options than it is to teach participants the differences between stocks and bonds, and the mechanics of diversification.

4. Today's state-of-the-art recordkeeping systems permit plan sponsors to set up and rebalance these structured options automatically.

Whatever the approach, the bottom line is that participants need to be educated about the impact their decisions are going to have on their financial future. Specifically, participants need to understand

- The need for the real rate of return available only from equities. They simply cannot retire on the earnings of fixed income assets.

- The need to start contributing now.

- The need to contribute as much as they can, especially if there is a plan sponsor match feature.

Common 401(k) Investment Choices

The following will describe some of the various investment alternatives typically considered by plan sponsors for participants in 401(k) plans.

GICs or Stable Asset Value Funds. A GIC is an insurance company contract that provides that the insurance company repays the participant's contributions plus interest at a guaranteed rate according to a schedule specified in the contract. There is a significant amount of DC assets invested in GICs—approximately $150 to $200 billion. A recent survey of investment managers revealed that while GICs continue to hold the largest market share of DC assets, from 1993 to 1994 that share decreased from 42 to 37 percent, with the loss in assets going mainly to equities (increasing from 28 to 33 percent across all DC plan assets).[8]

---

[8] "Defined Contribution News—Exclusive DC News Survey," *Institutional Investor,* Special Supplement, October 3, 1994.

The GIC is only as good as the financial viability of the insurance company that issues it. Although this alternative is designed to be stable, there have been instances where the issuing insurance company has failed or has been placed in receivership. Even though not required (and certainly not expected in the future), the plan sponsor has typically had to make good on losses since they bear the ultimate responsibility for the appropriateness and due diligence undertaken to select the carrier that provided the GIC.

The true cost of the GIC or stable asset value alternative is the opportunity cost of not having the funds invested in an alternative that may yield higher returns over the long term (e.g., stocks). This is just another example of the importance of educating plan participants.

Fixed Income.   One step up on the risk/return spectrum from GICs, fixed-income choices are also a common option. The choices usually contain a short-term (in average maturity) alternative and/or an actively managed core bond alternative. The participant must be reminded that these alternatives (over the long term) may not provide the after-inflation returns necessary to preserve the purchasing power of the funds invested.

Balanced.   As the middle ground, the balanced alternative is presented either to achieve the diversification sought by a participant by default or (more appropriately) to be used as the swing manager between asset classes. The critical aspect of the balanced alternative is that the participant is made aware of the asset classes contained in the balanced fund. As an example, the fund may contain foreign stocks or bond derivatives that surprise the participant when the markets take a downturn.

Domestic Equity.   The education and disclosure about this option should contain such critical information as

- Style of management, since blending styles of management (growth versus value) is a well-recognized tool to limiting interim fluctuations.

- The extent, if any, of nondomestic equity asset classes in the portfolio (e.g., cash, international equities, convertible bonds, and the like).

Company Stock.   A corporate plan sponsor can make its own stock one of the plan's investment options. Presumably, participants holding company stock are likely to have a greater interest in the success of their company. By its nature, employer stock is a nondiversified investment. The participation in company stock may not be appropriate as a diversified alternative if the participant already has stock options, stock grants, or other close ties to the plan employer's equity performance.

International.   Based on diversification benefits, international securities are becoming a more frequent option. The two major items to consider with this alternative are

- The extent to which the international equity alternative includes components of both the EAFE index and emerging markets.
- Whether the international alternative is international in name only. The fund could actually be a global balanced alternative and not a pure international fund.

DC Service Providers

Initially, DC plans were almost entirely served by so-called bundled providers, such as mutual fund families, insurance companies, banks, and brokerage firms. These firms provided administration, recordkeeping, and custody as well as investment management.

The growing trend is to unbundle these services and turn to outside specialists in each of the different service sectors. The coordination of the different components can be constructively packaged to provide a seamless web of services to plan sponsors. These programs have been advanced by strategic alliances formed by different vendors in the marketplace. One result of the alliances is that more light has been focused on fund performance and the cost of the individual services. Plan sponsors are able to select the best funds, then, on an ongoing basis, monitor the performance and replace funds, as required, without having to terminate the entire service contract.

Differences between DB and DC Plans

In conclusion, some of the practical differences between DB and DC plans are

- DC plans avoid the burdensome regulations and administration of DB plans. These factors are widely perceived as making DB plans too costly to continue. This has been compounded by the increase in the premiums paid to the PBGC to help shore up the government coffers in the event that failed plans have to be bailed out.

- DC plans can avoid the financial accounting rules (FASB 87) that require, in certain cases, plan sponsors to reflect unfunded DB pension liabilities on their balance sheets and to account for changes in the present values of those liabilities as charges against corporate earnings.

- Participants in DC plans do not have to spend an unbroken string of several decades with one plan sponsor to earn a pension. When participants leave, they can take the value of their vested account with them (portability feature).

- DC participants have an asset that ultimately can be left to their spouse and/or children upon their death. This is contrasted to a DB payment, which dies with the retiree (or the surviving spouse).

- DC plans offer participants the flexibility to contribute to their own retirement account in a tax-advantaged way. The participant knows the value of his or her account and how much of it is vested. Participants often misunderstand or fail to appreciate formula-derived calculations of their stake in a traditional DB plan. They seem to prefer watching their own account.

- Recordkeeping for DC plans can be more complicated due to demands for daily account valuation, switching or exchange capabilities, and loan features. Communication responsibilities to participants is also increased for DC plans.

- DC nondiscrimination testing limits the usefulness of these plans for highly compensated participants, sometimes even triggering a return of contributions during or after the plan year. This is an awkward problem for some plan sponsors attempting to convince senior participants that their company-sponsored retirement plan will take care of them during their retirement years.

- From a participant's perspective, the key disadvantage of DC plans is that they place the burden of investment results on the participant. Participants may be ill-equipped to make the appropriate long-term investment decisions that will maximize their account value. This situation can be exacerbated by plan sponsors that, seemingly relieved of financial responsibility for investment results, provide a poor set of investment choices and fail to adequately educate their participants.

APPENDIX 15–1
401(K) CHECKLIST
Defined Contribution Clients

I. BACKGROUND INFORMATION

Company Information: **Financial Advisor Information:**

Company: _____   Name: _____
Contact: _____   Firm: _____
Title: _____   Address: _____
Address: _____   _____

_____   _____

Phone: _____   Phone: _____

Business Information:

Type of business: ☐ Corporation   ☐ Partnership
                     ☐ Sole proprietorship   ☐ S corporation

Other (please specify) _____

Is the business part of a controlled group?   ☐ Yes   ☐ No
Is the business part of an affiliated service group?   ☐ Yes   ☐ No
Does the business use any leased employees?   ☐ Yes   ☐ No

II. PLAN SPECIFICS

Total number   Estimated number
of employees: _____   of eligible employees: _____

This will be: ☐ A new plan   ☐ An amendment to an existing plan
Is there another plan currently in place: ☐ Yes   ☐ No (if no, go to III)
If yes, type of plan (check all those that apply):
    ☐ 401(k)   ☐ Profit sharing   ☐ Money purchase   ☐ Defined benefit
    ☐ Target benefit   Other (please specify)_____
Plan name: _____
Plan assets: _____ Number of participating employees: _____
Plan year-end: _____ Original effective date: _____
    ☐ Union   ☐ Non-Union   ☐ Hourly   ☐ Salaried
Other plans: _____
Current recordkeeper: _____☐ Centralized   ☐ Decentralized
On-line with recordkeeper   ☐ Yes   ☐ No
Frequency of account valuations: _____
Current trustee (name of trust company or self-trusteed): _____

III. PAYROLL

Payroll vendor: _____   Number of locations:_____
☐ Centralized   ☐ Decentralized   Frequency of payroll:_____
Preferred transmission mode: ☐ Tape   ☐ Disc   ☐ RJE   ☐ Hardcopy
    Other (please specify) _____

IV. SERVICES REQUESTED

☐ Full service   ☐ Recordkeeping   ☐ Trustee   ☐ Investment management
Why considering a change?_____
_____
_____
Objectives of a change:_____
_____
Proposed conversion date?_____

V. CONTRIBUTIONS

Frequency: _____   Estimated annual contributions: $_____
Contribution types: ☐ Employee salary deferrals   ☐ Profit sharing
                        ☐ Employer match   ☐ Employee aftertax
                        How much_____ ☐ Employee rollover
                        ☐ Other_____
Vesting schedule (if any, explain)_____
_____

VI. DISTRIBUTIONS (In Service or Termination)

Types: ☐ Lump sum   ☐ Annuities   ☐ Installment
Frequency   Estimated annual
of processing:_____   withdrawals: $_____
Turnaround time for checks: _____
How are distributions currently being administered?_____
_____

VII. LOANS

Loans available?   ☐ Yes   ☐ No   Value of outstanding loans: $_____
Will loans be offered?   ☐ Yes   ☐ No   Frequency of processing:_____
Turnaround time for checks: _____   Estimated annual loans:_____
How are loans currently being administered?_____
_____

VIII. INVESTMENT CHANGES/TRANSFERS

☐ Daily   ☐ Monthly   ☐ Quarterly   ☐ Other (Specify)_____

Frequency of deferral rate change: _____

Current Fund Name:	Current Manager	Current Balance	Cash Flow (est.)
_____	_____	_____	_____
_____	_____	_____	_____
_____	_____	_____	_____
_____	_____	_____	_____

Are there any existing plan assets that will not be liquidated and transferred into the new plan (e.g., company stock, outside GICs, life insurance, etc.)? Please specify: _____

Are all investments participant directed? _____

What kind of GICs do they have? _____

GIC considerations (such as: are they expecting the new manager to take over an existing portfolio; is it an in-house portfolio or managed by an outside manager; who is trustee?) _____

Will they be changing their investment options?   ☐ Yes   ☐ No

Do they want to use: ☐ One outside manager   ☐ Multiple outside managers

Do they prefer: ☐ Separate vehicles   ☐ Commingled vehicles

Funds added:

_____

_____

Funds deleted:

_____

_____

IX. COMPANY STOCK (if applicable)

Publicly traded on open market	☐ Yes	☐ No
Widely traded	☐ Yes	☐ No
Are voting rights passed through to participants?	☐ Yes	☐ No
If ESOP, does it meet 404(c) requirements?	☐ Yes	☐ No
Is plan a leveraged ESOP?	☐ Yes	☐ No
Proxy solicitation required?	☐ Yes	☐ No

Preferred accounting treatment _____

Exchange traded on _____

X. ADMINISTRATION

	Currently Have	Would Like to Have
800 number currently in use	☐ Yes ☐ No	☐ Yes ☐ No
Voice response	☐ Yes ☐ No	☐ Yes ☐ No
Human operators	☐ Yes ☐ No	☐ Yes ☐ No
Combination of both	☐ Yes ☐ No	☐ Yes ☐ No
Inquiry only	☐ Yes ☐ No	☐ Yes ☐ No
Can initiate transactions	☐ Yes ☐ No	☐ Yes ☐ No

	Current Provider	Desired Provider
Benefit design consulting	_____	_____
IRS Form 1099-R	_____	_____
Financial information for 5500	_____	_____
5500 preparation	_____	_____
401(k) or 401(m) nondiscrimination testing	_____	_____

XI. PARTICIPANT COMMUNICATIONS

Statement frequency: ☐ Quarterly   ☐ Monthly   ☐ Other

Describe current communications support: _____

_____

_____

_____

_____

Additional communications desired:

_____Enrollment materials   _____Investment performance

_____Employee meetings   _____Training seminars (plan sponsor)

_____Other: _____

XII. OTHER ISSUES

Are you aware of any major changes that will be going on in the company (such as spinoffs, reorganizations)? _____

_____

_____

_____

Other special considerations: _____

_____

_____

APPENDIX 15–2
SAMPLE CONSULTANT ENGAGEMENT LETTER FOR
SELF-DIRECTED 401(K) PLAN

Mr. _____
Director, Human Resources
ABC Company

_____

_____

Re: ABC Company 401(k) Plan

Dear _____:

As a follow-up to our meeting on _____ , this letter will outline
the services XYZ Consultants, Inc., will be providing to ABC, Inc. (ABC).
We appreciate the opportunity to be of service to ABC. We look forward to
what is, hopefully, the first step in a long relationship together.

As we discussed, we will provide certain services and information pertaining to ABC's 401(k) Plan and Trust (ABC Plan). You have indicated the
desire to utilize Fiduciary Admin., Inc., as administrator and IJK Trust as custodian for the ABC Plan. Our services are independent of these vendors. We are
not receiving any commissions or other compensation from any of these sources.
You have provided us with a list of the mutual fund alternatives available to
the ABC Plan through IJK Trust. Based on this information, we will provide
the following services and reports to you:

1. We will review the mutual fund alternatives provided through IJK Trust.
Based on our examination of these alternatives, we will narrow the choices
down to three funds under each of the following investment objectives:

a. Short/intermediate bond fund.

b. Actively managed bond fund.

c. Balanced fund.

d. Equity growth fund.

e. International equity fund.

Our list will be based on both objective investment performance criteria and subjective characteristics of the funds presented. We will then review this short list with you (and other members that are involved in the selection process) to arrive at the final fund to be used in each investment objective category.

2. After the selection of the final fund to be utilized for each investment objective, we will issue a letter to you documenting the selection process, the criteria used, and the rationale behind the fund selection. This letter will satisfy ERISA guidelines in documenting that prudent procedures were utilized in making the fund selection. We will also provide you with historical return information on the funds selected so this information may be incorporated into the communications information you prepare for your participants.

3. We will also prepare an investment policy statement (IPS) for the Plan that reflects certain Plan characteristics, the funds selected, and the monitoring process that will be undertaken for the funds utilized. The IPS is required under ERISA and will satisfy the fiduciary duty you owe to ABC Plan participants in this area.

The fee for preparing these items and meeting with you and the other members of your committee will be $_____ , payable 50 percent on delivery of the letter specified under item 2 above and 50 percent on delivery of the IPS under item 3 above. We understand that the letter to be prepared under item 2 is a high priority. We anticipate issuing this letter no later than _____ , 199_____ , assuming we can meet with you and the other committee members on a timely basis.

As you may be aware, ERISA imposes a duty of supervision and monitoring once investment management choices have been made. Beginning with the quarter ending March 31, 199_____ , we will be glad to prepare a quarterly performance report for the ABC Plan that reflects the results obtained for each fund alternative selected. This will include rate-of-return data, any updated fund information we may possess, and comparative return information against the appropriate peer group. The initial fee to provide this data (for the quarters ending 3/31/9_____ , 6/30/9_____ , 9/30/9_____ , and 12/31/9_____) would be $_____ per quarter. This quarterly report would include data on each of the five funds selected. The fee includes meeting with the committee each quarter.

For disclosure purposes,

1. We are, with this letter, providing you with a copy of Part II of our Form ADV that has been filed with the Securities and Exchange Commission, receipt of which is acknowledged by you.

2. All information furnished by either party to the other shall be treated as confidential and not be disclosed to third parties except as agreed upon in writing or as required by law. This does not preclude the

disclosure of information to participants as part of normal participant communications.

3. Either party may terminate this agreement by providing the other party with written notice requesting termination.

4. Since our services are personal in nature, we may not assign the right to perform these services to any other party without your written consent.

Our services are designed to assist you in satisfying ERISA rules and regulations. We represent to you that the process we follow and the reports we issue are in compliance with current ERISA provisions, rules, and regulations. If this description of our services accurately describes the nature of our understanding, please sign in the place designated below and return a copy of this letter to me.

We are excited about being able to work with you in the selection of these funds for the ABC Plan. We think our services will be of enormous benefit to you and the Plan fiduciaries in evaluating and deciding on the investment choices. I look forward to working with you.

Sincerely yours,

XYZ Consultants, Inc.

Agreed and Accepted:

ABC Company, Inc.

By: _____

Its: _____

Enclosure

APPENDIX 15–3
INVESTMENT POLICY STATEMENT FOR SELF-DIRECTED 401(K) PLAN

ABC Company 401(k) Plan

Executive Summary

Type of plan: Participant-directed 401(k) plan.

Current assets: $9,509,856 (12/31/94 balance).

Fiscal year end: December 31.

Trustee/custodian: Trustworthy Trust Company.

Administrator/recordkeeper: Tick & Tie.

Benefit plan committee members: Director, Human Resources; CFO; Controller.

Risk tolerance: N/A—participant directed.

Asset allocation: N/A—participant directed.

Effective January 1, 1995, alternatives:

> Money market fund: No principal risk, variable rate.
> Short-term bond fund: Limited risk, variable return.
> Actively managed bond fund: Greater risk, but fixed income only.
> Balanced fund: Mix of equities/fixed income/cash.
> Equity growth fund: Equities only (cash to limit risk).
> Global equity fund: International and U.S. equities and fixed income.

Selected mutual funds for each alternative:

> Money market fund: Premier Advantage Money Market
> Short-term bond fund: Premium Short Duration
> Actively managed bond fund: Ultimate Fixed Income
> Balanced fund: Best Balanced Fund
> Equity growth fund: Maximizer Stock Fund
> Global fund: Around the World Fund

ABC Company 401(k) Savings Plan and Trust

Investment Policy Statement

I. Background

The ABC Company (ABC) 401(k) Savings Plan and Trust (Plan) was originally adopted effective January 1, 1988, and covers the employees of ABC and its subsidiaries: ABC Manufacturing, ABC Plan & Design, ABC Shipping, and ABC Trucking.

The goal of adopting and implementing the Plan was to provide a means for employees to save toward the goal of retirement and to reward those employees that remain with ABC by matching a portion of the funds an employee contributes toward this savings. The average age of participants in the Plan is 44. The average length of service is 14.6 years.

The Benefit Plan Committee (Committee) is appointed by the Board of Directors of ABC to be responsible for the operation and administration of the Plan for the benefit of the participants. Current members of this Committee are _____ , _____ , and _____ . Each member serves at the discretion and will of the Board of Directors of ABC. The members of the Benefit Plan Committee have executed this Investment Policy Statement in satisfaction of certain Employee Retirement Income and Security Act of 1974 (ERISA) requirements.

II. Current Status

The Plan currently covers 507 active employees. As of December 31, 1994, the Plan size was $9,509,856.

Participants of the Plan can make contributions up to 8 percent of their pay on a before-tax basis. In 1993, ABC matched the first 6 percent of participant compensation that was contributed into the Plan $.20 per $1.00. For 1994, the Board of Directors of ABC has approved the match of $.25 per $1.00 contributed, again limited to the first 6 percent of participant compensation contributed into the Plan. Participant contributions are 100 percent vested when made. Matching contributions are vested over a five-year period (20 percent per year). Participants may also contribute up to 4 percent of pay on an after-tax basis. Vested participant account balances are payable upon termination or withdrawal. Distributions are typically paid in lump-sum cash payments. Distributions are made the quarter after termination or withdrawal. Forfeited and unvested employer contributions are used to decrease the employer's required matching contribution.

Contributions are deposited into the Plan within five business days following each bimonthly payroll period. Withdrawals occur periodically during the year as distributions are paid to participants.

The Plan assets are invested as directed by each participant. The Plan is to comply with the provisions of Section 404(c) of ERISA. The participants are permitted to choose from at least three investment alternatives, each of which is diversified, has materially different risk and return characteristics, and, in the aggregate, enables a participant to achieve appropriate risk and return characteristics. Participants are afforded the opportunity to give investment instructions regarding the investment of their funds (both funds contributed and new funds being contributed) each quarter.

The Plan fiduciaries acknowledge their duty to consider the prudence of investment alternatives made available to participants under the Plan. This Investment Policy Statement is designed to accomplish this duty owed to participants of the Plan. The members of the Benefit Plan Committee will continue to evaluate and examine Plan assets in accordance with this Investment Policy Statement.

III. Investment Alternatives

In order to provide appropriate investment alternatives for participants, effective January 1, 1994, six investment choices were made available. These were as follows: (1) money market fund, (2) short-term bond fund, (3) actively managed bond fund, (4) balanced fund, (5) equity growth fund, and (6) global fund.

Money Market Fund. The fund is to have no principal risk (or have investment risk only commensurate with similar money market funds) and pay a competitive rate of interest. It is realized that the interest rate this fund will earn will be a function of short-term rates for assets held by the fund.

Short-Term Bond Fund. The goal is to provide participants with a fund choice that has limited risk in that it will only make short-term bond investments. This is necessary to limit principal risk if interest rates increase. The objective is to strongly limit risk and loss of principal while achieving a competitive rate of return that will (over the long term) be superior to money market returns.

Actively Managed Bond Fund. This fund should take advantage of returns that can be achieved in the bond market by aggressively working the bond portfolio up and down the yield curve in anticipation of interest rate trends. The desire is to provide a bond alternative that will take more risk and, hopefully, provide more return than the short-term bond fund or money market fund.

Balanced Fund. As a means to obtain appropriate diversification between stocks, bonds, and cash, a balanced alternative is also made available to participants. The balanced fund is designed to utilize the benefits of tactical asset allocation between these asset classes and be supported by a fairly good yield. It should not be designed to make large commitments to any one asset class. The desire of this alternative is to utilize the long-term advantage equities have in providing favorable returns while utilizing bonds and cash as a means to limit volatility.

Equity Funds. To provide an alternative that is tied primarily to the U.S. equity markets, the equity fund alternative is designed to utilize the expertise of a manager that can add value to overall U.S. stock market returns. The desire is to utilize a fund with a value and growth bias to achieve returns greater than the broad markets. Risk is acceptable given the commitment to equity securities; however, risk beyond the broad markets should be taken only if the incremental return justifies it.

Global Fund. To allow participants the right to have their funds placed in overseas markets, the desire is to have a global fund that will participate outside of the U.S. capital markets. The fund should not be limited to non–U.S. markets since the manager may perceive the U.S. investment markets as having attractive return potential. This will also allow participants diversification since only one U.S. stock investment alternative is provided (equity fund, above). Likewise, it is acceptable that stocks, bonds, and cash be utilized by the manager to control risk.

IV. Investment Objectives

A. Time Horizon. Since the accounts are participant directed, there is no time horizon to be expressed for the specific funds. However, since the funds are to be considered by participants as available for retirement purposes and since the average age of participants is 44, the desire is to have quality investment alternatives that can provide the participants with favorable long-term returns.

B. Overall Return Objectives. The investment return objective of the money market fund and short-term bond alternatives is to provide a rate of return at least equal to the annual rate of inflation as measured by the Department of Labor, Bureau of Labor Statistics Consumer Price Index (all cities average). The return objective for each of the other alternatives is to produce an overall annual rate of return at least equal to 2 percent plus the same annual rate of inflation return. This return objective is stated in order to acknowledge that the goal is to provide inflation-protected retirement benefits for the participants.

C. Complementary Return Objectives. Since the duration, direction, and intensity of inflation cycles vary from cycle to cycle, it is recognized that the return experienced by the assets over any one cycle may vary from this objective. A complementary investment objective of the assets is that the rate of return achieved competes favorably, when compared over comparable time periods, to broad investment indexes and similarly managed funds—both factors being dependent on the specific asset class (or classes) of each fund.

D. Risk Tolerance. The Benefit Plan Committee members recognize the difficulty of achieving the investment objectives in light of the uncertainties and complexities of the contemporary investment markets. To achieve the return objectives, risks must be minimized. To minimize this risk, any investment decisions will be viewed with a goal of diversification in an attempt to control risks and minimize losses. The members of the Committee have made a conscious decision to provide participants with a broad array of investment choices so they have alternatives that provide different levels of risk and return. The Committee members will undertake an educational process, as necessary, to fulfill the duty owed to Plan participants so they are fully informed of their fund alternatives.

V. Fund Selection

The Committee will utilize the services of an investment consultant to assist the Committee members in the selection of mutual funds for each investment alternative. The consultant's review of the funds will contain

1. An examination of the return and risk history.

2. The reputation of the fund and manager(s) in the industry.

3. The quality of the fund management company.

4. Name recognition by the public.

5. IRC Section 404(c) criteria.

6. Ratings and rankings by independent mutual fund tracking and monitoring services.

The following criteria will be used to select the final funds in each category. Each criterion was assigned a weight based on its relative importance. The weighting and criteria selection have been established as the guidelines by which any future fund choices will be made.

Criteria	Weight
1. Average annual return	40%
2. Limited downside risk	30
3. Expense ratio	10
4. Size of fund	10
5. Name recognition	10
6. Revenue sharing to offset administration expenses	0
Total	100%

There has been an intentional decision to assign a value of zero to the criterion that would allow a portion of the expenses to be used to offset administration expenses. ABC pays for these administration expenses from its own resources and not from Plan assets. To place the interests of the participants of the Plan ahead of ABC, it was decided that this criterion should have no relevancy.

VI. Performance Reviews

The investment performance of each fund selected will be reviewed each calendar quarter. Comparison will be made to results from other fund alternatives and conformity to the investment objectives specified in this Investment Policy Statement. In addition, periodic meetings will occur as necessary to verify that the objectives of this Statement are being carried out. The overall investment policy will be reviewed annually. The objectives and/or investments are subject to change or revision at any time.

This Investment Policy Statement is signed and dated this _____ day of _____ , 199_____ .

Benefit Plan Committee Members:

_____   _____

(Name)   (Name)

APPENDIX 15–4

DEFINED BENEFIT AND DEFINED CONTRIBUTION PLAN

Reporting Guidelines and Requirements

Item	*Description*	*Filing Date*	*Penalty*	*Filing Location*
IRS Form 5500				
Series	**Participants:**			
5500	100 or more	On or before last	Up to $1,000 per	IRS Service
5500C/R	Less than 100	day of the seventh	day for late filing.	Center indicated
5500 EZ	1 (owner and	month after close		in instructions to
	spouse)	of plan year. 2 ½		Form 5500
Schedules:		mo. extension if		
		Form 5558 filed		All schedules are
Sch. A	Insurance info.	and approved.		to be filed with
Sch. B	Actuarial info.			Form 5500
	(DB Plans)			
Sch. C	Service provider			
	and trustee info.			
Sch. E	ESOP info.			
Sch. P	Annual return			
	of fiduciary			
Sch. SSA	Annual registration		$1 per day up	
	statement for		to $5,000	
	separated part. with			
	deferred vested			
	benefits			
PBGC Form 1-ES	Estimated premium	Within 2 months of	Late payment	PBGC
	payment	end of plan year	penalty and interest	PO Box 105655
				Atlanta, GA 30348
PBGC Form 1	Annual premium	Within 8 ½ months	Late payment	PBGC
	payment	of end of plan year	penalty and	PO Box 105655
			interest	Atlanta, GA 30348
Summary plan	Summary of plan	Within 120 days		SPD Rm. N-5644
description	provisions in easy	of plan adoption.		PWBA
	to understand	If plan amended,		US Dept. of Labor
	language. Includes	every 5 years		200 Const. Ave. NW
	outline of	after initial filing,		Washington, DC
	participant rights.	otherwise every		20210
		10 years.		
Notice of	Material	Within 30 days of		SPD Rm. N-5644
reportable event	modifications to	reportable event or		PWBA
	plan or significant	210 days after plan		US Dept. of Labor
	plan events	year if material		200 Const. Ave. NW
		modification		Washington, DC
				20210
W-2P	Wage and tax	Participant by	$15–$50 for each	Social Sec. office
	statement for	Jan 31st. Social	late filed return	on instructions for
	payment of pension	Security Admin.		W-3 transmittal
	benefits	by 3/1.		form

16

PUBLIC FUNDS[1]

*"If you're not fired with enthusiasm,
you'll be fired with enthusiasm."*

Vince Lombardi

*"Good character is to be praised more than outstanding talent.
Most talents are, to some extent, a gift. Good character, by contrast,
is not given to us. We have to build it piece by piece—by thought,
choice, courage, and determination."*

John Luther

Retirement funds for state, county, city, and municipal employees do
not come under the federal jurisdiction of the DOL as do corporate funds.
Instead, each state and some municipalities have responsibility for legis-
lating the standards for trustee and fiduciary conduct, fund operations,
benefits, administration, and reporting. The public fund fiduciary has a
number of unique challenges to contend with, including (1) the
increasing growth of the size of public funds, (2) the lack of uniformity across state codes, and (3) citizens becoming more hostile to
increased taxes to pay for retirement funding shortfalls.

---

[1] Special thanks to Paul Troup for his contributions and insight.

While the absence of uniform state codes results in a broad variety of operating practices and regulations, it should not be suggested that public funds are poorly managed. Most states have adopted comparable language to ERISA, and in some instances have adopted more stringent standards than those under ERISA. Absent these specific restrictions, public fund fiduciaries will find that the adherence to the investment management process outlined in this book will satisfy most all of the duties owed to public fund participants (and, indirectly, taxpayers).

As of 1994, there was an estimated $1.0 trillion in public funds. These funds continue to receive substantial annual contributions. The California Public Employees Retirement System, the California State Teachers Retirement System, and the New York State Common Fund are some of the largest pools of pension assets in the country. The gap between the size of public funds and corporate DB funds will most likely continue to increase as many corporate funds shift their funds to defined contribution funds, such as 401(k) funds.

Public funds search for ways to control and limit retirement funding expenses. As with the corporate side, public funds have found that switching to defined contribution funds, or using defined contribution funds as a benefit offset, has tremendous appeal. Public funds can offer defined contribution funds, but funds started after 1986 have had to offer participants IRC *457* funds instead of *401(k)s*. A Sec. 457 fund has fewer administrative requirements than the 401(k), but the contribution levels are lower, there are no rollover provisions, and the assets are not vested to the participant (i.e., they could be seized in the event of a municipality bankruptcy). At various times, Congress has considered reinstating 401(k) funds for public employees, and most likely 401(k) funds will be available in the near future.

Funding Status

The first item of relevant information is the funding status of a public pension fund. As seen with defined benefit funds, this has a large impact on long-term investment strategy that can be undertaken. Public funds that are underfunded must handle the same two-edged sword as their corporate counterparts. On the one hand, the board must consider a more aggressive asset mix to increase the probability of narrowing the shortfall between liabilities and assets. On the other hand, a more aggressive mix also increases the probability that negative short-term performance of the capital markets could set the fund further behind, requiring additional contributions from the public entity (and ultimately the taxpayer).

> Faced with the stark realities of budget crunches and citizens more and more hostile to increased taxes, city and county government are wise to move cautiously and prudently as they fund for uncertain futures.[2]

Not all public funds are poorly funded, in spite of periodic publicity about specific funds. The typical public fund has about $76 in assets for every $100 in long-term liabilities. This is reasonably close to the same ratio for corporate pension funds. In certain cases, underfunding is not a result of poor investment funding but rather a function of when the public entity actually started making contributions into the retirement fund. The state of Massachusetts and the Washington, D.C., retirement funds, for example, began funding their pension liabilities in the 80s. It is rare for these younger funds to have a high degree of liability coverage. Funds that started making contributions decades ago (as an example, the Utah Retirement System) have better liability coverage because they have had longer time periods for their investment base to grow by significant amounts.

Board Composition

Most public funds vest fiduciary responsibility and management control at the board level. Board members are appointed or elected with a tenure of between two and five years. There are several difficult dilemmas public funds encounter that are not normally experienced by corporate pension funds:

1. The short board membership tenure means a high turnover of members. Maintaining the continuity of investment practices (further justification for the IPS) and educating new members can absorb a significant amount of the board's valuable time.

2. Public boards are generally composed of both appointed and elected members. There is a potential for conflicts of interest between the fiduciary requirement to make impartial decisions for the benefit of all participants, and the political and personal agendas of the individual board members. Every

---

[2] "Safeguarding Public Funds," *American City & County* 108, April 1993.

investment board—corporate, public, or private—is torn by conflicts, but the public fund board seems to face the greatest number of distractions because it is in the mainstream of politics and politicians.

3. The part-time nature of the board member's position can potentially clash with the full-time demands of the member's job. Some board members will invariably come from the rank and file of city employees. These members may be faced with investment management decisions for the first time in their professional careers. Corporate board members may also have full-time positions; however, these positions are oftentimes related to other finance or governance roles.

4. The public fund board also has the added responsibility of making benefit decisions for its participants. Benefit issues and investment management decisions are two very different areas, each requiring specialized expertise and management time. Whereas the corporate board rarely has to address day-to-day benefit issues, the typical public board is constantly having to deal with payment disputes, exceptions, appeals, and benefits calculations.

For these reasons, when dealing with public fund boards, the desire is to promote a spirit of cooperation and teamwork where individual and political agendas can be superseded by the desire to be proper stewards of retirement funds. Politics, by its very nature, breeds adversarial relationships. When the operation of a public retirement system is diseased by adversarial relationships, the fund will invariably end up with higher-than-average expenses, disappointing long-term investment results, periodic bouts of negative publicity, and the resulting distractions all these items present. Board members should recognize that while they are not required to be the best of friends with political adversaries, the realities are that the long-term interests of the fund participants must be served.

Optimizing the Portfolio

The importance of making the fund's investments work cannot be overstated. For most public retirement systems, it is projected that two out of every three dollars ultimately paid to retirees will need to come from investment growth and earnings, not contributions by the public entity. The greater the investment return from the assets, the less the funding burden will be borne by the taxpayers. The pressure is to achieve successful long-term results so that contributions can be decreased. Keeping the money working is critical to the long-term success of the fund.

Legal constraints at the municipal or state level may affect the asset classes utilized by the fund. The most common limits are on equity exposure or prohibitions against investing in specific asset classes. States such as West Virginia, South Carolina, and Indiana still have restrictions prohibiting investments in equities. States that have prohibitions on investing in international securities include Georgia, Kentucky, Nebraska, New Jersey, New Mexico, West Virginia, Wyoming, and several funds in Texas. Twenty other states have restrictions regarding alternative investments, such as real estate, commodities, and venture capital.[3] These types of legislative or policy restrictions must be dealt with and factored into the list of asset classes to be considered when asset allocation decisions are being formulated.

The Importance of the Investment Policy Statement

Because of political influences and ever-changing board membership, it is imperative that a well-thought-out and well-documented IPS be prepared for the public fund. Present and future board members need to be reminded that more than 90 percent of the growth of a fund is driven by the strategic asset mix and that long-term strategies should be adopted and put into place. These funds must transcend the tenure of board members and certainly any political turnover. By having an easily understood IPS, the public board members will not find it necessary to create significant policy changes during ensuing changes of command. A well-crafted IPS is also important from an audit perspective. Legislative audits and interested outside third parties will want to know where the fund is today and where it is headed in the future.

---

[3] "States Holding Their Breath," *Pension & Investment Age,* October 29, 1990.

Implementation

Most public funds experience relatively large positive cash flows as they make their contributions. Except for the most mature funds, contributions usually exceed current benefit payments and related expenses. Large incoming cash flows require innovation in diversification strategies and money manager funding. Periodic cash flows can be considered to have an inherent dollar cost averaging approach built in. As an example, the funding of an equity account may be made with significant dollars over a multi-year basis. This will tend to average the exposure of the fund's assets into equities over an established time period.

It must also be realized that certain money managers have difficulty accepting significant cash flows if their total assets under management are close to capacity. This is particularly true with small capitalization stock investments, where managers may limit their assets under management to prevent their transaction activity from disrupting trading markets.

With regard to money manager selection and implementation, public funds may also have special nuances or requirements not expected in the normal course of the investment management decision. As an example, some states will only allow a manager to make trades for a public fund if all of the trades are approved on a before-the-fact basis by the board. This is practically an impossibility since few managers would want to wait until a board can convene to implement any buy or sell recommendations.

Another area that is somewhat unique is that of socially responsive investing. This involvement has been partially a result of states passing legislation requiring an increased concern for social issues. Even if not a legislative requirement, pressure may be applied to a public retirement fund board for the consideration of socially responsive investing. Most board members, elected or appointed, are expected to respond to the needs of the constituents they represent, as well as behave as prudent fiduciaries. It is common for these two missions to conflict, as many political constituents fail to appreciate the singlefold mission of the retirement fund—to fund the long-term liabilities of the fund. The most common socially responsive investing pressures fall into three categories: (1) minority and women-owned business enterprises (MWBEs), (2) economically targeted investing (ETI), and (3) local involvement.

Social investing for public funds generally involves the use of MWBEs. It is not unreasonable for a municipality that has a large minority population to mandate that a certain percentage of the fund's services be provided by MWBEs. A number of respectable money management firms have been in place that specifically serve this market.

ETI frequently stands apart from social investing in a public fund. Creating partnerships with organizations that are taxpayer supported, such as the Office of Economic Development and the Housing Bureau, allows the pension fund to provide needed capital to these organizations while still receiving a market rate of return.

Using local talent to provide services to the retirement fund is normally the first issue with which a new fiduciary must deal. Over 20 states have laws that have specific set-aside provisions for local service providers. These provisions can come in three forms:

1. To prefer that securities transactions flow through local brokerage firms.
2. To give preference to the services of local money managers and/or service vendors.
3. To prefer that the funds be custodied at a local financial institution.

The basis for the set asides is simple. The local people are talented professionals, therefore, they should be benefiting from the pension fund assets. If the pension fund is located in New York, Boston, or Chicago, it might be possible to justify local preference because there is a large concentration of custodial, money management, and brokerage talent in these cities. It is rare, however, for a large public fund to be able to prudently diversify its portfolio and engage only local money managers who best fit their investment needs. The hiring of specialists can rarely be fully filled by local talent.

A more difficult issue is local brokerage. All states and most municipalities have offices of nationally recognized brokerage firms. Public fund board members may feel that local brokers should receive a portion of the transactions conducted on behalf of the fund. The board member must recognize that the commissions generated and price received or paid on securities transactions are an expense of the fund. The board members have an obligation to control these expenses. This obligation to the fund participants and taxpayers is more onerous than the obligation to a local broker.

Board members must recognize that any restrictions on the investment program have the potential to reduce the ability to achieve superior investment results over time. If certain restrictions or directives are adopted, there is the potential that increases in contributions must be made to offset the lost opportunity returns from the restricted or redirected assets.

One of the most difficult challenges facing a board member is staying focused on the big picture. Many find it difficult to step aside from their full-time jobs and take on part-time oversight responsibility. Other board members get too involved in day-to-day decision making and begin to take on the functions of the full-time staff charged with day-to-day administration. The disharmony created by these activities can frequently result in a breakdown of a team approach and add unnecessary expenses to the system.

Supervision

Because of board turnover, it is imperative that a formal monitoring process be developed and consistently applied. High standards of conduct that discourage the practice of *ex parte* communications should be utilized.

Board members cannot be expected to possess the skills necessary to deal with the operation of a retirement fund. A variety of money managers, actuaries, attorneys, and investment consultants may be needed to assist the board in the management and discharge of their fiduciary responsibilities. Occasionally, vendors may be interested in interfering with policy setting at the board level. These vendors will want board members to circumvent their normal procedures so the vendors can gain access to business opportunities. Formal operating policies and guidelines must be adopted that regulate the solicitation of business and quantify the monitoring and supervision activities.

Trends in the Public Retirement Fund Arena

There are those in public office who view retirement funds as being the property of the public, not the retirement participants. Over the last several years, there have been periodic discussions about granting public entities the right to borrow funds from retirement funds during budgetary shortfalls.

> Unfortunately, it is not always possible to arrive at a fully funded status in public pension funds that must rely on the actions of politicians to fund contributions with taxes, and which have no clear and consistent mandate to strive for full funding.[4]

This type of thinking can have a negative impact on the long-term investment success of public funds. Such action jeopardizes the safety and reliability of these funds to provide a competitive retirement benefit to an employee that has opted for public versus private service. If a public fund subsequently fails, it would not be surprising to see the federal government take over the jurisdiction of all public retirement funds. The failure of corporate entities to safeguard their retirement accounts was a major reason behind the passage of ERISA. Alternative proposals to guarantee the viability of these public funds have included a federal agency, such as the PBGC, that would be created to collect premiums and provide some assurance of the safety of the public retirement funds.

Another trend that has had periodic discussion is the federal taxation of public retirement fund investments within the fund. This has typically been included with discussions also dealing with the taxation of private retirement system assets.

Another trend (actually, an extension of conduct that has been around for decades) is the disruptive practice of placing the public retirement fund in the middle of political mudslinging. Political parties that are on the out have discovered that accusations of mismanagement and fraud by current board members makes good press. Often, the accusations are nothing more than grandstanding. Not all investment decisions can be anchored to quantitative research or objective search criteria. There is always an element of subjectivity—boards are, after all, comprised of people, not computers. It is these subjective decisions that come under the scrutiny of outsiders. If the trend continues, board members will inevitably seek the safety of mediocrity, which ultimately harms (1) the retirement fund beneficiary, by reducing the fund's ability to finance additional benefits with investment performance, and (2) the taxpayer, by requiring additional revenue sources to pay for competitive benefits.

---

[4] Clay B. Mansfield and Timothy W. Cunningham, *Pension Funds,* (Burr Ridge, IL: Business One Irwin, 1993), p. 27.

17

TAFT-HARTLEY PLANS

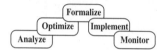

*"People ask the difference between a leader
and a boss . . . The leader works in the open
and the boss in covert.
The leader leads and the boss drives."*
Theodore Roosevelt

*"Leadership is the ability to get people to
do what they don't want to do and like it."*
Harry Truman

There exist differences in management between single-employer, single-plan sponsored retirement plans and those of labor unions, where multiple employers make contributions. Because of these differences, special legislation has been passed, and the plans, commonly referred to as Taft-Hartley plans, have taken on their own unique identity.

There are over 3,000 Taft-Hartley plans, with total assets of $1.5 trillion. Although the number of plans is relatively few compared to the total of 900,000 ERISA plans, their combined assets and the number of union members covered by the plans are substantial.

The Taft-Hartley Act

The legislative history of the labor movement and collective bargaining can be traced to the late nineteenth century. The foundation for modern jointly trusteed plans is the Labor Management Relations Act of 1947, more commonly referred to as the Taft-Hartley Act. A provision of the Taft-Hartley Act is the prohibition of passing money or other things of value from management to labor. However, Section 302(a) of the act permits payments to pension or welfare plans when the following conditions are met:

1. The basis for the payments is detailed in a written collective bargaining agreement. [ERISA requires certain trust documents to establish a qualified plan, but the Taft-Hartley plan has the additional requirement of having been created as a condition to a collective bargaining agreement.]

2. Management and labor are equally represented in the administration and management of the plan.

3. There is a procedure to select an impartial umpire in the event that disputes arise between or within members of the administrative board and/or the investment committee.

4. The plan is operated for the sole and exclusive use of covered members. [This language parallels ERISA, where the plan must be managed for the exclusive benefit of participants.]

5. Payments into the plan are made to specified types of benefit (pension and welfare) programs, such as[1]

Retirement plans	Accident insurance
Medical/hospital care	Insurance
Occupational illness/injury	Apprenticeship/training
Unemployment benefits	Educational scholarships
Life insurance	Child care centers
Disability/sickness insurance	Legal services

---

[1] Cynthia J Drinkwater, "History of Taft-Hartley Plans," in *Trustee Handbook,* 4th ed. (Brookfield, WI: International Foundation of Employee Benefit Plans, 1990), p. 2.

Board Composition

Of the requirements outlined above, potentially the biggest challenge is having investment and administrative decisions handled by a board of trustees composed equally of management and labor. By the very nature of the appointments, the Taft-Hartley investment committee faces challenges other retirement plans do not have.

Trustees will, more often than not, come from much more diverse educational and socioeconomic backgrounds. Information submitted before a Taft-Hartley board must be presented in a format that all members of the committee can understand, and can act on. Corporate pension boards, on the other hand, are often made up of members who have extensive education and experience in business, finance, and accounting.

The board has the additional challenge of suppressing long-standing mistrust and, at times, dislike for members representing opposing interests. Trustees are challenged to disregard their historical roles and make decisions for the good of all members. As with the trustees of public funds, there is absolutely no room for private agendas. This is not just a suggested moral standard, but a standard mandated and required by law.

Now and again, the suggestion is made to appoint professional trustees. After all, the argument is made, the ideal board should consist of attorneys, actuaries, accountants, and administrators—not carpenters, plumbers, brick layers, or stevedores. Those who make such suggestions have forgotten the principle reason for having trustees: *The trustee is to have a direct and material role in managing the retirement benefits of the members it represents. No one understands their members, their industry, and the jurisdiction of their particular trade union better than the appointed labor trustee.*

It should also be noted that the act of appointing trustees by labor or management carries fiduciary responsibilities similar in nature to those of appointing any professional investment adviser or consultant. A thoroughly documented due diligence process should be followed in selecting trustees. The courts have found a union to be a fiduciary to a trust in a case where the union selected the labor trustees, and it was later determined that the trustees were unfit to serve.[2]

---

[2] Ira Mitzner, *ERISA Litigation: A Basic Guide,* (Brookfield, WI: International Foundation of Employee Benefit Plans, 1993), p. 3.

Delinquent Contributions

Every retirement plan faces the risk that an employer will be unable to make a required contribution because of economic difficulties. The problem, however, is more common to Taft-Hartley plans. A basic duty of the trustee is to collect employer contributions. Failure to do so is a prohibited transaction—viewed as an extension of credit to a party-in-interest. If the noncollection continues, it can result in a finding of a breach of fiduciary duties and result in personal liability and/or removal as a trustee.

ERISA, as originally released, provided little leeway for the trustee to settle delinquent contributions without the trustee committing a prohibited transaction. However, forcing an employer that is facing economic difficulties to make contributions could very well drive the employer into bankruptcy, thereby eliminating many jobs held by union members. The trustee is naturally torn by the desire to protect the jobs of fellow members.

In 1976, the DOL and IRS provided some relief with class exemption, PTE 76-1. The exemption allows for partial payments and the ability to claim a payment as uncollectible as long as

1. The plan has made and recorded proper efforts to collect the delinquent payment, including

    a. Issuing written notices of delinquency.

    b. Establishing an auditing program to ensure that proper and prompt payments are made by employers.

    c. Notifying employers that delinquent payments will result in the employer incurring expenses for any litigation, and requiring the employer to post a bond to ensure payment.

2. Extensions, when granted by the trustees, are in writing and include reasonable terms for payment, including interest and liquidated damages.

3. The delinquency is referred to legal counsel.

To further assist the trustees in fulfilling their duties, Congress passed the Multi-employer Pension Plan Amendments Act of 1980 (MPPAA). MPPAA imposes liability on employers that withdraw early from unfunded plans and increases the premium payment to the PBGC. Requirements for the collection of delinquent payments were stiffened. A payment would be considered to be in arrears unless either of the following conditions are met:

1. The employer signs an agreement that the payment will be made within 60 days.
2. A third-party guarantees the payment, the delinquent amount will be made up within 24 months, and quarterly installments of principal and interest will be made.

Education and Training

The DOL once made Taft-Hartley plans a priority of their enforcement agenda. What turned the situation around was education and training. As a rule, Taft-Hartley trustees have made more of an effort to learn about their duties and responsibilities than any other group. The progress in large part is due to the efforts of organizations such as the International Foundation of Employee Benefit Plans, which produces excellent handbooks and regularly schedules courses and conferences for trustees.

Servicing the Taft-Hartley Plan

Because of the unique makeup of Taft-Hartley investment committees, service providers who plan to offer their services should be aware of certain decorum:

1. Ensure that business cards, stationery, and marketing material have been printed at a union shop and are printed with the union "bug."
2. Drive to the appointment in an American-made car.
3. Don't wear suspenders (braces) or European fashion.
4. Use UPS for overnight deliveries. (Federal Express is not unionized.)

And, finally, the trustee that has a drawl and states, "These new fangled investment ideas and products are way over my head. I'm not as smart as you Wall Street types," is usually the smartest member of the board.

18

CURRENT AND
FUTURE TRENDS

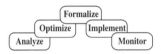

"We forecast. Magicians and fortune-tellers predict."[1]

Robert H. Smith, CEO, The Futures Group

*"I recalled an old epigram which had often comforted me,
that the future comes one day at a time."*[2]

Dean Acheson, former U.S. Secretary of State

The preceding chapters prescribed a timeless and flexible process for
the successful management of investment decisions. Once familiar with
the process, the investor will understand that no new investment product or technique will be good or bad per se, nor will it be valuable merely
because it worked for other investors. Furthermore, the process will help
investors to understand which new products and techniques fit into their
priorities, and which do not.

The intelligent and prudent management of investment decisions
merely requires that an investor maintain a rational, consistent investment program. It is also essential that the investor walk before he or

---

[1] Robert H. Smith, *Manhattan, Inc.* (1990)

[2] Dean Acheson, *Present at the Creation, My Years in the State Department* (New York,
NY: Norton Company, 1987), p. 28.

she runs. One will accomplish the lion's share of his or her critical investment objectives by implementing a basic investment strategy without any of the bells and whistles. Until then, the latest esoteric quantitative method to reduce risk is of even less value than a sail is to a motorboat. One should not let sales pitches, new product hype, the superficial analysis of popular investment periodicals, or one's own interests in the latest, greatest technologies sidetrack one's efforts.

Rather than being confined or limited to any particular investment type or strategy, this disciplined process will enable investors to distinguish valuable future enhancements from the occasional futile, if not counterproductive, innovations of Wall Street. The mind-boggling array of choices can understandably result in financial paralysis from information overload. Investors clearly need a framework for making investment decisions that allows them to consider developing investment trends and to thoughtfully navigate the possibilities. Otherwise, the likelihood of realizing value from future innovations would be random at best.

We would like to finish this book by outlining the current trends that either are already evolving or can be expected to emerge in the immediate future. Investors may find that these developments will allow one to fine-tune an already well-developed investment strategy, or to encourage an investor to scout his or her community for a new service provider that can provide an objective, comprehensive investment process. Or the investor may find of interest new tools that, for the first time, provide cost-effective access to the best available investment planning tools and information.

Multimedia Presentation Software.   Multimedia presentation software will combine the elements of asset allocation and manager/mutual fund databases. The delivery system, most likely a CD-ROM disk, would provide the convenience of both functions on one platform. Yet, the function of the two steps would be kept separate and distinct—as they should be. That is, an investor would first complete an asset allocation analysis and identify which asset classes and subasset classes would be appropriate for the particular situation. After that, the investor would click on a particular asset class and information on those mutual funds and/or separate account managers that passed particular search criteria would appear on the screen. The investor could scroll through detailed information on the managers and funds until the list was narrowed to a few candidates. At that point, the investor would click another button and a video presentation on each manager would begin. The managers, in their own words, would describe their investment philosophy and overall strategy and then detail their security selection process. This capability would streamline the decision-making process and reduce the expense (and presumably the investor's costs) associated with flying sales reps of the money managers all over the country to give presentations.

Investment Consulting Services.   Middle and retail market investors will be able to access a broad array of investment consulting services through smaller independent investment consulting firms. The services will be a mirror image of the scope of services that are provided to larger institutional investors. Costs will be dramatically reduced because the smaller firms will be able to operate at lower overheads and will be able to outsource most of their expensive back-office requirements to the major investment consulting firms that have excess capacity. The net result will be comprehensive services that will be affordable by just about any investor.

CPA Firms.   As an adjunct to the above, CPA firms will begin providing investment consulting services. CPAs have always been sought after for their advice or opinion on investment decisions. Until now, firms have been reluctant to give specific advice because it often meant being linked to a specific investment product, rendering the CPA in the same role as the broker. With the ability for CPA firms to associate with the major investment consulting firms, CPA firms will be able to offer truly independent, objective, third-party advice.

Risk Tolerance Software.   Risk is perhaps the most difficult of the asset allocation variables to quantify. Not only is it difficult to know one's bottom line until one experiences it, over time, education and experience will undoubtedly change one's perception of, and tolerance for, risk. Thus, advances in risk tolerance software will enable investors to simulate different economic scenarios and the resulting portfolio outcomes. An additional development will be software to measure an investment committee's groupthink. What individual dynamics are impacting the overall investment decision-making process? Who are the outliers— those individuals who are more conservative or aggressive relative to the group as a whole? Are the committee's decisions a true reflection of the makeup of the individual parts, or is there likely to be a major restructuring of a portfolio at the first market reversal?

Cost Effective Style or Asset Class–Specific Indexed Funds.   The industry has begun to build style-tilted (growth versus value) indexed funds. But the costs are greater than comparable active management products. One of the primary benefits of indexing should be that they offer a cost-effective means of implementing a specific asset allocation target.

The Slow Demise of the Commission-Oriented Investment Services Firms. Virtually every investment product now has a no-load alternative. Fee-only or asset-based advisers/consultants can now deliver the same array of products and services as the major brokerage firms, the major differences being that the fee-based adviser can be more objective and deliver the services at substantially reduced costs. Stockbrokers will resume their traditional roles—to transact individual shares of stocks and bonds. Those brokers that wish to pursue a consultative practice will set up new firms as independent registered investment advisers.

Defined Contribution Plans Unbundling Service Requirements.   When ERISA was first passed in 1974, the requirements appeared to be overwhelming and plan sponsors flocked to the major financial institutions (banks and insurance companies) that could provide a bundled solution. As plan sponsors became more comfortable with the different ERISA requirements and less satisfied with their bundled packages, they began looking for specialists in each of the different servicing areas. The same trend is repeating itself with defined contribution plans. Today plan sponsors prefer the bundled approach, but some are already discovering that when a particular component of the bundle fails, it is almost impossible to replace the broken piece. Plan sponsors are rethinking their approach, showing increased interest in consulting firms that can coordinate the activities of specialists. This provides the sponsor the convenience of one-stop shopping, but also the benefits of cost-effective specialists in each of the different areas.

Defined Benefit Plans.   The popularity of defined benefit plans will return as today's middle managers assume the reins of corporate responsibility. Studies are conclusive that defined contribution plans will not aggregate sufficient dollars for executives to retire in the same lifestyle as their predecessors. Nor are today's middle managers likely to see meaningful, if any, social security benefits. As the retirement crisis looms, corporations will reinstate defined benefit plans to make up the potential shortfalls.

Defined Contribution Plan Investment Options. Technology will enable larger defined contribution plans to set up discreet separate accounts as investment options. Most plan sponsors have opted to use retail-oriented mutual funds as their defined contribution investment options. New technology will enable plan sponsors to, in essence, create their own funds at reduced expenses. A major expense of a retail-oriented fund is the cost associated with shareholder services, an expense that becomes redundant when a defined contribution recordkeeper is maintaining the same information at the participant level. In addition, the ability for plan sponsors to create their own funds will enable the investment committee to do a more thorough job of monitoring the activities and performance of selected money managers—an almost impossible task when retail funds are selected.

The Information Highway. The information highway will provide more timely access to data and many other benefits of secured, shared databases. First, consultants, money managers, and custodians will be able to improve communications between each other. Client data collected at the consultant's level will be able to be shared with custodians and money managers, eliminating the wasted time of each separate entity creating its own data file on a client. Consultants will be able to do a better job of monitoring cash flows in and out of the custodian and monitor the investment decisions being made by the managers. Managers will be able to do two-way video conference calls with clients, reducing the need to put portfolio managers on the road to conduct quarterly client meetings. Portfolio managers will be able to stay focused on what they were hired to do—pick stocks and bonds, not travel the country answering the same questions posed by different plan sponsors.

As a final note, we can predict with a high degree of certainty that we will take a long-needed break before we attempt to write another full-length book. This has been a labor of love, and we hope that you have benefited in some small way from our efforts to distill the knowledge of the hard-working men and women with whom we have the pleasure of associating. To that end . . .

Bye-bye, and buy bonds—unless your asset allocation dictates otherwise!

GLOSSARY OF INVESTMENT TERMS

Accrual Basis Accounting Method　This method values assets based on accrued changes in values, not actual cash flows as in cash basis accounting. For example, dividends are included in the portfolio value (i.e., accrued) as of the ex-dividend date, rather than the payment date.

Active Cash　Managers whose objective is to achieve a maximum return on short-term financial instruments through active management. The average portfolio duration is typically less than one year.

Active Duration　A style of investing that employs either interest rate anticipation or business cycle timing. Portfolios are actively managed so wide changes in duration are made in anticipation of interest rate changes and/or business cycle movements. See the chart on the following page for a graphical depiction of various fixed-income styles and their relative maturities and returns.

Active Management　A form of investment management that involves buying and selling financial assets to earn positive risk-adjusted returns.

ADV Parts I, II　Disclosure document required to be filed (and updated annually) by a registered investment advisor with the Securities and Exchange Commission. This form details the advisor's practices, operations, fees, and individuals associated with the advisor, if registered as a firm. Part II of the Form ADV is required to be delivered to a client prior to or in conjunction with the entering into an agreement with an advisor (sometimes called the brochure rule). This may be satisfied by providing the client with the information contained on the form but in a format that is different from the actual

Fixed Income Styles

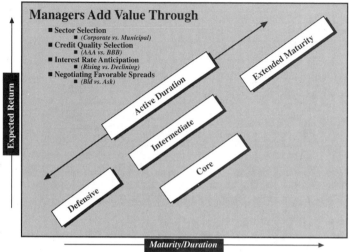

Copyright © 1995, Investment Management Council.

form filed. The advisor must at least annually offer to provide the client with a copy of this form. Part I is not required to be given to the client, but it should be requested since it also contains material information on the advisor.

AIMR   The Association for Investment Management and Research is the umbrella organization for the two big investment management advisers' groups, the Institute of Chartered Financial Analysts and the Financial Analysts Federation. This organization administers the annual examinations for the **CFA** designation and also publishes industry guidelines for performance measurement reporting and calculations. Presentation standards and topical articles are also issued by AIMR.

AIMR Performance Presentation Standards   These standards, effective January 1, 1993, are designed to promote full disclosure and fair representation in the reporting of investment results to provide uniformity in comparing manager results. These standards include ethical principles and apply to all organizations serving investment management functions. Compliance is verified at two levels: Level 1 and Level 2. (Level 2 is a more comprehensive verification process.) Specific information regarding these standards can be obtained by calling **AIMR** at (804) 980-3547.

Alpha   This statistic measures a portfolio's return in excess of the market return adjusted for risk. It is a measure of the manager's contribution to performance with reference to security selection. A positive alpha indicates that a portfolio was positively rewarded for the residual risk taken for that level of market exposure.

Alpha = Mean of excess returns of portfolio − Mean of excess returns of the index

Alternative Investments   These generally refer to institutional blind-pool limited partnerships that make private debt and equity investments in privately held companies, as well as hedge funds and other publicly traded derivatives–based strategies.

American Depository Receipts (ADRs)   Financial assets issued by U.S. banks that represent indirect ownership of a certain number of equity shares in a foreign firm. ADRs are held on deposit in a bank in the firm's home country.

Arbitrage   The simultaneous purchase and sale of the same or related securities in different markets to make a profit as unequal prices become equal; occasionally involves securities of companies to be acquired or merged; an investment management style that seeks arbitrage profits.

Arithmetic Return   The sum of the period returns divided by the number of periods. This is the simple average return and should be contrasted with **Geometric Return**.

Asset Allocation   The process of determining the optimal allocation of a fund's portfolio among broad asset classes.

Asset Allocation Variables

Internal: Set by Consultant		*External:* Set by Investor	
Callan:	**Risk premium model overlayed with econometric forecasts.**	R	Risk tolerance
1.	Projected returns of asset classes	A	Asset class preferences
2.	Projected levels of variability of returns (standard deviation)	T	Time horizon of investments
3.	Projected correlations (related movement) of asset classes	E	Expected returns

Source: Copyright © Investment Management Council.

Balanced Fund   An investment strategy that is a combination of equities and bonds in an effort to obtain the highest return consistent with a low-risk strategy. A balanced fund typically offers a higher yield than a pure stock fund and performs better than such a fund when stocks are falling. However, in a rising market, a balanced fund usually will not keep pace with an all-equity fund.

Basis Point   100 Basis Points = 1 percent.

Benchmark Portfolio   A portfolio against which the investment performance of a money manager can be compared for the purpose of determining the value added by the manager. A benchmark portfolio must be of the same style as the manager and, in particular, similar in terms of risk.

Best Execution   This is formally defined as the difference between the strike price (the price at which a security is actually bought or sold) and the fair market price, which involves calculating opportunity costs by examining the security price immediately after the trade is placed. Best execution occurs when the trade involves no lost opportunity cost—for example, when there is no increase in the price of a security shortly after it is sold.

Beta A statistical measure of the volatility, or sensitivity, of rates of return on a portfolio or security in comparison to a market index. The beta value measures the expected change in return per one percent change in the return on the market. Thus, a portfolio with a beta of 1.1 would move 10 percent more than the market.

Board Room Risk The risk that trustees will not ride out short-term volatility (and therefore wind up altering a sound long-term strategy) due to pressure put on them in their role as trustees. Other types of investment risk have been outlined in the chart below.

Elements of Investment Risk

Liquidity risk	Will there be sufficient cash to meet disbursement/expense requirements?
Boardroom risk	Are decision makers willing to ride out short-term volatility in favor of appropriate long-term strategies?
Purchasing power risk	Has an investment strategy been employed that will, at the very least, keep pace with inflation?
Funding risk	What is the probability that anticipated contributions will not be made?
Risk versus return	Are investment returns consistent with level of risk taken?
Asset allocation risk	Are assets optimally allocated to meet required return and risk parameters?
Lost opportunity risk	Have market timing strategies been inappropriately employed, exposing the investor to missed opportunities in the market?

Book Value The value at which an asset is carried on the balance sheet. In portfolio management, book value is the net worth per share of a company's stock. Book value is calculated by subtracting from total assets the following items: intangible assets, liabilities, and the par value of preferred stock. The sum is divided by the number of common shares of stock the company has outstanding. The deficiency of book value is that it is normally based on historical cost of assets (after depreciation). The fair market value of these assets may be far in excess of their historical cost, but it is used as an estimate of the company's break-up value.

Bottom-up Analysis An approach to valuing securities that first involves analyzing individual companies, then the industry, and finally the economy.

Callan Broad Market Index This index includes the 2,000 largest common stocks with capitalization ranging between $85 million and $75 billion dollars. The index is capitalization weighted.

Callan Large Cap Index   This index includes the largest 150 companies traded in U.S. markets. The capitalization ranges between $5 billion and $75 billion dollars. The index is capitalization weighted.

Callan Medium Cap Index   This index includes the next 350 issues in capitalization size trading in the U.S. markets. The capitalization range for this index is $1 billion to $5 billion dollars. The index is capitalization weighted.

Callan Small Cap Index   This index includes the remaining 1,500 issues in the Broad Market Index by capitalization. The capitalization range for this index is $85 million to $1 billion dollars. The index is capitalization weighted.

Callan Large-Medium Cap Index   An index of 500 stocks comprised of the 150 stocks in the Callan Large Cap Index and the 350 stocks in the Callan Medium Cap Index. The index is capitalization weighted.

Callan Medium-Small Cap Index   An index of 1,850 stocks comprised of the 350 stocks in the Callan Medium Cap Index and the 1,500 stocks in the Callan Small Cap Index.

Callan Micro Cap Index   This index includes an additional 1,000 companies not included in the Callan Broad Market Index. The stocks in this index have small capitalizations ranging from $25 million to $85 million dollars. The index is capitalization weighted.

Capital Asset Pricing Model   An equilibrium model of asset pricing that states the expected return of a security increases as the security's sensitivity to the market (i.e., **Beta**) increases. That is, as the expected return of a security or portfolio increases (decreases), risk increases (decreases) as well.

Capitalization-Weighted Market Index   A method of calculating a market index where the return of a security (or group of securities) is weighted by the market value of the security (or group of securities) relative to total value of all securities.

Cash Sweep Accounts   A money market fund into which all new contributions, stock dividend income, and bond interest income are placed (swept) for a certain period of time. At regular intervals, or when rebalancing is necessary, this cash is invested in assets in line with the asset allocation stipulated in the IPS.

CFA (Chartered Financial Analyst)   A designation awarded by the Institute of Chartered Financial Analysts (ICFA) to experienced financial analysts who pass examinations in economics, financial accounting, portfolio management, security analysis, and standards of conduct.

CFP (Certified Financial Planner)   A designation granted by the Certified Financial Planner Board of Standards for Planning to individuals who complete a series of educational requirements, courses, and examinations in the areas of personal financial and retirement planning and who pledge to a code of ethical standards and continuing education.

Commingled Fund   An investment fund similar to a mutual fund in that investors purchase and redeem units that represent ownership in a pool of securities. Commingled funds are usually offered through a bank-administered plan allowing for broader and more efficient investing.

Commission Recapture   An agreement by which a plan sponsor earns credits based on the amount of brokerage commissions paid. These credits can be used for services that will benefit the plan, such as consulting services, custodian fees, or hardware and software expenses.

Contrarian   Used to describe an investment style in which managers select stocks that are out of favor or have little current market interest, on the premise that gains will be realized when the stocks return to favor. Used to describe someone who believes "I think differently than everyone else," the dilemma being that most contrarians are self-proclaimed. (Everyone wants to be a successful contrarian since it implies that everyone else is wrong.)   Contrarians buy securities that nobody else wants (at the moment!). See also **Style**.

Convertible Bond   A bond that may, at the holder's option, be exchanged for common stock.

Convexity   Describes the shape of the price/yield relationship for fixed-income securities when it is bowed toward the origin. Convexity implies that prices rise at an increasing rate as yields fall and that prices decline at a decreasing rate as yields rise.

Core Bond   A fixed-income strategy that constructs portfolios to approximate the investment results of the Lehman Government/Corporate Bond Index with a modest amount of variability in duration around the index. The objective is to achieve value added from sector or issue selection.

Core Equity   An investment strategy where the portfolio's characteristics are similar to those of the S&P 500 Index, with the objective of adding value over and above the index, typically from sector or issue selection. See Equity Style Matrix below.

Equity Style Matrix

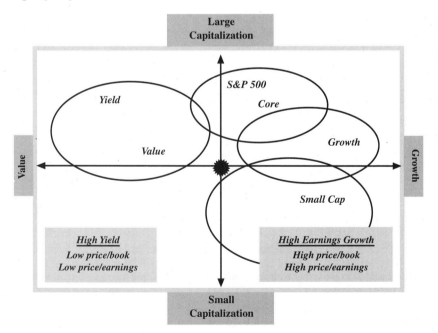

Correlation Coefficient   A statistical measure equivalent to covariance, in that it measures the mutual variation between two variables. The correlation coefficient is bounded by the values -1 and $+1$. A value of $+1$ indicates that the two variables are perfectly related to one another and a value of 0 indicates that there is no relationship between the two variables.

Coupon   Interest rate of a debt security the issuer promises to pay to the holder until maturity. The coupon is expressed as an annual percentage of the bond's face value. The term is used interchangeably with interest, as in "The bond has an 8 percent coupon," meaning it pays 8 percent interest per year ($80 per $1,000).

Covariance   A statistical measure of the mutual variation between two variables. It measures the degree to which returns on two assets move in tandem. A positive covariance means that assets move together. A negative covariance means they vary inversely.

Current Yield   The annual interest on a bond divided by the market price. The current yield is different from the yield to maturity in that it uses the actual income rate as opposed to the coupon rate. See also **Yield to Maturity**.

Defensive   A fixed-income investment strategy where the objective is to minimize interest rate risk by investing only in short- to intermediate-term securities. The average portfolio maturity is typically two to five years.

Defined Benefit Plan   A type of employee benefit plan in which employees know (through a formula) what they will receive on retirement or after a specified number of years of employment with an employer. The employer is obligated to contribute funds into the defined benefit plan based on an actuarially determined obligation that takes into consideration the age of the workforce, their length of service, and the investment earnings that are projected to be achieved from the funds contributed. Defined benefit plans are overfunded if the present value of the future payment obligations to employees is less than the current value of the assets in the plan. It is underfunded if the obligations exceed the current value of these plan assets. The **Pension Benefit Guarantee Corporation** insures a specified amount of these future pension benefit payments on a per-employee basis.

Defined Contribution Plan   A type of employee benefit plan in which the employer (sponsor) makes annual contributions (usually discretionary in amount or possibly based on a percentage of the profits of the company, e.g., **Profit-Sharing Plan**) to the plan for the ultimate payment to employees at retirement. Each employee's account value will be determined by the contribution made, the earnings achieved, and usually a vesting percentage (e.g., 20 percent per year after one year of service).

Directed Brokerage   Circumstances in which a board of trustees or other fiduciary requests that the investment manager direct trades to a particular broker so that the commissions generated can be used for specific services or resources. See **Soft Dollars**.

Dividend Yield   The current annualized dividend paid on a share of common stock, expressed as a percentage of the stock's current market price.

Dollar-Weighted Rate of Return   Method of performance measurement that calculates returns based on the cash flows of a security or portfolio. A dollar-weighted return applies a discounted cash flow approach to obtain the return for a period. The beginning and ending market values in a given time period are considered to be cash flows. Any other cash flows within the time period, such as a dividend payment, are entered into the discounted cash flow analysis. The discount rate that equates the cash inflow at the end of the period plus any net cash flows within the period with the initial outflow is the dollar-weighted rate of return. This return is also referred to as the internal rate of return (IRR).

Dow Jones Industrial Average   The Dow Jones is a composite of 30 major industrial companies. The index is a price-weighted average of the issues in the index.

Duration   A measure of the average maturity of the stream of interest payments of a bond. The value of a given bond is more sensitive to interest rate changes as duration increases, that is, longer duration bonds have greater interest rate volatility than shorter duration bonds. Duration is always shorter than **Maturity,** except for zero coupon bonds.

Earnings per Share   A firm's reported earnings divided by the number of its outstanding shares of common stock. The figure is calculated after paying taxes and after paying preferred shareholders and bondholders.

Economically Targeted Investment (ETI)   Investment where the goal is to target a certain economic activity, sector, or area to produce corollary benefits in addition to the main objective of earning a competitive risk-adjusted rate of return.

Efficient Market   A theory that claims a security's market price equals its true investment value at all times since all information is fully and immediately reflected in the market price.

Efficient Portfolio   A portfolio which offers maximum expected return for a given level of risk or minimum risk for a given level of expected return.

Employee Stock Ownership Plan (ESOP)   A retirement-oriented savings program in the employer's own stock. Usually the plan borrows to purchase the stock due to favorable benefits a lender can receive on such transaction. The individual owner/seller also receives favorable tax treatment on the sale of his or her stock in the company to the plan. May also be referred to as a leveraged ESOP transaction.

End Point Sensitivity   The performance of a manager/fund may vary depending on which ending time periods are used to analyze performance. Therefore, it is important to look at performance for a number of market cycles or time periods to gain an accurate assessment of the manager/fund's performance.

Equal Weighted   In a portfolio setting, this is a composite of a manager's return for accounts managed that gives equal consideration to each portfolio's return without regard to size of the portfolio. Compare to **Size Weighted**. In index context, equal weighted means each stock is given equal consideration to the index return without regard to market capitalization. The Value Line Index is an example of an equal-weighted index.

Equilibrium Spending Rate   Specific to foundations and endowments, the spending rate that offsets inflation and additional cost increases.

9.0%	−	3.5%	−	1.5%	=	4%
Return	−	Inflation	−	Cost increases	=	Equilibrium spending rate

ERISA   The Employee Retirement Income Security Act is a 1974 law governing the operation of most private pension and benefit plans. The law eased pension eligibility rules, set up the **Pension Benefit Guaranty Corporation**, and established guidelines for the management of pension funds.

Exculpatory   A clause or set of regulations, for example, the safe harbor rules, that generally free trustees from responsibility and liability.

Extended Maturity   A fixed-income investment strategy where average portfolio maturity is greater than that of the Lehman Brothers Government/Corporate Bond Index. Variations in bond portfolio characteristics are made to enhance performance results.

Family Office   The family office is typically a staff of at least one attorney and/or accountant and administrative support person established by wealthy families (generally families with more than $50 million in assets) who are responsible for planning the budget, paying the bills, and making investment decisions. The structure of the office, or the ownership of the assets, often takes the form of either a trust or corporation.

Family offices evolved from the need to (1) centralize the management of investable assets and provide recordkeeping, tax planning, and other personal services to the family members; (2) anticipate the need to serve more than one or two generations that required a more formal structure to be put in place; and (3) coordinate their philanthropic services, interests, and activities through one entity.

Fiduciary   Indicates the relationship of trust and confidence where one person (the fiduciary) holds or controls property for the benefit of another person—for example, the relationship between a trustee and the beneficiaries of the trust.

• Under **ERISA,** any person who (1) exercises any discretionary authority or control over the management of a plan or the management or disposition of its assets; (2) renders investment advice for a fee or other compensation with respect to the funds or property of a plan, or has the authority to do so; or (3) has any discretionary authority or responsibility in the administration of a plan.

• One who acts in a capacity of trust and who is therefore accountable for whatever actions may be construed by the courts as breaching that trust. Under **ERISA**, fiduciaries must discharge their duties solely in the interest of the participants and beneficiaries of an employee benefit plan. In addition, a fiduciary must act exclusively for the purpose of providing benefits to participants and beneficiaries in defraying reasonable expenses of the plan.

Sample Floating Bar Chart

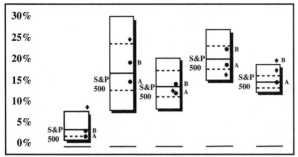

How to Read a Bar Chart

The top line of the bar indicates the top 10th percentile of the universe. The middle solid line is the median, which has a percent rank of 50. The 75th percentile is indicated by the lower dotted line and the 90th percentile is indicated by the bottom line.

	Last Quarter ▼	Last Year ▼	Last 2 Years ▼	Last 3 Years ▼	Last 5 Years ▼
Total Equity Database					
10th Percentile	7.58	30.17	19.91	25.73	18.84
25th Percentile	5.38	22.34	16.16	22.00	15.89
Median	3.69	15.91	13.17	19.21	14.44
75th Percentile	2.52	12.37	11.02	17.12	13.01
90th Percentile	1.50	7.96	8.76	15.33	11.79
S&P 500	2.57	12.99	12.01	18.09	14.69
Manager A	2.52	12.79	11.81	17.82	14.47
Manager B	3.30	18.30	13.32	20.87	19.58
Your Fund	9.34	23.78	12.55	16.36	17.16

10th Percentile

25th Percentile

◆ Fund Return

50th Percentile
—Median

75th Percentile

90th Percentile

Source: Copyright © 1994, Callan Associates Inc.

Funding Risk   The risk that anticipated contributions to the plan will not be made.

Funding-Support Ratio   The funding-support ratio (the fraction of the budget supported by the fund) is the key strategic variable used by experienced committees to track and manage contributions to an institution's or recipient's annual budget. Although increasing the spending rate increases the fund's current contribution to the overall budget, more spending obviously means less reinvestment, a smaller growth rate, and, all other things being equal, a lower funding-support ratio in the future. Stationary long-run financial equilibrium, where stationary means the fund-support fraction is constant over time (with a fixed spending rate), requires

1. *The funding growth rate to equal the budget growth rate.* The equilibrium spending rate is sufficient to maintain the funding-support ratio if the budget is only sustaining current activities (and thus growing at the rate of cost increases). Expansion will reduce the funding-support ratio.

2. *The spending rate to be consistent with the funding growth rate.* Budget growth can be offset by reduced spending (which increases the reinvestment), but that will reduce the current funding-support ratio. Budget growth can also be offset by changing the asset allocation to increase expected total return, and by increased gifts and other additions to the fund. The most common cause of sharp declines in the funding-support ratio is the decision to increase current spending to fund operating deficits.

Geometric Return A method of calculating returns that links portfolio results on a quarterly or monthly basis. This method is best illustrated by an example, and a comparison to **Arithmetic Return,** that does not utilize a time link. Suppose a $100 portfolio returned +25 percent in the first quarter (ending value is $125) but lost 20 percent in the second quarter (ending value is $100). Over the two quarters, the return was 0 percent—this is the geometric return. However, the arithmetic calculation would simply average the two returns: $(+25\%)(.5) + (-20\%)(.5) = +2.5\%$.

Global Equity Managers who invest in both foreign and domestic equity securities but exclude regional and index funds.

Growth Equity Managers who invest in companies that are expected to have above-average prospects for long-term growth in earnings and profitability.

Guaranteed Investment Contracts (GICs) Contract between an insurance company and a corporate profit-sharing or pension plan that guarantees a specific rate of return on the invested capital over the life of the contract. Although the insurance company takes all market, credit, and interest rate risks on the investment portfolio, it can profit if its returns exceed the guaranteed amount. For pension and profit-sharing plans, guaranteed income contracts are a conservative way of assuring beneficiaries that their money will achieve a certain rate of return.

Hard Dollars Specified fees paid for services rendered in cash directly against an invoice. Compare to **Soft Dollars**.

Hedge A transaction or strategy designed to reduce risk. This typically involves short selling, futures contracts, options, and similar strategies. The strategy usually also reduces potential reward.

High Yield A fixed-income investment strategy where the objective is to obtain high current income by investing in lower-rated, higher-default–risk fixed-income securities. As a result, security selection focuses on credit risk analysis. See **Junk**.

Index Fund A passively managed investment in a diversified portfolio of financial assets designed to mimic the performance of a specific market index.

Institute for Investment Management Consultants (IIMC) The IIMC is a national, nonprofit Phoenix-based professional society that offers education, professional recognition, and public relations for consultants, brokers, money managers, and other interested parties. The IIMC certifies consultants as Certified Investment Management Consultants (CIMCs) based on demonstrated knowledge and experience. Information can be obtained by calling (602) 265-6114.

Interest Rate Risk The uncertainty in the return on a bond caused by unanticipated changes in its value due to changes in the market interest rate.

Intermediate A fixed-income investment strategy where the objective is to lower interest rate risk by investing only in intermediate-term securities. The average portfolio maturity is typically five to seven years.

Investment Grade   Refers to the **Quality Rating** of bond issue. Securities rated AAA to BBB are typically referred to as investment grade securities. See also **Junk.**

Investment Management Consultants Association (IMCA)   IMCA is a Denver-based nonprofit association of over 900 members, founded in 1985. The association certifies consultants as CIMAs, Certified Investment Management Analysts, through an intensive program held at the Wharton School of Business. In addition to the certification program, IMCA offers two professional development conferences a year, as well as regional seminars, and publishes *The Monitor.* More information regarding IMCA can be obtained by calling (303) 770-3377.

Investor Responsibility Research Center (IRRC)   The IRRC, an independent, nonprofit research and publishing organization founded in 1972, provides its subscribers with research on issues related to global shareholders, social issues, corporate governance, environmental issues, and South Africa. More information can be obtained by calling (202) 833-0700.

Junk   Usually applied to below investment grade–rated debt securities (bonds). The term grew from the early 1980s as leveraged buyouts occurred and **High Yield** bonds were issued. Though widely used, it is not very specific because of its throwaway connotation.

Lehman Brothers Government/Corporate Index   The Government/Corporate Index is a composite of all publicly issued, fixed-rate, nonconvertible, domestic bonds. The issues must be rated at least BBB, have a minimum principal of $100 million for U.S. government issues and $50 million for other bonds, and have a maturity of at least one year. The index is capitalization weighted.

Liquidity   In general, liquidity refers to the ease with which a financial asset can be converted to cash.   Liquidity is often more narrowly defined as the ability to sell an asset quickly without having to make a substantial price concession.

Liquidity Risk   The risk that there will be insufficient cash to meet the fund's disbursement and expense requirements.

Load   The percentage commission or charge on a mutual fund or partnership. This includes both front-end and possibly ongoing (e.g., 12(b)(1)) charges borne by the investment.

Lost Opportunity Risk   The risk that, through inappropriate **Market Timing** strategies, a fund's portfolio will miss short-term or long-term market opportunities.

Manager Search   The selection of specific managers following the manager structure.

Due Diligence for Selecting Money Managers

1. Performance numbers	Time weighted, composite of actual results, quarterly returns, and net and gross of fees
2. Performance relative to assumed risk	Sharpe ratio and/or Alpha
3. Performance among peers	Third-party objective evaluations, long-term upper median performance
4. Performance of manager's adherence to stated investment style	Articulates investment strategy and demonstrates discipline to maintain strategy over time
5. Performance in both rising and falling markets	Clear defensive strategies and sell disciplines
6. Performance of key decision makers and their organizations	Growth in assets, track record attributed to same decision makers

Manager Structure   The identification of the type(s) of managers to be selected within each broad class of assets.

Marked-to-Market   The daily process of adjusting the value of a portfolio to reflect daily changes in the market prices of the assets held in the portfolio.

Market Capitalization   A common stock's current price multiplied by the number of shares outstanding. It is the measure of a company's total value on a stock exchange.

Market Risk   See **Systematic Risk**.

Market Timing   A form of **Active Management** that moves funds between asset classes based on short-term expectations of movements in the capital markets. (Not recommended as a prudent process.) It is very difficult to improve investment performance by attempting to forecast market peaks and troughs. A forecasting accuracy of at least 71 percent is required to outperform a buy-and-hold strategy.

Market Weighted   Typically used in an index composite. The stocks in the index are weighted based on the total **Market Capitalization** of the issue. Thus, more consideration is given to the index's return for higher market-capitalized issues than smaller market-capitalized issues.

Maturity ˡThe date on which a bond's par value becomes due and payable.

Modern Portfolio Theory (MPT)   An investment decision approach that permits an investor to classify, estimate, and control both the kind and amount of expected risk and return. Essential to portfolio theory are its quantification of the relationship between risk and return and the assumption that investors must be compensated for assuming risk. This portfolio approach shifts emphasis from analyzing the characteristics of individual investments to determining the statistical relationships among the individual securities that comprise the overall portfolio.

Money Markets   Financial markets in which financial assets with a maturity of less than one year are traded.

MSCI EAFE Index   The EAFE Index is composed of approximately 1000 equity securities representing the stock exchanges of Europe, Australia, New Zealand, and the Far East. The index is capitalization weighted and is represented in U.S. dollars.

Mutual Fund   Professionally managed investment company made up of commingled funds from multiple investors used to create a diversified portfolio of securities. Individuals typically buy and sell mutual funds like stocks by making the assumption they are a specific capital asset. Mutual funds are managed like large private accounts, but there are certain tax and economic differences between having an individually managed account and owning shares in a mutual fund.

Passive Management   For a given asset class, the process of buying a diversified portfolio that mimics the overall performance of the asset class (i.e., the relevant market index).

Pension Benefit Guaranty Corporation (PBGC)   The federal agency, established as a nonprofit corporation, charged with administering the plan termination provisions of **ERISA** Title IV and the Multi-employer Pension Plan Amendments Act of 1980. Employers pay premiums to the PBGC, which guarantees benefits for participants and beneficiaries when defined benefit plans terminate.

Performance Attribution The process of evaluating the factors that contribute to the total rate of return of a portfolio. Performance attribution is most commonly used in the monitoring of common stock portfolio performance, where breakdowns of sector performance are readily available for comparison. Two other types of performance attribution, total fund and style structure attribution, can be used to provide additional insight into the factors that contribute to the total return of a portfolio.

Plan Sponsor   Parent organization of a benefit plan, such as an employer or nonprofit entity.

Price-Earnings Ratio   The p/e ratio represents a measure of value of a company. It is equal to the firm's current stock price divided by its earnings per share. Earnings are typically trailing 12-month earnings, but estimated earnings may sometimes be used.

Price-to-Book   The price-to-book value is a measure of value for a company. It is equal to the market value of all the shares of common stock divided by the book value of the company. The book value is the sum of capital surplus, common stock, and retained earnings.

Private Placement   The direct sale of a newly issued security to one or a small number of large institutional investors.

Profit-Sharing Plan   Retirement plan that receives contributions as a percentage of the sponsoring company's profits. See **Defined Contribution Plan.**

Proxy Voting   A written authorization given by a shareholder to someone else to vote his or her shares at a stockholders' annual or special meeting called to elect directors or for some other corporate purpose.

Prudent Man   A concept born from the 1830 Massachusetts court decision of *Harvard College* v. *Armory* that described the duty owed by a trustee to beneficiaries: "All that can be required of a trustee to invest is, that he shall conduct himself faithfully and exercise sound discretion. He is to observe how men of prudence, discretion, and intelligence manage their own affairs, not in regard to speculation, but in regard to the permanent disposition of their funds, considering the probable income, as well as the probable safety of the capital to be invested."

Purchasing Power Risk   The risk that a portfolio will earn a return less than the rate of inflation, that is, a negative real return.

Qualified Plan or Trust   Tax-deferred plan set up by an employer for employees under tax law. Such plans usually provide for employer contributions—for example, a **Profit-Sharing Plan** or pension plan—and may also allow employee contributions. They build up savings, which are paid out at retirement or on termination of employment. The employees pay taxes only when they draw the money out. When employers make payments to such plans, they receive certain deductions and other tax benefits.

Quality Rating   The rank assigned a security by such rating services as Moody's and Standard & Poor's. The rating may be determined by such factors as (1) the likelihood of fulfillment of dividend, income, and principal payment obligations, (2) the nature and provisions of the issue, and (3) the security's relative position in the event of liquidation of the company. Bonds assigned the top four grades (AAA, AA, A, BBB) are considered **Investment Grade** because they are eligible bank investments as determined by the comptroller of the currency. Rating, whether for stocks or bonds, must be used with care due to a tendency of the rating service to recognize changes in financial condition after they occur rather than as they are anticipated to occur.

Real Estate Investment Trust (REIT)   An investment fund whose objective is to hold real estate–related assets, either through mortgages, construction and development loans, or equity interests.

Residual Risk   Residual risk is the unsystematic, firm-specific, or diversifiable risk of a security or portfolio. It is the portion of the total risk of a security or portfolio that is unique to the security or portfolio itself and is not related to the overall market. The residual risk in a portfolio can be decreased by including assets that do not have similar unique risk. For example, a company that relies heavily on oil would have the unique risk associated with a sudden cut in the supply of oil. A company that supplies oil would benefit from a cut in another company's supply of oil. A combination of the two assets helps to cancel out the unique risk of the supply of oil. The level of residual risk in a portfolio is a reflection of the bets the manager places in a particular asset class or sector. Diversification of a portfolio can reduce or eliminate the residual risk of a portfolio.

Restatement Third, Trusts (Prudent Investor Rule)   A set of new and more specific standards for the handling of investment process by fiduciaries. These standards were adopted in 1992 and rely heavily on modern investment theory.

Return on Equity   Return on equity is a measure of a company's profitability, specifically relating profits to the equity investment employed to achieve the profits. Return on equity focuses on the returns accruing to the residual owners of a company, the equityholders. It is equal to income divided by total common equity. Income excludes all expenses, which include income taxes and minority interest, but before provision for dividends, extraordinary items, and discontinued operations. Common equity includes common stock outstanding, capital surplus, and retained earnings. The earnings per share of a firm is divided by the firm's **Book Value** per share.

Risk-Adjusted Return   The return on an asset or portfolio, modified to explicitly account for the risk of the asset or portfolio.

Risk-Free Rate of Return   The return on 90-day Treasury bills. This is used as a proxy for no risk due to its U.S. government issuance and short-term maturity. The term is really a misnomer since nothing is free of risk. It is utilized since certain economic models require a risk-free point of departure. See **Sharpe Ratio**.

R-squared (R^2)   Formally called the coefficient of determination, this measures the overall strength or explanatory power of a statistical relationship. In general, a higher R^2 means a stronger statistical relationship between the variables that have been estimated, and therefore more confidence in using the estimation for decision making.

S&P Rating   The Standard and Poor's market-weighted average rating of all the rated securities in a portfolio. Stock ratings are intended to provide an objective measure of the risk of a company in terms of the perceived level of stability in earnings and dividends. Securities that are not rated by S&P are excluded from the weighted average rating.

Safe Harbor Rules   A series of guidelines set forth by the Department of Labor that, when in full compliance, *may* limit a fiduciary's liabilities.

Safe Harbor Requirements

Safe Harbor Rules Require:

1. The use of prudent experts

2. A due diligence process for selecting managers

3. Investment discretion be given to selected managers

4. Managers' acknowledgement of cofiduciary status in writing

5. Monitoring of the activities of selected managers

Salomon Brothers Non–U.S. Dollar World Bond   This index is comprised of government bonds, Eurobonds, and foreign bonds, excluding U.S. bonds. The issues must be rated at least AA with remaining maturities of at least five years. The index is weighted by the remaining principal outstanding of each issue and is expressed in terms of U.S. dollars.

Scattergrams   A graphical representation of a manager's risk/return profile within a peer group or related database—typically over a 5- or 10-year time period. Crosshairs depict appropriate comparative index.

How to Read a Scattergram

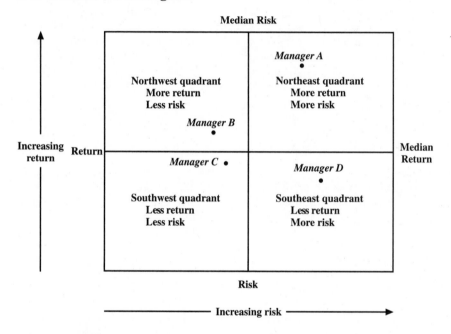

Settlor   The person or persons that establish and transfer their property to a trust.

Sharpe Ratio   This statistic is a commonly used measure of risk-adjusted return. It is calculated by subtracting the **Risk-Free Return** (usually three-month Treasury bill) from the portfolio return and dividing the resulting excess return by the portfolio's total risk level (standard deviation). The result is a measure of return gained per unit of total risk taken. The higher the Sharpe ratio, the better the fund's historical risk-adjusted performance.

Size Weighted   In a portfolio setting, this is a composite of a manager's return for accounts managed that weights each portfolio's return based on the size of the account. Compare to **Equal Weighted**. In index context, size weighted means each stock is given unequal consideration to the index return because it takes into consideration market capitalization of each stock. The Standard & Poor's 500 Index is an example of a size-weighted index.

Small Capitalization   Managers who invest in companies with relatively small **Market Capitalization**. The cut-off point for small capitalization varies from manager to manager, but on average targets firms with capitalization of $100–$800 million.

Socially Targeted Investment   An investment that is undertaken based on social, rather than purely financial, guidelines. See also **Economically Targeted Investment**.

Soft Dollars   The portion of a plan's commission expense incurred in the buying and selling of securities that is allocated through a **Directed Brokerage** arrangement for the purpose of acquiring goods or services for the benefit of the plan. In many soft-dollar arrangements, the payment scheme is effected through a brokerage affiliate of the consultant. Broker-consultants servicing smaller plans receive commissions directly from the counseled account. Other soft-dollar schemes are effected through brokerages that, while acting as the clearing/transfer agent, also serve as the conduit for the payment of fees between the primary parties to the directed fee arrangement.

Specific Risk   The part of a security's total risk that is not related to movements in the market and therefore can be diversified away.

Standard & Poor's 500 Composite Stock Index   An index of stocks composed of approximately 400 industrial, 40 utilities, 40 financial firms, and 20 transportation issues. The index is **Market Weighted**. The index is widely used as a benchmark for account performance measurement. Mutual funds and common trust funds have been organized to duplicate this index. See **Index Fund**.

Standard & Poor's MidCap Index   A composite of 400 medium capitalization domestic common stocks. Stocks in this index are not included in the Standard & Poor's 500 Index. The index is capitalization weighted.

Standard Deviation   A statistical measure of portfolio risk. It reflects the average deviation of the observations from their sample mean. Standard deviation is used as an estimate of risk since it measures how wide the range of returns typically is. The wider the typical range of returns, the higher the standard deviation of returns, and the higher the portfolio risk. If returns are normally distributed (i.e., have a bell-shaped curve distribution) then approximately $^2/_3$ of the returns would occur within plus or minus one standard deviation from the sample mean.

Strategic Asset Allocation   Rebalancing back to the normal mix at specified time intervals (quarterly) or when established tolerance bands are violated (±10 percent).

Style   The description of the type of approach and strategy utilized by an investment manager to manage funds. The style is determined by, as an example for equities, portfolio characteristics such as market capitalization of issues, price-to-earnings ratio, and dividend yield. Equity styles include growth, value, yield, core, and small cap.

Building the Style Groups

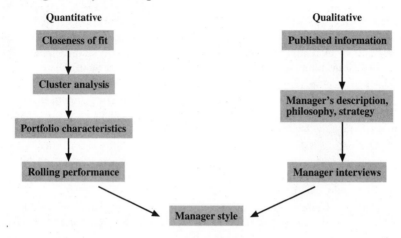

Systematic Risk Attributable to common macroeconomic factors and sometimes referred to as market risk. It is the part of a security's total risk that is related to movements in the market portfolio and therefore cannot be diversified away.

Tactical Asset Allocation The first cousin to **Market Timing**, as it uses certain indicators to make adjustments in the proportions of a portfolio invested in three asset classes: stocks, bonds, and cash.

Term to Maturity The time remaining until a bond's maturity date.

Time-Weighted Rate of Return Method of performance measurement that strips the effect of cash flows on investment performance by calculating subperiod returns before and after a cash flow and averaging these subperiod returns. Because dollars invested do not depend on the investment manager's choice, it is inappropriate to weight returns within a period by dollars. Time-weighted performance removes the impact of cash flows and, as a result, is widely accepted as the appropriate method of comparison for investment managers and market index returns. To remove the effect of a cash flow, the value of a security or portfolio must be known on the date of the flow. Using the value on this date, a subperiod return is calculated from the beginning of the subperiod to the end of the subperiod. Then a subperiod return is calculated from the cash flow date to the end of the period. The two subperiod returns are linked together to arrive at the full period return.

Total Return A standard measure of performance that includes both capital appreciation and depreciation as well as realized gains and losses and income. The term is widely misunderstood and sometimes bitterly debated. Total return is often a published investment objective, usually a compromise between those trustees that advocate growth and those that advocate income. It is a standard for performance comparison between funds because it includes both income and growth as the manager's entire contribution to the portfolio.

Total Risk Total risk is a measure of the total volatility of the excess returns of an asset or portfolio. The total risk is composed of two measures of risk: **Market** (nondiversifiable or systematic) **Risk** and **Residual** (diversifiable or firm-specific) **Risk.**

Trading Costs Behind investment management fees, trading accounts for the second highest cost of plan administration. Trading costs are usually quoted in cents per share. Median institutional trading costs range around 5 to 7 cents per share.

Treynor Ratio The Treynor ratio is a risk statistic that measures the excess return per unit of systematic market risk taken in a portfolio. The excess return is the total excess return without adjustment for risk. The ratio is equal to the excess return of the portfolio divided by the **Beta** of the portfolio.

Trustee A person, bank, or trust company that has responsibility over financial aspects (receipt, disbursement, and investment of pension funds). Where this responsibility is not exercised by a bank or trust company, it is usually exercised by a board of trustees in which the individual trustee has but one vote.

  • A person, bank, or trust company designated in the trust agreement as having responsibility for holding and investing plan contributions (and possibly having responsibility over other financial aspects of the plan).

  • One who acts in a capacity of trust as a fiduciary and to whom property has been conveyed for the benefit of another party. Under the terms of **ERISA**, a **Fiduciary** is "one who occupies a position of confidence or trust and who exercises any power of control, management or disposition with respect to moneys or other property of an employee benefit fund or who has authority or responsibility to do so."

Unsystematic Risk A risk pertaining to one element in a large environment or system. The risk of one stock is unsystematic, while the risk of the entire market of which it is an element is systematic. See **Systematic Risk**.

Value Equity Managers who invest in companies believed to be undervalued or possessing lower-than-average price/earnings ratios, based on their potential for capital appreciation.

Variance The variance is a statistical measure that indicates the spread of values within a set of values. For example, the range of daily prices for a stock will have a variance over a time period that reflects the amount the stock price varies from the average or mean price of the stock over the time period. Variance is useful as a risk statistic because it gives an indication of how much the value of a portfolio might fluctuate up or down from the average value over a given time.

Yield to Maturity Used to determine the rate of return an investor will receive if a long-term, interest-bearing investment, such as a bond, is held to its maturity. It takes into account time to maturity, current market price, and coupon yield.

INDEX